OPENNESS IN MEDIEVAL EUROPE

Cultural Inquiry

EDITED BY CHRISTOPH F. E. HOLZHEY
AND MANUELE GRAGNOLATI

The series 'Cultural Inquiry' is dedicated to exploring how diverse cultures can be brought into fruitful rather than pernicious confrontation. Taking culture in a deliberately broad sense that also includes different discourses and disciplines, it aims to open up spaces of inquiry, experimentation, and intervention. Its emphasis lies in critical reflection and in identifying and highlighting contemporary issues and concerns, even in publications with a historical orientation. Following a decidedly cross-disciplinary approach, it seeks to enact and provoke transfers among the humanities, the natural and social sciences, and the arts. The series includes a plurality of methodologies and approaches, binding them through the tension of mutual confrontation and negotiation rather than through homogenization or exclusion.

Christoph F. E. Holzhey is the Founding Director of the ICI Berlin Institute for Cultural Inquiry. Manuele Gragnolati is Professor of Italian Literature at the Sorbonne Université in Paris and Associate Director of the ICI Berlin.

OPENNESS IN MEDIEVAL EUROPE

EDITED BY
MANUELE GRAGNOLATI
ALMUT SUERBAUM

ISBN (Hardcover): 978-3-96558-031-2
ISBN (Paperback): 978-3-96558-032-9
ISBN (PDF): 978-3-96558-033-6
ISBN (EPUB): 978-3-96558-034-3

Cultural Inquiry, 23
ISSN (Print): 2627-728X
ISSN (Online): 2627-731X

Bibliographical Information of the German National Library
The German National Library lists this publication in the Deutsche Nationalbibliografie
(German National Bibliography); detailed bibliographic information is available online at
http://dnb.d-nb.de.

In Europe, the paperback edition is printed by Lightning Source UK Ltd., Milton Keynes,
UK. See the final page for further details.

The digital edition can be downloaded freely at: https://doi.org/10.37050/ci-23.

ICI Berlin Press is an imprint of
ICI gemeinnütziges Institut für Cultural Inquiry Berlin GmbH
Christinenstr. 18/19, Haus 8
D-10119 Berlin
publishing@ici-berlin.org
www.ici-berlin.org

Contents

Introduction
Medieval Openness
MANUELE GRAGNOLATI AND ALMUT SUERBAUM

Umberto Eco, the great semiotician but also medievalist, presents a compelling sketch of a history of art, science, and culture progressing in openness in his essay 'The Poetics of the Open Work'.[1] Works of art have always been open to interpretation, but in his account artists move from seeking to control the range of interpretation to encouraging it, as an 'imperial and theocratic society' with an 'authoritarian regime' (52) gave way to a more enlightened one, informed by a 'modern scientific universe' (57) that opens up towards empiricism and eventually post-Newtonian relativity and indeterminacy. Although there are some references to antiquity, Eco's history begins with the Middle Ages as the pinnacle of closure:

> In every century the way that artistic forms are structured reflects the way in which science or contemporary culture views reality. The closed, single conception in a work by a medieval artist reflected the conception of the cosmos as a hierarchy of fixed, preordained orders. (57)

The present volume challenges in different ways such a diagnosis of non-openness, albeit without claiming that medieval works are open

---

1   Umberto Eco, 'The Poetics of the Open Work', in *The Role of the Reader: Explorations in the Semiotics of Texts* (London: Hutchinson, 1979), pp. 47–66. See also his *The Open Work*, trans. by Anna Cancogni (Cambridge, MA: Harvard University Press, 1989).

in Eco's sense. Here, we would like to highlight that Eco's notion of an open work relies on a modern conception of the work of art and that this conception enacts its own closures.

Eco is quite explicit in situating his argument within an aesthetic theory that 'aspires to general definitions', and applies them 'to a whole variety of experiences, which can range from the *Divine Comedy* to, say, electronic composition', but that rests on a closely circumscribed notion of a 'work of art' in relation to its author:

> [O]ur Western aesthetic tradition forces us to take 'work' in the sense of a personal production which may well vary in the ways it can be received but which always maintains a coherent identity of its own and which displays the personal imprint that makes it a specific, vital, and significant act of communication. (63)

However, such a notion of a work of art is not merely Western, but also modern; and even if Dante was perhaps among the first to perform it, more recent scholarship on medieval music, visual art, and literature has shown that conceptions of openness and, in the words of modern textual scholarship, *mouvance* were pervasive in medieval culture.[2]

In referring to medieval theories of the fourfold sense of Scripture, which could be read not only literally but also allegorically, morally, and anagogically, Eco admits that medieval art may have 'a measure of openness', but contends that

> in this type of operation, 'openness' is far removed from meaning 'indefiniteness' of communication, 'infinite' possibilities of

---

2 For medieval music, see *Manuscripts and Medieval Song: Inscription, Performance, Context*, ed. by Helen Deeming and Elizabeth Eva Leach (Cambridge: Cambridge University Press, 2015). *Leaves from Paradise: The Cult of John the Evangelist at the Dominican Convent of Paradies bei Soest*, ed. by Jeffrey Hamburger (Cambridge, MA: Houghton Library of the Harvard College Library, 2008), analyses the ways in which scribes and artists in medieval convents used their knowledge of exegetical and iconographical traditions to compose new and often striking juxtapositions and interpretations. For *mouvance* within textual transmission, see Paul Zumthor, *Essai de poétique médiévale* (Paris: Edition du Seuil, 2000); Simon Gaunt, 'Discourse Desired: Desire, Subjectivity and *Mouvance* in *Can vei la lauzeta mover*', in *Desiring Discourse: The Literature of Love, Ovid through Chaucer*, ed. by James Paxson and Cynthia Gravlee (Selinsgrove, PA: Susquehanna University Press, 1998), pp. 89–110; Almut Suerbaum, '*Es kommt ein schiff, geladen*: Mouvance in mystischen Liedern aus Straßburg', in *Schreiben und Lesen in der Stadt: Literaturbetrieb im spätmittelalterlichen Straßburg*, ed. by Stephen Mossman, Nigel F. Palmer, and Felix Heinzer (Berlin: De Gruyter, 2012), pp. 99–116.

form, and complete freedom of reception. What in fact is made available is a sense of rigidly preestablished and ordained interpretative solutions, and this never allows the reader to move outside the strict control of the author. (51)

While Eco cites Dante merely as an example and insists on a much longer tradition developed by authors writing in Latin (from St Jerome and Augustine to Hugh and Richard of St Victor, Bonaventure, and Aquinas) and referring to the exegesis of the Scriptures and classical texts, also written in Latin, we highlight the novelty of Dante's attempt to enact the kind of closure practised for classical texts and the Scriptures on his own vernacular texts.

Indeed, by focusing on Dante one can speak of the birth of the modern author and work of art, and describe this process as a move towards increasing closure.[3] In this respect, the case of the *Vita Nova* is particularly instructive insofar as it lays out the textual strategies exerting control and fixity over a material that was fluid and open: while Dante, following contemporary custom, had begun his activity as a lyric poet by composing *rime*, i.e. stand-alone, independent poems that were not meant to be related to one another and whose meaning was often left open to the interpretation of fellow poets, the *Vita Nova* collects thirty-one of these lyrics and, through a prose commentary that is meant to specify their meaning once and for all, inserts them into a unitary and teleological first-person narrative describing the protagonist's ideal discovery of a correct form of desiring and writing. In this way, a new, individualized authorial figure emerges: the figure of the modern author controlling and guaranteeing the work's identity, coherence, and meaning.[4]

The *Vita Nova*'s performance of an author proved so successful that subsequent readers have taken it at face value and found it hard to undo Dante's imposition of a rigid, new meaning on the *rime* and to recover the openness they originally had — something made even more difficult by the decision of most editions of the *rime* to exclude

---

3   See Albert Ascoli, *Dante and the Making of a Modern Author* (Cambridge: Cambridge University Press, 2008).

4   See Manuele Gragnolati, 'Authorship and Performance in Dante's *Vita nova*', in *Aspects of the Performative in Medieval Culture*, ed. by Manuele Gragnolati and Almut Suerbaum (Berlin: De Gruyter, 2010), pp. 123–40.

the lyrics included in the *Vita Nova*.[5] Thus, the *Vita Nova* represents a model for how modern notions of work of art and authorship have retroactively curtailed the open, fluid, and indeterminate character of much medieval cultural production. At the same time, even for Dante's *Divine Comedy* one may question — as Nicolò Crisafi does in this volume — whether it is as closed as Eco suggests by mentioning it at one end of the range of experiences that his aesthetic theory narrates as a progression towards open works. Nonetheless, Eco's account remains inspiring insofar as it highlights how those works that in his conception are the most radically open — by leaving their interpreters and readers the freedom to finish them in all kinds of unpredictable ways — rely on an equally radical closure that ensures their 'coherent identity' bound to the imprint of their author, who ultimately functions like the God of Spinoza.

The essays in this volume seek to understand manifold kinds of medieval openness that become visible when one refrains from modern assumptions, and are also interested in how articulations of openness in the Middle Ages often stand in creative tension with forms of closure and can even be empowered by them.[6] The chapters highlight the complex relationship between author, work, and text,[7] but also explore several, often paradoxical, ways in which medieval culture mobilizes forms, practices, and experiences of openness without having a single abstract concept for it.[8]

---

5   See Manuele Gragnolati, 'The Lyric Poetry', in *Dante's 'Other' Works*, ed. by Zygmunt Baranski and Theodore J. Cachey, Jr (Notre Dame: Notre Dame University Press, 2022), pp. 1–34.

6   On the inevitable interconnectedness of openness and closure, see Cary Howie, *Claustrophilia: The Erotics of Enclosure in Medieval Literature* (New York: Palgrave Macmillan, 2007).

7   Roland Barthes, 'From Work to Text', in his *Image, Music, Text*, trans. by Stephen Heath (London: Fontana Press, 1977), pp. 155–64, provides a framework for these distinctions; on Barthes and medieval studies see *The Case for a Medieval Barthes*, ed. by Jennifer Rushworth and Francesca Southerden (= *Exemplaria*, 33.3 (2021)). For a medieval context and the new modes of reading developed in the thirteenth century, see Vincent Gillespie, 'From the Twelfth Century to c.1450', in *The Cambridge History of Literary Criticism*, 9 vols (Cambridge: Cambridge University Press, 1990–2013), II, ed. by Alastair Minnis and Ian Johnson (2005), pp. 145–235; Lukas Rösli and Stefanie Gropper, in the introduction to *In Search of the Culprit: Aspects of Medieval Authorship*, ed. by Lukas Rösli and Stefanie Gropper (Berlin, De Gruyter, 2021), pp. 9–16, provide a discussion of the relationship between work and text in the context of *mouvance* in transmission.

8   The most commonly used term in Latin is *aperire* (to open), which can refer to physical as well as metaphorical or interiorized opening; see Byrne in this volume on

Recent interest in the materiality of medieval culture, the physical dimension of textuality and transmission, as well as the performative nature of medieval writing and reading has shed light on the range of levels on which readers and listeners engage with a text.[9] The 'material turn' of medieval studies has insisted that manuscripts are physical objects, and that the tactile handling of these objects was an integral part of medieval reading practices. Medieval thinkers and artists therefore frequently highlight the physical act of opening a book, and in turn reflect on the act of reading as an opening up of the mind or the text.[10] Medieval readers would have been reminded of the significance of reading, speaking, and opening one's mind at the start of each day when reciting the opening words of Psalm 51: 'Domine labia mea aperies' [Lord, open thou my lips].

While the Divine Office, the recitation of psalms across each day and week, was developed for monastic settings, the practice spread to lay circles as well. Psalm 51 opens the *Hours of the Virgin*, a compilation of psalms and prayers with a focus on Mary which became increasingly popular in prayer books for lay readers, especially women.[11] The

---

its use in scholastic thought, and Giusti on its significance in Augustine's *Confessions*, whereas Otter discusses the literary uses in Geoffrey of Monmouth's *Vita Merlini*. For vernacular terminology, Gragnolati and Southerden discuss Petrarch's use of *m'aperse* (to open) in the *Rerum vulgarium fragmenta*, whereas Otter and Suerbaum highlight the paradoxical nature of Gottfried's Middle High German term *offenlîche* (openly) with its tensions between public and secret; this association between openness and public space is addressed in Sutherland for the Latin and Middle English accounts of the biblical stable which leaves its inhabitants *al opene* (exposed) to the elements.

9   See, for instance, *Aspects of the Performative in Medieval Culture*, ed. by Gragnolati and Suerbaum; Mary Carruthers, *The Book of Memory: A Study of Memory in Medieval Culture*, 2nd edn (Cambridge: Cambridge University Press, 2008) and *The Craft of Thought: Meditation, Rhetoric, and the Making of Images, 400–1200* (Cambridge: Cambridge University Press, 2000); Armando Petrucci, *Writers and Readers in Medieval Italy: Studies in the History of Written Culture*, ed. and trans. by Charles M. Radding (New Haven, CT: Yale University Press, 1995); Laurel Amtower, *Engaging Words: The Culture of Reading in the Later Middle Ages* (New York: Palgrave, 2000); *Orality and Literacy in the Middle Ages: Essays on a Conjunction and its Consequences in Honour of D. H. Green*, ed. by Mark Chinca and Christopher Young (Turnhout: Brepols, 2005).

10   On reading practices and the shift from corporeal to mental images, see Susie Nash, 'Meditation and Imagination', in her *Northern Renaissance Art* (Oxford: Oxford University Press, 2008), pp. 271–88, and Jeffrey Hamburger, *The Visual and the Visionary: Art and Female Spirituality in Late Medieval Germany* (New York: Zone Books, 1998).

11   On the *Little Hours of the Virgin*, see Rachel Fulton Brown, *Mary and the Art of Prayer: The Hours of the Virgin in Medieval Christian Thought* (New York: Columbia University Press, 2017), and the review by Barbara Newman in *Speculum* 93.4 (2018), pp. 1169–71.

Figure 1. Jean Pucelle, *The Hours of Jeanne d'Evreux, Queen of France* (c. 1324–28), Metropolitan Museum of Art, New York, The Cloisters Collection, Accession No 54.1.2, fol. 16ʳ. © bpk Bildagentur / The Metropolitan Museum of Art.

psalm is inserted into the office of Matins, marking the start of the day. Liturgically, the *Hours of the Virgin* associate Psalm 51 with the Annunciation bringing salvation to humankind. The office therefore blends the start of the physical day with a contemplation on salvation history. It also allows the reader to associate herself with Mary receiving the angel's message and with Christ, whose incarnation and infancy the *Hours of the Virgin* memorialize.

Considering an individual example of such a prayer book illustrates the different levels at which the manuscript engages the reader.

A fourteenth-century book of hours for the French queen Jeanne d'Evreux, third wife of Charles IV of France, which was illuminated by the artist Jean Pucelle and which juxtaposes scenes from Christ's Passion with scenes from his infancy, opens the text of Psalm 51 with a historiated initial of the letter *D* in two registers: the lower one depicts Queen Jeanne reading a book, while the upper one represents the Annunciation, with the Virgin Mary holding a book as Gabriel addresses her (Figure 1).[12] The illumination combines and conflates different layers of meaning: physically, it is part of a book of hours and offers the reader a reflection of her own actions. In opening the book, she confronts the figure of Mary as a reader and mirrors herself in the Virgin, who is portrayed in contemporary clothes and in a contemporary interior setting. Textually, the initial highlights the first in a series of psalms whose recitation structures the monastic day of nuns and monks: while lay women are not bound by the same monastic rules, the books of hours highlights that prayer and the imaginative mapping of one's own lived time against the life of Christ and salvation history also imbues secular life. Iconographically, since the Incarnation, in the words of John 1. 1, is the word become flesh, the initial points to this aspect of salvation history and, indeed, the act of reading the psalter is a common representation of the Annunciation: reading is therefore not just a reflection of physical human activity, but a form of *imitatio Christi* in which the reader imaginatively inhabits the role of Mary and through her, can contemplate the Incarnation. Experientially, this imitation of Christ is possible only because the reader, by the divine grace sought in the opening prayer, is receptive to the mysteries of salvation history, and affected or transformed by them.

Psalm 51 thus takes on a special significance, marking the beginning of the hour of Matins and daybreak, while inviting the reader to reflect on salvation history; to experience, rather than to know, that the Annunciation offers the hope of redemption to all human beings. Such reflection may raise anxieties, since the hope of salvation also evokes the spectre of eternal damnation, yet it also offers reassurance,

---

12   Jean Pucelle, *The Hours of Jeanne d'Evreux, Queen of France* (c. 1324–28), Metropolitan Museum of Art, New York, The Cloisters Collection, Accession No 54.1.2, fols 15ᵛ–16ʳ <https://www.metmuseum.org/art/collection/search/470309>. See Beth Williamson, *Christian Art: A Very Short Introduction* (Oxford: Oxford University Press, 2004).

since the act of accepting human sinfulness and vulnerability is also
the condition in which divine grace may offer hope. Within the prayer
book, the meditation shifts from the act of opening the book, through
the articulation of prayer, towards an inner state of openness. Opening
up lips and heart, as the psalm commentaries set out, may thus be the
start of a devotional practice which required guidance and habituation
as well as scriptural knowledge. Notably, such opening up goes hand
in hand with the introduction to a closed, exclusive, or even secret
space — the royal chamber of the Song of Songs, the wine cellar, or the
Hortus conclusus, the enclosed garden in which against all expectations,
the human bride and her divine bridegroom may become one.

The example of the prayer book highlights different levels on
which even a simple, everyday act of devotion involves different forms
of openness: on a physical level, the opening of the book at daybreak
marks both a moment in physical time and the tangible start to the
act of reading. At the same time, it encourages an interiorized experience in which the act of reading allows for reflection on the universal
perspective of salvation history, but it is also transformative for the
individual reader, who opens up to Christ and Mary's model and is
shaped by it. Situated at the interface between institutional monastic
practice and individual devotion by lay people, between Latin and
the vernaculars, between fixed liturgical texts and individual paratexts
which guide the transformation of readers, the example of the prayer
book also illustrates a creative interplay between openness and closure
— in this case closed physical spaces, fixed ritual practices and horizons of interpretation, as well the creation of interiority and space for
individual responses. It is the richness of such creative tensions, fluid
movements, and transformative experiences which the chapters of the
current volume explore.

This volume is divided into three parts: 'Texts', 'Experience and Subjectivity', and 'Community' but chapters often overlap with one another and could also be arranged differently. The first part addresses
forms of openness in medieval practices of making, reading, and appropriating texts. As the example of the prayer book illustrates, medieval
culture conceives of reading as a complex activity which may involve
the ability to inhabit several roles simultaneously. Where this involves

reading scriptural texts, it is predicated on assuming an absolute truth which the act of exegesis can reveal or unveil. Augustine, whose *Confessions* reflect on the importance of such acts of reading, became a seminal text for medieval readers precisely because it focused on the reciprocal acts of opening required — a God who is willing to open up to those who are radically different from the Divinity, and readers who are willing to accept the word revealed to them. Monastic institutions, and later the universities, provided structures through which readers could acquire and practise such ways of uncovering the revealed truth, yet the essays in this section also explore what happened when such practices were disseminated beyond the walls of the monasteries, to women and secular audiences.

Augustine provides the most widely disseminated model of reading as a transformative experience. Drawing on Derrida's and Lyotard's re-reading of Augustine, Giusti argues that an implicit conceptualization of openness runs through the whole of the *Confessions*. He identifies different layers: on the most practical one, the opening of a book marks a gesture of inclusion, because in sharing the book as material object, the act of reading encourages reciprocal disclosure between readers. Giusti contrasts this with the mimetic identification evidenced in the episode of Paolo and Francesca in Dante's *Inferno*. In Augustine's reading, the Scriptures — which open up to readers while retaining a veil of mystery — can have multiple meanings for different readers, though this openness to interpretation is not unlimited. It can therefore be argued to bear similarities with contemporary literary theory, especially Attridge's concept of authoredness: conveying intentions while leaving room for each reader. Giusti therefore argues that reading requires an act of faith as a performative search for truth. By ending the *Confessions* with a statement in the passive voice — 'thus will it be opened to us' — Augustine highlights that this search is not ultimately a matter of intention or referential truth, but a performative act: in being open to the text, readers are ready to be transformed.

Medieval institutions of learning nevertheless aim to regulate such acts of transformative reading, as the chapter by Philippa Byrne demonstrates. Focusing on the meaning of the verb *aperire* and its cognates in the commentaries and treatises of authors like Alan of Lille, Honorius Augustodunensis, Peter of Poitiers, Peter Abelard, Hugh of St

Victor, and Robert Grosseteste, Byrne's chapter explores the development of the concept of 'opening' a text in scholastic thought from the mid-eleventh to the mid-thirteenth century. At first, the 'opening up' of Scripture was associated with the revelation of truths according to a model of divine action and intervention in the created world: scholars sought knowledge, but understanding was granted to them by God through an act of revelation which stood outside the human mind, and the process was continuous and would, until the end of the *saeculum*, remain incomplete. Subsequently, another strand of theological thought began to associate the act of 'opening' a text with the application of dialectical reasoning — primarily to Scripture, but also to philosophical works and classical writing. In this sense, a text was 'opened' by the correct application of human reason, and in such a way that its meaning could be followed by readers or listeners. In this newer model, if a conclusion was 'open' (*apertus*), or proven openly (*aperte*), it could be considered clear, manifest, or evident — it was beyond challenge. The final part of the chapter highlights that the act of opening a text was given a polemical stance and became part of an argument about correct interpretation and intellectual pre-eminence which was not limited to the world of the schools but also informed Christian anti-Jewish disputational literature: from the late eleventh century onwards, authors like Gilbert Crispin, Peter Alfonsi, and Peter Abelard claimed that only Christian reason was capable of opening up the Old Testament, while Jewish irrationality and tradition was not.

While Latin learning is available only to select groups, who seek to differentiate themselves externally, as in the anti-Jewish defences of the faith, and internally, by highlighting the skill and training required to achieve ultimate clarity about divine truth, those reading vernacular texts face different constraints, but also opportunities, in a textual culture which often differs significantly from Eco's model of strong authorship and stable texts. Brian McMahon's chapter focuses on Icelandic sagas and highlights their textual openness, retaining features of orality even in the written forms which are their only mode of survival across time. While most scholarship has focused on the process of textualization and its aim to solidify the written text, McMahon foregrounds the freedom which the written texts afforded to reciters. Using prolegomena as a contemporary commentary on how the sagas should be transmitted, McMahon argues that the comparative open-ness of oral versions was 'enclosed' in manuscript traditions, which furthermore restricted access to a closed community of readers. Never-theless, prologues and epilogues defy this tendency towards strict control, and their variations allow a glimpse of the ways in which com-pilers understood their role. Focusing in particular on Oddr's *Óláfs saga Tryggvarsonar*, McMahon argues that the saga presents the text as an authorized redaction, the result of first opening up the text to com-mentary and then 'closing' it in an agreed version. Where epilogues offer the first and only instance of a first-person narrator, this can therefore be seen as an act of opening up the saga to a wider audience, marking a shift in the relationship between narrative voice and reader.

Such porousness is observable not just in vernacular literary forms traditionally associated with anonymity and collective tradition, but also extends to paradigms which are often evoked as the beginnings of modern authorship and its production of self-contained, stable texts and works. Nicolò Crisafi's chapter engages Dante's *Commedia* in a dialogue with Umberto Eco's concept of the 'open work' and contests the commonplace, shared by Eco himself, that Dante's poem is com-pletely self-enclosed and perfectly reflects its internally coherent moral universe and the 'tetragonal' persona of its narrator. Crisafi explores a number of instances in the poem and its afterlife where this ideal air-tightness is challenged or threatened. He focuses on the 'veiled threats of narrative interruption' (Barolini) from the obvious obstacles in the protagonist's path of *Inferno* I–II and VIII–IX to the more subtle anxiety of unfinishedness in *Paradiso* V and XIII, and investigates the safety valves in Dante's poem which vent the pressure of 'total coherence' (Contini, Ascoli) that is built into, and projected onto, the *Commedia*. In this way, Crisafi reclaims the material vulnerability of the text and of its author, showing that far from being a postmodern invention, the picture of Dante as a fragile and vulnerable author that emerges from these passages is picked up by his earliest admirer: in his tale of the lost cantos of the *Paradiso*, Boccaccio invites readers to consider a *Commedia* left unfinished and wide open. In thus blurring the line between the author's biography and the fate of his poem, between the narrator and his narrative, Boccaccio's account is attuned to the ways in which the *Commedia* involves the *poeta* in the perilous and open-ended journey of writing.

The final chapter of this section argues that modern academic practice and its unspoken assumptions and tendencies to erect boundaries need to be challenged in the interest of true scholarly accuracy. Alastair Matthews's chapter shows that premodern German-language writing from the area now referred to as Denmark has often been marginalized. Situating his project within the context of recent scholarly debates, his chapter makes the case for moving beyond a philological discourse which has its origins in the nineteenth century and has therefore been shaped by concepts of nation states. Matthews argues that the cultures of northern Germany and Denmark were closely connected in the medieval period, but that the use of German as a writing language in Denmark has been largely ignored by scholars of Danish literary history. The chapter sets out four different methodological pathways for redressing this imbalance: analysing the plurality of languages (Latin, German, Danish) in the region; tracing the trajectory of texts translated from one of these languages into another; studying individuals and institutions; and investigating the material circulation of texts across territorial borders. Opening up a scholarly investigation which hitherto has been constrained by preconceptions of national boundaries would allow a more nuanced view of a literary landscape of mutual contact and exchange.

Whereas the first part of the volume addresses medieval forms of textuality, the chapters of the second part explore the open subjectivity that they articulate, shape, and produce. For instance, as already became evident in the earlier chapters, opening up can be presented as a path towards greater clarity and illumination. Yet, as the late medieval example of the Lüne nuns highlights, such openness can also be perceived as a state of exposure and vulnerability.

Monika Otter's chapter on Geoffrey of Monmouth's *Vita Merlini* (*c.* 1150) draws on an unusual architectural space, enclosed and yet open to the elements, which Geoffrey appears to have invented: the observatory in the woods, built to Merlin's specification with seventy doors and seventy windows, where Merlin finds refuge after surviving a disastrous battle and losing his reason. The open-sided house is somewhere between a compromise and a paradox, almost a riddle: a house that is not a house, a building that is both enclosed and not, indoors and outdoors, safe and open, companionable and solitary. Otter takes the building as a structuring emblem of Merlin's state of mind and, by extension, the poem's poetics and epistemology. First, she shows that the prophetic mind is both lucid and translucent, perspicacious but also alarmingly open to the outside and vulnerable to it. It is indeed significant that Merlin is relieved when he loses his prophetic gift and that gift is passed on to his sister Ganieda. Then, Otter argues that the project itself of the *Vita* could be described as negotiating a way of knowing and a way of writing that are open but not too open, that admit the outside world and permit communication with it in ways that nonetheless do not leave the speaker overly exposed and vulnerable. Finally, Otter claims that the sudden and abrupt end refers to Geoffrey himself and represents not so much a proud conclusion to a successful career but a sad, disillusioned abdication: the poem's vatic voice has also found the open poetic mind too much of a strain, and like Merlin, he is relieved to relinquish his prophecy as rapidly as possible.

Whereas Geoffrey's conceit of the half-open tower expresses aspects of existential vulnerability in its potentiality and attractiveness as well as danger, Annie Sutherland's chapter shows that a very similarly constructed 'house without walls' can be read very differently within a scriptural and theological framework. Sutherland investigates medieval presentations of the birth of Christ and argues that the association of the nativity with a stable as a narrow, confined space is widespread, but not supported by biblical text or indeed medieval exegesis. Sutherland demonstrates that medieval exegetes foreground the *diversorium* as a public space or structure, open to all. Medieval devotional writing explores the affective potential of this openness and multiplicity: drawing on the dialectic of enclosure and exposure, Bonaventure presents it as a space both empty and filled, sealed off yet open. In Anglo-Norman meditations, the stable thus becomes a 'house without walls', an image which Sutherland has established elsewhere as having a particular resonance for anchoritic audiences. The chapter highlights that these images in fact also inflect sermons for lay audiences. In focusing on Christ's birthplace as an open, liminal space, the English tradition therefore also centres on Christ's vulnerability — opening up the closed book of the Old Testament, interacting openly with those who love him. Within the framework of salvation history, therefore, even extreme vulnerability can be contained, because it offers the hope of divine grace.

As the organ through which the soul interacts with the world, the medieval body takes up a position as a portal or gateway through which openness and its corollary of closedness can be articulated. Johannes Wolf's chapter argues that the devotional literature of the later Middle Ages places this tension centre-stage and, focusing on two Middle English texts and engaging them in a dialogue with Rosi Braidotti's concept of 'becoming' as an opening up of the self and an activation of intensity, shows that they make visible a set of unstable propositions about radical openness and the possibility of breaking down distinctions between individuals, identities, and even species. First, Wolf explores *The Book of Margery Kempe*, where the eponymous protagonist moves across geographies, communities, and identities in a shifting and mobile fashion, which frustrates her contemporaries, and reacts to visions of Christ's Passion in such a violent way that it unsettles both her physical frame and stable ontological distinctions. Wolf also shows that Kempe's compassionate imagination even seizes upon the image of a suffering animal in the street, offering a momentary glimpse of interspecies affect that disrupts the assumptions of a text otherwise calmly involved in the systematic exploitation and abuse of animals. Then, Wolf considers *The Life of Christina Mirabilis*, which also describes a body whose capacities scorn the dictates of nature and convention: Christina flies, lives in the river, and transforms into a limbless 'rownde gobbet' as she meditates; her transformations are explicitly associated with animals and especially with birds; and as her body prefigures the remade flesh of the Last Judgement, she also frustrates ontological distinctions and participates in a process of becoming-animal. Wolf also argues that while both texts reflect a medieval fascination with the transhuman and interspecies potential of the 'human' body, they also elicited anxiety in the masculine/male clerical elite and social institutions, which tried to control and suppress that fascination.

As Matthews's essays in the first section argued, our understanding of medieval texts is often influenced by modern academic and editorial practices and their unspoken and sometimes unreflected assumptions.

In a similar vein, Almut Suerbaum's chapter argues that Middle High German vernacular religious songs have often been marginalized because they do not conform to aesthetic norms which privilege stable forms and single, male authorship over the open textuality and collaborative modes characteristic of religious women's writing. Thirteenth-century courtly writing had developed a form of exclusive inclusion by encouraging readers to reject ignorant or mundane behaviour and thus demonstrating that they belong to a select group. Gottfried von Straßburg's *Tristan* pushes this strategy to paradoxical extremes by portraying his protagonists as both representative and exceptional, offering social and aesthetic role models which are open to every listener while insisting on their utter singularity. While Gottfried's exclusivity is ultimately aesthetic rather than social, contemporary mystical theology develops a similar tension: an unmediated encounter with the Divine which is both utterly exceptional and yet obtainable for all who are willing to leave everything behind in a state of spiritual nakedness. Eckharts's speculative theology is as exclusive as Gottfried's poetry, yet it finds its way into vernacular songs by and for women who open up forms of discourse that had hitherto been the exclusive prerogative of the universities and monasteries. These songs therefore offer a glimpse of poetic practices which are both collective and inclusive.

In the concluding chapter of this section, Manuele Gragnolati and Francesca Southerden offer a comparative reading of two poems by Petrarch, *Rerum vulgarium fragmenta* 23, known as the *canzone delle metamorfosi* [canzone of the metamorphoses], and 228, the sonnet 'Amor co la man dextra il lato manco'. In related but different ways, these poems explore the poetic subject's transformation into, or implantation with, the laurel tree that normally represents the poet's beloved, Laura, and imply a reversal in the traditional dynamics of desire, which — on the model of the Ovidian myth of Apollo and Daphne — consists of pursuit of the beloved, attempt at possession, and ensuing frustration By bringing Petrarch's poems into dialogue with philosophical works that consider the nature of plant existence as a form of interconnectedness and porosity to the outside, this chapter shows that the becoming tree of the Petrarchan 'I' opens up new possibilities in terms of both subjectivity and desire. In particular, Gragnolati and Southerden read the loss of subjective autonomy, vulnerability, and opening to the outside expressed in Petrarch's two poems through Rosi Braidotti's concept of 'becoming' (which she develops from Deleuze and Guattari and which incorporates what she calls a 'polymorphous vitalism'), and argue that, unlike most other poems in Petrarch's collection, *Rvf* 23 and 228 express a sense of desire not as lack but as intensity.

The final part of the volume considers instances in which openness can also be a category of intersubjective encounter and connection, establishing communities even where acts of exclusion are evoked. Damiano Sacco's chapter proposes a speculative notion of openness that embeds individual experience within a messianic horizon promising the eschatological reconciliation of differences, and considers the Franciscan form of life as an attempt to inhabit this promise as a community. It develops this notion of openness in the work of Giorgio Agamben by reading the question of man and animal in *The Open: Man and Animal* together with the promise of the Franciscans' vow, or *sacramentum*, in *The Highest Poverty: Monastic Rules and Form-of-Life*. These two texts unfold the themes of openness and promise in thirteenth-century settings instantiated, firstly, by the discussion of an eschatological miniature depicting a form of reconciliation between animal and human natures, and, secondly, by the analysis of the vow or promise pledged by the Franciscans upon entering monastic life. Through a discussion of the different forms of openness that, according to Heidegger, distinguish man from the animal, Agamben presents his own notion of openness as that of a constitutive element of the concept of life itself. Openness here stands for a certain void of representation that articulates the very separation between human life and animal life through which the human constitutes itself in the Western philosophical and political traditions. At the same time, this notion of openness relates to a certain structure of the promise, namely a messianic horizon that allows for a life that, as in the case of the righteous ones depicted in the eschatological miniature, is not premised upon excluding what Agamben calls 'bare life'. According to Agamben's *The Highest Poverty*, the Franciscans' *experimentum vitae* is one of the most successful attempts in the Western tradition at constituting a life that inhabits this promise and this openness, which, Sacco argues, the miniature of *The Open* had set as the very horizon of messianicity. Sacco concludes by pointing to the common ground that underlies the two instances of openness and promise presented in *The Open* and in *The Highest Poverty*, namely the openness and promise of language itself.

As Agamben suggests, medieval institutions, especially those of the monastic orders, are predicated on conceptions of belonging, developing a sense of differentiation or even exclusion in order to foster radical openness for those who are initiated into the community. In a survey of almost a thousand years of monasticism, Benjamin Thompson's chapter argues that one of the key fault-lines in the history of English monasticism is the extent of the convent's openness to the society around it. It offers a three-part survey that scrutinizes a selection of texts from nearly a millennium of monastic history. First, it considers the Rule itself, Lanfranc's Cluniac-influenced customs for post-Conquest English monasticism, and the early Cistercian statutes, showing that the moral and physical enclosure of monks and nuns is central to the founding documents of Western monasticism but also the need for monasteries to interact with their societies through recruits, hospitality, and the monastic economy. Second, the papal reform proposals of the 1330s provide a focus for the state of enclosure at that point: addressing a more developed society, they tried to reinforce the old ideals of isolation and enclosure, but the competing functions of monasticism and pressures on the monastery resulted in a series of compromises with the world. Finally, focusing on visitation records in fifteenth- and sixteenth-century England, Thompson shows how difficult it was to negotiate enclosure for monasteries that increasingly felt society's demand that they justify their existence by providing a range of social and economic as well as religious and ecclesiastical services. As the government under Thomas Cromwell ordered the religious back into enclosure, they found themselves with little core function by which to justify their existence. Thus, ironically, the most reformed and austere houses, whose prestige at the top end of the monastic spectrum might have enabled them to argue for survival on the grounds of their faithfulness to the Benedictine ideal, led resistance to reform (thus very much engaging with the political world outside the enclosure) and in the process made themselves the prime targets for Dissolution.

Whereas Thompson considers English monasticism and attitudes to enclosure in a diachronic panorama, Edmund Wareham's chapter consists of a detailed study of the paradoxical dynamics between enclosure and opening in a group of convents in northern Germany in the fifteenth century. These convents were part of the contemporary reform movement advocating a return to strict enclosure for nuns, yet reveal a close engagement with the society around them which, in the case of the convent of Lüne, has left tangible traces in the form of extensive correspondence. In his chapter, Wareham situates these Lüne letters, written in a mix of Low German and Latin, within the context of fifteenth-century concerns about how to access God's mercy. Written by enclosed nuns, the letters maintain a link with the outside world, often in very pragmatic ways, while simultaneously reflecting on their enclosed status and role in society. Wareham argues that references to the convent as 'closed' rather than 'open' reflect the introduction of fifteenth-century monastic reform, focusing on obedience and strict enclosure. While nuns where therefore excluded from a culture which, in Gumbrecht's terms, placed particular importance on visual participation and presence, their letters are a way of transcending spatial and temporal distance. At the same time, the nuns reflect on the fact that enclosure allows them a special openness to Christ, which they in turn communicate to others. This link between presence and openness was reinforced when devotional images were attached to these letters — most poignantly when the image sent is that of the open, wounded heart of Christ.

While late medieval convents thus provide examples of a physical seclusion that paradoxically enables greater exploration of vulnerability, yet also connectedness, within a framework which prioritizes the collective, the monastic experience is often contrasted with early humanist individuality. In the last chapter in this section, Oren Margolis undermines such binary oppositions by exploring the significance which open books play in humanist portraiture. In his exploration of a Holbein portrait of Hermann von Wedigh, in which the sitter is portrayed holding a half-open book, Margolis argues that the book is a potent simile of the work of art. Noticing that unlike the Steelyard portraits, with which it has sometimes been associated and which depict their sitters with business letters or bills, this portrait foregrounds a book, Margolis rejects the assumption that it might be a Lutheran Bible. He argues, instead, for an association with Erasmus of Rotterdam, whose humanist circle of friends Holbein joined in Basel. In evoking Erasmus, the book thus foregrounds Holbein's own authority as an artist and author. Margolis draws attention to the unusual state of the book, with one clasp fastened, the other opened, and the slip of paper protruding from it. By identifying the text as an Erasmian adage, Margolis inserts Holbein into a context in which reading is a process of creative tension between interpretative openness and a need for concealment. At the same time, viewing the portrait thus becomes an act akin to that of a sharing of the self in reading, indeed a shared reading such as occurs between humanist friends.

The chapters of this volume present medieval conceptions of openness which complement Eco's focus on the 'open work' as an aesthetic whole, allowing for multiple, though not necessarily infinite ways of reading (Byrne, Giusti, Margolis). Yet it is striking how often premodern contexts evoke a sense of incompleteness — even in works, like Augustine's *Confessions* and Dante's *Comedy*, that are usually associated with completion (Giusti, Crisafi), or in the humanist circles with which Holbein was associated (Margolis). While the binary opposition of inclusion and exclusion can serve to support a stable sense of identity and textual authority (Byrne, Thompson), the more common mode is one of fluidity, embracing motion, porous boundaries, and shifts which challenge notions of fixity, whether linguistically, in code-switching between Latin and the vernacular (Wareham); on a textual level (McMahon, Matthews, Suerbaum); by breaking aesthetic norms (Suerbaum, Wolf, Wareham); or experientially, by preferring a sense of vulnerability and becoming to enclosed or stable ontological conceptions of self (Gragnolati-Southerden, Otter, Sacco, Sutherland, Wolf). Often, the chapters show a culture where these forms of openness coexist with forms of enclosure and containment, in a creative tension that unsettles binaries and clear-cut distinctions. At the same time, they illustrate the extent to which modern conceptions of open or closed aesthetic or societal norms have influenced readings of the medieval material which may be unduly reductive (Matthews, Suerbaum, Gragnolati-Southerden). Finally, they demonstrate the significant role which gender plays in these explorations: the examples discussed in the volume illustrate repeatedly how reading as contemplation rather than rapture allows a model of womanhood which is both spiritual and intellectual — in a fitting tribute perhaps to the *spiritus loci* of Somerville College as a former women's college.

***

The current volume is the result of an interdisciplinary collaboration which had its origins in the medievalist community at Somerville College, but has since then opened out to encompass a larger group. What has remained the same, across the volumes *Aspects of the Performative in Medieval Culture,*[13] *Polemic: Language as Violence in Medieval and Early Modern Discourse,*[14] *Medieval Temporalities: The Experience of Time in Medieval Europe,*[15] and *Openness in Medieval Culture,* is a sense of open dialogue across subject boundaries, periods, and languages.

The project took shape at an initial workshop held in Somerville College on 25 June 2016 — a day of contrasts etched into the memories of many participants, when the large-scale political results of the Brexit referendum, opting to erect new boundaries, stood in stark contrast with the sense of solace derived from multilingual dialogue about a shared cultural space. It was this sense of openness which imbued our conference in Berlin in July 2019, when we enjoyed the hospitality of the ICI Berlin as a congenial location for intellectual exchange and convivial encounter. When editing the final versions of these papers during the pandemic, the echoes of those conversations provided a different form of solace: a reminder that scholarship can create a sense of community and open up horizons even during a lock-down.

---

13   *Aspects of the Performative*, ed. by Gragnolati and Suerbaum.

14   *Polemic: Language as Violence in Medieval and Early Modern Discourse*, ed. by Almut Suerbaum, George Southcombe, and Benjamin Thompson (Farnham: Ashgate, 2015).

15   *Medieval Temporalities: The Experience of Time in Medieval Europe*, ed. by Almut Suerbaum and Annie Sutherland (Woodbridge: Boydell & Brewer, 2021).

I. TEXTS

An Interminable Work?
The Openness of Augustine's *Confessions*

FRANCESCO GIUSTI

> Quis exaperit istam tortuosissimam
> et inplicatissimam nodositatem?
>
> Augustine, *Confessions*, II. 10. 18

OPENING AND BEING OPENED

'To open' is an important verb in Augustine's *Confessions* both in its active form, *aperio* (to open something), and in its passive form, *aperior* (to be opened). This is, in fact, the word with which Augustine decides to put an end to his work, without bringing it to completion, and once again he quotes Matthew 7. 7–8 (also in Luke 11. 9): 'a te petatur, in te quaeratur, ad te pulsetur: sic, sic accipietur, sic invenietur, sic aperietur' (Of You we must ask, in You we must seek, at You we must knock. Thus only shall we receive, thus shall we find, thus will it be opened to us; XIII. 38. 53).[1] In the following pages, I will discuss various uses

---

1   All quotations are from Augustine, *Confessions*, trans. by Francis J. Sheed, ed. by Michael P. Foley, intro. by Peter Brown, 2nd edn (Indianapolis: Hackett, 2006). For the Latin original, cf. Augustine, *Confessions*, trans. by William Watts, Loeb Classical Library, 26–27, 2 vols (Cambridge, MA: Harvard University Press, 1912). All quotations of the biblical texts outside of Augustine's text are from the New Revised Standard Version.

of this verb in the *Confessions* using selected occurrences. Augustine deploys 'to open' in four main senses: the action of opening books to read them; the opening of the words therein contained to the reader, or more precisely, the disclosure of their meanings; the continuous effort at opening one's heart to God; and finally, the eventual opening up of God's mysteries to human beings.

The hypothesis is that it may be possible to trace an implicit conceptualization of *openness* through the *Confessions*. Passive or active, literal or metaphorical, rhetorical or theological, bound to human interpretation or wholly revealed in the self-disclosure of the divine: openness and the 'act-event' of opening — the constitutive entanglement of *aperio* and *aperior* — may on the one hand acquire philosophical significance, on the other hand point to a certain way of creating and approaching human works.[2] The entire trajectory, whose final purpose is to find repose in God, rests on the grounds which are already contained in this prayer in I. 5. 5:

> So speak that I may hear, Lord, my heart is listening; open [*aperi*] it that it may hear Thee say to my soul *I am Thy salvation.* Hearing that word, let me come in haste to lay hold upon Thee. Hide not Thy face from me. Let me see Thy face even if I die, lest I die with longing to see it.

The prolonged effort embodied in the *Confessions* is constantly directed towards an opening up of the speaker's heart (and writing) so that he can hear God speaking in him (and in his writing) and eventually see God's unhidden face.[3] The human work of confession, in

---

2   I adopt here the compound 'act-event' proposed by Derek Attridge to indicate both the active and passive dimensions of the encounter of a reader with a literary text (*The Singularity of Literature* (London: Routledge, 2004), pp. 26, 150–51 n. 16; *The Work of Literature* (Oxford: Oxford University Press, 2015), pp. 59–60).

3   In his introduction to the *Confessions*, James J. O'Donnell writes: 'We are presented throughout the text with a character we want to call "Augustine", but we are at the same time in the presence of an author (whom we want to call "Augustine") who tells us repeatedly that his own view of his own past is only valid if another authority, his God, intervenes to guarantee the truth of what he says. Even the self is known, and *a fortiori* other people are known, only through knowing God. So Augustine appears before us winning self-knowledge as a consequence of knowledge of God; but his God he searches for and finds only in his own mind.' Truth, however, is made in writing: 'The *Confessions* offer no unedited transcript, but a careful rhetorical presentation. But the writing of this text was itself part of Augustine's life. "Confession" for Augustine, that act of "making the truth", was itself an important part of his religion, somewhere

Augustine, is predicated upon this double speech: the 'I' speaks in order to (be able to) hear the other speaking in him. The 'I' exists and performs his confession only in so far as he is, at the same time, the 'me' who is subject to the other's action upon him.[4] Although in quite different manners, in the last decade of the twentieth century both Jacques Derrida in his own 'Circonfession' (1991) and Jean-François Lyotard in his unfinished book *La Confession d'Augustin* (1998) recognized, and in turn pursued in their own writing, the peculiar double voice and continuous act of address to the other that characterize Augustine's confession.[5] Their approaches to the early medieval text underpin the idea of Augustine's writing as a constitutively *open work* that these pages aim to elucidate on its multiple levels. As Maria Muresan writes about the passage from the *Confessions* (v. 1. 1) that Lyotard inserts in the section 'Oblivion' with no quotation marks, as usual in the double voice of this text in which the other speaks in 'me' while remaining other:

> My inner is all you, who touches me said Lyotard-Augustine, 'receive here the sacrifice of my confessions, de manu linguae mea, from the hand of my tongue which thou hast formed and stirred up to confess unto thy name.' My inner is shaped by your strokes, it is nothing other than my openness to you, an instrument-support (suppôt) of your writing.[6]

---

between doctrinal disputation and cult act — perhaps even forming a link between the two' (Augustine, *Confessions*, ed. by James J. O'Donnell, 3 vols (Oxford: Clarendon Press, 1992), I: *Introduction and Text*, pp. xviii, xxx).

4   On Augustine and his 'hetero-biography' in postmodern thought, see John D. Caputo, 'Augustine and Postmodernism', in *A Companion to Augustine*, ed. by Mark Vessey with the assistance of Shelley Reid (Malden: Wiley-Blackwell, 2012), pp. 492–504; *Augustine and Postmodernism: Confessions and Circumfession*, ed. by John D. Caputo and Michael J. Scanlon (Bloomington: Indiana University Press, 2005).

5   Jacques Derrida, 'Circonfession', in Geoffrey Bennington and Jacques Derrida, *Jacques Derrida* (Paris: Seuil, 1991), English version in Geoffrey Bennington and Jacques Derrida, *Jacques Derrida*, trans. by Geoffrey Bennington (Chicago: University of Chicago Press, 1993); Jean-François Lyotard, *La Confession d'Augustin* (Paris: Galilée, 1998), English version in Jean-François Lyotard, *The Confession of Augustine*, trans. by Richard Beardsworth (Stanford: Stanford University Press, 2000).

6   Maria Muresan, 'Belated Strokes: Lyotard's Writing of *The Confession of Augustine*', *Romanic Review*, 95.1–2 (2004), pp. 151–69 (pp. 159–60).

READING TOGETHER

Let us begin with the most practical sense of the verb 'to open'. The
act of opening a book recurs two times in the famous scene of Augustine's conversion (it has already appeared in VIII. 6. 14, when Alypius
picked up and opened (*aperuit*) Paul's Epistles, which Augustine was
reading), right after he hears, in a moment of profound anguish and
spiritual turmoil, a voice from some nearby house repeating: 'Tolle
lege, tolle lege' (Take and read, take and read; VIII. 12. 29). He understands these words as a divine command to open his book of Pauline
Epistles and read the passage found. So, he returns to the place where
Alypius was sitting and where he had put down Paul's book, and opens
it at a randomly chosen page, which happens to be Romans 13. 13–14.
In this scene of reading — of which Francesca's reverse conversion in
Dante's *Inferno* v sounds almost like a deliberate parody, in particular
the resonance of Augustine's sentence 'nec ultra volui legere, nec opus
erat' (I had no wish to read further, and no need) with Dante's 'quel
giorno più non vi leggemmo avante' (that day we read no further; v.
138)[7] — the act of opening is insistently repeated (VIII. 12. 29–30):

> Damming back the flood of my tears I arose, interpreting the in-
> cident as quite certainly a divine command to open [*aperirem*]
> my book of Scripture and read the passage at which I should
> open. [...] So I was moved to return to the place where Alypius
> was sitting, for I had put down the Apostle's book there when I
> arose. I snatched it up, opened [*aperui*] it and in silence read the
> passage upon which my eyes first fell: *Not in rioting and drunk-*
> *enness, not in chambering and impurities, not in contention and*
> *envy, but put ye on the Lord Jesus Christ and make not provision*
> *for the flesh in its concupiscences.* I had no wish to read further,
> and no need. For in that instant, with the very ending of the

---

7   Dante Alighieri, *La Commedia secondo l'antica vulgata*, ed. by Giorgio Petrocchi, 4 vols
     (Milan: Mondadori, 1966–67); *The Divine Comedy*, trans. by Mark Musa, 3 vols (Har-
     mondsworth: Penguin, 1984–86), I: *Inferno* (1984), p. 113. Augustine has no need
     to read further because the passage he has just read quenches his spiritual thirst and
     shows the way out of his torments; for Dante's infernal lovers, the reading is interrupted
     by the sudden satisfaction of carnal desire: at that point, in fact, the trembling Paolo
     kisses Francesca. It is worth noting that what in Augustine is a resolution of the will
     becomes an event that befalls the two lovers in Dante. For a discussion of these scenes,
     see Elena Lombardi, *The Wings of the Doves: Love and Desire in Dante and Medieval*
     Culture (Montreal: McGill–Queen's University Press, 2012), pp. 223–15.

sentence, it was as though a light of utter confidence shone in all my heart, and all the darkness of uncertainty vanished away.

Then leaving my finger in the place or marking it by some other sign, I closed the book and in complete calm told the whole thing to Alypius and he similarly told me what had been going on in himself, of which I knew nothing. He asked to see what I had read. I showed him, and he looked further than I had read. I had not known what followed. And this is what followed: *Now him that is weak in faith, take unto you.* He applied this to himself and told [*aperuit*] me so.

This scene of reading deserves close attention. One notices that the act of opening the book is not the intentional action of a solitary, autonomous self: the command 'Take and read' comes in fact from God, at least according to the eavesdropper's interpretation, and Augustine's reading in turn prompts Alypius to do the same. As Cary Howie writes, opening the book entails a gesture of inclusion:

> Augustine's book, newly marked, is opened to include Alypius, to speak to him just as Augustine has been spoken to. In fact, it is a contiguous sentence that will address itself to Augustine's friend, just as the two men are contiguous to one another within the garden where they have now closed and opened and closed and reopened the Epistles. Their proximity to one another outside the book is, from this moment on, unthinkable outside of their proximity inside the book, the extent to which two adjacent Pauline sentences have not just reproduced but reinforced the fact of these friends' being together.[8]

Yet another interesting phenomenon occurs in this scene. Augustine comes to understand that those words could be a command from God by associating what is happening to him with a story that he was told about Antony: happening upon a reading of the Gospel, Antony had felt that he was being urged to respond to Jesus's call, 'as though what was being read was being spoken directly to himself' (tamquam sibi diceretur quod legebatur; VIII. 12. 29).[9] He had been immediately

---

8   Cary Howie, *Claustrophilia: The Erotics of Enclosure in Medieval Literature* (New York: Palgrave Macmillan, 2007), p. 1.

9   Augustine refers back to the story of Antony's conversion that Ponticianus told him in VIII. 6; the passage quoted comes from Matthew 19. 21. It is the advice given by Jesus to the rich young man who had asked him what he lacked to reach a more perfect state: 'Jesus said to him, "If you wish to be perfect, go, sell your possessions, and give the money to the poor, and you will have treasure in heaven; then come, follow me."'

converted to God by this divine message. Something similar befalls Augustine and Alypius in their reading together a passage from Paul's Epistles. After having read the sentence that he applies to his own case, Augustine closes the book and serenely informs Alypius of what is going on in himself. Alypius similarly discloses to Augustine what is happening in himself. Alypius asks to see the passage Augustine has just read, and he looks at the following sentence, applies it to his own case ('quod ille ad se rettulit'), and reveals ('aperuit') this to Augustine. In its third occurrence, the verb 'to open' acquires the meaning of 'to disclose, to tell, to reveal'. The shared experience of reading induces a moment of openness in Alypius. The admonition found in Paul leads to a confirmation of his intent: after this experience, he gives himself over to God's will, ready to support the weaker Augustine.

This scene presents a case of double identification that could be called, more properly, triangulated substitution: as Antony had done, Augustine takes the random passage in Paul's Epistle as addressed to him; as Augustine just did, Alypius places himself in the position of the addressee of the next sentence. Paul's Epistles appear to be considered as transtemporal and transcontextual words that can be made one's own by different readers. Through the opening of the book as a (shared) material object and the openness of the words contained in it to the reception of each individual, Augustine and Alypius are also prompted to open themselves to each other in a moment of unexpected intimacy. To acknowledge his surprise, Augustine even admits that he did not know anything about what was going on in Alypius before this reciprocal self-disclosure, which also seems to confirm their respective experiences of the text.[10] Brian Stock comments:

---

10   Brian Stock examines the relationship between the process of conversion and the experience of reading in the sequence of three interrelated stories of conversion, each told by a different person, in book VIII: Simplicianus tells Augustine of the conversion of Marius Victorinus; Ponticianus tells Augustine and Alypius of the conversion of two state agents; and finally, Augustine describes his and Alypius's conversions in the garden in Milan. See Brian Stock, *Augustine the Reader: Meditation, Self- Knowledge, and the Ethics of Interpretation* (Cambridge, MA: Belknap Press of Harvard University Press, 1996), pp. 75–111. Here Stock identifies Alypius's role as that of a witness. See also Brian Stock, *After Augustine: The Meditative Reader and the Text* (Philadelphia: University of Pennsylvania Press, 2001), p. 45: 'Alypius, whose stories are related in book 6, is the appropriate witness to Augustine's conversion in book 8. However, he is a witness on the outside. He tells the story of the internal changes in his friend as a narrative that is understood only through what he observes taking place in his body.

A significant moment in Augustine's account occurs when he says that he does not know what was in Alypius' heart: it had to be revealed to him (8.12.41). This is a cumulative statement of his position on 'other minds.' In his view, we can never *really* penetrate another person's thoughts. We know them only through language, that is, through the linguistic conventions by which what is private is made public. If we do not know ourselves (that is, if we cannot express what it is about ourselves that we know), then we cannot know others or express anything about them. Moreover, to this revision of an ancient paradox, Augustine makes a unique contribution: his is the earliest analysis of the potential part played by reading in the creation of intersubjective thinking. Stated formally, the mediator between the private experience of two persons can be a single text. In the case of Ponticianus and Augustine, the recognition is based on a prereading. In the case of Augustine and Alypius, where different texts are involved, the common experience is reading itself.[11]

Paul's book not only mediates a double conversion to God; it also mediates the strengthening of an old friendship as a turning towards each other in a closer proximity.

When Alypius reads Romans 14. 1, 'Welcome those who are weak in faith', he seems to position himself as the addressee of that exhortation, much as Augustine positions himself among the 'us' of Romans 13. 13–14:

> let us live honorably as in the day, not in reveling and drunkenness, not in debauchery and licentiousness, not in quarreling and jealousy. Instead, put on the Lord Jesus Christ, and make no provision for the flesh, to gratify its desires.

Stock concludes that, for Augustine:

> Our understanding of our lives is inseparable from the stories by which we represent our thoughts in words. Every understanding, therefore, is a reading of ourselves, every genuine insight, a rereading, until, progressing upwards by revisions,

---

He does not penetrate Augustine's thoughts. In the end, Augustine has to tell him that he has decided to take up the religious life. When Alypius does the same, he too has to relate what has transpired within himself by means of words. One would expect the anecdotes about Alypius in book 6 to prepare the way for this situation. This is what they do.'

11   Stock, *Augustine the Reader*, pp. 110–11.

we have inwardly in view the essential source of knowledge, which is God. Reading, though not an end in itself, is a means of gaining higher understanding; the contents of the mind can in turn be conceptualized through the sensory relations of reading — listening and seeing. Augustine is the first to present a consistent analysis of the manner in which we organize the intentional structure of thought through this activity: he suggests that through reading a 'language game' can become a 'form of life.'[12]

However, in contrast to the episode of Paolo and Francesca in Dante's *Inferno* v, where the reader finds a case of mimetic identification of the two lovers with the narrated characters (Lancelot and Guinevere) of the romance they are reading, here the two friends, and now fellow-believers, are also brought together by their response to the act of address to them that they perceive in the text. In the open referentiality of their pronominal deixis, these isolated sentences point to them as the referents of their exhortative speech acts. There is no doubt that the stories of conversion previously told by Simplicianus and Ponticianus have prepared Augustine and Alypius for this decisive moment, but now they are fully receptive to the openness of the text which calls upon them.

A similar operation, after all, is what initiated the entire episode. When the utterance 'Tolle lege, tolle lege' randomly reaches his ears, Augustine ponders and eventually renounces the option of considering it as an overheard verbal exchange between others: 'I ceased weeping and immediately began to search my mind most carefully as to whether children were accustomed to chant these words in any kind of game, and I could not remember that I had ever heard any such thing' (VIII. 12. 29). Not finding a possible explanation in his own knowledge, he embraces the interpretation that it is a divine command directly addressed to him. This turn from a possible imitation of someone else's story towards a repositioning of oneself as the addressee of God's words marks the moment of conversion.[13] Now, in fact, Augustine is able to recall and understand the relevant event in

---

12 Ibid., p. 111.
13 'Up to this point he has been in volitional lockdown. Now he can will one thing: his willingness to be addressed' (James Wetzel, *Augustine: A Guide for the Perplexed* (London: Continuum, 2010), p. 103).

the example provided by Antony's conversion: 'For it was part of what I had been told about Antony, that from the Gospel which he happened upon he had felt that he was being admonished, as though what was being read was being spoken directly to himself' (VIII. 12. 29).[14] Antony's story is not to be taken simply as a conversion narrative to be imitated, but rather it is recognized as a preceding case of opening oneself to an act of address coming from the other.[15]

WHAT THE AUTHOR KNOWS

It is interesting to consider the phenomenology of reading delineated in the scene of conversion in the garden in Milan in the context of what Augustine writes in XII. 31. 42 about the multiplicity of meaning, another passage in which openness occurs:

> Thus when one man says to me, 'Moses meant what I think,' and another 'Not at all, he meant what I think,' it seems to me the truly religious thing to say, 'Why should he not have meant both, if both are true; and if in the same words some should see a third and a fourth and any other number of true meanings, why should we not believe that Moses saw them all, since by him the one God tempered Sacred Scripture to the minds of many who should see truths in it yet not all the same truths?'

---

14   According to Elena Lombardi, 'for a moment the soon-to-be converted character and the reader witness the suspension of the naked sign. "Tolle! Lege!" as an imperative from God finds its first reference in the story of Anthony, a *signum translatum* that points to Augustine's own story' (*The Syntax of Desire: Language and Love in Augustine, the Modistae, Dante* (Toronto: University of Toronto Press, 2007), pp. 45–47 (p. 46)).

15   Michael Keevak analyses the complex system of exemplarity involved in Augustine's conversion, but he maintains a model of imitation and prioritizes the 'hermeneutic' moment over the 'performative': 'There are two sorts of reading that the text invites: hermeneutic and performative. The story of the conversion in book 7 and 8, however, suggests that although the goal is undoubtedly the latter, it is only through the former that it is achieved and even facilitated'; for him, 'the thrust of the text is that there is really no difference between being a reader and being a witness, since "reading" Augustine's conversion is a performative act that is not properly understood until the hermeneutic experience of reading is translated into the reader's *own* experience (or act) of conversion via the actions that are represented in that text' (Michael Keevak, 'Reading (and Conversion in) Augustine's *Confessions*', *Orbis litterarum*, 50 (1995), pp. 257–71 (pp. 267, 261)). Augustine, however, properly associates himself with Antony (or acknowledges the possible imitation of the model) only when he manages to assume, with respect to 'Tolle lege, tolle lege', the position that Antony assumed with respect to Matthew 19. 21.

For Augustine, the proper approach to Scripture entails that the text can have diverse meanings for different readers and that its writer — Moses in this case — saw them all. God, in fact, inspired him and adjusted Scripture to the minds of all possible readers. The human writer, divinely inspired, wholly sees and realizes whatever truth readers have been and will ever be able to find in it. All those truths are there to be found. Philip Burton connects these observations with the events seen in the scene of conversion and with Augustine's response to the exhortation 'Tolle lege, tolle lege':

> Though recognizing that it might be part of some children's game, Augustine chooses to interpret it as a divine command to pick up his codex of Paul. In short, he interpreted the words as *he* meant them, the meaning he put on them being not that of the child. Claiming direct communication from God is, of course, dangerous for one's reputation for sanity; Augustine avoids this (perhaps) by claiming responsibility for his own interpretation of the words he has heard. Again, the notion of *voluntas* is not far off. Augustine 'did not mean' (or 'meant not') to read (*nec ultra volui legere*) further than he did. 'Interpreting as one means' is, then, not simply what one does to books, but potentially to any form of sign.[16]

Then Augustine continues his reflections on the writing of Scripture with a peculiar conditional sentence, admittedly quite bold, in which he presents himself as a possible example (XII. 31. 42):

> Certainly — and I say this fearlessly and from my heart — if I had to write with such vast authority I should prefer so to write that my words should mean whatever truth anyone could find upon these matters, rather than express one true meaning so clearly [*apertius*] as to exclude all others, though these contain no falsehood to offend me. This being so, I would not be so rash, O my God, as to believe that so great a man did not merit this gift at Your hands. When he was writing these words he wholly saw and realised whatever truth we have been able to find in them — and much beside that we have not been able to find, or have not yet been able to find, though it is there in them to be found.

---

16   Philip Burton, *Language in the* Confessions *of Augustine* (Oxford: Oxford University Press, 2007), p. 107.

If Augustine were in Moses' position, and such an enormous author-ity were bestowed upon his own writing, he would choose a kind of writing in which words are open to readers' interpretation, rather than express too clearly (*apertius*) one single truth to the exclusion of all other possible truths. God grants the vision of the truth to the hu-man writer invested with such an authority, but this does not restrict the reader's possibility of finding multiple meanings in those words. Augustine, here, seems to use *apertius* (clear, manifest, evident) in a negative sense. When words are too 'open', readers are prevented from pursuing their own interpretation. The openness to a variety of meanings is predicated upon the fact that those words do not express clearly one single meaning that would rule out all other possible mean-ings. However, although there can be multiple interpretations of a text, interpretation seems to be endless, but not unlimited.[17]

Augustine had used the adjective 'open' in relation to Scripture in VI. 5. 8, this time in a positive sense:

> Now that I heard them expounded so convincingly, I saw that many passages in these books, which had at one time struck me as absurdities, must be referred to the profundity of mystery. Indeed the authority of Scripture seemed to be more to be revered and more worthy of devoted faith in that it was at once a book that all could read and read easily, and yet preserved the majesty of its mystery in the deepest part of its meaning: for it offers itself to all in the plainest words [*verbis apertissimis*] and the simplest expressions, yet demands the closest atten-tion of the most serious minds. Thus it receives all within its welcoming arms, and at the same time brings a few direct to You by narrow ways: yet these few would be fewer still but for this twofold quality by which it stands so lofty in authority yet draws the multitude to its bosom by its holy lowliness.

---

17   According to Johanna Schumm, '[i]n spite of his critique of language, Augustine does not abandon faith and the search for an absolute truth. For him, the simultaneous existence of differing interpretations points to an unclear, but in no way uncertain truth, to the divine "spiritu[s] ueritatis" (Augustine, *Confessiones*, XII, xx, 29) ("spirit of truth"). Truth still exists, even though it can never be found with the means of human language. In Derrida's concept of différance, on the other hand, the place of truth is vacant. Derrida made this particularly clear when he distinguished his own concept from negative theology, saying that différance did not point to a "supraessentialité," and when he declared the differential "principe postal" to be neither "principe, ni une catégorie trascendentale" (Derrida, *La Carte Postale*, 206)' (Johanna Schumm, 'Quoted Confessions: Augustine's *Confessiones* and Derrida's "Circonfession"', trans. by Jan Schönherr, *Comparative Literature Studies*, 52.4 (2015), pp. 729–56 (pp. 737–38)).

Now that Augustine has heard Scripture persuasively illustrated by Ambrose, he sees that many passages, which in the past struck him as absurd because indemonstrable and even erroneous if taken literally, must be interpreted spiritually and therefore referred to the profundity of sacred truth. Scripture offers itself to all readers in the plainest words ('verbis apertissimis') and the simplest style of expression ('humillimo genere loquendi'), yet invites profound reflection in those who do not have 'a shallow mind' (Sirach 19. 4). In this way, it welcomes all readers to its open bosom, but also offers more demanding paths towards God to others. Those few others, however, are much more numerous than they would be if Scripture did not possess this twofold quality: on the one hand it reaches such high peaks of authority, on the other hand it welcomes crowds to the womb of a holy humility. Vocabulary and style must be open, but the truth must not be expressed too clearly. In order to be spiritually open, words must preserve their mystery behind the veil of their simplicity. Scripture does not convey truths that can be rationally demonstrated; rather, it asks the reader to have faith and love.[18]

Without pushing the association too far, one could venture that Augustine's approach to Scripture bears similarities with certain trends in contemporary literary theory. Not so much, I think, with Umberto Eco's 'open work', which is predicated on the ambiguity of signs in modern literature and art,[19] or with Roland Barthes's textual openness based on the 'death of the author' and therefore on the possibility of a purely synchronic reading of the text. For Barthes, 'a text is not a line of words releasing a single "theological" meaning (the "message" of the Author-God) but a multi-dimensional space in which a variety of writings, none of them original, blend and clash'; '[i]n the multiplicity of writing, everything is to be *disentangled*, nothing *deciphered*'.[20] For

---

18   For a brief account of Augustine's progress in reading Scripture, see Catherine Cony-
      beare, *The Routledge Guidebook to Augustine's* Confessions (New York: Routledge,
      2016), pp. 51–57.

19   Umberto Eco, *Opera aperta: Forma e indeterminazione nelle poetiche contemporanee*
      (Milan: Bompiani, 1962). English version: Umberto Eco, *The Open Work*, trans. by
      Anna Cancogni, intro. by David Robey (Cambridge, MA: Harvard University Press,
      1989).

20   Roland Barthes, *Image, Music, Text*, ed. and trans. by Stephen Heath (New York: Hill
      and Wang, 1977), pp. 146–47.

Augustine, human interpretation is an endless operation, both because one reader can never exhaust the signification of the (sacred) text and because there can be as many interpretations as individual readers, but it is not unlimited.

The reader has to acknowledge the 'authoredness' of the work, to use Derek Attridge's apt coinage: not the author as an individuated being, who may remain just as much unknown as their intentions, but the fact that the work has been authored, that there are intentions in it, even though the reader will never know them with certainty.[21] This authoredness limits interpretation in principle, but does not impose on the work one single meaning. It only ensures that there is a meaning to be found and makes the act of interpretation worth pursuing. Otherwise, the text would dissolve into a series of unrelated and unintended signs, and interpretation would be directionless and maybe even futile. In other words, to posit that the specific arrangement of signs in a text is intended and potentially meaningful allows for its openness. Its words must be plain enough, but their meaning must not be too clear and explicit, otherwise they would not make room for their reader. The *Confessions* are meant to be similarly open if, as Catherine Conybeare remarks, '[w]e, as readers, are crucial to the meaning of the *Confessions*. We do not complete its meaning, for the whole point is that we — any person, any people — cannot. But we continue its meaning.'[22]

AN ACT OF LOVE

Granting the text its authoredness without knowing the author and their intentions is, to a certain extent, part of the act of faith and love

---

21   'This underlying sense of purposiveness is manifested as what we may term "authored-ness," the presupposition that the words we are reading are the product of a mental event or a number of such events whereby the processes of linguistic meaning are engaged. We may know nothing about the author of a particular text, not even his or her name, but we read the text on the assumption that it is authored, that it is the work, however mediated, of at least one, almost certainly human, mind. Authoredness arises not from communion with the creator but, like all aspects of the work's meaning, from the social and cultural context within which art is received' (Attridge, *Singularity of Literature*, p. 101; see also Attridge, *Work of Literature*, pp. 27–28).

22   Conybeare, 'Reading the *Confessions*', in *A Companion to Augustine*, ed. by Vessey with Reid, pp. 99–110 (p. 100).

that Augustine requires from readers, both from the readers of Scripture and the readers of his *Confessions*. Indeed, he writes in x. 3. 3:

> But because charity believes all things — that is, all things spoken by those whom it binds to itself and makes one — I, O Lord, confess to You that men may hear, for though I cannot prove to them that my confession is true, yet those will believe me whose ears charity has opened [*aperit*] to me.

The *Confessions*, which are also a tentative act of interpretation of Scripture, ask for *caritas* from their readers.[23] As Augustine has faith in Scripture, so readers must have faith in his work, in which he is not so much expressing the truth he has achieved, as he is performatively seeking it (xi. 22. 28):

> My mind burns to solve this complicated enigma. O Lord my God, O good Father, for Christ's sake I beseech Thee, do not shut off these obscure familiar problems from my longing, do not shut them off and leave them impenetrable but let them shine clear for me in the light of Thy mercy, O Lord. Yet whom shall I question about them? And to whom more fruitfully than to Thee shall I confess my ignorance: for Thou art not displeased at the zeal with which I am on fire for Thy Scriptures. Grant me what I love: for it is by Your gift that I love. Grant me this gift, Father, *who dost know how to give good gifts to Thy children*. Grant it because *I have studied that I might know and it is a labour in my sight* until Thou shalt open [*aperias*] it to me.

However active and zealous Augustine's exploration of the conundrum of time might be, the ultimate unknowable author, the authority able to disclose the secret, is God. His investigation is a fruitful confession of ignorance. Only God can grant knowledge; even Augustine's love for knowledge is a gift from God. Augustine both empowers and weakens

---

23   Referring to *Confessions*, IX. 12. 33, and to the passage on Moses discussed in the previous section, Burton, *Language*, p. 105, writes: 'What matters is not that their reading of Augustine should be the same as his own, but that it should be informed by Christian charity towards him. A similar theory is advanced in Book 12, where Augustine declines to reject any interpretation of the opening words of the Book of Genesis ("In the beginning God made heaven and earth"), "except the carnal ones", while denying any exegete's claims to authoritative interpretation of Moses' meaning (the verb used here is *sentire* rather than *velle*, but there is little if any practical distinction). In this case, however, Augustine turns aside at the last minute from the possibility that Genesis might contain a true meaning *not* meant by Moses, in favour of the belief that Moses meant *all* the possible true interpretations (*Confessions* 12. 31. 42).'

the human author. The human author is not just God's mouthpiece, the mere scribe of his words, as some previous oriental traditions considered prophets to be;[24] at the same time, in order to write, to perform his research, ultimate authorship must be displaced onto God. The *Confessions* themselves are an act of writing in which believing in God comes to coincide with the quest for him enacted in them. For this reason, they become an interminable work that can bring together prayer directly addressed to God and the highest philosophical investigation, performance, and reflection. Truth-seeking, as much as truth-telling, is a matter of direction; it is a path that leads to God.

In fact, the hope for an eventual opening up of what remains secret for the human being in this world finds its ideal formulation in the quotation from Matthew 7. 7–8 (also in Luke 11. 9):

> Ask, and it will be given you; search, and you will find; knock, and the door will be opened for you. For everyone who asks receives, and everyone who searches finds, and for everyone who knocks, the door will be opened.

References to these verses recur with variations throughout the *Confessions* and become emblematic of how the words of Scripture can be applied to the individual case, to Augustine as part of that 'you', of that 'everyone':

> A great hope has dawned: the Catholic faith does not teach the things I thought and vainly accused it of. Catholic scholars hold it blasphemy to believe God limited within the shape of a human body. Do I hesitate to knock, that other truths may be opened [*aperiantur*]? (VI. 11. 18)
> See, Father: gaze and see and approve: and may it be pleasing in the sight of Thy mercy that I should find grace before Thee, that the inner secret of Thy words may be laid open [*aperiantur*] at my knock. (XI. 2. 4)
> My heart is deeply wrought upon, Lord, when in the neediness of this my life the words of Your Holy Scripture strike upon it. Thus it is that so often the poverty of the human intellect uses an abundance of words: for seeking uses more words than finding, petitions take longer to utter than to obtain, and

---

24 Raymond F. Collins, 'Inspiration', in *The New Jerome Biblical Commentary*, ed. by Raymond E. Brown, Joseph A. Fitzmyer, and Robert E. Murphy (London: Chapman, 1989), pp. 1023–33.

> knocking means more work for the hand than receiving. But
> we have the promise: who shall destroy it? *If God be for us,*
> *who is against us? Ask and you shall receive, seek and you shall*
> *find, knock and it shall be opened to you. For everyone that asks,*
> *receives: and he that seeks, finds: and to him that knocks, it shall*
> *be opened* [*aperietur*]. These are Your promises, and who need
> fear to be deceived when Truth gives the promise? (XII. 1. 1)
>
> I consider all these things as far as You give me the power,
> O my God, as far as You incite me to knock and open [*aperis*]
> to my knocking. (XII. 12. 15)

The verses from Matthew underlie Augustine's engagement with openness up to the very last words of the *Confessions*. That promise both
legitimizes the long enquiry and attests the close dialogue that is being
established with the beloved Scripture.[25] The intertwining of the problem of the disclosure of the word's meaning and the continuous effort
at opening one's heart to God can be traced throughout the book. In
book V, Augustine first realizes that even the famous Manichean orator
Faustus does not open or clarify (*aperire*) the questions that trouble
him (V. 7. 12):

> For when I realised that he was unlearned in those matters in
> which I had thought he excelled, I began to despair of his being
> able to clarify [*aperire*] and solve for me the questions that
> troubled me — though as I now realise he might have been
> able to hold the truth of piety even though he was a man of
> no learning, if he had not been a Manichean.

Then he recounts some advancements towards the final openness of
which only God is capable. Those advancements depend on God's
words slowly penetrating into his mind — which, back then, was still
susceptible to the pleasures of rhetoric — through its exposure to
Ambrose's words in Milan (V. 14. 24):

> Thus I did not take great heed to learn what he was saying but
> only to hear how he said it: that empty interest was all I now had
> since I despaired of man's finding the way to You. Yet along with
> the words, which I admired, there also came into my mind the
> subject-matter, to which I attached no importance. I could not
> separate them. And while I was opening [*aperirem*] my heart

---

25 For a discussion of the *Confessions* as conversation, prayer, and praise, see Conybeare,
    Guidebook, pp. 32–36 (and, on the 'restless motion of questioning', pp. 36–39).

to learn how eloquently he spoke, I came to feel, though only gradually, how truly he spoke.

In VI. 4. 6, Ambrose is acknowledged as able to open the veils of the mystery, but Augustine is not yet ready to see the truth in those words, to assent to that truth:

> And it was a joy to hear Ambrose who often repeated to his congregation, as if it were a rule he was most strongly urging upon them, the text: *the letter killeth, but the spirit giveth life*. And he would go on to draw aside the veil of mystery and lay open [*aperiret*] the spiritual meaning of things which taken literally would have seemed to teach falsehood. Nothing of what he said struck me as false, although I did not as yet know whether what he said was true. I held back my heart from accepting anything, fearing that I might fall once more, whereas in fact the hanging in suspense was more deadly.

If taken literally, words can teach perverse doctrines. Even when confronted with someone who can open them spiritually, however, one needs to be open to their spiritual meanings in order to receive the life they can give. What is required, here, is not rational or sensory certainty, to which Augustine is still attached, but an act of assent.

A WORK ALWAYS IN THE MAKING

At the very end of the *Confessions*, the passionate request addressed to God in I. 5. 5 —

> So speak that I may hear, Lord, my heart is listening [the ears of my heart are before thee]; open [*aperi*] it that it may hear Thee say to my soul *I am Thy salvation*. Hearing that word, let me come in haste to lay hold upon Thee. Hide not Thy face from me. Let me see Thy face even if I die, lest I die with longing to see it[26]

— has not been entirely fulfilled yet. Augustine has undoubtedly been running 'after that voice' for quite a long time now, but the full disclosure of the divine is not to be experienced in this life. The book,

---

26   Augustine is referring to and applying to himself Psalm 35. 3: 'Draw the spear and javelin against my pursuers; say to my soul, "I am your salvation."'

indeed, ends with a sequence of verbs in the passive voice and in the future tense that culminates with the desired manifestation of the divine.[27] The entire endeavour of opening oneself up actively, or more precisely co-actively, undertaken in the *Confessions* aims at this final passive openness, which is (always) yet to come, just as much as human *opera* are (always) yet to come to completion (XIII. 38. 53):

> We see the things You have made, because they are; and they are, because You see them. Looking outside ourselves we see that they are, and looking into our own mind we see that they are good: but You saw them as made when You saw that they were to be made.
>
> At the present time we move towards doing good, since our heart has so conceived by Your Spirit; but at an earlier time we moved towards doing ill, for we had gone away from You. But You, God, who alone are good, have never ceased to do good. Some indeed of our works are good through Your grace, but they are not eternal: after them we hope that we shall find rest in the greatness of Your sanctification. But You, the Good, who need no good beside, are ever in repose, because You are Your own repose.
>
> What man will give another man the understanding of this, or what angel will give another angel, or what angel will give a man? Of You we must ask, in You we must seek, at You we must knock. Thus only shall we receive, thus shall we find, thus will it be opened [*aperietur*] to us. Amen.

As Augustine had written in the discussion on will in VIII. 10. 24, any number of possible courses of action can open up for the will at the same time, but this does not mean that there is an equal number of diverse substances: there is only one soul.[28] In VIII. 11. 27, the possibility of the chaste dignity of continence was opening itself up (*aperiebatur*) for him, but he trembled to go.[29] Augustine has come

---

27 'The last word of the *Confessions* is a verb in the future tense and the passive voice: "it will be opened". Thirteen books have passed at a passionate stretch. The reader has placed herself in readiness. And everything is yet to come' (Conybeare, *Guidebook*, p. 135; see pp. 131–35 on these final paragraphs).

28 The question of will in Augustine is complex and much debated; for a particular interpretation, see James Wetzel, 'Augustine on the Will', in *A Companion to Augustine*, ed. by Vessey with Reid, pp. 339–52.

29 This is the irresoluteness of the will that will find an answer in Romans 13. 13–14, when Augustine picks up and reads Paul's Epistles in VIII. 12. 29. It is the personal question he brings to the text.

a long way from that timorous trepidation, which Alypius witnessed in silence; yet, at the very end of his *Confessions*, he is still longing for the opening up of the mysteries of God. He is now aware that this is the ultimate destination of his efforts and his full intention is directed towards that destination, but the final opening has not happened yet. The quote from Matthew emphasizes, in an exhortative mode, the activity and passivity of this endless search. The human being can only keep knocking on that door, waiting for the door to be opened by God, and God alone. Comparing Augustine's *Confessions* with Derrida's 'Circumfession', Johanna Shumm points out:

> These similarities [between the two thinkers] can be seen in their confessional texts and mainly consist in an orientation towards the future and in a valorization of linguistic form. First, confessions are always future-oriented speech acts, as they always expect the reaction of an addressee. In their Christian version, this expected reaction is forgiveness. The speaker in Augustine's *Confessiones* expects the future unification with God (still pending after the conversion); that is the object of writing the text and also influences Augustine's hermeneutic work. The *Confessiones* end with a prospect of future understanding [...].[30]

Augustine seems to be suggesting a specific philosophical and theological reflection on human works (*opera nostra*) in this last section, including what he has being doing in the *Confessions*, the act of confession itself. Bound to the world of time, human beings can see things created by God: externally, they can see that they exist through the senses, and internally, they can see that they are good through reflection. But they cannot see their maker and his intentions behind them: God alone 'saw them as made' when he 'saw that they were to be made'. Human beings change over time, Augustine added: 'we' are now moving towards doing good, but at an earlier time 'we' moved towards doing evil and away from him. God, instead, has always done good. Some human works are good thanks to divine grace, but they are not eternal: rest can be found only in God. God alone, who is not in need of any additional good because he is the Good, is always in repose, because he is his own repose. Until human beings finally join God's

---

30   Schumm, 'Quoted Confessions', p. 738.

rest beyond this life subjugated to time, they can only put all their effort into directing their intention to the right destination, into doing good in an interminable work.[31]

It seems that Augustine, here, is providing an ontological ground for what he has been saying in epistemological terms about the multiplicity of human interpretations and the openness of human works. While intention and created work immediately coincide in God, they do not coincide for human beings. While God experiences his own works as the full realization of his intentions for them, there is always a discrepancy between work and intention for the human being. Therefore, the latter is bound to endless interpretation and the work itself, literary or otherwise, is necessarily open from a human perspective. The entire endeavour of the *Confessions*, after all, can be seen as a tireless attempt to bring together work and intention in the form of a prolonged performance of love, rather than an accomplished task, a finished *work*.[32] For Conybeare,

> [t]he *Confessions* is a song of unlikeness. Augustine is not concerned just with incompleteness and imperfection and with trying again and again to put words to that endless open-endedness; he is trying, through the incompleteness, to gesture toward something utterly other, which is God.[33]

In confession, 'truly' or 'verily' speaking, for the confessant, does not seem to be primarily a matter of referential truth — that is, the content of the speech is unmistakably true — but a quality of the performance, which needs to perform a good intention. Augustine, as any other medieval author, is perfectly aware of intertextuality, of the fact that a text is always, as Barthes points out, a 'woven fabric' made of quota-

---

31 'At the beginning, we are reading the words of David's psalmody, not Augustine's own. At the end, we are only at the beginning. And the *Confessions* is, quite simply, a song' (Conybeare, 'Reading the *Confessions*', p. 99).

32 Conybeare sees the 'incompleteness' of the *Confessions* reflected in the use of the imperfect as the 'incomplete' tense and of the 'technique of instant negation'. 'If we are truly "singing with" Augustine, we must acknowledge the incompleteness of our own interpretations too. We are "anyone," but we cannot be "everyone," and so, although we may propose a multiplicity of meanings, there may always be more' (ibid., pp. 104–05).

33 Ibid., p. 106.

tions,[34] but he admits that there is an intention in the text. When the 'text' is the life of an individual seen in retrospect, as the life narrated in the *Confessions* is, the intention behind it is not his or her own, but God's.[35] The question is: how can readers respond to an intention they do not (yet) know? Augustine's answer seems to be: not by understanding, but by love, by being open to the text, by being ready to be reoriented and transformed by its words. The performance embodied in the *Confessions* appears as a double process never fully completed: on the one hand, a gradual accord or attunement of the reader's intention with the intention of the text that is being read, on the other hand, a gradual accord or attunement of the intention of the text that is being written with the author's intention.[36]

---

34   'The plural of the Text depends, that is, not on the ambiguity of its contents but on what might be called the *stereographic plurality* of its weave of signifiers (etymologically, the text is a tissue, a woven fabric)' (Barthes, *Image, Music, Text*, pp. 155–64 (p. 159)).

35   For a brief discussion of the *Confessions* as autobiography and of meaning as 'always a retrospective achievement' for humans, see Paula Fredriksen, 'The Confessions as Autobiography', in *A Companion to Augustine*, ed. by Vessey with Reid, pp. 87–98 (p. 96).

36   'It is the emotional sympathy generated by singing that Augustine so loves and fears'; '[t]he *Confessions*, for all that it is promulgated in writing, is a social work — conceived as one to be shared, one that expects the aspiring imitative involvement of its hearers. If they lay their ear to Augustine's heart — if they expect to hear him confessing "what I am like inside" (*quid ipse intus sim*) — then they must lay themselves open to being changed within as well' (Conybeare, 'Reading the *Confessions*', p. 102). Augustine's example, and especially his use of, and remarks on, song and singing may lead to interesting reformulations of the notion of the reader's 'attunement' to a text, as opposed to interpretation. See Rita Felski, *Hooked: Art and Attachment* (Chicago: University of Chicago Press, 2020).

What Was Open in/about Early Scholastic Thought?

PHILIPPA BYRNE

INTRODUCTION: DIFFICULT OPENINGS

In the urgent and bitterly fought disputations of the high scholastic period, one of the claims frequently made in dialectical treatises is that a concept has been 'clearly shown' or 'clearly proved' (*constat aperte, probat aperte*).[1] In the late thirteenth and early fourteenth centuries, such phrases are commonly found in arguments about the nature of the authority wielded by the institutional Church. Franciscan writers asserted that the principles of mendicant life could be made out *aperte* from reading the text of the Gospel and understanding the life of Francis.[2] The same methodological point was asserted in an even more polarized intellectual context when William of Ockham, James of Viterbo, and Marsilius of Padua each claimed that their own definition

---

1   For example, Henry of Ghent, *Opera omnia*, 38 vols (Leuven: Leuven University Press, 1979–2018), VI: *Quodlibet II*, ed. by R. Wielockx (1983), q. 8, p. 39: *sequitur apertissime*; q. 17, p. 122: *apertissime declaratur*. Henry uses these in relation to expounding the meaning of Origen's *Commentary on Exodus* and Avicenna's *Commentary on Aristotle's Metaphysics* respectively.

2   See e.g. Bonaventure, *Bonaventurae opera omnia*, ed. by PP. Collegii S. Bonaventurae, 10 vols (Quaracchi: Collegium S. Bonaventurae, 1882–1902), V: *Quaestiones disputatae de perfectione euangelica* (1891), q. 4, a. 3, conclusio, p. 195.

of papal *potestas* — and the limits they placed on it — resulted from a clear or open (*apertus*) interpretation of Scripture, Aristotelian political theory, and the evidence of the canons.[3] Each of these scholastic authors asserted that his reading was both 'open' and the only correct interpretation of the authorities. These were not merely speculative or hypothetical arguments, but disputes with sharp practical edges, often concerning how the competing legal and moral jurisdictions of the most powerful institutions in medieval Christendom were to be reconciled.

The appeal to something shown *aperte*, or an argument that a 'major premise is clear' (*maiora est aperta*), runs through these later scholastic texts.[4] These authors also use the verb *aperire* to similar effect, for example in a construction like *aperire digneris*: if this is your premise, you ought to show me or demonstrate it.[5] In this high scholastic world, once something is understood *aperte*, it is demonstrated beyond question — it is an established premise which can be built upon in the next stage of the argument, or in the next *distinctio*.[6] Ac-

---

3   James of Viterbo, *De regimine christiano*, ed. and trans. by R. W. Dyson (Leiden: Brill, 2009), II. 5, p. 192; II. 10, p. 324. Cf. Marsilius of Padua, *Defensor pacis*, ed. by C. W. Previté-Orton (Cambridge: Cambridge University Press, 1928), I. 9. 5, p. 33: *ut apparet ex Aristotelis aperta sententia*; I. 9. 9, p. 35: *quamvis indubie tenendum secundum veritatem, et Aristotelis apertam sententiam*; I. 11. 4, p. 45: *Et his amplius dicit aperte Aristoteles IV Politicae [...]*; II. 5. 5, p. 151: *de his enim loquitur Apostolus aperte, cum dixit [...]*.

4   William of Ockham, 1 *Dialogus*, III. 4: *Maior est aperta; minor exemplo et ratione probatur* (The major premise is clear; the minor is proved by example and by argument). The text of the *Dialogus* used here is taken from the British Academy's online edition, edited and translated by John Kilcullen and others <https://www.thebritishacademy. ac.uk/pubs/dialogus/ockdial.html> [accessed 22 December 2019].

5   William of Ockham, 1 *Dialogus*, v. 12: *Unde si possunt trahere hoc ex scripturis autenticis, aperire digneris* (So if they can extract this out from genuine writings, would you kindly show me). This is Ockham's student seeking explanation from his master about the different meanings that can be drawn out of the phrase *Romana ecclesia*.

6   Cf. Hugh of St Victor, *Didascalicon*, ed. by Charles H. Buttimer (Washington, DC: Catholic University Press, 1939), III. 8, p. 58: *aperta significatio* is a meaning which can be understood straightforwardly, without further investigation — the first and most obvious meaning of a word; cf. also III. 5, p. 56, for the idea that something which can be understood *apertius* can also be understood *brevius*. In v. 3, p. 97, Hugh promises an example which will be *brevi et aperto*. There is probably an association here with something which can be understood quickly, as soon as the physical text has been opened. For a translation of this text, see *The Didascalicon of Hugh of St. Victor: A Medieval Guide to the Arts*, trans. by Jerome Taylor (New York: Columbia University Press, 1961).

cordingly, in these works, the term *apertus* (open) is not opposed to *clausus* (closed), but is more typically contrasted with *obscurus*: that which is obscure, a text or authority which does not readily disclose its information, or one requiring further investigation and exposition by a master skilled in reading such texts.[7]

It goes without saying that this appeal to a text which has been successfully 'opened' is as much, if not more, a rhetorical as a logical strategy. When William of Ockham notes that he has demonstrated a proposition *aperte*, he is not describing a particular kind of scholastic methodology, but is rather stating that an idea or principle has been expounded to his own intellectual satisfaction. Indeed, the claim *videtur apertissime* is often made after William has brought forward the most contentious part of his argument — whether about the designation of heretics, the power of the Pope alone or in council, or the status of Rome before Constantine.[8] It serves as a way of indicating that a question has been settled, and that an incorrect interpretation has been put right. The same blurring of logical and rhetorical claims can be found in Dante's *Monarchia*. There Dante expounds on the relationship between temporal and spiritual powers, seeking to make the case for the necessity of a single world emperor. He turns to the text of Luke 2. 1, recording Augustus's decision to impose a tax across the Roman Empire. In Dante's reading, one can 'clearly perceive' (*aperte intelligere possumus*) from this passage that, at the time of Christ's birth, 'the Romans exercised jurisdiction over the whole world'.[9] This statement, in turn, becomes the basis for Dante's claims about the providential nature of Roman imperial authority. Both Dante and Ockham were making particular and specific arguments which, when taken together, were intended to redefine quite drastically the sphere of papal authority. In short, propositions presented as *aperte* were often far from settled.

---

7   This is a point made most clearly in introductory guides for the study of Scripture, e.g. Hugh of St Victor, *Didascalicon*, VI. 4, pp. 117–22.

8   William of Ockham, 1 *Dialogus*, V. 35 (on erring against faith).

9   Dante, *Monarchia*, ed. and trans. by Prue Shaw (Cambridge: Cambridge University Press, 1995), II. 8, pp. 82–84: Exivit edictum a Cesare Augusto, ut describeretur universus orbis; in quibus verbis universalem mundi iurisdictionem tunc Romanorum fuisse aperte intelligere possumus.

When this high scholastic disputational literature has been translated into English, the term *aperte* usually ends up as 'clearly', 'plainly', or 'evidently'. This is typically done with little consistency, but used to indicate the certainty and force behind the speaker's argument. This is not inaccurate insofar as it conveys the sense of the locution, but, as a practice of translation, it tends to elide *aperte* with terms like *patenter* or *manifeste*.[10] Such practices of translation make it more difficult to appreciate why *aperte* was a particularly meaningful term for scholastic theologians, and the polemical edge it contained, with implications about correct interpretation. If nothing else, then, this contribution is a plea for intellectual historians to read closely and consistently the small words and phrases which scholastic theologians used to underline their arguments.

I have begun with some of the many appearances of *aperire* in high scholastic thought, where its rhetorical and logical functions can be seen plainly. But those functions were a legacy of how the term had been integrated into the technical vocabulary of early scholasticism in the eleventh and twelfth centuries. *Aperire* was, of course, not a new term; but it was adapted and its old associations developed and redesigned for use in the dialectical teaching practices of the schools and universities. Thus, as a word in the scholastic lexicon (I make no claims for anywhere else), studying the meaning of *aperire/aperte* over the course of two centuries — from *c.* 1050 to *c.* 1250 — can provide a revealing way of thinking about the development of scholastic thought, and the relationship between dialectic and rhetoric.

Charting the scholastic use of *aperire* also compels the historian to consider the development of scholastic method and scholastic attitudes towards the pages on which their authorities could be read. It brings us to the now-classic argument of Mary and Richard Rouse that one of the key features of scholasticism — what distinguished it from forms of learning and teaching which preceded it — was that it provided a new model for the organization of knowledge.[11] Schools

---

10   While *patenter* and *manifeste* both convey the same idea of 'opening', they describe a state rather than suggesting the same agency, dynamism, or movement implied by *aperte/aperire. Patenter* (from *patere*) denotes being open, *manifeste* (*manifestare*) something which is exhibited or shown.

11   Richard H. and Mary A. Rouse, '"Statim invenire": Schools, Preachers, and New Attitudes to the Page', in *Renaissance and Renewal in the Twelfth Century*, ed. by Robert L. Benson and Giles Constable (Oxford: Oxford University Press, 1982), pp. 201–28.

needed texts which were readily searchable, capable of use by multiple students, which adhered to a somewhat standardized framework and recognizable models (hence, for example, the increasing importance of an alphabetical approach). Scholasticism is defined by a reorganization of the page, and a new relationship with what is on the page. By the same token, examining the shifting technical sense of *aperire*, we find an echo of this: the term came to denote a more standardized process of expounding and explication.

Over the course of a century and a half, the meaning of *aperire* underwent significant change. It moved from describing God as opening the human senses or performing acts of revelation to describing a mode of textual analysis undertaken by the *magister*, something closer in meaning to *ostendere* or *intelligere* (the three were increasingly used as synonyms). This was not a straightforward or consistent process. Nevertheless, the changing meaning of *aperire* does in some way map onto the way in which dialectic came to supersede older commentary traditions. This is not to suggest that we should resurrect old stereotypes of the hard and fast distinctions between long-standing 'monastic' and newer 'scholastic' forms of learning, or that a new and brutal public rationalism trampled over and superseded an earlier meditative and private approach to Scripture.[12] Certainly, however, the turn of the eleventh century saw a new interest in the different ways in which one might divide up authoritative texts and the techniques for exploring their meaning. Moreover, once *aperire* was increasingly associated with the interpretation of a text by a master, and given a technical meaning, it also gained a rhetorical function. It allowed the lines between those who could and could not correctly 'open' the text to be drawn more sharply; it allowed the process of textual interpretation to be turned to a more polemical purpose.

---

12   Cf. Jean Leclercq, *The Love of Learning and the Desire for God: A Study of Monastic Culture*, trans. by Catherine Misrahi (New York: Fordham University Press, 1982). Note that at least two of the authors examined here — Gilbert Crispin and Honorius Augustodunensis — were members of monastic communities.

FROM REVELATION TO INTERPRETATION

Let me begin in the later decades of the twelfth century, with Alan of Lille's *Distinctiones*.[13] This is a text Alan prepared as a reference tool for preachers, as a digest of theological learning, a work which, assembled in alphabetical order, provides entries defining the meanings and associations of terms which a scholar or preacher might need to know — ranging from *abyssus* to *zelotes*. Alan also notes significant scriptural passages featuring the word in question. Some of these words have obvious doctrinal or religious significance, such as *prophetare* or *Psalterium*; but other terms — even small ones such as *pro* — require discussion because understanding their meaning will shape one's reading of Scripture. Typically, Alan provides more detailed entries for words which recur often in Scripture or which can sustain multiple meanings.[14]

While we might associate Alan with an experimental approach to new intellectual forms, and the 'white heat' of scholastic learning, he provides a discussion of *aperire* which maintains its connection to an act of opening undertaken by God, i.e. the meaning of the term found in older monastic commentaries. In those earlier medieval texts, *aperire* describes the revelation or the exposure of divine truths — either on a small scale or a large scale.[15] It is an act performed by God, which changes the lives of humans on earth, or through which some aspect of the divine is made known to humankind in a way which they could not grasp of their own accord without provision made by God.[16] This meaning lies somewhere between a sense of preparation and revelation. Alan's examples are God 'opening' the heavens, or Christ's actions in ushering in the Resurrection and Last Judgement.

---

13   Gillian R. Evans, 'Alan of Lille's Distinctiones and the Problem of Theological Language', *Sacris erudiri*, 24 (1980), pp. 67–86.

14   A good example is the term *oculus* (*Patrologia Latina* [henceforth: PL] 210. 879–81). Alan notes that it can represent the contemplative life, but one can also speak of the *oculus Dei* which distinguishes between the good and the bad. From this Alan then moves to discuss the significance of the pupil, distinguishing light from dark.

15   See e.g. Gregory the Great, *Moralia in Iob*, ed. by Marc Adriaen, 3 vols (Turnhout: Brepols: 1979–85), I (1979), V. XXXVI. 66, pp. 264–66, explaining that there are some aspects of the divine too great for the human mind to be opened to, and in such cases the mind is kept reverentially shut.

16   Alan of Lille, *Distinctiones*, PL 210. 703B–C.

Aperire can also refer to God's actions in 'opening' the senses of a single individual, providing them with some special knowledge. In short, *aperire* describes a model of divine action and intervention in the created world: the human sinner makes a request, but divinity does the opening. Alan gives the example of Psalm 118. 19: 'open to me the gates of righteousness' (*aperite mihi portas justitiae*).[17]

There are limitations to what we can infer about theological change from Alan's *Distinctiones* alone. They belong to a genre of texts intended as a point of reference for theological terms, not as a comprehensive guide to the complexities of scriptural interpretation. Yet this text still shows evident continuity with earlier medieval senses of *aperire*.[18] Alan's use of the term has much in common with pre-twelfth-century glosses on Matthew 7. 7: *pulsate et aperietur vobis* (knock and it shall be opened unto you). Earlier commentators understood this passage as describing the fact that while humans must prepare themselves to receive divine revelation, knowledge is only bestowed upon them (*opened* for them) by God.[19] Alan of Lille's succinct description of the sense of *aperire*, however, does not fully represent the complexity of the discussions taking place in the schools around this term. Twelfth-century scholastic commentaries on the Old Testament seem to be — gradually, fitfully — moving towards a definition of opening which placed an emphasis on the process of human exposition rather than divine revelation, and towards an understanding of opening which is most closely associated with the handling of a text rather than the opening of (for example) the human heart or human mind. This is not a uniform development, but it is discernible in multiple commentaries. Moreover, this is most visible when commentators discuss how to treat the books of the Old Testament.

---

17 This meaning was not lost in later centuries — given its scriptural foundations, it continued to be employed, e.g. in Dante, *Monarchia*, II. 7, pp. 76–78, which describes the act of trial by combat as a way of God's judgement being 'opened' up to humankind.

18 See e.g. Bede's commentary on Song of Songs 5. 5: *surrexi ut aperirem dilecto meo*, discussing how the process of opening is one of opening to the Lord. See Bede, *In Cantica canticorum*, IV. 5.19, PL 91. 1157B.

19 See e.g. Pascasius Radbertus, *Expositio in Matheo*, ed. by Beda Paulus, 3 vols (Turnhout: Brepols, 1984), I, pp. 434–35; cf. Bede, *In Cantica canticorum*, III. 3.13, PL 91. 1123A.

This is the case in Abelard's commentary on the *Hexameron*, which probably dates to the early to mid-1130s.[20] I take Abelard because, at least here, he looks rather similar to his contemporaries — caught between two different meanings of *aperire*. Abelard begins his commentary allegorically, and associates the act of 'opening' with the different ages of the world: Christ's decisive intervention in human history, through the Incarnation, has opened a new age.[21] Likewise, the other act of opening he discusses is that associated with Genesis 1. 3 ('let there be light'). There, God brought light into being and thus opened the world, making it intelligible through light.[22] Elsewhere in this *Hexameron* commentary, however, Abelard begins to describe the process of opening in quite a different way, and one which puts considerably more emphasis on human ability to pursue the meaning of the text. To 'open' is to discover what can be understood from the text, and then to teach it. If Genesis can be opened *diligenter*, then one is also able to learn and explain many things about the human body and the human soul.[23]

This sense of *aperire* as exposition could also move beyond a purely scholastic audience, into texts concerned with the wider instruction and edification of a Christian laity; this is the sense in which the early twelfth-century theologian Honorius Augustodunensis sometimes employed the term. Although the details of his career remain obscure, Honorius's intellectual programme involved translating the essential premises of scholastic knowledge into a more readily comprehensible format.[24] His use of *aperire* reflects this desire. Honorius's commentary on the Psalms begins with a contrast between knowledge that is hidden *per involucra et aenigmatica tecta*, and those things which are available *aperta*.[25] The Psalms can be read; but they must be accessed through the Incarnation — Christ is the interpretive key to

---

20   Abelard, *Expositio in Hexameron*, ed. by Mary Romig (Turnhout: Brepols, 2004), p. lxxiv.

21   Ibid., [8], p. 5: *ut, qui prophetae verba largitus est, ipse nobis eorum aperiat sensum*.

22   Ibid., [45], p. 17.

23   Ibid., prologue, p. 5: the act of commentary on Genesis is to expound what is *obscura*.

24   For some discussion of the complicated problem of his identity and career, see V. I. J. Flint, 'The Career of Honorius Augustodunensis : Some Fresh Evidence', *Revue bénédictine*, 82.1–2 (1972), pp. 63–86.

25   Honorius Augustodunensis, *Expositio Psalmorum*, PL 172. 269C.

understanding its figurations. Honorius goes some way to explaining how this may be done as he sets out for the reader how individual Psalms may be broken down and divided up for scrutiny.[26] One task for the reader is to understand what the text would mean if its meaning were stated openly (*ac si aperte dicat*).[27] This relationship between 'open' knowledge and systematic exposition is evident elsewhere in Honorius's writings. He introduces his *Sacramentarium* as a text which is intended to open (*aperiatur*) the complexities of the divine office to the ignorant (*ignaris*).[28] Opening here is connected to new methods of learning and exposition, an attempt to teach and instruct. The purpose of instruction may require the restructuring or reframing of a text by a master. Honorius, however, never goes as far as to suggest that everything in the Bible can be read *aperte* or rendered open;[29] and he maintains (like many other authors, and in keeping with the text of Scripture) that *aperire* can be an injunction addressed to God, in the hope of divine revelation or fulfilment.[30] Overall, however, like many of those who would follow him in the twelfth century, Honorius equates the master's job in the expounding of Scripture with the work of opening.[31]

As with so much of medieval exegesis, ambivalence in meaning and emphasis was the order of the day: commentators could use *aperire* either to afford priority to divine power or to underline the efforts of the human master in the act of opening. Within the twelfth-century schools, there remained scope to invoke the idea of opening

---

26   See e.g. ibid., *PL* 172. 284B–C: *de divisione hujus Psalmi.*

27   Honorius Augustodunensis, *Expositio in Cantica canticorum*, I. 1, *PL* 172. 360B. This is of course a common phrase in much medieval writing, and is not particular to Honorius.

28   Honorius Augustodunensis, *Sacramentarium*, prologue, *PL* 172. 737C.

29   Honorius Augustodunensis, *Quaestiones et responsiones in Proverbia*, *PL* 172. 325C.

30   Honorius Augustodunensis, *Expositio Psalmorum*, on Psalm 50. 17: *Domine, labia mea aperies.*

31   See e.g. Peter the Chanter's *Verbum abbreviatum*, ed. by Monique Boutry (Turnhout: Brepols, 2004); in I. 1, p. 19 (glossing Matthew 27. 51), Peter develops an analogy about how the meaning that was hidden and concealed in the writing of the Prophets is made comprehensible — opened — when one relates those texts to the life of Christ (*ad intelligendum aperta et manifesta facta sunt*). One might also cite Hugh of St Victor's *Didascalicon*, another text for those beginning the study of Scripture; VI. 6, p. 123, discusses the relationship between *obscuris* and *apertis*: the Old Testament promises the truth but hides it, the New Testament announces it and makes it manifest.

in a more traditional and less technical fashion, according to a model in which God opened the text to human senses in order to permit human understanding. This usage was more equivocal about the association between *aperire* and *intelligere*; it continued to ascribe the act of opening to God. It can be seen in Peter of Poitiers's *Allegoriae super tabernaculum Moysi*, a work of the 1170s/80s.[32] The nature of glossing is discussed in the prologue: glossing is the process by which we see that the parts of Scripture that were once obscure and impenetrable can become intelligible.[33] This is not an act performed by humans alone — Peter of Poitiers relies on the model of *pulsate et aperietur vobis* (Matthew 7. 7): God opens mysteries to human comprehension; humans then set to work on them. Nevertheless, Peter of Poitiers's prologue does, at the very least, associate the act of glossing with the receipt of 'opened' information, and the opened information provided exclusively to Christians through Scripture.[34] Broadly speaking, in the context of the schools of twelfth-century northern France, *aperire* was being lined up as something less mystical, something increasingly more like the process of *expositio*, and something more closely aligned to the teaching of a text, just as that process of teaching was in itself becoming more clearly defined.[35]

The above examples of opening demonstrate that this language was applied to many different kinds of texts; but most commonly these twelfth-century discussions of how to open a text were focused on the interpretation of the Old Testament and how the seemingly obscure, occasionally contradictory, passages of those books could be explicated.[36] The centrality of the Old Testament in this process of scholastic opening is best illustrated by considering Hugh of St Victor's writing on Noah's ark. This encompasses two works composed between 1125 and 1130: *De arca Noe morali* and the *De arca Noe mystica*

---

32 Peter of Poitiers, *Allegoriae super tabernaculum Moysi*, ed. by Philip S. Moore and James A. Corbett (Notre Dame: University of Notre Dame Press, 1938).

33 Ibid., prologue, p. 1.

34 Ibid., I, p. 31.

35 Cf. Hugh of St Victor, *Didascalicon*, III. 9, pp. 58–59; VI. 12, pp. 129–30, emphasizing that a text is examined through dividing it into parts.

36 Cf. Abelard, *Sic et non*, ed. by Blanche B. Boyer and Richard McKeon (Chicago: University of Chicago Press, 1976–77), prologue, p. 97, recognizing the particular difficulty of opening the meaning of the Old Testament Prophets.

(also known as the *Libellus de formatione arche*). The two texts tend towards the same point: encouraging the reader to take the ark as a model for their own spiritual advancement, as well as a key to understanding the history of salvation.[37] The *Moral Ark* examines the different ways in which the ark might be interpreted, according to the four senses of Scripture: historically, in the sense of physical dimensions of the ark;[38] morally, as the institutional Church;[39] allegorically, as standing for wisdom;[40] and anagogically, as a model for the operation of grace.[41] These three latter kinds of interpretation are only possible if one has the correct understanding of the historical ark — its size and construction. Hugh is, first and foremost, concerned that any 'opening' of the text begin from certain and established historical parameters. Imagining the ark is one way in which scriptural history can be grasped: through it the Old Testament can be understood, and through it one can perceive parts of a history of salvation that is yet to come.

Hugh is particularly concerned with the allegorical significance of the opening of the windows of the ark, and how this conveys the relationship between human activity and divine revelation.[42] Noah opened the windows of the ark in order to send out birds to search for land; this kind of opening provides a model for the way in which the human soul might use reason to search out its heavenly destination.[43] But while humans may be capable of opening the windows of the ark, the doors could only be opened (or reopened) by the Lord, allowing humankind to finally leave the ark and continue on their journey to salvation. Hugh accords scope to the scholastic master and human intellect, but continues to recognize the importance of divine grace. The same idea is conveyed in the *Mystic Ark*, where Hugh returns to the opening of doors and windows: God will open the door and the

---

37   Hugh of St Victor, *De archa Noe, Libellus de formatione arche*, ed. by Patrice Sicard (Turnhout: Brepols, 2001). For a detailed discussion, see Conrad Rudolph, *The Mystic Ark: Hugh of Saint Victor, Art, and Thought in the Twelfth Century* (New York: Cambridge University Press, 2014).

38   Hugh of St Victor, *De archa Noe*, I. 4, pp. 18–23.

39   Ibid., I. 5, pp. 23–32.

40   Ibid., II. 1, pp. 33–34.

41   Ibid., III. 2, p. 57.

42   Ibid., II. 2, pp. 35–37.

43   Ibid., II. 2, p. 35.

good will walk through it, while the wicked will try to break down the doors to salvation, but will not be admitted.[44]

Hugh of St Victor underlined the active part taken by the human intellect in the process of opening up salvation history to understanding. His act of opening went beyond the page. Hugh 'opened' the text of the Old Testament by creating a wall painting to accompany the text: a complex diagram depicting both Christ and the ark which was reproduced on the walls of St Victor and could be used as an image for teaching. Indeed, Conrad Rudolph has argued that the text of the *Mystic Ark* represented an instruction manual for reproducing that image, enabling scholars outside St Victor to depict Noah's ark as a visual representation of salvation history.[45] This emphasis on understanding is repeated throughout the texts of the *Moral Ark* and the *Mystic Ark*: one of the challenges for the teacher is to convey to the reader or listener what could be understood through a simple unfolding of the text.[46] Only when the complete image had been depicted and made visible to the eye would it be possible to understand the relationship between parts and whole.[47] This was, in a certain sense, the 'opening up' of the text further by translating it into an image through which Scripture could be understood, certainly a process of opening in the sense of making it fit for teaching, recognizing divisions and subdivisions. Most importantly, Hugh's act of opening was an act of teaching: it was being done before an audience and for the improved understanding of that audience.

A similar practical aim can be traced further on into the thirteenth century, in Robert Grosseteste's commentary on the *Hexameron*.[48] Like many before him, Grosseteste tries to explain what it means to 'open' the text. The first point he makes is about the relationship between the teacher/expounder and his listeners or readers. Although this is a *Hexameron* commentary, Grosseteste here takes the example

---

44   Hugh of St Victor, *Libellus de formatione arche*, VII, p. 152.

45   Conrad Rudolph has argued that the text of the *Mystic Ark* should be understood as a *reportatio* (*'First, I Find the Center Point': Reading the Text of Hugh of Saint Victor's The Mystic Ark* (Philadelphia: American Philosophical Society, 2004), pp. 9–32).

46   Cf. Hugh of St Victor, *De archa Noe*, I. 4, p. 23.

47   Ibid., I. 3, p. 10.

48   Robert Grosseteste, *Hexaëmeron*, ed. by Richard C. Dales and Servus Gieben (Oxford: Oxford University Press, 1982).

of the Gospels. The Gospels, he explains, are sadly brief. That is because not every event of Christ's life could be written down in detail: if one held the writers of the Gospels to this standard, then the world would not be able to contain everything that could be related about the life of Christ.[49] Instead, the authors were obliged to offer a brief summary, along with rules for living. Grosseteste believes that Scripture contains everything (including the whole of the supernatural, details of human-kind's restoration and future glory) but for this to be realized it must be expounded.[50] That, then, means that the work of those who come after is to open out Scripture, an act of instructive expansion, in order to spell out what should be done to restore humankind.

Aperire in the twelfth century was undergoing a significant redefin-ition. As the examples above suggest, it was coming to be more closely aligned with the dialectical method and the technique of scholastic instruction. The complexity of the Old Testament drove scholastic theologians to think about what it meant for a text to be opened; it was increasingly associated with the application of human ratio: many of the seemingly obscure mysteries of Scripture were capable of being opened — if the student took the right interpretative approach.

OPENING AND POLEMIC

The above twelfth-century discussions of aperire are, for the most part, concerned with correct reading for the sake of improvement of Chris-tian understanding, particularly in deciphering the status of the Old Testament and its relationship to the post-Incarnation world. Mat-ters of 'clear' interpretation or opening are not yet enlivened by the later political arguments about the status of poverty, the correctness of Aristotelian political principles, or the proper ordering of institu-tional hierarchies within the Church. Ostensibly, then, it seems that twelfth-century commentaries offer increasingly 'practical' ideas about opening, but nothing as sharply polemical as later thirteenth-century texts. But to assume this would be to draw a false contrast. There was one context in which arguments about 'opening' served an explicitly

---

49   Ibid., I. 4. 1, pp. 51–52.
50   Ibid., I. 4. 1, p. 52.

argumentative purpose: in anti-Jewish disputational literature. In such texts, the difference between Christianity and Judaism is constructed upon the Christian ability to interpret the Old Testament correctly, and Jewish inability or unwillingness to do so.

Anti-Jewish diatribes were not, of course, new in the twelfth century, but the twelfth century certainly saw an expansion of a literature in which Christian and Jewish speakers disputed the merits of their relative religious practices and beliefs, and their access to spiritual truth. Some of these texts were based on real exchanges between Christian and Jewish scholars; others were clearly more 'abstract' exercises, written for the purpose of defining and vindicating Christian orthodoxy.[51] As has long been recognized, this disputational literature is in itself evidence of hardening Christian attitudes towards the presence of Jewish communities in Latin Europe, and one facet of increasing Christian violence against Jews in these societies.[52] A central claim in the texts of many of these debates is that what sets a Christian reader apart from a Jewish one is the ability to interpret Scripture in accordance with reason. One can here see how the concept of *aperire* impinged on these arguments; to use that Latin term was to claim that even 'obscure' passages of the Old Testament were capable of being opened, and that it was possible to distinguish between correct and incorrect openings of the text through the application of human reason. Thus, in the disputational literature of Gilbert Crispin, Peter Alfonsi, and Peter Abelard, it is Jewish unwillingness to appreciate the Christian method which is the problem. Christians explain the tools for opening the Old Testament, but Jewish readers refuse to utilize them. In these texts, *aperire* does not merely describe a process of textual exposition; it denotes the superior Christian ability to access the divine truths hidden in holy texts.

That association between Christian reason and correct opening is repeatedly asserted in Gilbert Crispin's *Disputatio Iudei et Christiani*,

---

51   The literature on this point is plentiful, but see esp. Anna Sapir Abulafia, 'Jewish–Christian Disputations and the Twelfth-Century Renaissance', *Journal of Medieval History*, 15.2 (1989), pp. 105–25.

52   Cf. M. Soifer, '"You say that the Messiah has come ..."': The Ceuta Disputation (1179) and its Place in the Christian Anti-Jewish Polemics of the High Middle Ages', *Journal of Medieval History*, 31.3 (2005), pp. 287–307.

written in the last decade of the eleventh century.[53] Gilbert, abbot of Westminster, had been a student of both Lanfranc and Anselm at Bec; as Alex Novikoff has argued, Gilbert's approach to the dialogue form was undoubtedly shaped by his training at Bec, an experience which also imbued him with a concern for how Christian truth could be accessed through human reasoning.[54] In Gilbert's *Disputatio*, the Christian speaker sets out the difference between Jewish and Christian interpretations of the Old Testament. He explains that Christians have opened up those profound mysteries, while the Jews have not. Here the act of opening becomes tied up with the idea of correct interpretation: through Christ the text has been opened to humans, and thus Scripture can be understood (*intelligere*). This is supported by invoking the words of Psalm 77. 2: *aperiam in parabolis os meum; loquar propositiones ab initio* (I will open my mouth in parables, I will explain things that were hidden from the beginning).[55] Rather than a process of revelation by God to man, this is Christian knowledge speaking to Jewish ignorance. In the *Disputatio*, it is Christian learning that opens up the Prophets and the law, converting *enigmata* to *aperta*;[56] the Christian who comes to the text of the Bible will understand the message it seeks to convey *apertissime*.[57] It is striking that in Gilbert's *Disputatio*, *aperire* is used almost exclusively by the Christian speaker: the term is characteristic of Christian claims about Scripture; it is not a word associated with the Jewish participant.

---

53   Gilbert Crispin, *Disputatio Iudei et Christiani*, in *The Works of Gilbert Crispin, Abbot of Westminster*, ed. by Anna Sapir Abulafia and Gillian R. Evans (London: British Academy, 1986), pp. 1–53. For the influence of Gilbert's dialogue beyond the context of Jewish–Christian disputation, see David Berger, 'Gilbert Crispin, Alan of Lille, and Jacob ben Reuben: A Study in the Transmission of Medieval Polemic', *Speculum*, 49.1 (1974), pp. 34–47; Berger's point is that the rhetorical techniques used by Gilbert Crispin against Jews went on to be used against heretics in the twelfth century.

54   See Alex J. Novikoff, 'Anselm, Dialogue, and the Rise of Scholastic Disputation', *Speculum*, 86.2 (2011), pp. 387–418 (esp. pp. 408–12). Gilbert's dialogue is also notable for the fact that he introduces it as based on a real debate with a Jewish merchant from Mainz.

55   Crispin, *Disputatio*, 31, p. 15.

56   Ibid., 104, p. 35.

57   Ibid., 94, p. 32. The use of the superlative here and elsewhere is striking, and indicates the metaphorical use and scholastic development of the term *aperire*. On a literal level, 'open' is a binary state, not one of degree; something is either opened or closed.

A decade or so after Gilbert's *Disputatio*, Peter Alfonsi's anti-Jewish *Dialogus* (*c.* 1110) yoked the term *aperire* to *demonstrare*. Alfonsi's *Dialogus* begins not with Scripture, but with the Christian speaker (Peter, modelled on Alfonsi himself, a convert to Christianity) discussing with the Jew the nature of the created universe — matters of climate, time, and astronomy. Even in the world of natural science, the Christian demonstrates his superior ability to open up the knowledge of the universe. Where the *Dialogus* differs from the *Disputatio* is in the fact that Alfonsi's Jew — named Moses — is keen to learn how the Christian scholastic methodology of opening texts works — whether applied to philosophical matters or the text of Scripture; he is an interested student of *ratio*. Thus Moses asks Peter to 'speak more plainly' (*quaeso apertius loquere*) and to explain through analogy, in order that he might follow the subtleties of the Christian argument.[58] Peter explains to his Jewish interlocutor how to decipher information on the page, explaining that what Moses seeks to understand about the orbit of the sun is made comprehensible through viewing a diagram.[59] Before they arrive at the topic of Scripture, the Christian speaker has been positioned as the individual able to open up the meaning of the written word. From this point, Peter moves into more familiar arguments about the Old Testament, a text which is not 'sufficiently open to all' (*nec omnibus satis aperta*).[60] It is only those who recognize that the Prophets of the Old Testament speak in allegories, prefiguring the future, who can open the text in accordance with reason (*ratio*) and who are capable of understanding (*intelligere*). Throughout the first several books of the *Dialogus*, the Jew wishes to be able to open the texts (*apertius intelligere volo*), but must turn to the Christian for instruction in the method of doing so.[61] In turn, he praises the Christian for using 'the most open and most unchallengeable arguments' to make

---

58   Petrus Alfonsi, *Dialogus*, I, PL 157. 544C: *adhuc, quaeso, apertius loquere, et per aliquam similitudinem rem tam subtilem ostende*. Translation: Petrus Alfonsi, *Dialogue against the Jews*, trans. by. Irven M. Resnick (Washington, DC: Catholic University of America Press, 2006), p. 55.

59   Ibid., I, *PL* 157. 548C: *oculis subjecta aperte demonstrate descriptio*.

60   Ibid., I, *PL* 157. 553A (trans. by Resnick, p. 72).

61   Ibid., I, *PL* 157. 556A–B; see too III, *PL* 157. 586C, in which the Jew thanks his Christian interlocutor for explaining that which he was ignorant of, but still wishes for one further point to be opened for him (*sed unum restat quod mihi postulo aperiri*).

his case.[62] It is not until book IV of the *Dialogus* that discussion of the process of 'opening' turns to Mosaic law and the Prophets of the Old Testament.[63] Moses challenges Peter to explain how Scripture can be opened — Peter responds by working through the texts set before him, line by line. This is not a meditation on Scripture but an induction into a scholastic method of opening texts; the text which has been opened then provides a convincing proof of Christian truth.

Lastly in this sequence of dialogues, we can consider Peter Abelard's *Collationes*, written between the late 1120s and early 1130s. Abelard's text is distinct in that it is a three-part dialogue between a Christian, a Jew, and a Philosopher. The latter figure represents a kind of classical (pagan) philosophy; he recognizes a divine if natural principle but does not recognize the authority of Christian Scripture. The work begins with a dialogue between Christian and Jew before moving on to a dialogue between Christian and Philosopher.

On multiple occasions, Abelard's Christian informs his Jewish interlocutor that Jewish social and religious practices, supposedly informed by Mosaic law, are wrong, premised on a straightforward misunderstanding of the text: *unde te aperte legis scriptura reprehendit* (the biblical text of the law openly shows that you are wrong).[64] Scripture *aperte docet* (openly teaches) the opposite of Jewish practice.[65] On the one hand, this is an appeal to a technical theological process (i.e. interpretation of specific Old Testament passages). On the other, it is also explicitly polemical — in the context of a debate between a Christian and a Jew to explain who has mastery of scriptural interpretation. The idea of opening the texts is allied to the idea of providing *testimonia* — evidence for the understanding of Christian writers.[66]

---

62 Ibid., IV, PL 157. 593B: *et apertissimarum et inexpugnabilium luce rationum, hujus a me infidelit tis errorem tulisti* (you have lifted the error of infidelity from me with the clearest and most unconquerable arguments; trans. by Resnick, p. 139).

63 See too ibid., VIII, PL 157. 619C, in which Peter explains that there are multiple statements from the Prophets which can demonstrate still more clearly (*apertius ostendere*) Christian arguments about the status of Christ as both God and man.

64 Abelard, *Collationes*, ed. and trans. by J. Marenbon and G. Orlandi (Oxford: Clarendon Press, 2001), I. 48, p. 58. Marenbon translates *aperte* as 'clearly' rather than 'openly'.

65 Ibid., I. 51, p. 60.

66 For testimonies and how they might be used, according to audience, see ibid., I. 26, p. 36; II. 143, p. 152.

The world of the *Collationes* is one in which the texts of Scripture are to be cracked open by human enquiry — rather than waiting for revelation by God.[67] This approach is most apparent when the Christian explains his intellectual method not to the Jew but to the (pagan) Philosopher. The Philosopher complains that the Christian is not arguing from reason (the agreed-upon basis for their discussion), but from the authority of Scripture, which the Philosopher does not accept and therefore cannot find persuasive. The Christian's response is that 'my purpose is not to put to you my own view, but to open up to you the common faith and teaching of our fathers' (*sed commune maiorum nostrorum tibi fidem seu doctrinam aperire*).[68] These are put before the Philosopher so they may be understood, so he may be able to comprehend the basis for the Christian's arguments. To put something openly (*aperte dicere*) is to explain its meaning;[69] *aperte ratione* (open reasoning) describes the process by which Christians work through Scripture.[70]

Two points should be drawn out of this discussion of anti-Jewish disputational literature. The first is a caveat: *aperire* was one important way of marking the distinction between Christian and Jew, but it was not the only tool for drawing such contrasts; other techniques were available. For instance, Peter the Venerable's attack on both the Jews and the Talmud, *Adversus Iudeorum inveteratem duritiem*, written in the mid-1140s, was more focused on the idea of Jewish 'blindness' than a Jewish failure to open up, divide, or analyse texts.[71] The second is that *aperire* was applied in one way in dialogues between Christians and Jews, and in quite another way in works intended to educate Christian students. A useful point of comparison is the *Elucidarium* of Honorius

---

67   More broadly, this parallels other twelfth-century discussions about how wisdom should be extracted from texts, including those over the significance of allegory and *integumenta*. It was understood that ancient authors had concealed profound theological or moral truths under literary 'veils', which only adept interpreters would be able to uncover. Strange, unusual, or disturbing language and images were not to be taken straightforwardly, but understood as such veils. The idea was applied both to Scripture and to classical texts, especially Ovid.

68   Abelard, *Collationes*, II. 168, p. 178.

69   Ibid., II. 221, p. 216.

70   Ibid., II. 223, p. 220.

71   Peter the Venerable, *Adversus Iudeorum inveteratam duritiem*, ed. by Yvonne Friedman (Turnhout: Brepols, 1985).

Augustodunensis, a pastoral text probably intended for the training of
priests of limited learning. Here the Christian *discipulus* asks a series
of questions of the Christian *magister*, each relating to the doctrines,
traditions, and practices of the Church. The *magister* elaborates, the
explanation serving the honour of God and the utility of the Church.[72]
This is not a discussion of method premised on a need to vindicate
a particular reading of religious authorities, but a straightforward and
very unspeculative explication of ideas. The Christian student never
doubts the way in which the master has come to his answer — i.e.
his method for reading text and tradition — he merely seeks further
knowledge.[73]

CONCLUSION: WHO WAS OPENING FOR?

This contribution began by considering the 'academic' use of *aperire*
in biblical commentaries before coming to its more polemical use in
scholastic anti-Jewish disputational literature. This structural choice
should not be taken as implying that the former chronologically preceded the latter; quite evidently, that was not the case. The use of
aperire in theological commentaries overlapped and interacted with
its use in disputational literature. Christian belief about why Jews
misinterpreted the Old Testament informed Christian theologians'
understandings of how they should approach Scripture, and vice versa.
The twelfth-century Latin scholastic world valued, above all things, the
correct application of methodology and argument: the schools shaped
a vision of Christianity which was not simply defined by the doctrines
derived from Scripture, but by the technical way in which Christians
handled and dissected Scripture.

Finally, we should consider whether tracing out the dimensions of
aperire in this way provides us with anything new in thinking about the
dimensions and development of scholastic thought. There can be little
doubt that the scholastic method did introduce a new sense of what
it meant for a text to be opened. Even as more technical terms were
being developed for the way in which one read, taught, or commented

---

72   Honorius Augustodunensis, *Elucidarium*, I, PL 172. 1109.

73   Ibid., I, PL 172. 1133C.

on Scripture, scholastic thought was also repurposing the older term *aperire* and providing it with new, technical dimensions. But those technical aspects equally gave rise to a rhetorical and disputational function. That may have begun with a focus on the methodological opening of the Old Testament, but it would soon come to be applied to the opening of any kind of authoritative text, including texts which had not been written by Christians but which could be put to use in the construction of Christian political society.

The changing associations of *aperire* help us perceive some of the new aspects of early twelfth-century scholastic method. This was about a 'public' culture of teaching: the text opened not just for the individual master, but for the instruction of students, according to a process that could be followed and imitated. *Aperire* had to be made explicable; it came to stand for a methodology (closely associated with logical and dialectical processes) that could reach greater numbers of students and which could be replicated across different schools, each time arriving at a successful 'opening' of the text. There is a dismal irony implicit in this process. Making the process of 'opening' a text a demonstration of scholastic reason allowed others to be cast as unreasonable interpreters. To expound a text — to open it up, whether on the page or on the walls of St Victor — had the effect of making Christendom narrower.

Speech-Wrangling
Shutting Up and Shutting Out the Oral Tradition in Some Icelandic Sagas

BRIAN MCMAHON

The ultimate origins of the Icelandic sagas are lost in the mists of time. The word *saga* (from Old Norse *segir*) means 'that which is said or reported'; however, the written prose texts which describe themselves as *sagas* bear all the hallmarks of having been composed by literate authors and are now the only evidence that attests to a once apparently thriving oral storytelling milieu.[1] We do not know precisely when the Icelanders began to write their sagas down, but it is highly unlikely that the practice began in earnest before the middle of the eleventh century, and its development was certainly gradual.[2] Since many sagas contain apparently accurate historical details inherited from the earliest settlers in the late ninth century, it follows that at least these snippets of information, embedded in narratives of indeterminate length, had been in circulation for some two hundred years before the literate sagamen began their task of composing — or, at least, redacting — written saga

---

1   See Paul Bibire, 'On Reading the Icelandic Sagas: Approaches to Old Icelandic Texts', in *West over Sea: Studies in Scandinavian Sea-Borne Expansion and Settlement before 1300*, ed. by Beverley Ballin Smith, Simon Taylor, and Gareth Williams (Leiden: Brill, 2007), pp. 3–18 (p. 3).

2   Margaret Clunies Ross, *The Cambridge Introduction to the Old Norse-Icelandic Saga* (Cambridge: Cambridge University Press, 2010), p. 48.

texts. We seldom know who these authors were, although the scribes of some manuscripts have been identified, but we do know that they ranked among the literate social and cultural elite in Iceland, primarily made up of clergy, lawyers, and landowning chieftains.[3]

The oral tradition through which folk memory was given voice before the advent of literacy in Iceland was, by definition, comparatively open. Anyone who reported news was, in the literal sense of the word, telling a *saga*. Early writers thus had access to a diffuse nexus of stories from which to draw and shape the versions of the stories they would imprint upon the page. Stephen Mitchell imagines the authors of the great family sagas, for which we rarely have any witnesses dated earlier than the late thirteenth century, as each more closely resembling 'a medieval Burns or Scott (or, perhaps more aptly, a medieval Paul Anderson or Michael Crichton)' rather than a diligent antiquarian or folklorist determined to preserve the pure distillation of some ephemeral oral *ur*-saga.[4] Tommy Danielsson has employed the metaphor 'det muntliga havet' (the oral sea) to express the fluid relationship between different oral iterations of the same stories which resist assuming a fixed form, since every recitation and repetition will differ from the last.[5] By contrast, as Ward Parks writes, 'the written text could be defined as memory concretized [...] fixed in durable form that frees it, apparently, from the effects of time'.[6] The written sagas might therefore be conceived of as islands rising up out of the oral sea — discrete; with shorelines that erode just a little over time but retain their essential integrity; and solid rather than fluid, manifesting a particular version of the story, closed off from its original sources and influences, which remains *in situ* as the waters recede and the oceans drain away. There is

---

3   Pernille Hermann, 'Literacy', in *The Routledge Research Companion to the Medieval Icelandic Sagas*, ed. by Ármann Jakobsson and Sverrir Jakobsson (Abingdon: Routledge, 2017), pp. 34–47.

4   Stephen A. Mitchell, 'The Sagaman and Oral Literature: The Icelandic Traditions of Hjörleifr inn Kvensami and Geirmundr heljarskinn', in *Comparative Research on Oral Traditions: A Memorial for Milman Parry*, ed. by John Miles Foley (Columbus, OH: Slavica, 1987), pp. 395–423 (p. 413).

5   Tommy Danielsson, *Sagorna om Norges kungar: Från Magnús góði till Magnús Erlingsson* (Hedemora: Gidlunds Förlag, 2002).

6   Ward Parks, 'The Textualisation of Orality in Literary Criticism', in *Vox Intexta: Orality and Textuality in the Middle Ages*, ed. by A. N. Doane and Carol Braun Pasternack (Madison: University of Wisconsin Press, 1991), pp. 46–61 (p. 58).

every reason to suppose that the growth of the written sagas occurred in the context of a sustained oral tradition and that, at some stage, the two forms of any given story — the written and the oral — might have come into contact and, indeed, competition with one another.[7] Yet they were distinct in modal terms: the liquid oral tradition was an open one; the process of inscribing texts on parchment sealed them off, to some extent, from further innovation. Where different or contradictory written variants emerged, their differences and contradictions could no longer be elided through dialogue and exchange between living storytellers passing on mutable stories; the writing down of sagas was, in this respect, an act of closure.

Given these circumstances, it is quite remarkable that there is such uniformity within the surviving corpus of the written sagas. Certainly, there are differences of expression which distinguish one redaction from the next — sometimes amounting to the inclusion or omission of whole episodes — and certainly, as Carol Clover has written, 'the sagas share characters, dovetail matter, and refer and defer to one another in a way that suggests that they were not conceived as self-contained wholes but as interrelated or interdependent members of a larger undertaking'.[8] Yet for all that, there is just one surviving *Njáls saga*, just one *Grettis saga*, a single *Laxdœla saga*. These exist in variant versions, but each clearly descends from a common source — although that source itself may once have been compiled from different oral influences. As Gísli Sigurðsson has argued,

> it is not unlikely that the plot and subject-matter of the sagas was derived from a living tradition of oral story-telling, where it was moulded by performers interacting with their audiences until it eventually received its fixed form in a written saga designed to be read[9]

Of course, the promulgation of the written saga does not exclude the likelihood that various versions of the same narrative continued to

---

7   A common phenomenon in medieval Europe, discussed at length in D. H. Green, *Medieval Listening and Reading* (Cambridge: Cambridge University Press, 1994).

8   Carol Clover, *The Medieval Saga* (Ithaca: Cornell University Press, 1982), p. 41.

9   Gísli Sigurðsson, 'Another Audience — Another Saga: How Can We Best Explain Different Accounts in *Vatnsdœla saga* and *Finnboga saga ramma* of the Same Events?', in *Text und Zeittiefe*, ed. by Hildegard L. C. Tristram (Tübingen: Narr, 1994), pp. 359–76 (p. 375).

circulate and evolve orally. The proliferation of manuscripts attests to the enduring popularity of these stories, and they frequently invoke one another, but the lack of competing traditions — different sagas telling the same story, rather than variant versions of the same saga — is certainly striking and significantly at odds with the mythological and heroic verse literature recorded during the same period. Two obvious solutions present themselves: either Icelandic institutional memory really was so exceptional that the same version of the same story persisted throughout the country for more than two centuries; or at some stage an editorial process took place through which unauthorized sagas were excluded from the written corpus in favour of a single, preferred, 'best-text' iteration of each story. Such a process, if it occurred, would be difficult to examine, since by definition it would have involved the expunging of competing sagas dealing with the same individual, area, or episode, but it may be possible to deduce its likelihood from the evidence of cultural attitudes which the surviving sagas provide. Editing the corpus in this way — redacting the oral tradition into authorized written versions of the sagas — would represent a process of closing off access to divergent versions in favour of a single approved iteration.

In addition to Tommy Danielsson's metaphorical 'oral sea', I would like to propose an analogy with the modern concept of copyright. The oral tradition must have been comparatively open to revision from a range of sources — susceptible to changes emerging in the narrative, focus, and *ductus* of the sagas — but by constraining or 'enclosing' the story within a manuscript and fixing it within the limits of the page, its early editors began to restrict these possibilities, gradually confining the saga within set narratological, orthographical, and codicological boundaries. The act of inscribing a saga on parchment required literacy, scribal expertise, and the expenditure of resources. As such, the process of writing down a particular redaction of the narrative conferred a certain status upon it. Writing the saga down therefore represented a challenge to alternative versions of the story then in circulation. The act of writing also represented the imposition of limitations on the scope of the story — a beginning and end within which this discrete saga took place. An oral storyteller, working from memory rather than from a manuscript, might improvise and innovate in the course of a recitation, modulating his or her performance in response to live audience feedback, but the writing down of the saga restricts the private reader from taking similar liberties. Emendation would be possible, insofar as there was space on the page, but the skeleton of the text would now be fixed. The opening and closing of the book controlled access to the written saga, and therefore access to the book was necessary to access this high-status redaction of the traditional story. Additionally, the writing down of sagas restricted access to those who could read — in other words, the literate elite.

Whereas the practice of oral storytelling was potentially open to all sectors of society, written sagas were available only to a closed community of readers — those who both enjoyed access to the manuscripts and possessed the literate skills necessary to glean their content from them. This community might be opened up to a wider audience through the reading aloud of sagas from a manuscript, but such a process should still be considered less 'open' than the preliterate oral tradition, since it could only take place subject to the availability of a manuscript and the presence of a suitably qualified (i.e. literate) reader. At the very least, the production of written saga texts introduced a three-tier system for the reception of these stories: they were either spoken aloud from memory, read aloud from a manuscript, or read privately by a sufficiently competent individual, who was also therefore exposed to paratextual material which might not necessarily be communicated through an oral performance.[10] This emerging distinction between the written word and oral culture, potentially freighted with hierarchical associations for each means of reception, was doubtless in Oddr Snorrason's mind when he cautioned readers of his *Óláfs saga Tryggvasonar* to prefer his written redaction of the saga over other competing stories which they might have heard: 'Ok betra er slict með gamni at heyra en stivp meðra saugvr, er hiarðar sveinar segia, er enge viet hvart satt er' (And it is better to listen to such [tales] with enjoyment than to stepmothers' stories, which shepherd-boys tell, which nobody knows the truth of).[11] It is significant that Oddr appears to

---

10   D. H. Green refers to texts designed with an eye to public as well as private transmission
      as an 'intermediate mode' of storytelling ('Orality and Reading: The State of Research
      in Medieval Studies', *Speculum*, 65.2 (April 1990), pp. 267–80).

11   *Saga Óláfs Tryggvasonar*, ed. by Finnur Jónsson (Copenhagen: Gads Forlag, 1932), p.
      2. Translations, except where otherwise stated, are my own.

criticise both the source of these 'stivp meðra saugvr' (stepmothers'
stories) and their mode of transmission — spoken rather than read.
Both characteristics appear to indicate their low status in this author's
mind, a fact perhaps reflective of his dual profession as a Benedictine
monk and a scribe. In both capacities, Oddr would have been a natural
champion of Scripture and the written word, predisposing him to look
sceptically at oral tradition as a potential vehicle for pagan (or, at least,
unorthodox) wisdom and practices.[12] His subject, Óláfr Tryggvason,
actively fought paganism in Scandinavia, and Oddr's awareness of the
novelty of monastic life in Iceland (his monastery at Þingeyrar being
the first to be founded there in 1133) would have provided him with
an incentive to be a champion of written, authorized, Christian histories over and above competing oral iterations of the same stories.
In this respect, his warning reflects a wider medieval tension between
pre-Christian oral narratives and their post-conversion written descendants.

The high medieval Icelandic elite had ample motive for wanting
to control and 'authorize' the writing down of the sagas. As Theodore
Andersson writes, 'the content of the stories was no doubt agreed on
by many people, but the selection and ordering of the stories was left
to the individual teller or writer who shaped them.'[13] This 'shaping'
amounts to the imposition of control over the sagas, and this is especially pertinent in the case of the family sagas (*Íslendingasǫgur*) which,
along with *Landnamabók* (a medieval record of the early settlement
of Iceland, possibly first compiled in the late eleventh century) and
Íslendingabók (an early twelfth-century history of Iceland by Ári Þorgilsson), comprise the story of the founding of Iceland, Europe's only
medieval commonwealth, by a proud and independent people whose
descendants had a vested interest in their commonly agreed content.
History is written by the victors — that is, the ruling elite, and it would
be in their interests to establish a widely circulated and accepted basis
for their present high status. As Kirsten Hastrup has written,

---

12   On Oddr's prologue, see Judy Quinn, 'From Orality to Literacy in Medieval Iceland',
      in *Old Icelandic Literature and Society*, ed. Margaret Clunies Ross (Cambridge: Cam-
      bridge University Press, 2000), pp. 30–60 (pp. 38–40).

13   Theodore M. Andersson, *The Growth of the Medieval Icelandic Sagas* (Ithaca: Cornell
      University Press, 2006), p. 19.

> In Icelandic, *saga* means both story and history. It is literally
> what is 'said' about previous events, periods, or people. Telling
> makes history. The Icelandic sagas are stories of different his-
> torical veracity, but the point is that in the concept of *saga*,
> story and history are one.[14]

Paul Bibire goes still further in claiming that any attempt to impose a
modern distinction between 'literature' and 'history' is 'irrelevant to
the study of Norse'.[15] This disjunction between modern and medieval
attitudes towards history naturally extends beyond the Norse-speaking
world. The Latin term *historia* is similarly multivalent, meaning both
'history' and 'narrative'; however, the Old Norse word *saga* is still more
complicated because of the explicit allusion to speech which it contains.
The adoption of this term for written texts suggests a certain conser-
vative desire either to retain the impression of spoken history or to
appropriate and control it by imprinting it on vellum. Thus, while the
reluctance to distinguish between fiction, legend, and history which
frustrates modern historians reflects a widespread medieval European
mindset, the Old Norse sagas conflate not only fact with fiction but also
the spoken word with the written. Most of the early surviving redactions of these sagas were written in the Sturlung Age (1220–64), when
internecine warfare threatened the stability of Iceland and imperilled its
independence.[16] During and after this period there were strong reasons
to compose a record — however embellished — of the country's earlier
glory. In Hastrup's words, 'by stressing the unity of people, history, and
language an ideology of Icelandicness [was] created'.[17] Additionally,
we know that many sagas were commissioned, with the name of their
commissioner being associated with them rather than that of the author, compiler, redactor, or scribe. In this sense they bore the authority
of *he who caused them to be made*, and he — who was, of necessity,
wealthy — would likely resist the persistence of alternative forms of the
same saga which undermined or contested his proxy composition.

Insofar as surviving texts of the sagas *do* vary, the variation tends
to be most extreme in the prologue or epilogue appended to the text

---

14   Kirsten Hastrup, *A Place Apart: An Anthropological Study of the Icelandic World* (Ox-
     ford: Clarendon Press, 1998), p. 23.
15   Bibire, 'On Reading the Icelandic Sagas', p. 15.
16   Iceland became a vassal state under the Norwegian Crown in 1262.
17   Hastrup, *A Place Apart*, p. 90.

in certain redactions. Here we occasionally encounter the voice of the scribe — or possibly the author; it is always difficult to distinguish between the two — emerging from behind the mask of studied anonymity which he otherwise wears throughout.[18] These fragmentary contributions from different periods and iterations in a saga's development provide a rare glimpse into the agendas of those involved in its transmission, and are consequently a rich source of information about how authors, scribes, and compilers conceived of their respective roles in this process. Differentiating between these interacting voices is rarely straightforward, but the prolegomena which do survive deserve serious attention because they provide snatches of the discourse which took place between the saga texts and their medieval audiences, and potentially help to illuminate the designs of those who commissioned them in their written forms. One obvious example of an epilogue acting as a critical commentary on a saga text occurs at the end of Oddr's *Óláfs saga Tryggvasonar*. As Andersson points out, this passage 'stakes an Icelandic literary claim: in effect, it copyrights the biography of Olaf Tryggvason', appropriating this famous king of Norway as an honorary Icelander.[19] This distinction would have been significant for many Icelanders, who continued to regard their commonwealth as having been in tension with the Kingdom of Norway ever since the earliest Scandinavian settlers in Iceland broke with King Haraldr hárfagri in the ninth century. Despite often relying on the patronage of the Norwegian kings, Icelandic saga heroes are typically proud of their fledgling commonwealth's independence, and therefore any Icelandic history of a king believed to be descended from Haraldr — as Óláfr Tryggvason was — would be sensitive to the competing claims of oral biographies circulating between mainland Scandinavia and Iceland.[20]

---

18   Such narrative interventions are more common in kings' sagas, but they can be found in some redactions of *Íslendingasǫgur*, including the epilogues to *Droplaugarsona saga* (see below) and *Bolla þáttr Bollasonar* (which describes how many accounts of Bolli's journey are in circulation). For a thorough discussion of narratology in the sagas, see Heather O'Donoghue, *Narrative in the Icelandic Family Saga: Meanings of Time in Old Norse Literature* (London: Bloomsbury Academic, 2021).

19   Andersson, *Growth of the Medieval Icelandic Sagas*, p. 204.

20   See further Theodore M. Andersson, 'The First Icelandic King's Saga: Oddr Snorrason's "Óláfs saga Tryggvasonar" or "The Oldest Saga of Saint Olaf"?', *Journal of English and Germanic Philology*, 103.2 (2004), pp. 139–55.

If Oddr's version of the saga was to achieve the status of being the definitive record, he would need to authenticate it in some way and indemnify it against future competition from competing versions, both oral and, potentially, written. He appears to attempt this in an additional chapter appended to the saga in one manuscript, AM 310 4to (c. 1250–75), which contains the following passage:[21]

> Þessa sogu sagþi mer Asgrimr abboti Uestliða s. Biarni prestr Bergþors s. Gellir Þorgils. s. Herdis Daða dottir. Þorgerðr Þor-steins. d. Inguðr Arnors. d. Þessir menn kendu mer sua sagu Olafs konungs T. s. sem nu er sogð. Ec synda oc bokina. Gitsure Hallz s. oc retta ec hana eptir hans raðe.[22]

> (I was told this story by Abbot Ásgrímr Vestliðason, the priest Bjarni Bergþórsson, Gellir Þorgilsson, Herdís Daðadóttir, Þór-gerðr Þorsteinsdóttir, [and] Inguðr Árnórsdóttir. These people instructed me in the saga of King Óláfr Tryggvason as it is now told. I showed the book to Gízurr Hallsson and corrected it with his counsel.)

This careful referencing of multiple sources and deference to an es-tablished authority for correction represents a marked attempt to set the text apart from its oral antecedents which, so far as we can tell, deliberately avoided association with particular sources, being framed rather as a continuance of unbroken (and thus relatively 'open') oral discourse — a convention also to be found in Ári Þorgilsson's *Íslendingabók* (c. 1122–33). That phrase 'sem nu er sogð' (as it is now told) is especially instructive, since it implies a conscious effort to distinguish the present iteration from any competing — allegedly spurious — versions. The written text is not merely 'the saga' but 'the saga as told here' — the authorized redaction. This effect is substan-tially amplified by the litany of authorities to which the redactor refers. Rather than offering himself as a reliable source per se, the author of this passage cites the names and credentials of prominent Icelanders

---

21 Its source, though, may have been his fellow monk Gunnlaugr Leifsson. See further Bjarni Aðalbjarnarson, *Om de norske kongers sagaer* (Oslo: Dybwad, 1937), pp. 85–86, for the case against Oddr having shown his text to Gizurr Hallsson. This argument is persuasively refuted in the introduction to Andersson's more recent translation: *The Saga of Olaf Tryggvason*, trans. by Theodore M. Andersson (New York: De Gruyter, 2003), pp. 3–4.

22 *Saga Óláfs Tryggvasonar*, p. 247.

with a reputation for wisdom (reputations in turn burnished in many of the so-called 'contemporary' sagas, or *samtíðarsǫgur*). The rhetorical effect is to suggest the conferring of authenticity by consensus. The scribe depicts a process by which he first 'opens' his text for comments and contributions from a wider polity of knowledgeable experts before emphatically 'closing' it by inscribing it on parchment as an approved testamentary record.[23]

This insight may also shed light on the famous coda to *Droplaugarsona saga*, which reads: 'Þorvaldr átti son, er Ingjaldr hét. Hans sonr hét Þorvaldr, er sagði sǫgu þessa' (Þorvaldr had a son, and he was called Ingjaldr. His son was called Þorvaldr, who told this story).[24] Tempting as it has always been to consider this a generically typical third-person reference to the author of the extant saga, it is surely more likely that the informant, Þorvaldr, is named as an authenticating voice only, and not, as Peter Hallberg thought, 'enough to prove that the family sagas were not in principle regarded as anonymous'.[25] Pragmatically, identifying an author would do nothing to authenticate the saga — it may, in fact, have had the opposite effect of suggesting literary or editorial innovation rather than faithful historical chronicling — whereas naming the saga's source preserves a sense of proximity to the action it relates. Þorvaldr may indeed have *sagði* (told) the news, but it was *samansetta* (assembled) by others from the raw material of history and tradition. The voice of ancient sources speaks louder for the saga's authenticity than that of even the most erudite later author. A similar attempt to associate a saga with a known authority (who is most unlikely to have authored it per se) can be found in one redaction of *Gunnlaugs saga ormstungu*, which claims to follow the version of the story given by Ári Þorgilsson, prefacing the saga text with a single sentence that contains no fewer than three references to his renowned wisdom, which

23   For a discussion of similar appeals to authority in relation to Old Norse legal texts, see Stefan Brink, 'Minnunga mæn: The Usage of Old Knowledgeable Men in Legal Cases', in *Minni and Muninn: Memory in Medieval Nordic Culture*, ed. by Pernille Hermann, Stephen A. Mitchell, and Agnes S. Arnórsdóttir (Turnhout: Brepols, 2014), pp. 197–210.

24   *Droplaugarsona saga*, ed. by Jón Jóhannesson, Íslenzk Fornrit, 11 (Reykjavik: Hið Íslenzka Fornritafélag, 1950), p. 180.

25   Peter Hallberg, 'The Syncretic Saga Mind: A Discussion of a New Approach to the Icelandic Sagas', *Mediaeval Scandinavia*, 7 (1974), pp. 102–17. For an alternative view, see Ralph O'Connor, 'History or Fiction? Truth-Claims and Defensive Narrators in Icelandic Romance-Sagas', *Mediaeval Scandinavia*, 15 (2005), pp. 101–69 (p. 114).

it thereby seeks to co-opt and associate with the text that follows.[26] This gambit is presumably intended to pre-emptively close down any opportunity for dissent.

Implicit in these passages is the desire among the literate classes to create a canon of accepted story variants — an agenda frequently discernible in the text of later written sagas such as *Grettis saga Ásmundarsonar*, which at one point attempts to resolve a perceived disparity between divergent reports about its hero through an appeal to popular consensus:

> Grettir var jafnan með Birni, ok reyndu þeir margan frœknleik, ok vísar svá til í sǫgu Bjarnar, at þeir kallaðisk jafnir at íþróttum. En þat er flestra manna ætlan, at Grettir hafi sterkastr verit á landinu, síðan þeir Ormr Stórólfsson ok Þórálfr Skólmsson lǫgðu af aflraunir.[27]

> (Grettir was staying with Bjarni, and they tried many bouts, and it is said in *Bjarnar saga* that they were called equal at sports. But it is most people's belief that Grettir was the strongest man who lived in the country since Ormr Stórólfsson and Þórálfr Skólmsson ended their strength-contests.)

By first acknowledging and then subsequently contradicting the earlier account, using popular opinion as authenticating proof, this saga seeks to establish a definitive version of events. Saga authors and scribes, at least by the fourteenth century, were clearly confident of the need both to acknowledge and to seek to supersede alternative narratives which recounted the same happenings, often offering a pre-emptive riposte to readers or listeners who might dispute their interpretation. Where a writer found himself not inclined or not able to proffer a definitive account, he would make reference to another saga and cede to it the greater authority concerning a particular subject.

Although the *Íslendingasǫgur* are famously circumspect concerning their redactors' motivations, they do not avoid the topic altogether. *Grettis saga* is particularly distinguished by the attention it pays to the purpose of saga-telling, remarking after an account of the Battle

---

26 The manuscript in question is Holm. Perg. 18 4to in the Royal Library, Stockholm.

27 *Grettis saga Ásmundarsonar*, ed. by Guðni Jónsson, Íslenzk Fornrit, 7 (Reykjavik: Hið Íslenzka Fornritafélag, 1936), p. 187.

of Havsfjord (*c.* 885) which occurs early on that 'koma hér ok flestar
sǫgur við, því at frá þeim er jafnan flest sagt, er sagan er helzt frá gǫr'
(the majority of sagas refer to it [the battle], because it is such matters that sagas usually refer to).[28] Whether the writer of these words
had in mind only written sagas or written and oral sagas circulating
simultaneously remains uncertain; what is noteworthy is the assertion
that the saga is not an entirely open form but rather exists as a vehicle
for certain kinds of material, of which this battle, part of the founda-
tional narrative of Iceland, is an example. The author of this passage
had strong evidence to support his claim, moreover, since a substantial
number of *Íslendingasǫgur* do indeed begin with genealogies — often
of Norwegian kings rather than Icelanders — followed immediately
by a synopsis of the settlement. The term 'Saga Age', used by modern
scholars as a device for distinguishing between *Íslendingasǫgur* and
other genres of saga literature, indicates an enclosed period of time
beginning shortly before the settlement (frequently dealt with in the
prologue, even if it has little direct bearing on the nominal subject of
the saga) and concluding with the conversion to Christianity (often
supplemented by epilogues which assert the Christian credentials of
saga protagonists, such as when Guðrún becomes a nun at the end of
Laxdœla saga). These sagas are not simply a record of 'what is said', but
rather of what is thought to be important by those chronicling this two-
hundred-and-fifty-year period. The *Íslendingasǫgur* collectively close
off this period from the present, confining pre-Saga Age genealogies
to the prologue and most post-conversion concerns to the epilogue.

These observations help to account for the cursory tone often
adopted at the end of *Íslendingasǫgur*, and it is noteworthy that these
sparse epilogues afford virtually the only opportunity for the narrator,
scribe, or author of the saga to address the reader directly. This is the
case in *Njáls saga*, the longest and greatest in scope of the *Íslendingasǫgur*, which concludes with the words 'Ok lýk ek þar Brennu-Njáls
sǫgu' (And thus I end Burnt Njáll's saga),[29] and much the same formula appears at the end of *Sneglu-Halla þáttr*: 'Lýk ek þar sǫgu frá

---

28   *Grettis saga Ásmundarsonar*, p. 5.
29   *Brennu-Njáls saga*, ed. by Einar Ólafur Sveinsson, Íslenzk Fornrit, 12 (Reykjavik: Hið
      Íslenzka Fornritafélag, 1954), p. 464.

Snegu-Halla' (And so I conclude the story of Sarcastic Halli).[30] In both
cases the formulation is striking, since it represents the reader's first
and only direct encounter with the narrator of the story referring to
himself in the first person. In this sense a direct encounter takes place
only at the last possible moment, and the effect is akin to the removal
of a mask or, perhaps, the laying aside of a manuscript from which the
reciter of the saga has been reading so as to enable direct eye-contact
with the audience. In the context of an oral recitation, this device
might serve a number of purposes: to help ease the transition from the
storyworld of the saga, closed off in historical time, to the present day;
or to differentiate between the scribe and the reader. We might, for
instance, consider the likelihood that these final sentences were not
intended to be read aloud, but rather as a private remark for the eye
of the literate reader, rather than the ear of his audience. They might
communicate the subtext that this is a particular redaction of the saga
— one compiled and controlled by the figure who identifies himself as
'ek' (I) in the closing lines, effectively signing off his authorized version
of the story.[31] The act of reading the saga aloud would represent an
opening up of its contents to a wider audience, yet certain aspects of
what appeared on the page might remain obscure to them, intended
for the eye of the reader rather than the ear of the audience.

A contrasting, though similarly brief epilogue concludes *Þórðar
saga hreðu*, and reads a little like a disclaimer, perhaps intended for
the literate reader in the first instance and then, at his discretion, for
members of a wider audience. This is the remark that 'Þórðr hreða varð
sóttdauðr. Höfum vér ekki fleira heyrt með sannleik af honum sagt'
(Þórðr the Menace died in his bed. We have not heard any more true
facts about him).[32] Two observations can be made here: first, the quali-

---

30   *Sneglu-Halla þáttr*, in *Eyfirðinga sǫgur*, ed. by Jónas Kristjánsson, Íslenzk Fornrit, 9
     (Reykjavik: Hið Íslenzka Fornritafélag, 1956), pp. 261–95 (p. 295). A third example
     may be found at the end of *Finnboga saga*.

31   Green, 'Orality and Reading', p. 277. See also Else Mundal, 'How Did the Arrival of
     Writing Influence Old Norse Oral Culture?', in *Along the Oral–Written Continuum*, ed.
     by Slavica Ranković, Leidulf Melve, and Else Mundal (Turnhout: Brepols, 2010), pp.
     163–81. For a wider discussion of medieval attitudes towards orality and textuality,
     see M. T. Clanchy, *From Memory to the Written Record*, 3rd edn (Chichester: Wiley-
     Blackwell, 2013), esp. p. 298.

32   *Þórðar saga hreðu*, in *Kjalnesinga saga: Jökuls þáttr Búasonar, Víglundar saga, Króka-refs
     saga, Þórðar saga hreðu, Finnboga saga, Gunnars saga keldugnúpsfífls*, ed. by Jóhannes

fication that the saga's compiler knows of no more *true* facts recalls the language used in the prologue to Oddr's *Óláfs saga Tryggvasonar*, and appears to suggest the continuing circulation of false reports which require shutting up and shutting out of the authorized record. Second, the use of the first-person plural pronoun distinguishes these closing comments from those examined above, since it implies a kind of corporate authorship — as though this redaction of the saga was the work of a committee, perhaps comprised of learned men like those listed by Oddr in his prologue or referred to in the closing lines of *Droplaugarsona saga*. This impression might again be intended for the eye of the private reader rather than the ear of an audience, but in any event it represents another attempt to refine — and thereby close down — the narrative of Þórðr's life. Of course, an alternative reading of this coda might be to interpret it as an invitation; were the text of this epilogue to be read aloud, it is possible that a historically minded audience might wish to contribute 'true' stories from their own additional store of knowledge. What appears to be an act of closure might, if the literate reciter chose to read the whole passage aloud, prove rather an opening up of the storytelling ritual to accommodate a reciprocal exchange of knowledge or tradition about the life of Þórðr. Any claim to authenticity for the 'true facts' exchanged in this way would surely rely on the reputation of those who contributed them, with those participants known to be gifted with long memories, and perhaps those descended from Þórðr, likely to have been credited with special wisdom — perhaps exceeding even that codified in the book. It might be helpful to regard the process of writing the saga down as one of closure, and the reading of the saga aloud as one of opening up.[33]

Alternatively, the use of the first-person plural pronoun may reflect an attempt to imitate or pay homage to the oral tradition through which the narrative is understood to have passed before reaching this fixed, static form. This kind of fictional orality, defined by Almut Suerbaum and Manuele Gragnolati as 'the creation of a spoken, collective voice evoking poetic presence, but doing so by means of a

Halldórsson, Íslenzk Fornrit, 14 (Reykjavik: Hið Íslenzka Fornritafélag, 1959), pp. 161–226 (p. 226).

33 Stephen M. Tranter, 'Reoralization: Written Influence, Oral Formulation', in *Text und Zeittiefe*, ed. by Tristram, pp. 45–54.

consciously literate and literary written text', is common to various medieval texts and genres, from the *Nibelungenlied* to the opening lines of *Beowulf* to numerous romances.[34] The use of the first-person pronoun remains strikingly uncommon in the *Íslendingasǫgur* corpus, however, and whatever its intended effect, the fact that its rare occurrences are almost entirely limited to prologues and epilogues reinforces the impression that the relationship between the narrative voice and the reader or audience is understood to shift here, at the limits of the text, a natural boundary between closed (i.e. formalized and monodirectional) and open discourse.[35]

Similar passages which appear to contain the subtextual invitation to share knowledge occur in other sagas and *þættir* ('short sagas' or 'fragmentary saga episodes'), suggesting that the storytelling community was not so closed as is sometimes thought, nor exclusively made up of literate Icelanders. For example, in *Þorleifs þáttr jarlsskálds* the narrator remarks: 'ok gengr af honum [Hallbjǫrn] mikil saga bæði hér á landi ok útlendis, þó at hon sé hér eigi rituð' (and there is a saga about him [Hallbjǫrn] that is well known here in Iceland and abroad, though it is not written here).[36] Any encounter with the written *þáttr*, whether as a private reader or member of the audience, must lead one to wonder about this story and seek to supply it from one's external knowledge of these persons and events where possible. In this sense, the manuscript containing the *þáttr* represents as much a prompt book as a complete and enclosed narrative; the story of Þorleifr was written down in a kind of authorized redaction, but it continued to allude explicitly to supplementary material which was perhaps only available in the oral

---

34 Almut Suerbaum, in collaboration with Manuele Gragnolati, 'Medieval Culture "betwixt and between": An Introduction', in *Aspects of the Performative in Medieval Culture*, ed. by Manuele Gragnolati and Almut Suerbaum (Berlin: De Gruyter, 2010), pp. 1–12 (p. 1). For a discussion of how the term 'fictional orality' can be applied in Old Norse contexts, see Stephen Mitchell, 'Memory, Mediality, and the "Performative Turn": Recontextualizing Remembering in Medieval Scandinavia', *Scandinavian Studies*, 85.3 (2013), pp. 282–305.

35 Slavika Ranković, 'The Performative Non-Canonicity of the Canonical: *Íslendingasǫgur* and their Traditional Referentiality', in *The Performance of Christian and Pagan Storyworlds*, ed. by Lars Boje Mortensen, Tuomas M. S. Lehtonen, and Alexandre Bergholm (Turnhout: Brepols, 2013), pp. 247–72.

36 *Þorleifs þáttr jarlsskálds*, in *Eyfirðinga sǫgur*, ed. by Jónas Kristjánsson, pp. 213–29 (p. 229).

tradition at the time of writing or not immediately available to the
redactor in a form which he considered to be authoritative.

Despite the impression either of anonymity or corporate authorship which the *Íslendingasǫgur* present, their narrators are not always
hesitant about asserting their editorial powers and anticipating certain
objections which their readers might raise. *Eyrbyggja saga*, for instance,
announces itself as the 'saga of the people of Eyri', but early on the
narrative voice remarks that 'þarf hér ekki at segja frá þeira manna
landnámum, er eigi koma við þessa sǫgu' (there is no need to speak
here about the settlements belonging to people who do not come into
our story).[37] Taken together with a similar remark from *Grettis saga* —
'Mart bar til tíðenda um sameign þeira byskups ok Norðlendinga, þat er
ekki kemr við þessa sǫgu' (There are many stories about the exchanges
between the bishop's men and the men in the north, but these are not
part of this saga)[38] — this has again the look of a disclaimer, reflecting
the writer's need to account for the decisions made in promulgating
this particular redaction of the story. It is noteworthy that these statements do not pronounce on the importance of the redacted material,
merely on its relevance to the narrative, or the extent to which it is
suitable content for a text in the saga genre. Comments of this kind,
common throughout the corpus, contribute to our impression of a
collective endeavour towards dividing up the 'oral sea' and imposing
static order upon it. This process might be termed 'canonization' and
is, in any event, an act of enclosure, separating one saga — one set of
incidents — from the next.

One of the enduring curiosities concerning the *Íslendingasǫgur*
— and Old Norse sagas more generally — is that they should have
been written in the vernacular. If the agenda of those who committed
them to parchment was straightforwardly to generate a high-status
written record of early Icelandic history, perhaps one thought to be of
interest to the peoples of Scandinavia and wider Europe, then writing
in Latin would have been the obvious choice. In any event, we might
reasonably expect to find a mixture of languages, as we do a mixture
of prose and verse, but in fact Latin passages — even Latin rubrics

---

37   *Eyrbyggja saga*, ed. by Einar Ólafur Sveinsson and Matthías Þórðarson, Íslenzk Fornrit,
     4 (Reykjavik: Hið Íslenzka Fornritafélag, 1935), p. 11.

38   *Grettis saga Ásmundarsonar*, p. 35.

— are remarkably scarce. There is every reason to suppose at least some Latin literacy among most of the scribes responsible for the sagas, and therefore the fact of their being written in Old Norse indicates a specific and deliberate preference. One suggestive insight is offered by the anonymous author of the *First Grammatical Treatise*, a work dated to the mid-twelfth century, or early period of vernacular saga writing:[39]

> J flestvm londvm setia menn a bækr annat tveggia þann froðleik er þar innan landz hefir giorz eða þann annan er minnisam-ligaztr þikkir þo at annars sdaða[r hafi] helldr giorz eða lǫg sin setia menn a bækr hverr þioð a sína tvngv.[40]

> (In most countries men record in books either the [historical] lore [relating to events] that have come to pass in that country, or any other [lore] that seems most memorable, even though it [relates to events that] have taken place elsewhere, or men commit their laws to writing, each nation in its own tongue.)

The implied connection between law and history suggests a common interest in maintaining records of both, while the mention of nations keeping these records 'a sína tvngv' (in their own tongue) suggests a closed linguistic community. The situation is made slightly more complicated by the fact that modern linguistic distinctions were not necessarily recognized in the Middle Ages. The witness of *Gunnlaugs saga ormstungu* attests that the saga writer believed the language of the Anglo-Saxons and the tenth-century Icelanders to have been at least contiguous if not actually identical.[41] If this view was widely shared, it would suggest that differentiating between groups and cultures on the basis of language was less straightforward than the modern designation of the language used in in saga writing as 'Old Norse' (or, more spe-cifically, 'Old West Norse' or 'Old Norse-Icelandic') initially implies. Nonetheless, the important point remains that the language is not

---

39   Einar Haugen, '*First Grammatical Treatise*: The Earliest Germanic Phonology', *Lan-guage*, 26.4 (1950), pp. 4–64 (p. 6).

40   Text and translation from *The First Grammatical Treatise: Introduction, Text, Notes, Translation, Vocabulary, Facsimiles*, ed. by Hreinn Benediktsson (Reykjavik: Institute of Nordic Linguistics, 1972), pp. 206–07.

41   For the relevant passage, see *Gunnlaugs saga ormstungu*, in *Borgfirðinga sögur: Hœnsa-Þóris saga, Gunnlaugs saga ormstungu, Bjarnar saga Hítdœlakappa, Heiðarvíga saga, Gísls þáttr Illugasonar*, ed. by Sigurður Nordal and Guðni Jónsson, Íslenzk Fornrit, 3 (Reykjavik: Hið Íslenzka Fornritafélag, 1938), pp. 40–108 (pp. 70–71).

Latin — the lingua franca of the elite — but a vernacular tongue particular to the descendants of those about whom the sagas were written. While immediate access was therefore restricted to those who could read, the oral recitation of a saga from a manuscript would have been widely understood because of the choice to record it in the vernacular tongue. The editorial control exercised by those who wrote sagas down was not wholly intended as an act of foreclosure, but rather of control and curation for a wide (though predominantly Icelandic) audience.

Scribes such as Oddr Snorrason had access to Latin texts and, indeed, often wrote their own compositions in Latin (the surviving Old Norse translations of his *Óláfs saga Tryggvasonar* appear to derive from a Latin original). Since Latin was the language of the Church and the universal language of European scholarship, the determination to write in the vernacular always represented a deliberate and particular choice. Many medieval Old Norse texts written in Iceland were translated from Latin exemplars, but the instinct to compose in the vernacular seems to have been unusually strong when compared to continental European cultures. Margaret Clunies Ross points out that the act of translating high-status texts such as saints' lives into the vernacular likely had the effect of elevating the vernacular as a suitable language for expressing high-status ideas.[42] While Latin was plainly thought suitable for many kinds of texts, including some sagas, the *Íslendingasǫgur* were invariably written in Old Norse, this being the language of Iceland, and were therefore most immediately accessible to the descendants of their storied protagonists — a quasi-closed linguistic community around which the notion of a nation, independent from the Scandinavian mainland and, indeed, the European continent, was being formed.

Íslendingasǫgur are, without exception, anonymous.[43] While this condition is common among medieval texts, the fact that it should be true for an entire genre raises a number of pertinent questions and possibilities. The names of many skaldic poets are diligently recorded in the sagas, so it might be that saga authorship was understood to

---

42 Clunies Ross, *Cambridge Introduction to the Old Norse-Icelandic Saga*, p. 47.

43 Notwithstanding Sigurður Nordal's spirited attempt to demonstrate that Snorri Sturluson was the author of *Egils saga*, compelling proof has yet to be produced. See the introduction to *Egils saga Skalla-Grímssonar*, ed. by Sigurður Nordal, Íslenzk Fornrit, 2 (Reykjavik: Hið Íslenzka Fornritafélag, 1933), pp. liii–xcv.

be either a lower artistic form or one less indebted to the creative agency of an individual when compared with skaldic verse. The scribes who wrote or copied the written sagas may have thought of themselves (or wished to present themselves) as recorders of an extant oral tradition rather than innovators of original written works. A further possibility is that sagas were not considered to be literary works, but something more akin to chronicles, and therefore authorship was thought to matter less. The reasons for this ubiquitous anonymity are frequently debated.[44] For our purposes, however, the fact of this genre-wide anonymity is telling in itself. By removing the intermediary figure of the author from the frame, the sagas give the impression of speaking with a common, corporate voice. This sense is reinforced by their frequent habit of intertextually referencing one another — for instance, in *Laxdœla saga*: 'Gunnarr hafði sekr orðit um víg Þiðranda Geitissonar ór Krossavík, sem segir í sǫgu Njarðvíkinga' (Gunnarr had been outlawed for slaying Þiðrandi, Geitir's son, of Krossavík, as is told in the *Saga of the People of Njarðvík*).[45] Or, in another instance, in *Þorskfirðinga saga*: 'Þeir Guðmundr félagar urðu sárir nökkut, ok fóru þeir utan um sumarit, sem ætlat var, ok er mikil saga af þeim í Nóregi frá viðskiptum þeira Ölvis hnúfu' (Guðmundr and his companions were somewhat wounded, and they travelled to Norway that summer, as they had intended, and there is a great saga about them in Norway and their dealings with Qlvir Hump).[46] Or, in a third case, in *Grettis saga*: 'þaðan af gerðisk saga Bǫðmóðs ok Grímólfs ok Gerpis' (the *Saga of Bǫðmóðr, Grímólfr, and Gerpir* describes the events that followed).[47] What emerges from these examples is the sense of a network of literate authors attempting to create the impression of a unified saga corpus which, in order to be fully understood, needs to be accessed as a whole. The naming conventions used in the first and last of these

44 Andersson, *Growth of the Medieval Icelandic Sagas*; Clover, *Medieval Saga*; Gabriel Turville-Petre, *Origins of Icelandic Literature* (Oxford: Clarendon Press, 1953).

45 *Laxdœla saga*, ed. by Einar Ólafur Sveinsson, Íslenzk Fornrit, 5 (Reykjavik: Hið Íslenzka Fornritafélag, 1934), p. 202.

46 *Þorskfirðinga saga*, in *Harðar saga: Bárðar saga, Þorskfirðinga saga, Flóamanna saga*, ed. by Þórhallur Vilmundarson and Bjarni Vilhjálmsson, Íslenzk Fornrit, 13 (Reykjavik: Hið Íslenzka Fornritafélag, 1991), pp. 173–227 (p. 226).

47 *Grettis saga Ásmundarsonar*, p. 32. No saga of this name exists in the surviving corpus, so we may assume that it was either lost or never written.

examples suggest the existence of discrete sagas, whether written or oral, known by those names and sufficiently static that each author could be confident the incident they were alluding to would appear in every redaction to which their audience might have access. This device reinforces the imperative for readers to accept the emerging authorized canon of written sagas, since divergent oral iterations might not supply these cross-references so reliably.

As the Middle Ages wore on and the written word attained primacy over the spoken word in Iceland, a process of closure took place by way of which an authoritative canon of saga variants began to enter circulation. Part of this process involved the appending of prolegomena to written sagas. These used a range of rhetorical strategies to stress the authenticity of the particular redactions which they introduced and concluded. Where oral discourse was open and fluid, the very practice of containing and constraining the sagas — 'that which is said' — on the page involved the generating of a hierarchy which sought to privilege the written saga over any competing spoken traditions; the closed book over the open oral exchange. Despite the strong imperatives in favour of the written saga as a means of imposing editorial control on the form, this process of textualization and its effects were gradual and piecemeal. While the act of inscribing a particular redaction on parchment closed down certain possibilities for the simultaneous circulation of several mutually contradictory yet equally authoritative versions of a given saga, the existence of saga manuscripts written in the vernacular also enabled a process of opening up the corpus, which had previously been enclosed in the minds and memories of a knowledgeable few, to successive generations. Since the primary mode of reception remained oral well into the high Middle Ages, through a process of listening as sagas were read aloud, the writing down of sagas opened a new range of performative possibilities couched in the interplay between the voices of the author, scribe, compiler, reader, and, potentially, the contributing voices of audience members. Far from fixing the sagas in a static form, these manuscripts might be better understood as vessels containing the fluid stories for a time, but ultimately intended to be opened up with each rereading to a new generation of Icelanders.

Interrupted and Unfinished
The Open-Ended Dante of the *Commedia*

NICOLÒ CRISAFI

'THE CLOSED [...] CONCEPTION IN A WORK BY A MEDIEVAL ARTIST'

In his essay 'The Poetics of the Open Work', Umberto Eco makes an argument for the correlation between the 'artistic forms' that arise across different centuries and places, and the ways in which the discourses of 'science or [...] culture' of a period 'view reality'.[1] From this perspective, the Middle Ages appear to Eco as the very opposite of openness. The essay characterizes the period as a time of 'closed' 'hierarchical' systems whose artistic manifestations express a 'fixed' and 'preordained' order.[2] In contrast to this spirit and aesthetics of the age, Eco hails the art forms of the Baroque as having a more 'open', fluid, polycentric, subversive character alive to the 'multiplicity of possible orders', which mark what Eco calls 'the open work':[3]

---

1   Umberto Eco, *The Role of the Reader: Explorations in the Semiotics of Texts* (Bloomington: Indiana University Press, 1979), pp. 47–66 (p. 57).

2   Ibid.

3   Ibid., p. 60.

The closed, single conception in a work by a medieval artist reflected the conception of the cosmos as a hierarchy of fixed, preordained orders. The work as a pedagogical vehicle, as a monocentric and necessary apparatus (incorporating a rigid internal pattern of meter and rhymes) simply reflects the syllogistic system, a logic of necessity, a deductive consciousness by way of which reality could be made manifest step by step without unforeseen interruptions, moving forward in a single direction, proceeding from first principles of science which were seen as one and the same with the first principles of reality. The openness and dynamism of the Baroque mark, in fact, a new scientific awareness.[4]

Although Eco never mentions Dante in his essay, it is clear that his discussion of the Middle Ages is informed by his understanding of the *Commedia*. The essay's line of argument implies a reading in which the *Commedia* is the antithesis of an 'open work'. Firstly, the 'rigid internal pattern of meter and rhymes' that Eco ascribes to a typical medieval artwork surely alludes to the *Commedia*'s closed structure of three canticles, over one hundred cantos, linked together in the interlocking rhyming pattern of *terza rima*.[5] Secondly, Eco's reference to a 'syllogistic system' alludes to the poem's many doctrinal discussions, echoing another common assumption about Dante's poem, first championed by Benedetto Croce, who claimed that doctrinal passages in the *Paradiso*, in particular, were excessively 'theological' in content and on occasion forwent more 'poetic' elements.[6] But most importantly, the idea that reality could be made manifest 'step by step without unforeseen interruptions, moving forward in a single direction' can serve as a rough plot summary of the *Commedia* as a whole — the story of a journey of progressive knowledge oriented toward Dante's final vision of transcendence, which ends happily despite the many difficulties encountered along the way. While Dante's journey does indeed proceed 'step by step', as the protagonist makes his way on foot through the three realms of the afterlife of Hell, Purgatory, and Paradise, in what

---

4   Ibid., p. 57.

5   Zygmunt G. Barański, 'Terza rima, "Canto", "Canzon", "Cantica"', in *Dante Now: Current Trends in Dante Studies*, ed. by Theodore J. Cachey, Jr (Notre Dame: University of Notre Dame Press, 1995), pp. 3–41.

6   Benedetto Croce, *La poesia di Dante* (Bari: Laterza, 1921). Incidentally, Croce's monograph was instrumental in the success of the comparison of the *Commedia* to a Gothic cathedral in Italian Dante Studies (pp. 68–69).

follows I will show how his steps are by no means 'without unforeseen interruptions'. It is precisely through interruptions that a particular kind of openness emerges through the cracks of the *Commedia* as a counterpoint to the ahistorical image of its text as a monolithic whole. I intend to contest the characterization of medieval artworks as rigidly structured, self-contained, and hostile to interruptions and unforeseen elements by asserting the very category of openness that Eco denies them. As committed to textual airtightness as it certainly is, the *Commedia* also offers a meditation on the text's fragility and its vulnerability to the damage, loss, misplacement, unfinishedness that were part of manuscript culture in Dante's time,[7] the more so for an author who, like Dante, lived in precarious circumstances as an exile. In my argument, the *Commedia* is an open work in the most literal of senses: a work that reflects on the risk of not finding closure while it engages with the prospect of its own, and its author's, material vulnerability to circumstance. As I will show, spectres of interruption and unfinishedness haunt not only the poem but also its early reception, starting from the most perceptive of Dante's first readers, Boccaccio. This essay will analyse select passages of the poem where threats of interruption and unfinishedness bring a specific kind of openness into the text: its potential lack of closure due to accidents beyond the author's control. The *Commedia* thematizes denied closure on three different levels: the protagonist's fictional journey is interrupted and appears to go awry; the act of narration is shown to be vulnerable to suspension, if only momentarily; and finally, the material text itself is exposed to the danger of unfinishedness or loss.

Running through these episodes, as I will show, is a common thread marked by a specific kind of language that I call the language of possibility. This is constituted by the counterfactuals, subjunctives, and ellipses that, in these passages, help imagine the protagonist's journey and the poem that narrates it in a state other than it is, thus opening its tale and the universe of the *Commedia* to alternative outcomes and non-normative interpretations. Attending to the text's thematizations of openness and the language of possibility in the *Commedia* allows

---

7   Mark Bland, *A Guide to Early Printed Books and Manuscripts* (Chichester: Wiley-Blackwell, 2010), p. 212.

a different picture of its author to emerge, one that is more attuned to his vulnerable biographical circumstances as an exile and to the precarious material conditions of writing and manuscript transmission in fourteenth-century Italy. By thematizing unfinishedness and interruption, Dante experiments with, exorcizes, and exceeds precisely the kinds of expectations of a complete, airtight artwork with a concluded plot that are now associated with the *Commedia*'s supposedly fixed poetic structure and self-contained universe. It is my contention that a personally vulnerable Dante and materially precarious *Commedia* are at least as important as the self-fashioned but ahistorical image of Dante as an infallible, monolithic author and the *Commedia* as a complete, infallible text above all circumstance. Indeed, Dante's thematization of interruption and unfinishedness exposes the very narrative mechanisms by means of which the *Commedia* presents itself as airtight and monolithic, and challenges its readers to complicate this first impression, imagine the poem as open-ended, and thus take into their own hands the business of interpreting it.[8]

THREATS OF INTERRUPTION FOR THE PILGRIM

The risks of interruption are most evidently thematized as a plot point when they concern the protagonist's fictional journey through the three realms of the afterlife. A broken bridge and a gang of pesky devils force Dante and his guide, Virgil, to detour in *Inferno* xx–xxi, and the beginning of the journey of *Purgatorio* is delayed by over four cantos as the protagonist and his guide try to find their way up Mount Purgatory. The idea that the journey might be cut short is stressed from the very beginning, as the first two cantos of the *Inferno* repeatedly stop-start the protagonist's progress:[9] the dangers are allegorical and

---

8   For an argument for Dante as an author who is 'more surprising and less monolithic, who often raises questions rather than solving them, and who, over the course of time, finds himself in vulnerable situations and takes "minoritarian" decisions that may be less evident at first', see Manuele Gragnolati, 'Insegnare un classico: La complessità di Dante e lo spirito critico', in *In cattedra: Il docente universitario in otto autoritratti*, ed. by Chiara Cappelletto (Milan: Raffaello Cortina, 2019), pp. 179–216 (p. 180; my translation).

9   On the stop-start narration of the first cantos of the *Inferno*, see Teodolinda Barolini, *The Undivine 'Comedy': Detheologizing Dante* (Princeton: Princeton University Press, 1992), pp. 21–47.

externalized, as in the case of the leopard (traditionally interpreted as a symbol of lust), lion (pride), and she-wolf (greed) that hinder Dante's path in the first canto and nearly force him to retreat (*Inferno*, I. 31–60); or they are psychological and come from the protagonist's own insecurities regarding his ability and worthiness ahead of such a perilous enterprise (*Inferno*, II). Such episodes have the narrative purpose of raising the stakes of Dante's journey and creating some suspense in its otherwise linear progression. In both these instances, the impasse is solved by the intervention and words of the Latin poet Virgil, who becomes Dante's guide through the first two-thirds of the journey and promises to help lead his journey to its intended conclusion.

I focus here on one particular episode where that conclusion is momentarily placed out of reach and Virgil is rendered helpless. Having progressed through the upper Hell, Dante and his guide Virgil must enter the gates of the infernal city of Dis but find themselves locked out of its walls, unable to continue on their journey. It is the first time that the borders between the circles of Hell are closed off to Dante. The city walls appear as an emblem of exclusion — not the last time in the poem, as I will show later in this chapter — as Dante is mocked by more than a thousand devils that are garrisoned inside (*Inferno*, VIII. 82). Their taunts, questioning Dante's right to traverse the realm of the dead ('Chi è costui che sanza morte | va per lo regno de la morta gente?'; Who is this, who is not dead | yet passes through the kingdom of the dead?; *Inferno*, VIII. 84–85), hit the protagonist closest to home, playing on the self-doubts he had voiced at the start of the journey:[10]

> Ma io, perché venirvi? O chi 'l concede?
> [...]
> me degno a ciò né io né altri crede. (*Inferno*, II. 31–33)

> (But why should I go there? Who allows it?
> [...]
> Neither I nor any think me fit for this.)

---

10   Quotations from Dante's poems are from *La Commedia secondo l'antica vulgata*, ed. by Giorgio Petrocchi, 2nd edn, 4 vols (Florence: Le Lettere, 1994). All translations from the *Commedia* are from Robert and Jean Hollander's *Inferno* (New York: Anchor, 2000), *Purgatorio* (New York: Anchor, 2003), and *Paradiso* (New York: Doubleday, 2007).

The journey seems seriously threatened with a premature end, and for the first time Virgil is unable to help him. To Dante's dismay, the devils insinuate that the guide alone should be granted access to Dis, leaving Dante to retrace his steps through the upper Hell by himself (*Inferno*, VIII. 88–93) in a repeat of his earlier encounter with the three beasts at the start of the poem. Not only is Virgil unable to talk his way out of the situation, but the prospect of interruption puts a strain on his otherwise confident use of language ('parola ornata'; ornate style; *Inferno*, II. 67) to the point of fragmenting it:

> 'Pur a noi converrà vincer la punga',
> cominciò el, 'se non… Tal ne s'offerse.
> Oh quanto tarda a me ch'altri qui giunga!'.
>   I' vidi ben sì com'ei ricoperse
> lo cominciar con l'altro che poi venne,
> che fur parole a le prime diverse;
>   ma nondimen paura il suo dir dienne,
> perch'io traeva la parola tronca
> forse a peggior sentenzia che non tenne. (*Inferno*, IX. 7–15)

> ('Yet we must win this fight,' he began,
> 'or else… Such help was promised us.
> long it seems to me till someone comes!'
>   I clearly saw that he had covered up
> His first words with the others that came after,
> Words so different in meaning.
>   Still I was filled with fear by what he said.
> Perhaps I understood his broken phrase
> To hold worse meaning than it did.)

It is a commonplace of the scholarship to notice here how this passage is engineered to show Virgil's limits as a guide in the new poetic universe of the *Commedia*. Virgil's fallibility is here emphasized rhetorically in a clash of two registers expressing two sides of his character: on the one hand, the Latin *auctoritas* who composed the epic *Aeneid*; on the other, the vulnerable pagan who is out of his depths in a Christian poem. Virgil's speech begins pugnaciously: the line 'Pur a noi converrà vincer la pugna' (Yet we must win this fight; *Inferno*, IX. 7) stresses the providential necessity of their journey through the afterlife with the decisive future tense 'converrà' (we must) and by employing Latinisms virtually synonymous with the martial epic that Virgil is identified with ('vincer la punga'; win this fight). And yet, the epic march of the sentence is cut short in an ellipsis which denies it closure by exploiting interruption for dramatic effect: 'se non...' (or else...; *Inferno*, IX. 8). The brief suggestion that things might go differently is enough to wreck the rest of the sentence, effectively throwing into disarray the incipit's carefully constructed rhetoric as the authoritative epic poet's turn of phrase is broken off. It is a clash of poetics, with Virgil's martial incipit beset by an unfamiliar sense of uncertainty and the nightmarish visions it lets into the poem's imaginary. Confronted with the open-endedness of Virgil's truncated sentence, Dante's imagination becomes crowded with fearful possibilities that take on very dark hues.[11] The open space left by 'la parola tronca' (the broken phrase; *Inferno*, IX. 14) is filled with Dante's fear, the sentence's implications growing worse in Dante's imagination than Virgil perhaps meant ('perch'io traeva la parola tronca | forse a peggior sentenzia che non tenne'; Perhaps I understood his broken phrase | To hold worse meaning than it did; *Inferno*, IX. 14–15).

The episode is by no means rhetorically unique in the *Commedia*,[12] but it is emblematic of the disruptive force of interruption when it comes to the familiar mechanisms of the poem. When Virgil's otherwise authoritative speech is denied its closure, it becomes literally open-ended, its interpretation up for grabs. Suddenly, the character Dante is tasked with the imaginative business of filling in the gaps left by the guide on whose authority he used to count.

THREATS OF UNFINISHEDNESS FOR THE NARRATOR

The anxiety about the open future displayed by the protagonist of the *Commedia* in this passage is traditionally explained in moralized terms as a function of its narrative structure. Scholars of the *Commedia* distin-

---

11 For a reading of this passage's 'anacoluthon' and Dante's 'pessimistic fantasy', see Justin Steinberg, *Dante and the Limits of the Law* (Chicago: University of Chicago Press, 2013), p. 106.

12 Nicola Gardini reflects on this passage in his *Lacuna* (Turin: Einaudi, 2014), p. 46, dedicating a chapter to this and other instances of *reticentia* in the *Commedia* (pp. 46–55). Gianfranco Contini, *Un'idea di Dante* (Turin: Einaudi, 1970), p. 143, calls Dante 'lo scrittore, i cui silenzî, le cui reticenze, le cui oscurità e ambiguità sono ferree quanto tutto il resto'.

guish between two Dantes behind the first-person 'I' in the poem:[13] on the one hand, the character whose journey through the afterlife is told in the past tense; on the other, the narrator who writes of the journey in retrospect after having returned to earth and comments on it in the present tense. In this view, Dante-character and Dante-narrator have different attributes and different tasks. The character is more naive, more prone to mistakes, while the narrator can comment on his experience and assess it from a more mature and knowing vantage point. The general shape of the *Commedia*, in this view, is linear, the forward journey bending back self-reflexively in its retelling, thus closing off the poem in a reassuring circularity.[14] Dante-character does not yet have the benefit of knowing the triumphant conclusion of his journey, which is reserved for the narrator. Yet gradually, as the poem unfolds, the *Commedia* also starts involving the act of narration in the dangers of interruption, as is the case in one of the narrator's addresses to the reader, when Dante calls upon them to envision precisely 'the event of a sudden interruption of the canticle':[15]

> Pensa, lettor, se quello che qui s'inizia
> non procedesse, come tu avresti
> di più savere angosciosa carizia. (*Paradiso*, v. 109–111)

> (Merely consider, reader, if what I here begin
> Went on no farther, how keen would be
> Your anguished craving to know more.)

---

13 Charles S. Singleton, *Dante's 'Commedia': Elements of Structure* (Baltimore: Johns Hopkins University Press, 1954), pp. 9–11. The twin protagonist of this story is what Gianfranco Contini, *Un'idea di Dante*, pp. 33–62, called Dante 'personaggio-poeta'. On Singleton's and Contini's writings about the Dante narrator-character, see Justin Steinberg, 'The Author', in *The Oxford Handbook of Dante*, ed. by Manuele Gragnolati, Elena Lombardi, and Francesca Southerden (Oxford: Oxford University Press, 2021), pp. 3–16.

14 On the 'grand, circular, closed construction that celebrates the end of a long arduous journey, and this sense of absolute closure', see Jennifer Rushworth, *Discourses of Mourning in Dante, Petrarch, and Proust* (Oxford: Oxford University Press, 2016), p. 135. Rushworth contrasts the closure of the *Commedia* with the open-endedness inherent in the promise of future writing in Dante's youthful work *Vita nova*.

15 Elena Lombardi, *The Syntax of Desire: Language and Love in Augustine, the Modistae, Dante* (Toronto: University of Toronto Press, 2007), p. 156. Lombardi discusses the triangulation of desires between the pilgrim, the souls, and the reader on pp. 156–57. On Dante-narrator teasing the reader 'with the possibility of resistance of any form of closure', see Rushworth, *Discourses of Mourning*, p. 147.

As the narrator's tale is confronted with a 'veiled threat of narrative interruption',[16] the desire for knowledge that usually propels Dante forward ('di più savere [...] carizia') is here deformed by a similar kind of anxiety ('angosciosa', lit. 'anguishing'; *Paradiso*, v. 111) to that which took over Dante-character in the fiction when he heard Virgil's truncated speech. Here, however, Dante addresses readers, appealing to them 'to imagine what [they] would have felt had Dante the narrator stopped at this point'.[17] The possibility of the poem's interruption is presented as a known quantity, conceivably part of the everyday experience of both the author and his contemporaries, whom the threat of narrative interruption concerns in different ways but equal measure. The readers may be counted upon to entertain a scenario where the poem is unfinished or its manuscript transmission incomplete — all the more so if they are familiar with the precarious material culture of the time, not to mention its author's track record and well-publicized circumstances. Indeed, the author Dante Alighieri was no stranger to unfinished writing. By the time he was penning the *Paradiso*, he had left unfinished two treatises (*Convivio* and *De vulgari eloquentia*). Before that, in his early *Vita nova*, he had flirted with the potential failure of writing by including in the book the sonnet with two beginnings 'Era venuta ne la mente mia' and the interrupted *canzone* 'Sì lungiamente m'ha tenuto Amore', and leaving its conclusion open-ended with the promise of future writing.[18] In writing the *Commedia*, he was composing his most ambitious work in precarious conditions as an exile, its copies circulating in batches over whose integrity and reliability he had no control.[19] No matter how self-enclosed and tightly structured, his poem still relied on its material conditions. How would it be transmitted, received, and interpreted? In thematizing unfinishedness, the *Commedia* expresses Dante's anxiety that he would never see his work bound in a single volume. This fear, of course, turned out to be warranted.

---

16   Barolini, *The Undivine 'Comedy'*, p. 190.

17   Leo Spitzer, 'The Addresses to the Reader in the *Commedia*', Italica, 32.3 (1955), pp. 143–65 (pp. 151–52).

18   On the promise of future writing at the conclusion of the *Vita nova*, see Rushworth, *Discourses of Mourning*, pp. 129–162.

19   John Ahern, 'Binding the Book: Hermeneutics and Manuscript Production in *Paradiso* 33', *PMLA*, 97.5 (1982), pp. 800–09 (p. 800).

THREATS OF INTERRUPTION FOR THE HISTORICAL DANTE: BOCCACCIO'S TAKE

It was Dante's admirer Giovanni Boccaccio who first responded to the *Commedia* as a text vulnerable to interruption. In the *Trattatello in laude di Dante*, a short work where he embellishes Dante's biography with his own 'innate talent for narrative', Boccaccio comments precisely on the difficult circumstances of the *Commedia*'s composition.[20] Reading Boccaccio's take on exile is important for two reasons. His account gives important historical evidence of the material difficulties of writing as an exile, as well as responding creatively to Dante's own anxiety about leaving his *Commedia* in an unfinished state:

> conoscer dobbiamo così alta, così grande, così escogitata impresa [...] non essere stato possibile in picciolo spazio avere il suo fine recata; e massimamente da uomo, il quale da molti e varii casi della Fortuna, pieni tutti d'angoscia e d'amaritudine venenati, sia stato agitato.[21]

> (we must understand that it was not possible [...] to bring to its end such a high, great, and contrived undertaking; and especially on the part of a man who was troubled by the many and varied chances of Fortune, full of anguish and poisoned with bitterness.)

Writing an ambitious poem such as the *Commedia* takes a long time, as Boccaccio testifies; all the more so for a poet in Dante's situation. Showing the ways in which both the author and his poem were once vulnerable to hazards and circumstance, Boccaccio proceeds to relate two 'accidents that occurred around the time of the beginning and end of the composition of the *Commedia*', which nearly prevented the poem from reaching its conclusion ('il suo fine'; its end). As Boccaccio writes, the first accident was caused by Dante's sudden exile in 1302 ("l gravoso accidente della sua cacciata, o fuga che chiamar si convegna'; the terrible accident of his exile, or escape, whatever one should call

---

20   Martin McLaughlin, 'Biography and Autobiography in the Italian Renaissance', in *Mapping Lives: The Uses of Biography*, ed. by Peter France and William St Clair (Oxford: Oxford University Press, 2004), pp. 37–65 (pp. 47–48).

21   Giovanni Boccaccio, *Trattatello in laude di Dante*, ed. by Vittore Branca (Milan: Mondadori, 1974), xxvi. Translations from the *Trattatello* are my own.

it). In his tale, exile forced the poet to abandon the first seven cantos in Florence as he wandered through Italy in perpetual insecurity ('per lo quale egli e quella e ogni altra cosa abandonata, incerto di se medesimo, più anni con diversi amici e signori andò vagando'; which, after he abandoned both Florence and all other things, caused him to roam back and forth and stay with several friends and lords, uncertain of himself). The practical man that he is, Boccaccio does not see exile as a fortifying experience or as an allegory of Dante's spiritual journey. Instead, he focuses squarely on the practical problems of exile. The first problem is Dante's sudden displacement, which forced him to abandon his manuscript in Florence and interrupt his writing only seven cantos into the poem. Eventually, the interruption was resolved when Dante's patron, Marquis Morello Malaspina, was sent the cantos and, led on by the *plaisir du texte*, entreated Dante to pick up where he had left off so as to avoid leaving the work unfinished ('che gli piacesse di non lasciare senza debito fine sì alto principio'; that it may please him to not leave such a lofty beginning without a proper conclusion).

The second accident that befell the integrity of the *Commedia* is a direct consequence of Dante's exile. Boccaccio tells us that the last thirteen cantos of the *Paradiso* were lost, as death caught up with the poet before he could bind his work into an authorized copy. Even if apocryphal, the tale is revealing: it responds imaginatively to Dante's own concerns about leaving his text unfinished and unbound, while giving us an insight into what could plausibly be believed to be the material conditions of the *Commedia*'s composition and transmission in times of exile. Boccaccio reflects on the ways in which the loss of the final cantos affects so systematic, so structured a poem as the *Commedia*. He has a keen sense for the fact that the *Commedia* is, in its design, a strong coherent whole. He repeatedly refers to the idea of a 'proper conclusion' of the poem, which, though materially lost, still informs and constricts its architecture.[22] So strong is this ideal completeness, that, in Boccaccio's tale, Dante's sons Iacopo and Pietro Alighieri feel compelled to reconstruct the integrity of their father's text based on what is left of the poem in an attempt to 'supplire la

---

22   On ways to mark the proper end of works of literature in the Middle Ages, see John Ahern, 'Dante's Last Word: The *Comedy* as a *liber coelestis*', *Dante Studies*, 102 (1984), pp. 1–14.

paterna opera, acciò che imperfetta non procedesse'; to add to their father's work, so as to avoid leaving it incomplete'; *Trattatello*, xxvi). Their attempt to not let the *Commedia* remain 'imperfect' confirms the fundamental tension between the vulnerability of the material text and the integrity of its architectural design.[23] Boccaccio is perfectly attuned to this important ambiguity. On the one hand, his tale pays homage to the ways in which the *Commedia* is structurally whole and textually bound by design, and invites completion independently of its material circumstances. On the other hand, however, Boccaccio is attuned to Dante's own emphasis on the open-ended nature of writing and textual transmission, and his condition as the vulnerable author of a vulnerable text. Although the design of the *Commedia* invites binding, the physical manuscripts could still be left unbound. No matter how much closure the author built into his text, its final appearance would still be out of his hands, as 'once the long-awaited final *quaderno* had been released [Dante's] readers would be faced with the choice of leaving the text in its vulnerable unbound condition or going to the expense of having it bound'.[24]

THREATS OF INTERRUPTION FOR THE AUTHOR

As I have shown, there is an important ambiguity in Dante's writing between this desire for a strong architecture and a strong voice on the one hand, and the poet's painful experience and need to dramatize that experience of vulnerability on the other. The last instance of this ambiguity can be seen in *Paradiso* xxv, one of the final cantos of the *Paradiso*. *Paradiso* xxv is a canto on hope and begins with Dante's most treasured hope: that of a return from exile. This hope turns on a big 'if':

> Se mai continga che 'l poema sacro
> al quale ha posto mano e cielo e terra,
> sì che m'ha fatto per molti anni macro,

---

23   On the 'sort of idealism' implicit in scribal attempts to reconstitute the completeness of a text, see Daniel Wakelin, *Scribal Correction and Literary Craft: English Manuscripts 1375–1510* (Cambridge: Cambridge University Press, 2014), pp. 246–74 (p. 246).

24   Ahern, 'Binding the Book', p. 801. On the tension between aesthetically 'closed' texts and their awareness of their 'openness' to material circumstance beyond Dante Studies, see the classic study by Thomas M. Greene, *The Vulnerable Text: Essays on Renaissance Literature* (New York: Columbia University Press, 1986), esp. the essay 'Vulnerabilities of the Humanist Text' (pp. 1–17).

vinca la crudeltà che fuor mi serra
del bello ovile ov'io dormi' agnello,
nimico ai lupi che li danno guerra;
    con altra voce omai, con altro vello
ritornerò poeta, e in sul fonte
del mio battesmo prenderò 'l cappello. (*Paradiso*, xxv. 1–9)

(Should it ever come to pass that this sacred poem
to which both Heaven and earth have set their hand
so that it has made me lean for many years,
    should overcome the cruelty that locks me out
of the fair sheepfold where I slept as a lamb,
foe of the wolves at war with it,
    with another voice then, with another fleece,
shall I return a poet and, at the font
where I was baptized, take the laurel crown.)

Here the narrator is pictured as visibly leaner after years in exile, his voice and hair no longer what they used to be (*Paradiso*, xxv. 3, 7). This very famous passage has been interpreted in a variety of ways, but I would like to focus on its inbuilt open-endedness. As a text that mentions a changed voice, the passage is in fact dependent on the shifts in the tone of one's reading. Does one voice the passage with defiance, emphasizing its gravitas?[25] Or does one voice it more cautiously, as the delicate hope of an ageing and emaciated man — placing the emphasis on the language of possibility: the tentative mood of hypotheticals and subjunctives, and the fact that it is the narrator (his life on earth still unfolding, his story still unresolved) that speaks these lines?[26] Typically of the Dante I am describing, the passage alternates between these major and minor chords. It uses the resounding prophetic mode through triumphant future indicatives ('ritornerò poeta'; shall I return a poet; 'prenderò 'l cappello'; [I shall] take the laurel crown; *Paradiso*, xxv. 8–9), but modulates it through the subjunctives on which they are conditional ('Se mai continga che [...] vinca la crudeltà';

---

25   For the biblical intertexts in *Paradiso* xxv, see Giuseppe Ledda, 'L'esilio, la speranza, la poesia: Modelli biblici e strutture autobiografiche nel canto xxv del *Paradiso*', *Studi e Problemi di Critica Testuale*, 90.1 (2015), pp. 257–77.

26   Albert Russell Ascoli describes the Dante represented here as '"human, all too human". Dante's coronation [...] is posited as radically contingent, subject to the constraints of history' (*Dante and the Making of a Modern Author* (Cambridge: Cambridge University Press, 2008), p. 402).

Should it ever come to pass that [...] [the poem] should overcome;
Paradiso, xxv. 1–4).[27] From the narrator's perspective, his life remains
open-ended, his future unknowable. Naturally, reading the incipit after
Dante Alighieri's death, it is impossible to suspend one's knowledge
that, if these lines were ever meant to be prophetic, they failed — one
of very few such failures in the author's oeuvre.[28] We can only imagine
whether the 'molti anni' (many years) spent in exile did make Dante as
'macro' (lean) as he paints the narrator here (*Paradiso*, xxv. 33), and
whether age did alter his 'voce' (voice) and 'vello' (fleece [i.e. hair];
Paradiso, xxv. 7).[29] What we do know, however, is that Dante Alighieri
never returned to Florence and that the contingent prophecy of being
poet laureate expressed here was never fulfilled. From this perspective,
at least, a more cautious reading of *Paradiso* xxv seems justified: these
hypotheticals and subjunctives, with their doubts and fears, do not
conceal the vulnerability of his narrator and his text, but place it at the
heart of the *Commedia*. In this case, the minor chord of vulnerability
eventually turned out to be more truthful. As we know, for the author
of the poem Dante Alighieri, the open-endedness expressed by the incipit's 'could be's had the last word over the confidence of the prophetic
'will be'.

The early iconographic tradition of Dante Alighieri reflects this
ambiguity in certain ways. Whereas the earliest depictions of Dante
in manuscripts, panels, or frescos represent him as 'giovanile, sereno,
chiaro d'incarnato' (youthful, serene, of fair complexion) and wearing
his distinctive cap, two iconographic innovations begin to appear in
the second half of the fifteenth century.[30] On the one hand, Dante appears more mature and gaunt, as he already did in such early fifteenth-

---

27   On the shift in mood in the first tercet, see Claire E. Honess and Matthew Treherne,
      'Introduction', in *Se mai continga ... : Exile, Politics and Theology in Dante*, ed. by Claire
      E. Honess and Matthew Treherne (Ravenna: Longo, 2013), pp. 7–10 (p. 8).

28   According to Robert Wilson, Dante prefers obscurity and ambiguity to the possibility
      of incorrect prophecy. Rare examples of failed prophecy are found in *Epistola* VI
      and *Purgatorio*, XIII. 91–111 (Robert Wilson, *Prophecies and Prophecy in Dante's
      'Commedia'* (Florence: Olschki, 2008), pp. 96–97).

29   On Dante's leanness, see Ledda, 'L'esilio, la speranza, la poesia', p. 261 n. 1, and
      bibliographical references therein.

30   Anna Maria Francini Ciaranfi, 'Iconografia', in *Enciclopedia Dantesca* (1970) <http://
      www.treccani.it/enciclopedia/iconografia_(Enciclopedia-Dantesca)/> [accessed 30
      May 2020] (my translation).

century manuscripts as Strozzi 174 (Florence, Biblioteca Medicea Laurenziana), fol. 4^v, and Riccardiano 1040 (Florence, Biblioteca Riccardiana), fol. 1^v; on the other, he wears the laurel crown that alludes to his poetic coronation.[31] The earliest representation of Dante to feature both these iconographic innovations is perhaps the best-known one: the fresco painted by Domenico di Michelino in the Duomo of Florence in 1465 for the bicentenary of Dante's birth (Figure 1). Here Dante appears at the centre of the frame, gaunt and laurelled, holding his *Commedia*, surrounded by Hell to the left, Purgatory in the background, and the spheres of Heaven above him. On the right-hand side of the composition lies Florence, such that the poet appears locked out of the gates of his own home city. Behind the city walls, the skyline is dominated by Florence's Duomo, which contains this very fresco where Dante is represented. Through this *mise en abyme* — the fresco of Dante in the Duomo containing the fresco of Dante in the Duomo — the poet simultaneously appears both outside and inside the city: outside, because we see him standing outside of the city walls; inside, because we know that the painted Duomo inside the gates holds Dante's portrait. Thus, the painting preserves the ambiguity of *Paradiso* xxv and Dante's language of possibility, remaining faithful to the poem's own open-endedness when employing counterfactuals and future tense at the time of writing.[32] The 'resilient validation of the spiritually, politically and poetically transformative nature of Dante's experience of banishment from Florence' coincides, specifically, with Dante's laureation and ageing, both performed by his poetic use of possibility and performing the two complementary sides of it, bringing closure to the myth of Dante while not erasing his vulnerability.[33] As the last five centuries of Dante iconography demonstrate, his *Commedia* gained him the poetic laurels with which he is now always represented, but also left traces of the arduous and uncertain journey of its writing in representing the poet as emaciated and gaunt.

---

31   Ibid.

32   Cf. Catherine Keen, 'Florence and Faction in Dante's Lyric Poetry: Framing the Experience of Exile', in *Se mai continga ...*, ed. by Honess and Treherne, pp. 63–83 (p. 82).

33   Robert Hollander, on *Paradiso*, xxv. 1–9. See also the comment by Daniele Mattalia on *Paradiso*, xxv. 9, from the Dartmouth Dante Project, available online at <https://dante.dartmouth.edu/> [accessed 30 May 2020].

Figure 1. Domenico di Michelino, Dante and his Poem. 1465. Fresco.
Cathedral of Santa Maria del Fiore, Florence.
Copyright: Wikimedia Commons.

EPILOGUE

I would like to conclude with a quote from Kierkegaard. In a chapter of
The Sickness unto Death called 'Necessity's Despair Is to Lack Possibility', the philosopher writes about the breath of fresh air that is afforded
by thinking in terms of possibility:

> When someone faints, we call for water, eau de Cologne,
> smelling salts; but when someone wants to despair, then the
> word is: Get possibility, get possibility, possibility is the only
> salvation. A possibility — then the person in despair breathes
> again, he revives again, for without possibility a person seems
> unable to breathe.[34]

Possibility brings a breath of fresh air to the *Commedia* in a number
of ways. The passages I have analysed in this discussion of the inter-

---

34   Søren Kierkegaard, *The Sickness unto Death: A Christian Psychological Exposition for
      Upbuilding and Awakening*, ed. and trans. by Howard V. Hong and Edna H. Hong
      (Princeton: Princeton University Press, 1980), pp. 38–39.

ruptions and unfinishedness that make the *Commedia* an open work all displayed the language of possibility. Dante's fears of premature and inappropriate endings to the journey through the afterlife and to the journey of writing about it, his hopes for return from exile that I have discussed — these all revolve around counterfactuals, 'if's, and subjunctives: Virgil's elliptical 'se non...' (*Inferno*, IX. 8), the narrator's 'se [...] non procedesse' (*Paradiso*, V. 110), Dante's 'Se mai continga' (*Paradiso*, XXV. 1). Dante character-narrator is not only the monolithic author in control of the architecture of his poem but also represents himself as involved in the open-ended course of human life. No matter how strongly conceived, the poem itself is equally vulnerable to unfinishedness, corruption, loss. The future of what might happen is for Dante and his poem still open, uncertain, and undivinable. When Dante uses the language of possibility regarding his own open future as an author and exile, this Dante shows himself more vulnerable and exposed to chance and mishap than the Dante that carefully controls his narrative and its retrospective interpretation. Attending to the language of possibility in the text thus allows us to take a breath of fresh air as interpreters. Less concerned with the coherence of the *Commedia* and its seemingly incontestable authority as a hermeneutic criterion, readers of possibility can discover a new side of Dante that dwells on alternatives and uncertainty. Retrospective storytelling risks making a life appear necessary, predetermined, its outcome conclusive. To balance this perspective, a focus on possibility allows the teleological linearity of the *Commedia* to open out on possibilities and destinies not taken, representing life not as understood in retrospect but as lived forward, with all the attendant risks of interruption and unfinishedness. Thus, if we return to the Eco quotation with which this essay started, we will find that 'The Poetics of the Open Work' sets out to describe as 'open' precisely the kind of storytelling of which the *Commedia* constitutes a special case. The writing of the *Commedia* does not forget the debt it owes to circumstance for its completion, but dilates its space in the text; it does not disown the need it has for readers or listeners for its fruition, but reminds them of their responsibility in receiving the text and deciding on its interpretation; it does not simply wish to appear as absolutely resolved and self-contained but preserves and lingers in the time when it was 'in time', 'in movement [...]', 'incomplete'.[35] It is this kind of 'open work' that, as Eco puts it, is 'characterised by the invitation to make the work together with the author'.[36] This commitment to open-endedness even in the moment of closure constitutes the paradoxical double movement of the *Commedia*.

35   Eco, *Role of the Reader*, p. 56.
36   Ibid., p. 63.

Medieval Denmark and its Languages
The Case for a More Open Literary Historiography
ALASTAIR MATTHEWS

INTRODUCTION

Embracing, or at least including a nod toward, the rhetoric of openness is by now almost *de rigueur* when it comes to setting the agenda for research on the literature of the Middle Ages.[1] The origins of national

1   I would like to thank Simon Skovgaard Boeck, Steffen Hope, Lars Boje Mortensen, and the editors of the present volume for reading and commenting on drafts of this chapter. — For the trends in medievalism described here, cf. e.g. Joep Leerssen, 'Literary Historicism: Romanticism, Philologists, and the Presence of the Past', *Modern Language Quarterly*, 65 (2004), pp. 221–43; *Mittelalter im Labor: Die Mediävistik testet Wege zu einer transkulturellen Europawissenschaft*, ed. by Michael Borgolte and others (Berlin: Akademie Verlag, 2008); Nadia R. Altschul, *Geographies of Philological Knowledge: Postcoloniality and the Transatlantic National Epic* (Chicago: University of Chicago Press, 2012); *Histories of Medieval European Literatures: New Patterns of Representation and Explanation* (= *Interfaces: A Journal of Medieval European Literatures*, 1 (2015)) <https://doi.org/10.13130/interfaces-4960>; *Europe: A Literary History, 1348–1418*, ed. by David Wallace, 2 vols (Oxford: Oxford University Press, 2016); Mark Whittow, 'Sources of Knowledge; Cultures of Recording', *Past and Present*, 238, suppl. 13 (2018), pp. 45–87; Peter Frankopan, 'Why We Need to Think About the Global Middle Ages', *Journal of Medieval Worlds*, 1.1 (2019), pp. 5–10 <https://doi.org/10.1525/jmw.2019.100002>. The rise of these interests is also reflected in the appearance of journals and book series such as *Medieval Worlds: Comparative & Interdisciplinary Studies* (<http://www.medievalworlds.net/medieval_worlds?frames=yes> [accessed 20 January 2020]) and Beyond Medieval Europe (ARC Humanities Press; <https://arc-humanities.org/our-series/arc/bme/> [accessed 20 January 2020]).

philologies in the context of nineteenth-century nation-building are widely recognized, and with this awareness has come the pursuit of more open discourses that cross, question, and break down the disciplinary, political, and cultural boundaries associated with modern nation states. These efforts to rethink approaches to literature before the current era have made much of adopting, on the one hand, a European perspective and questioning, on the other, what is meant by 'Europe' and how it functions as a potentially limiting point of orientation. This in turn dovetails with the growing scholarly interest in a 'global' Middle Ages. Work on the 'insular Middle Ages', the Atlantic, northern and eastern Europe, Byzantine Studies, Africa, or connections with the Arab world — the list is not exclusive — can all be seen as an expression of this process.[2]

Yet tensions remain — imbalances in the attention being given to different regions, languages, and approaches that may be due to more than just the truism that it is not possible to cover everything. The present chapter responds to one particular case in point. It follows on from my Marie Curie Fellowship, 'Northern Narratives: The Poetics of Cultural Contact between Germany and Scandinavia in the Middle Ages' (2015–17). One of the conclusions to emerge from that project is that there is still a pressing need to open up the writing of medieval literary history in the case of German in Denmark. I say 'still' because the desideratum is not a new one. It, and the intellectual context behind it, had already been identified by Vibeke Winge almost thirty years ago, long before topics such as multilingualism and the questioning of nationally oriented scholarship became fashionable in the philologies:

---

2   *Crossing Borders in the Insular Middle Ages*, ed. by Aisling Byrne and Victoria Flood (Turnhout: Brepols, 2019); *Studies in the Medieval Atlantic*, ed. by Benjamin Hudson (New York: Palgrave Macmillan, 2012); *Historical Narratives and Christian Identity on a European Periphery: Early Historical Writing in Northern, East-Central, and Eastern Europe (c. 1070–1200)*, ed. by Ildar H. Garipzanov (Turnhout: Brepols, 2011); Ian Johnson, 'A Perspective from the Far (Medieval) West on Byzantine Theories of Authorship', in *The Author in Middle Byzantine Literature: Modes, Functions, and Identities*, ed. by Aglae Pizzone (Boston: De Gruyter, 2014), pp. 277–94; François-Xavier Fauvelle, *The Golden Rhinoceros: Histories of the African Middle Ages*, trans. by Troy Tice (Princeton: Princeton University Press, 2018); *A Sea of Languages: Rethinking the Arabic Role in Medieval Literary History*, ed. by Suzanne Conklin Akbari and Karla Mallette (Toronto: University of Toronto Press, 2013).

Aus einer größeren Perspektive gesehen ist es m.E. notwendig, die dänische Kultur-, Sprach- und Literaturgeschichte unter dem Aspekt der Mehrsprachigkeit darzustellen. Bis heute ist das jedoch noch nie versucht worden. Das Verhältnis zu unserem südlichen Nachbarn spielt in historischen Darstellungen immer eine große Rolle, jedoch ist diese infolge einer Rückprojezierung der nationalen Konflikte des 19. und 20. Jahrhunderts meistens eine recht negative.[3]

(From a wider perspective, it is in my view necessary to present Danish cultural, linguistic, and literary history in terms of multilingualism. Up to now, however, that has never been attempted. Relations with our southern neighbour always play a significant role in historical accounts, but it is, as a consequence of the back-projection of the national conflicts of the nineteenth and twentieth centuries, generally a markedly negative one.)

The following pages advocate and lay the groundwork for a project that would finally begin to fill this gap where premodern literature is concerned. I begin with a necessarily brief overview (or reminder) of the extent of the German presence in Denmark in the period, before demonstrating how it has been marginalized in Danish literary historiography in recent decades. I consider possible explanations for this, including a continued influence of the factors mentioned by Winge. I then present some ways in which Danish, German, and Latin could be brought together in a genuinely inclusive history of literature in the broadest sense of the term. Finally, I consider how such a project could be developed further, from its potential to inform our understanding of specific locations, such as Odense, to the connections that could be drawn with current themes, such as diversification and multilingualism, in Modern Languages teaching and research.

GERMANS AND GERMAN IN DENMARK

It is a fact that the history and culture of (generally northern) Germany and Denmark were intertwined in the Middle Ages. Following

---

3   Vibeke Winge, *Dänische Deutsche — deutsche Dänen: Geschichte der deutschen Sprache in Dänemark 1300–1800* (Heidelberg: Winter, 1992), pp. 4–5. Translations are my own unless otherwise indicated.

the breakdown of the Danish 'North Sea empire', 'the major ambitions of Danish kings were [...] directed [...] east and south along
the land frontiers of Jutland and the shores of the Baltic Sea. [...] In
each case Danish ambitions came into conflict with the interests of
German princes, institutions, and populations.'[4] Large parts, or even
all, of the realm were pawned and effectively in the hands of German ar-
istocrats at various points.[5] Numerous Danish kings and queens were
of German descent,[6] and there was a substantial presence of German
merchants and craftsmen — not entirely without conflict, but marked
also by a degree of convergence evident in, for instance, intermarriage.[7]
This state of affairs went hand in hand with the use of German in
Denmark.[8] Early linguistic influence is apparent in a twelfth-century
tombstone in Føvling (Jutland) on which part of the name is a loan-
word from Low German,[9] and evidence of proficiency in German
can be found in the account in Saxo's *Gesta Danorum* (History of the

---

4   For a historical overview, see Alan V. Murray, 'The Danish Monarchy and the Kingdom
     of Germany, 1179–1319: The Evidence of Middle High German Poetry', in *Scandinavia
     and Europe 800–1350: Contact, Conflict, and Coexistence*, ed. by Jonathan Adams and
     Katherine Holman (Turnhout: Brepols, 2004), pp. 289–307 (pp. 289–92; quotation:
     pp. 289–90).

5   See e.g. Anders Leegaard Knudsen, 'Kongeriget Danmark i 1332 — et fallitbo', *Histo-
     risk Tidsskrift* [Denmark], 108 (2008), pp. 321–40.

6   For the German royal connections following Margaret I, see Steinar Imsen, 'The Union
     of Calmar — Nordic Great Power or Northern German Outpost?', in *Politics and
     Reformations: Communities, Polities, Nations, and Empires: Essays in Honor of Thomas
     A. Brady, Jr.*, ed. by Christopher Ocker and others (Leiden: Brill, 2007), pp. 471–89.

7   See Bjørn Poulsen, 'Late Medieval Migration across the Baltic: The Movement of
     People between Northern Germany and Denmark', in *Guilds, Towns, and Cultural
     Transmission in the North, 1300–1500*, ed. by Lars Bisgaard, Lars Boje Mortensen,
     and Tom Pettitt (Odense: University Press of Southern Denmark, 2013), pp. 31–56
     (pp. 47–49 on intermarriage); importantly, Poulsen also addresses the two-way nature
     of migration between Germany and Denmark. On the specifically Hanseatic aspect,
     see Kilian Baur, *Freunde und Feinde: Niederdeutsche, Dänen und die Hanse im Spät-
     mittelalter (1376–1513)* (Vienna: Böhlau, 2018), pp. 231–40, 333–38 (with extensive
     references). For the shifting extent to which 'nationalistic' sentiment was expressed
     in medieval Danish historical writing, see Anders Leegaard Knudsen, 'Interessen for
     den danske fortid omkring 1300: En middelalderlig dansk nationalisme', *Historisk
     Tidsskrift* [Denmark], 100 (2000), pp. 1–32.

8   The indispensable study remains Winge, *Dänische Deutsche — deutsche Dänen*. It
     should, however, be born in mind that it is not an exhaustive catalogue of material, and
     that details may need reassessing in the light of more recent research, some of which is
     also drawn into this chapter.

9   See Niels Houlberg Hansen, 'The Transformation of the Danish Language in the
     Central Middle Ages: A Case of Europeanization?', in *Denmark and Europe in the Middle
     Ages, c. 1000–1525: Essays in Honour of Professor Michael H. Gelting*, ed. by Kerstin
     Hundahl, Lars Kjær, and Niels Lund (London: Routledge, 2014), pp. 111–38 (p. 128).

Danes) of a legate sent by Valdemar I to Henry the Lion in 1176: 'Waldemarus [...] Henricum, quem stabulo suo preposuerat, Germanice uocis admodum gnarum in Saxoniam dirigi curat' (The Danish king [...] arranged to have Henrik, his master of the horse, sent to Saxony, because the man was tolerably conversant with the German tongue).[10] It is also very likely that the northern German poet Rumelant von Sachsen performed strophes concerned with Danish politics on a visit to Denmark in the later thirteenth century.[11] The written record, however, does not begin until the fourteenth century. Alongside the production of numerous *Urkunden* in (Low) German for private, political, and administrative purposes — the *schra* of the so-called Elende Lav (Foreigners' Guild) in Odense (1435) is one well-known example — historiographical and legal texts were translated into German.[12] This material needs to be viewed alongside Danish works based on German sources or models, such as *Dværgekongen Laurin* (Laurin the Dwarf King; earliest manuscript *c.* 1500), the Danish *Lucidarius* (generally dated to the fourteenth century), or *De gamle danske Dyrerim* (The Old Danish Rhyming Bestiary; fifteenth century).[13]

---

10   Saxo Grammaticus, *Gesta Danorum*, ed. by Karsten Friis-Jensen, trans. by Peter Fisher, 2 vols (Oxford: Clarendon Press, 2015), XIV. 54. 18. See Winge, *Dänische Deutsche — deutsche Dänen*, p. 36.

11   The strophes concerned (v. 8, VI. 10, x. 3–5) relate to the 1286 assassination of Eric V and to his successor, Eric VI; they are best read alongside the commentary in *Die Sangspruchdichtung Rumelants von Sachsen: Edition — Übersetzung — Kommentar*, ed. and trans. by Peter Kern (Berlin: De Gruyter, 2014). See further Murray, 'Danish Monarchy', pp. 294–306 (also covering other German political poetry on Danish kings, for which the case for performance in Denmark is less convincing); Reinhold Schröder, 'Rumelant von Sachsen, ein Fahrender aus Deutschland in Dänemark', in *The Entertainer in Medieval and Traditional Culture: A Symposium*, ed. by Flemming G. Andersen, Thomas Pettitt, and Reinhold Schröder (Odense: Odense University Press, 1997), pp. 15–44.

12   An initial overview is provided in Winge, *Dänische Deutsche — deutsche Dänen*, pp. 46–85; the historiographical material is discussed in more detail below.

13   On these and other texts, see *Dansk litteraturs historie*, ed. by Klaus P. Mortensen and May Schack, 5 vols (Copenhagen: Gyldendal, 2006–09), I (2007), pp. 132–39; Winge, *Dänische Deutsche — deutsche Dänen*, pp. 78–83; the survey of translations in Vibeke Winge, 'Zur Übersetzungstätigkeit Niederdeutsch-Dänisch und Dänisch-Niederdeutsch von 1300 bis Ende des 16. Jahrhunderts', in *Niederdeutsch in Skandinavien*, 6 vols (1987–2005), III, ed. by Lennart Elmevik and Kurt Erich Schöndorf, Beihefte zur Zeitschrift für deutsche Philologie, 6 (Berlin: Schmidt, 1992), pp. 30–36; Marita Akhøj Nielsen, 'Dværgekongen Laurin: Litteraturhistorisk baggrund', in *Tekster fra Danmarks middelalder og renæssance 1100–1550 — på dansk og latin* <https://tekstnet.dk/dvaergekongen-laurin/about> [accessed 12 February 2020]; Britta Olrik

DANISH LITERARY HISTORIOGRAPHY

The treatment of the German tradition in existing literary histories of Denmark stands at odds with the situation that has just been described.[14] Consider, for instance, *Dansk litteraturs historie* (Danish Literary History; 2006–09), a multivolume collaborative survey that has the status of a 'standard work'. The project aims emphatically to understand Danish literature from a European and international perspective.[15] As the foreword puts it: 'Den danske litteratur sættes derfor ind i en europæisk og — for nyere perioders vedkommende — international sammenhæng, som tydeliggør, hvordan dansk litteratur til stadighed har udfoldet sig i et samspil med andre litteraturer og kulturstrømninger' (Danish literature is therefore set in a European and — where more recent periods are concerned — international context that makes clear how Danish literature has constantly unfolded in an interplay with other literatures and cultural currents).[16] In many respects, the project lives up to these ambitions. Where the German-speaking areas in the premodern period are concerned, we learn, for instance, about Johan Snell, the first printer in Denmark, who came to Odense from Lübeck in the late fifteenth century, or the German sources for most of the stories in the late medieval/early modern *folkebøger*.[17]

Only marginally addressed, however, is the use of German for textual production within Denmark. In the 188 pages that cover developments up to 1500 — to take an arbitrary cut-off point — this is recognized in no more than three sentences; the sole text to be mentioned by name in this context is the *Jyske Lov* (Jutish Law), which was translated into Low German in the fourteenth century.[18] This state

---

Frederiksen, 'Dyrerim, De gamle danske', in *Medieval Scandinavia: An Encyclopedia*, ed. by Phillip Pulsiano and Kirsten Wolf (New York: Garland, 1993), p. 145.

14 For a discussion of national literary historiography — including two of the surveys considered here — in the Scandinavian countries, see Annika Olsson, 'Challenging the Bodies and Borders of Literature in Scandinavia: Methodological Nationalism, Intersectionality and Methodological Disciplinarity', in *Rethinking National Literatures and the Literary Canon in Scandinavia*, ed. by Ann-Sofie Lönngren and others (Cambridge: Cambridge Scholars Publishing, 2015), pp. 30–51.

15 See p. 112 below on the intellectual context for this.

16 *Dansk litteraturs historie*, ed. by Mortensen and Schack, I, p. 13.

17 Ibid., I, pp. 200–01, 132–34.

18 Ibid., I, pp. 22, 89, 92. For an introduction to the German translation of the *Jyske Lov*, see Seán Vrieland, 'A Reunited Law: AM 6 8vo', *Manuscript of the Month*, 15 Febru-

of affairs cannot, as the examples later in this chapter will show, be explained simply by a lack of surviving material in German to include; and it is all the more striking when compared with the attention that is given to the literary use of Latin in Denmark. The imbalance can thus be seen not as a result of simply excluding anything that is 'not (in) Danish' but to indicate a challenge posed by German in particular.[19] The ironic result is that, despite the programme laid out in the foreword, the sense of Denmark as set apart from what is now the larger neighbour to the south is reinforced: there is a readiness to acknowledge influence *from* (primarily northern) Germany, but the notion of literary activity in German *within* Denmark seems difficult to countenance in any detail.

This is not an isolated example; similar tendencies can also be observed in other literary histories. Three can be mentioned here, one from another collaborative study and two from enterprises with a single author. (i) *Hovedsporet: Dansk litteraturs historie* (The Main Line: Danish Literary History; 2005) also reflects to a degree on concepts of Danish identity and the European context for Danish literature.[20] But German is all but written out of the linguistic-literary developments in the Middle Ages, which are presented in terms of the schematic sequence: orality–written Latin culture–written Danish culture.[21] Consequently, the discussion of the medieval period concentrates on writing in Latin and Danish; German is mentioned only twice in over eighty pages (translations of the *Compendium Saxonis* and the *Jyske Lov*).[22]

(ii) Pil Dahlerup's *Dansk litteratur: Middelalder* (Danish Literature: Middle Ages; 1998) and its later extension, *Sanselig senmiddelalder* (Late Middle Ages of the Senses; 2010), do mention German material on occasion (e.g. the translations of the *Rimkrønike* (Rhym-

---

ary 2020 <https://manuscript.ku.dk/motm/a-reunited-law-am-6-8vo/> [accessed 7 April 2020].

19 But see also pp. 120–21 below on the need to consider languages other than German as well.

20 *Hovedsporet: Dansk litteraturs historie*, ed. by Jens Anker Jørgensen and Knud Wentzel ([n.p.]: Gyldendal, 2005), e.g. pp. 17–18, 20–22.

21 Ibid., pp. 85, 103–04.

22 Ibid., pp. 97, 102; the discussion of the medieval period spans pp. 59–142. For the *Compendium*, see p. 116 below.

ing Chronicle) and the *Jyske Lov*),[23] but there is no effort to address German systematically alongside the Danish and Latin traditions. Emblematic of this is the framework formulated for the *Middelalder* volume, where the starting point is the 'national language', broadened where necessary to include Latin:

> Jeg har valgt det hovedprincip, at 'dansk' her betyder *tekster der foreligger på dansk sprog*. [...] Princippet kan imidlertid ikke strengt overholdes. Det brydes for dette binds vedkommende af latindigterne, hvor 'dansk' betyder, personer, der kan tale dansk, men ikke gør det, eller personer bosiddende i Danmark, der skriver (om danske emner) på et fremmed sprog.[24]

> (The main principle I have chosen is that 'Danish' here means *texts that are found in the Danish language*. [...] The principle, however, cannot be strictly observed. In this volume, it is set aside in the case of the Latin poets, where 'Danish' means people who can speak Danish but do not, or people living in Denmark who write (about Danish subjects) in a foreign language.)

(iii) The first volume of Anne-Marie Mai's *Hvor litteraturen finder sted* (Where Literature Takes Place; 2010–11), finally, addresses the problem of German/Danish identities, particularly with regard to language,[25] mentions the multilingual nature of later centuries,[26] and

---

23   Pil Dahlerup, *Dansk litteratur: Middelalder*, 2 vols (Copenhagen: Gyldendal, 1998), II, pp. 99–100; Pil Dahlerup, *Sanselig senmiddelalder: Litterære perspektiver på danske tekster 1482–1523* (Aarhus: Aarhus Universitetsforlag, 2010), p. 89. Saxo ebook. For the *Rimkrønike*, see p. 116 below.

24   Dahlerup, *Dansk litteratur*, I, p. 38 (italics in original). Dahlerup's confused understanding of the relationship between language and 'Danishness' is obvious on the only occasion when she acknowledges the extent of the German presence. In the context of the relatively late appearance of the courtly romance in Denmark, she suggests as a possible alternative to the assessment that Denmark had been 'bagefter' (left behind) in this respect: 'Ridderromaner kan være blevet læst højt på tysk gennem hele middelalderen, en sandsynlig hypotese pga. den store tyske kulturindflydelse og de mange tyske dronninger' (The courtly romances may have been read aloud in German throughout the Middle Ages, a likely hypothesis given the considerable German cultural influence and the many German queens; II, p. 238). The extensive role of German evidently *can* be recognized when it is convenient — in order to support a particular image of Danish literary history — so the reader cannot help but ask why it is treated as an afterthought elsewhere.

25   Anne-Marie Mai, *Hvor litteraturen finder sted*, 3 vols ([n.p.]: Gyldendal, 2010–11), I: *Fra Guds tid til menneskets tid 1000–1800* (2010), pp. 12–16. Saxo ebook.

26   See e.g. ibid., I, pp. 348, 369, 480.

acknowledges earlier German connections and the Low German translation of the *Rimkrønike*.[27] But the latter is the exception that proves
the rule in the picture drawn of the manuscript culture of medieval
Denmark: 'Håndskrifternes sprog var oftest latin, men også dansk
sprog blev anvendt, og der findes både håndskrifter med runer og med
latinske bogstaver' (The language of the manuscripts was most often
Latin, but the Danish language was also used, and manuscripts are
found with both runes and Latin letters).[28]

THE INTELLECTUAL CONTEXT

The reasons for the infrequent juxtaposition of the German and Danish
literary-historical strands, as we might call them, are complex, and
should not be seen reductively in any one national context alone.[29]
The East Norse tradition, to which Danish belongs, has historically
tended to receive relatively little attention of any kind compared to the
more 'canonical' West Norse/Icelandic material,[30] and institutional
structures in the United Kingdom, for instance, do not necessarily
lend themselves to the building of bridges between Old Norse and
German Studies. The particular definition of literature that is adopted

---

27 Ibid., I, pp. 52, 158, 57.
28 Ibid., I, p. 57; similarly the section on 'Håndskrifter på latin og dansk' (Manuscripts in
    Latin and Danish; pp. 70–74).
29 Noteworthy in this respect, for instance, are the remarks in the foreword to a literary
    history (albeit of Scandinavia more generally) edited by a Swiss scholar and released
    by a German publisher: 'Bereiche, die [...] gar nicht oder nur ansatzweise behandelt
    werden, sind etwa die in fremden Sprachen (Lateinisch, Deutsch [...]) verfasste
    Dichtung' (Areas that [...] are not treated at all, or only in outline, include literature
    composed in foreign languages (Latin, German [...]); Jörg Glauser, 'Vorwort', in
    Skandinavische Literaturgeschichte, ed. by Jörg Glauser, 2nd edn (Stuttgart: Metzler,
    2016), pp. viii–xviii (p. xv)). On the Glauser history, see Lars Boje Mortensen and
    Tuomas M. S. Lehtonen, 'Introduction: What Is Nordic Medieval Literature?', in *The
    Performance of Christian and Pagan Storyworlds: Non-Canonical Chapters of the History
    of Nordic Medieval Literature*, ed. by Lars Boje Mortensen and Tuomas M. S. Lehtonen
    with Alexandra Bergholm (Turnhout: Brepols, 2013), pp. 1–41 (pp. 14–15). See also
    the remarks on *Europe: A Literary History*, ed. by Wallace, on pp. 119–20 below. It
    would be rewarding, but beyond the scope of this chapter, to look beyond Denmark
    and envisage a medieval literary history of the wider Nordic and/or Baltic literary space
    in terms of the languages that were actually used there.
30 See Jonathan Adams, 'Indledning: Østnordisk filologi — nu og i fremtiden', in *Østnor-
    disk filologi — nu og i fremtiden*, ed. by Jonathan Adams (Copenhagen: Universitets-
    Jubilæets danske Samfund, [n.d.]), pp. 11–13.

in any given case will also affect the range of material that is included. Nonetheless, it is highly likely that modern cultural interpretations of Denmark's relationship with Germany are also involved. As alluded to in Winge's remarks (p. 105 above), against the background of the two Schleswig wars in the nineteenth century and the German occupation in World War II in the twentieth, tensions (if not outright antagonism) have marked not only academic scholarship but also more popular mindsets.

Images of the Hanseatic League that position it as a German force in opposition to Danish interests are an obvious example of this: the Peace of Stralsund that concluded the war between Denmark and the League in 1370 has been interpreted as 'Unterdrückung durch ein expansives Deutschland' (subjection by an expanding Germany).[31] Such understandings appear to have become so deeply set as to prevent even a single Danish town from joining the 'Hanse Today' network, the aim of which is explicitly 'to bring about closer economic, cultural, social and national ties across Europe'.[32] Something of this mentality was captured by the linguist, academic, and publisher Jørn Lund when he acerbically commented: 'Tysk er det sprog og den kultur, der har påvirket dansk mest gennem hele det historiske forløb. Men det er der mange, der ikke vil være ved' (German is the language and culture that has had the greatest influence on Danish through the whole course of history. But there are many who do not want to acknowledge this).[33]

Nevertheless, some aspects of the situation to which Winge and Lund refer have begun to change. In the public sphere, one could point to the 2020 Danish–German 'friendship year' declared to mark the centenary of the plebiscites that led to North Schleswig/Southern Jutland becoming part of Denmark.[34] In an academic context, meanwhile, scholarship from various angles has argued against setting Den-

---

31   See Baur, *Freunde und Feinde*, p. 11.

32   See ibid., pp. 11–12, 15–36. For the 'Hanse Today', see <https://www.hanse.org/en/> [accessed 18 September 2020].

33   Professor Higgins [Jørn Lund], 'Tysk', *Folkeskolen*, 26 May 2006 <https://www.folkeskolen.dk/42837/tysk> [accessed 17 April 2019]. On the pseudonym, see 'Jørn Lund', in *Wikipedia* <https://da.wikipedia.org/wiki/Jørn_Lund_(professor)> [accessed 17 April 2019].

34   'The 2020 Commemoration' <https://genforeningen2020.dk/the-2020-commemoration/> [accessed 21 January 2020].

mark apart from Germany in particular and from the European cultural sphere more generally. This includes, for example, work on the German–Danish borderlands in which 'the sharp edges of national boundaries begin to blur, and several layers of identity surface side by side'.[35] Danish historiography on the Middle Ages has likewise been concerned to question the paradigm of 'essential differences between the societies of Western Europe on the one hand and Denmark and the Scandinavian countries on the other', and to approach medieval Denmark in an emphatically European context instead.[36] The influence of Middle Low German on the Scandinavian vernaculars, including Danish, has also long been recognized.[37] When it comes to the role played by German in the specifically literary history of the Danish Middle Ages, however, the picture remains fragmented. Studies on individual themes and works can be found, particularly in the context of projects on the wider German–Scandinavian literary and linguistic interface,[38] but a comprehensive account is lacking.

---

35 Peter Thaler, *Of Mind and Matter: The Duality of National Identity in the German–Danish Borderlands* (West Lafayette: Purdue University Press, 2009), p. 19.

36 Kerstin Hundahl and Lars Kjær, 'Introduction', in *Denmark and Europe in the Middle Ages*, ed. by Hundahl, Kjær, and Lund, pp. 1–7 (p. 2). Further examples would include Nils Hybel, *Danmark i Europa 750–1300* (Copenhagen: Museum Tusculanums Forlag, 2003); *Danmark og Europa i senmiddelalderen*, ed. by Per Ingesman and Bjørn Poulsen (Aarhus: Aarhus University Press, 2000).

37 The literature here is extensive. Starting points may be found in *Contact between Low German and Scandinavian in the Late Middle Ages: 25 Years of Research*, ed. by Lennart Elmevik and Ernst Håkon Jahr (Uppsala: Kungl. Gustav Adolfs Akademien för svensk folkkultur, 2012); Vibeke Winge, *Pebersvend og poltergejst: Tysk indflydelse på dansk* (Copenhagen: Gyldendal, 2000); *Niederdeutsch in Skandinavien*, vols 1–4, Beihefte zur Zeitschrift für deutsche Philologie, 4–7 (Berlin: Schmidt, 1987–1993), vols 5–6 [in one] (Frankfurt a.M.: Lang, 2005). See further also Hansen, 'Transformation of the Danish Language', pp. 128–36.

38 Cf. e.g. contributions to 'Deutsch-Skandinavische Literatur- und Kulturbeziehungen im Mittelalter', ed. by Sieglinde Hartmann and Stefanie Würth, *Jahrbuch der Oswald von Wolkenstein Gesellschaft*, 16 (2006/07), 1–346, and *Niederdeutsch in Skandinavien*, III, ed. by Lennart Elmevik and Kurt Erich Schöndorf, IV, ed. by Hubertus Menke and Kurt Erich Schöndorf. Conversely, other accounts give no more than perfunctory attention to the medieval period; e.g. *Scandinavia and Germany: Cultural Crosscurrents*, ed. by Jennifer M. Hoyer and Jennifer Watson (= *Scandinavian Studies*, 91.4 (winter 2019)).

TOWARDS AN INCLUSIVE APPROACH

The closest existing counterpart to the project I have in mind is Winge's study. Yet its focus — and it does not claim otherwise — is on linguistic history: the primary concern is to describe the German used in Denmark in terms of dialectal features, the transition from Low to High German, the social background of its users, and so on.[39] Matters such as textual or narrative structure, differences between source and translation, or the circulation and function of themes, motifs, and genres are addressed at best tangentially in an analysis of this kind. Second, although it recognizes the fundamentally multilingual nature of medieval Denmark,[40] Winge's study introduces the Danish and Latin traditions primarily where they inform discussion of the German material in any particular case, rather than covering them in parallel to it. What forms might an attempt to do just that in a new literary history take? Some possibilities, with examples drawn primarily from historical writing, are presented below; in practice, there will obviously be overlaps between them.

(i) One possibility is to present the material in terms of cross-language rubrics such as the emergence of a written tradition on parchment (later also paper) in roman script for the three languages.[41] In this context, Latin is documented from the eleventh century; the oldest known coherent text of Danish origin is Canute IV's 1085 letter of donation to the church of St Lawrence in Lund (the earliest copy is

---

39   See e.g. Winge, *Dänische Deutsche — deutsche Dänen*, pp. 1–5.

40   Ibid., pp. 1–2, 4–5. See also pp. 120–21 below.

41   The formulation is intentionally narrow for the purposes of this example, and excludes other media (such as inscriptions, runic and otherwise) and the use of runes in manuscripts (on the latter see e.g. Britta Olrik Frederiksen, 'The History of Old Nordic Manuscripts IV: Old Danish', in *The Nordic Languages: An International Handbook of the History of the North Germanic Languages*, ed. by Oskar Bandle and others, 2 vols (Berlin: De Gruyter, 2002–05), i (2002), pp. 816–24 (p. 821)). Introductions to such matters can be found in Nils Hybel and Bjørn Poulsen, *The Danish Resources c. 1000–1550: Growth and Recession* (Leiden: Brill, 2007), pp. 82–95; Robert Nedoma, 'Der Beginn volkssprachlicher Schriftlichkeit im alten Skandinavien: Eine Skizze', in *Anfangsgeschichten: Der Beginn volkssprachiger Schriftlichkeit in komparatistischer Perspektive/Origin Stories: The Rise of Vernacular Literacy in a Comparative Perspective*, ed. by Norbert Kössinger and others (Paderborn: Fink, 2018), pp. 275–301 (pp. 275–82, 298–99); Jakob Povl Holck, 'Cultural Contacts and Genres of Runes — Danish Literacy around 1300', in *Literacy in Medieval and Early Modern Scandinavian Culture*, ed. by Pernille Hermann (Odense: University Press of Southern Denmark, 2005), pp. 151–63.

preserved in a twelfth-century manuscript),[42] and the earliest specifically narrative text is the *Passio Kanuti* (Passion of Canute), written in Odense by an anonymous author between 1095 and 1101 (but known only from a sixteenth-century copy).[43] We know that Danish was being used to write down legal texts from as early as around 1170.[44] The first texts in German, finally, appear to have been the fourteenth-century *Urkunden* mentioned above; the earliest that can be said with certainty to have originated in Denmark is from 1329, issued by Christopher II in Ringsted.[45] Identifying the appearance of these strands is merely one way in which one can do justice to the co-existence of the three languages. It is not intended to valorize a search for 'firsts' of which our knowledge can only ever be conditional because of the possibility of lost material. Instead, it points to how the interest in beginnings and origins that is associated with the narratives of national philologies[46] can be redirected (or expanded) to address this plurality, rather than levelling it in order to map teleologically the course of one single future national language. A juxtaposition along these lines could, for example, be used to compare and contrast the rise of Danish and German as vernaculars in terms of stages such as literization, literarization, and librarization.[47]

(ii) The trajectory of particular texts as they passed from one language to another can also be traced. An example of this is the afterlife of Saxo's *Gesta Danorum* in languages other than Latin.[48] His influence

---

42 'Knud den Helliges gavebrev, 1085', *danmarkshistorien.dk* <https://danmarkshistorien.dk/leksikon-og-kilder/vis/materiale/knud-den-helliges-gavebrev-1085/> [accessed 17 February 2020].

43 For the dating, see Haki Antonsson, 'Sanctus Kanutus rex', in *Medieval Nordic Literature in Latin: A Website of Authors and Anonymous Works c. 1100–1530*, ed. by Stephan Borgehammar and others <https://wikihost.uib.no/medieval/index.php/Sanctus_Kanutus_rex> [accessed 24 January 2020].

44 See Per Andersen, 'Dating the Laws of Medieval Denmark: Studies of the Manuscripts of the Danish Church Laws', in *Denmark and Europe in the Middle Ages*, ed. by Hundahl, Kjær, and Lund, pp. 183–202; Per Andersen, *Legal Procedure and Practice in Medieval Denmark* (Leiden: Brill, 2011), p. 71.

45 Winge, *Dänische Deutsche — deutsche Dänen*, p. 49.

46 See e.g. Norbert Kössinger and others, 'Introduction', in *Anfangsgeschichten/Origin Stories*, ed. by Kössinger and others, pp. 7–8 (p. 8).

47 On this sequence, see Lars Boje Mortensen, 'Latin as Vernacular: Critical Mass and the "Librarization" of Book Languages', in *Anfangsgeschichten/Origin Stories*, ed. by Kössinger and others, pp. 71–90 (pp. 71–80).

48 It is worth noting that changes in the accentuation of the 'anti-German' aspect of Saxo's original work do not necessarily map onto changes in the language of its

can be felt in the *Gesta Danorum pa danskæ* (History of the Danes in Danish),[49] and the *Compendium Saxonis* (a compressed and stylistically simplified version; c. 1342–46)[50] was one of the sources for the fifteenth-century Danish *Rimkrønike*.[51] The *Rimkrønike* was in turn translated into German (very likely still in Denmark, in the orbit of the royal household) as the *Niederdeutsche Chronik aller koninge tho Dennemarken* (Low German Chronicle of All the Kings of Denmark).[52] In addition, the *Compendium* was translated directly into German in two versions, both of which can be linked to a Danish context. Copenhagen, Royal Library, Gammel kongelige Samling 819 2°, a manuscript of one of these versions, was 'completed 22 February 1476 at Skanderborg Castle, Jutland' and 'written for Erik Ottesen Rosenkrantz (ca. 1427–1503), who [...] held the highest office in the royal household'; the other version, the *Denscke Kroneke* (Danish Chronicle), was very probably printed (on the basis of an earlier manuscript) by Matthäus Brandis in Odense in 1502.[53]

---

adaptations/reuses; see Anders Leegaard Knudsen, 'The Use of Saxo Grammaticus in the Later Middle Ages', in *The Birth of Identities: Denmark and Europe in the Middle Ages*, ed. by Brian P. McGuire (Copenhagen: Reitzel, 1996), pp. 147–60.

49   The modern reader should be aware that this text is not a straightforward translation of Saxo into Danish but a short work that draws on a range of earlier material. See Anders Leegaard Knudsen, *Saxostudier og rigshistorie på Valdemar Atterdags tid* (Copenhagen: Museum Tusculanums Forlag, 1994), pp. 17–19 (with a dating to c. 1300); 'Gesta Danorum: Kulturhistorisk baggrund', in *Tekster fra Danmarks middelalder og renæssance 1100–1550 — på dansk og latin* <https://tekstnet.dk/gesta-danorum/about> [accessed 14 February 2021] (with a dating to the late fourteenth century).

50   See Lars B. Mortensen, 'Compendium Saxonis', in *The Encyclopedia of the Medieval Chronicle*, ed. by Graeme Dunphy, 2 vols (Leiden: Brill, 2010), I, p. 484 (the *Encyclopedia* is henceforth abbreviated as *EMC*).

51   Knudsen, *Saxostudier og rigshistorie*, pp. 67–68.

52   Reimer Hansen, 'Bruder Nigels dänische Reimchronik niederdeutsch', *Niederdeutsches Jahrbuch*, 25 (1899), pp. 132–51 (pp. 132–33).

53   See e.g. Anders Leegaard Knudsen, 'Compendium Saxonis & Chronica Jutensis', in *Medieval Nordic Literature in Latin*, ed. by Borgehammar and others <https://wikihost.uib.no/medieval/index.php/Compendium_Saxonis_%26_Chronica_Jutensis> [accessed 20 February 2020] (quotation); Knudsen, *Saxostudier og rigshistorie*, pp. 37–62; Mortensen, 'Compendium Saxonis'; Christine Stöllinger-Löser, '"Denscke Kroneke"', in *Die deutsche Literatur des Mittelalters: Verfasserlexikon*, 2nd edn, 14 vols (Berlin: De Gruyter, 1978–2008), XI (2004), cols 344–46; Martin Przybilski, 'Denscke Kroneke', in *EMC*, I, p. 516. Various datings and places of printing for the *Denscke Kroneke* will be encountered in the literature. I follow here Wolfgang Undorf, 'Print and Book Culture in the Danish Town of Odense', in *Print Culture and Peripheries in Early Modern Europe: A Contribution to the History of Printing and the Book Trade in Small European and Spanish Cities*, ed. by Benito Rial Costas (Leiden:

(iii) Alternatively, specific individuals and institutions can be fore-grounded. For instance, Johannes Nicolai/Jens Nielsen from Ålborg — plausibly the prior of the Helligåndskloster — not only copied (at least a large part of) Copenhagen, Arnamagnæan Institute, 372 2° (completed in 1482), which contains a Middle Low German *Historien-bibel*, but also produced a number of manuscripts in Danish, featuring in particular the *Jyske Lov*.[54] The Cistercian abbey of Ryd/Rüde in Schleswig,[55] meanwhile, is well known to scholars of medieval Danish history and historical writing as the place where the Latin *Annales Ryenses* (Annals of Ryd) were probably composed in the late thirteenth century. The influence of the annals on Danish historiography and their 'strong anti-German tone' is often noted.[56] That the

Brill, 2012), pp. 227–48: 'Its publication has been attributed by bibliographers to either Lübeck or to the Danish provincial towns of Schleswig or Ribe, and the publication date has been established as between 1490 and 1502. We now know that it was most likely printed by Matthaeus Brandis during his stay in Odense 1502' (p. 244). For the relation of the print to the manuscripts and the Latin text, see Vibeke Winge, 'De denscke kroneke — der niederdeutsche Saxo', in *Vulpis Adolatio: Festschrift für Hubertus Menke zum 60. Geburtstag*, ed. by Robert Peters, Horst P. Pütz, and Ulrich Weber (Heidelberg: Winter, 2001), pp. 919–28. On Rosenkrantz, see Henry Bruun, 'Rosenkrantz, Erik Ottesen', in *Dansk biografisk leksikon*, 3rd edn, ed. by Sv. Cedergreen Bech, 16 vols (Copenhagen: Gyldendal, 1979–84), xii (1982), pp. 332–33 <http://denstoredanske.dk/Dansk_Biografisk_Leksikon/Monarki_og_adel/Hofmester/Erik_Ottesen_Rosenkrantz> [accessed 13 March 2020].

54   Jürgen Wolf, *Die Sächsische Weltchronik im Spiegel ihrer Handschriften: Überlieferung, Textentwicklung, Rezeption* (Munich: Fink, 1997), pp. 90–91, 174–76; Brigitte Derendorf, 'Die mittelniederdeutsche "Historienbibel VIII"', *Niederdeutsches Wort*, 36 (1996), pp. 167–82 (esp. pp. 170–71, 180–82). AM 372 2° also contains Old Danish material (on fol. 138^v). consisting of two sententiae in Latin and Old Danish translation. A digitization of the manuscript can be viewed at <https://handrit.is/en/manuscript/imaging/da/AM02-372> [accessed 13 August 2020]. Views differ on whether Nicolai was the manuscript's only scribe, but this does not affect the argument here. On the other manuscripts produced by Johannes Nicolai, see Ellen Jørgensen, *Studier over danske middelalderlige Bogsamlinger* (Copenhagen: Bianco Lunos bogtrykkeri, 1912), p. 65 n. 1 (NB: Wolf's claim that Nicolai was also the scribe of 'Lobund Preisbücher[]' would appear to be the result of a mistranslation of Jørgensen's 'Lovbøger'); Britta Olrik Frederiksen, '57. The Jutland Law', in *Living Words & Luminous Pictures: Medieval Book Culture in Denmark: Catalogue*, ed. by Erik Petersen ([n.p.]: Det Kongelige Bibliotek; Moesgård Museum, 1999), pp. 44–45.

55   This should be seen in the wider context of the role played by religious institutions in cultural mediation, most obviously perhaps the Vadstena abbey, where, for instance, it is likely that the lost source of the Swedish and Danish versions of the Middle Low German *Seelentrost* (Consolation of the Soul) originated; see Margarete Andersson-Schmitt, '"Siælinna thrøst" und seine Varianten', in *Niederdeutsch in Skandinavien*, iii, ed. by Elmevik and Schöndorf, pp. 70–76. See also pp. 120–21 below.

56   Lars B. Mortensen, 'Annales Ryenses', in *EMC*, i, p. 85 (quotation); *Danmarks middelalderlige annaler*, ed. by Erik Kroman (Copenhagen: [n. pub.], 1980), p. 149.

abbey also helped to mediate historical writing in German in later medieval Denmark, however, is not so widely recognized: the manuscript Copenhagen, Royal Library, Gammel kongelige Samling 1978 4°, which includes a version of the so-called *Sächsische Weltchronik* (Saxon World Chronicle), was copied there by Johannes Vicken in 1434.[57] The version of the *Weltchronik* in that manuscript is also of interest because it appears to have been used in a work known as the *Mittelniederdeutsche Weltchronik* (Middle Low German World Chronicle); the manuscript Copenhagen, Arnamagnæan Institute, 29 2° of the latter contains a preface noting that it was written/copied at the behest of Eggert Frille, son of a Schleswig nobleman and an influential associate of Christian I of Denmark.[58]

(iv) Finally, the material circulation of texts across territorial borders can be investigated. The surviving text of the *Niederdeutsche Chronik aller koninge tho Dennemarken*, for example, is a copy made by Johann Russe of a (now lost) source captured from the Danes in the Battle of Hemmingstedt in 1500. Russe's copy was then itself captured — along with the other historiographical texts he assembled in the same codex, such as the 'anti-Danish' *Holsteinische Reimchronik* (Rhymed Chronicle of Holstein) — when Ditmarschen was conquered by the Danes in 1559.[59] To cases such as this we could add further material such as the Low German translation of

---

57 Wolf, *Sächsische Weltchronik*, pp. 85–86.

58 It is appealing to postulate a connection with Ryd and/or the manuscript of the *Sächsische Weltchronik* there, as has in fact been done in the past. The two earliest manuscripts of the *Mittelniederdeutsche Weltchronik* are indeed both from the fifteenth century, but the chronicle itself extends only to the mid-fourteenth century and could thus have been completed prior to the copying of the Ryd manuscript. Winge, *Dänische Deutsche — deutsche Dänen*, pp. 82–83; Wolf, *Sächsische Weltchronik*, pp. 229–31; Els Oksaar, 'Eine neuentdeckte mittelniederdeutsche Weltchronik des 15. Jahrhunderts', *Niederdeutsches Jahrbuch*, 85 (1962), pp. 33–46. On Frille, see Thelma Jexlev, 'Frille, Eggert', in *Dansk biografisk leksikon*, ed. by Bech, v (1980), pp. 13–14   <http://denstoredanske.dk/Dansk_Biografisk_Leksikon/Samfund,_jura_og_politik/Myndigheder_og_politisk_styre/Rigsråd/Eggert_Frille> [accessed 13 March 2020].

59 For the circumstances, see Hansen, 'Bruder Nigels dänische Reimchronik niederdeutsch', pp. 132–33; Paul H. Freedman, *Images of the Medieval Peasant* (Stanford: Stanford University Press, 1999), pp. 199–201; William L. Urban, *Dithmarschen: A Medieval Peasant Republic* (Lewiston: Mellen, 1991). For the content of the manuscript, see *Holsteinische Reimchronik*, ed. by Ludwig Weiland, in MGH Deutsche Chroniken, 2 (Hanover: Hahnsche Buchhandlung, 1877), pp. 609–33 (p. 612); Ursula Kundert, 'Holsteinische Reimchronik', in *EMC*, i, p. 812 (quotation).

the *Speculum humanae salvationis* (Mirror of Human Salvation) that was probably produced in Germany but came to Denmark by or in the sixteenth century, during which it was annotated in Danish.[60] In many cases, of course, a reconstruction of the exact circumstances of such transfer processes is no longer possible. Adam of Bremen's *Gesta Hammaburgensis ecclesiae pontificum* (History of the Archbishops of Hamburg-Bremen), to take an example involving writing in Latin, was used in several works of Latin historiography originating in Denmark (including Saxo) and has a clear Danish transmission in the guise of the *B* manuscripts, but precisely how the work made its way to Denmark or what form its early circulation there took is unknown; particular attention has been given to the so-called Sorø manuscript, which is believed to have existed in Denmark in the twelfth century.[61]

PRACTICALITIES AND FURTHER PERSPECTIVES

The suggestions above are not exhaustive; they represent merely four ways in which the material can be organized, four pathways that can be taken through it. The focus has primarily been on the production of texts, understood in a broad sense that encompasses copying and translation as well as 'original' output, but future work could give greater prominence to readers and the consumption of texts in the literary space; the circulation of Latin works that entered Denmark from the German sphere, on which the case of Adam of Bremen touches, is one example of this. Other approaches could also be added with the help of contemporary projects that explore the writing of literary history outside a national framework. The place-based 'itineraries [...] drawn

---

60   Hans Blosen, 'Ein mittelniederdeutsches "Speculum humanae salvationis" in dänischem Gebrauch', in *Vulpis Adolatio*, ed. by Peters, Pütz, and Weber, pp. 71–88. Digitization: <http://www5.kb.dk/permalink/2006/manus/219/eng/> [accessed 13 August 2020].

61   See Bernhard Schmeidler, 'Einleitung', in Adam von Bremen, *Hamburgische Kirchengeschichte*, 3rd edn, ed. by Bernhard Schmeidler, MGH SS rer. Germ. (Hanover: Hahn, 1917), pp. vii–lxvii (pp. xvii–xxix); Inger Ekrem, 'Essay on Date and Purpose', in *Historia Norwegie*, ed. by Inger Ekrem and Lars Boje Mortensen, trans. by Peter Fisher (Copenhagen: Museum Tusculanum Press, 2006), pp. 155–225 (p. 159); Werner Trillmich, 'Einleitung', in *Quellen des 9. und 11. Jahrhunderts zur Geschichte der hamburgischen Kirche und des Reiches*, ed. by Werner Trillmich and Rudolf Buchner, 7th edn, Freiherr vom Stein-Gedächtnisausgabe, 11 (Darmstadt: Wissenschaftliche Buchgesellschaft, 2000), pp. 137–58 (pp. 155–56).

together through links of travel, trade, religious practice, language, and literary exchange' employed in the recent *Europe: A Literary History, 1348–1418*, edited by David Wallace, are just one possibility.[62] Given that not a single location in modern-day Denmark features in the anthology,[63] it would be all the more rewarding to trace such currents and connections in the case of locations such as Odense.[64] That city has already figured several times in the preceding pages, from the *schra* of the Elende Lav, to the printer Johan Snell, to Brandis's print of the *Denscke Kroneke*. We might add to this the adaptation of Alanus de Rupe from Latin into Danish by an Odense priest, Herr Michael, in 1496. He was commissioned by the consort of King John of Denmark, Christina of Saxony, who was also active in the mediation of cultural activity more widely, such as — if one is concerned to draw links with Art History — supporting the workshop of the German artist Claus Berg, likewise in Odense.[65]

It would ultimately be important to bring further languages into the picture as well, particularly if we consider the extent of the areas under Danish control at one time or another in the Middle Ages.[66]

---

62   David Wallace, 'Introduction', in *Europe: A Literary History*, ed. by Wallace, I, pp. xxvii–xlii (p. xxviii).

63   Most of the material I have discussed falls outside the chronological scope of the Wallace history, so a direct criticism on that level would be unfair. However, in the introduction, the project is framed emphatically as an effort to overcome restrictive understandings of Europe and the limits of national approaches to medieval literary history. This agenda is bound so closely to the chronological points of reference that one could be forgiven for thinking the period has a representative status. This becomes problematic when the demarcation silently perpetuates one of the very imbalances that the anthology aspires to campaign against. For further criticism of the structuring of literary history in terms of such narrow parameters, also with reference to Wallace and Denmark, see Lars Boje Mortensen, 'Litteraturhistorisk tid — kan middelalderen afskaffes?', *temp — tidsskrift for historie* (forthcoming).

64   I am planning a separate study on this topic.

65   See Mette Nordentoft, 'Zum (nord)europäischen Stemma des Passionstraktates Hein-richs von St. Gallen', in *Niederdeutsch in Skandinavien*, IV, ed. by Menke and Schön-dorf, pp. 168–95 (pp. 189–92); Bridget Morris, 'Christian Poetry: East Norse', in *Medieval Scandinavia*, ed. by Pulsiano and Wolf, pp. 72–73 (p. 73). Worth mentioning in the present context is Nordentoft's theory that Christina was also behind the translation into Danish of Heinrich von St. Gallen's German-language *Extendit manum* tract. Figures such as Berg can be set in a wider context; cf. e.g. the case of the German artist Albertus Pictor, who painted the interior of churches in Sweden: *Den mångsidige målaren: Vidgade perspektive på Albertus Pictors bild- och textvärld*, ed. by Jan Öberg, Erika Kihlman, and Pia Melin (Stockholm: Sällskapet Runica et Mediævalia, 2007).

66   Cf. Winge, *Dänische Deutsche — deutsche Dänen*, p. 2: 'Dänemark war im hier untersuchten Zeitraum (1300–1800) ein multilinguales Land mit dänisch-, norwe-

The question of geographical and chronological demarcation would require a separate discussion, but the Kalmar Union (1397–1523), at least, must be mentioned briefly. Several of the texts we have encountered enter into connections with the Swedish textual tradition in this context. A Swedish translation of the *Gesta Danorum pa danskæ*, for instance, is preserved in a *Sammelhandschrift* (Stockholm, Royal Library, D 4) that was probably produced in Vadstena in the first half of the fifteenth century and contains material in Swedish, Latin, and Low German.[67] *Dværgekongen Laurin*, meanwhile, is preserved in a manuscript (Stockholm, Royal Library, K 47; *c.* 1500), apparently written by scribes from Jutland, that also includes the Danish versions of the Old Swedish *Eufemiavisor* (Eufemia Poems), which were crucial in the mediation of courtly narrative and culture to Denmark.[68] Finally, one of the questions raised by the *Rimkrønike* is whether it or the Swedish *Lilla rimkrönika* (Little Rhyme Chronicle; fifteenth century) should

gisch-, schwedisch- und deutschsprechenden Bürgern' (Denmark was, in the timespan considered here (1300-1800), a multilingual country with Danish-, Norwegian-, Swedish-, and German-speaking inhabitants).

67   See Knudsen, *Saxostudier og rigshistorie*, p. 17; Jonas Carlquist, *Handskriften som historiskt vittne: Fornsvenska samlingshandskrifter — miljö och funktion* (Stockholm: Sällskapet Runica et Mediævalia, 2002), pp. 97–103; Elena Brandenburg, *Karl der Große im Norden: Rezeption französischer Heldenepik in den altostnordischen Handschriften* (Tübingen: Narr Francke Attempto, 2019), pp. 67–75.

68   See the description of K 47 in *Tekster fra Danmarks middelalder og renæssance 1100–1550 — på dansk og latin* <https://tekstnet.dk/manuscript-descriptions/stockholm-k47-lang-beskrivelse> [accessed 28 January 2020]; Regina Jucknies, 'Through an Old Danish Lens? Precious Stones in the Late Medieval Danish Reception of Courtly Literature', in *The Eufemiavisor and Courtly Culture: Time, Texts and Cultural Transfer*, ed. by Olle Ferm and others (Stockholm: Kungl. Vitterhets Historie och Antikvitets Akademien, 2015), pp. 162–75 (pp. 163–64); Britta Olrik Frederiksen, '61. Courtly Romances', in *Living Words & Luminous Pictures: Catalogue*, ed. by Petersen, pp. 48–49. The findings of the conference 'The *Eufemiaviser* and the Reception of Courtly Culture in Late Medieval Denmark' (Zurich, September 2018) should provide an important contribution to our understanding of the Danish *Eufemiaviser* (programme at <https://www.ds.uzh.ch/_files/uploads/agenda/821.pdf> [accessed 4 March 2020]). The case of the *Eufemiavisor* once again underlines the wider cross-cultural context for this project: the Old Swedish originals were themselves translations, in part from 'continental' sources, commissioned by Queen Eufemia of Norway some two centuries earlier, very likely in the context of the project of marrying her daughter to Duke Eric Magnusson of Sweden; see e.g. Stefanie Würth, 'Eufemia: Deutsche Auftraggeberin schwedischer Literatur am norwegischen Hof', in *Arbeiten zur Skandinavistik: 13. Arbeitstagung der deutschsprachigen Skandinavistik, 29.7.-3.8.1997 in Lysebu (Oslo)*, ed. by Fritz Paul (Frankfurt a.M.: Lang, 2000), pp. 269–281 (pp. 278–80).

be credited with primacy in introducing the monologue form.[69] Recognizing the roughly contemporary circulation of historical writing in German *in addition to* the question of Swedish influence promises a better understanding of the environment in which this canonical work of Danish vernacular historiography appeared.

A project of this kind would require a substantial amount of research both to assemble the material to be considered and to establish some of the basic facts about it — or at least to acknowledge uncertainty where it is present. In the *Encyclopedia of the Medieval Chronicle*, one of the standard reference works in the field, for instance, the *Mittelniederdeutsche Reimchronik* mentioned earlier is categorically stated to have originated in Germany.[70] This is not an unreasonable assertion per se, particularly if one assumes completion of the work in chronological proximity to the final events mentioned in it.[71] Apart from the modern locations of the manuscripts, however, no indication is given of the Danish textual networks in which the work participated and without which its context cannot be fully understood. Seemingly straightforward statements of this kind become problematic when considered from the broader perspective advocated in this chapter. A reassessment of them depends on philological basic research that may not necessarily be glamorous or easily 'marketable', but is nonetheless necessary if an accurate understanding of the wider picture is to be obtained. Some of the relevant information and material is readily accessible, some of it less so; it is scattered across well-known handbooks and niche specialist literature from a number of medieval philologies, as well as other disciplines such as History and Religious Studies. Even this work — let alone that of subsequent interpretation, presentation, and analysis — is likely to go beyond what could be fully accomplished by a single person on their own.

What I have sought to do here is to demonstrate the breadth and inherent interest of the material, as well as the need finally to do justice to it; in realizing that objective, collaboration and sharing would be

---

69   See Pernille Hermann, 'Politiske og æstetiske aspekter i Rimkrøniken', *Historisk Tidsskrift* [Denmark], 107 (2007), pp. 389–411 (pp. 402–03 with n. 14); on the *Lilla rimkrönika*, Olle Ferm, 'Lilla rimkrönikan', in *EMC*, ii, p. 1032.

70   Stephen Mark Carey, 'Mittelniederdeutsche Weltchronik', in *EMC*, ii, p. 1115.

71   See n. 58 above.

crucial. The result would not only provide a much-needed understanding of medieval literary culture in a neglected part of northern Europe, but also allow connections to be drawn with more far-reaching debates. One could ask, for instance, whether the one-sided focus on Danish alongside and/or in opposition to Latin in existing literary histories is related to instrumentalization of the concept of a 'vernacular' in a colonialist context.[72] Such questions, in turn, point to the relevance of this project beyond Medieval Studies alone. My 'home' discipline, German Studies, for example, is characterized by its own concern with openness in the guise of calls such as that — to quote just one initiative — to embrace 'texts in or about German culture [...] written by or about under-represented and historically marginalised groups, with the aim of helping to expand and diversify the German Studies curriculum'.[73] The relevance of the sources discussed here to themes such as marginalization, migration, multilingualism, and diversity, and to the teaching and study of texts outside the traditional canon, ought to be obvious.[74] It is in wider contexts such as this that the project I envisage is ultimately to be understood.

---

72   Starting points for such reflection include Shyama Rajendran, 'Undoing "the Vernacular": Dismantling Structures of Raciolinguistic Supremacy', in *Critical Race and the Middle Ages* (= *Literature Compass*, 16.9–10 (September–October 2019)); Lars Jensen and others, 'Denmark and its Colonies', in *A Historical Companion to Postcolonial Literatures — Continental Europe and its Empires*, ed. by Prem Poddar, Rajeev S. Patke, and Lars Jensen (Edinburgh: Edinburgh University Press, 2008), pp. 57–103; *Anfangsgeschichten/Origin Stories*, ed. by Kissinger and others; *The Vulgar Tongue: Medieval and Postmedieval Vernacularity*, ed. by Fiona Somerset and Nicholas Watson (Princeton: Princeton University Press, 2003).

73   *Expanding German Studies: An Interactive Bibliography for Teachers and Lecturers* <https://germanstudiesbibliography.wordpress.com/> [accessed 18 September 2020]). Mention should also be made of similar efforts in Scandinavian Studies, such as the anthology *Rethinking National Literatures*, ed. by Lönngren and others.

74   Appreciation of this relevance is not necessarily to be taken as a given. At the time of writing, for instance, out of over one hundred entries in the *Expanding German Studies* bibliography, merely four covered the medieval period. For a recent demonstration, focusing on Lübeck, of the potential of Low German sources to inform understandings of transnationalism in a premodern context, cf. Elizabeth Andersen, 'Translation, Transposition, Transmission: Low German and Processes of Cultural Transformation', in *Transnational German Studies*, ed. by Rebecca Braun and Benedict Schofield (Liverpool: Liverpool University Press, 2020), pp. 17–41.

II. EXPERIENCE AND SUBJECTIVITY

Merlin's Open Mind
Madness, Prophecy, and Poetry in Geoffrey of Monmouth's *Vita Merlini*

MONIKA OTTER

My point of departure in Geoffrey of Monmouth's *Vita Merlini* (*c.* 1150), is the startling image of Merlin's refuge in the woods, built to his specifications.[1] Chief among the compound's buildings is to be a circular house, a kind of observatory with seventy doors and windows:[2]

> Ante domos alias unam compone remotam
> cui sex dena decem dabis hostia totque fenestras,

---

1   In describing this arcade-like circular structure, might Geoffrey have been thinking among other things of Stonehenge, another building associated with Merlin in his *History of the Kings of Britain*? It is there referred to as 'the giant's dance', not a building, but the visual analogies are striking (Geoffrey of Monmouth, *The History of the Kings of Britain*, ed. by Michael D. Reeve, trans. by Neil Wright (Woodbridge: Boydell, 2007), pp. 172–75). It would not have much bearing on the present discussion, except for the tantalizing suggestion that as early as the twelfth century, someone perhaps considered that Stonehenge could have had an astronomical purpose. On Stonehenge and Merlin, see Irène Fabry-Tehranchy, 'Écrire l'histoire de Stonehenge: Narration historique et romanesque (XIIe–XVe siècles)', in *L'Écriture de l'histoire au Moyen Âge: Contraintes génériques, contraintes documentaires*, ed. by Etienne Anheim and others (Paris: Garnier, 2015), pp. 131–47.

2   Geoffrey of Monmouth, *Life of Merlin/Vita Merlini*, ed. and trans. by Basil Clark (Cardiff: University of Wales Press, 1973). I am using Clarke's edition as well as his facing-page prose translation (henceforth cited by line number in the text).

per quas ignivomum videam cum Venere Phebum
inspiciamque polo labentia sydera noctu,
que me de populo regni ventura docebunt,
totque notatores que dicam scribere docti
assint et studeant carmen mandare tabellis. (555–61)

(Before the other buildings build me a remote one to which
you will give seventy doors and as many windows, through
which I may see fire-breathing Phoebus with Venus, and watch
by night the stars wheeling in the firmament; and they will
teach me about the future of the nation. Let there be as many
secretaries trained to record what I say, and work to commit my
song to writing tablets.)

The basic plot of the *Vita* is quickly told: after surviving a disastrous battle that killed many of his friends, Merlin loses his reason and escapes
from the court to live in the woods. After several unsuccessful attempts
by his loved ones to lure or force him back indoors, he suggests the
woodland compound as a compromise: a comfortable dwelling and
observatory, catered and staffed with secretaries. There he is joined
by the prophet 'Telgesinus' (Taliesin), by 'quidam vesanus' (another
madman) named Maëldin, also a battle-survivor, and finally, after her
husband dies, by his sister Ganieda, who to his great relief takes over
his prophetic gift. They spend their time researching and conversing,
and almost incidentally Merlin is cured of his mental disturbance at
some point. The open-sided house is thus somewhere between a compromise and a paradox, almost a riddle: a house that is not a house, a
building that is both enclosed and not, indoors and outdoors, safe and
open, companionable and solitary.[3]

It is also, quite overtly, a metonymy of Merlin's mind, as well as
a metapoetic allegory of writing. In the passage quoted above, Merlin
proposes to use his retreat to continue his prophetic activity. But the
nature of his enquiries and knowledge production evolves as the poem
progresses, becoming more circumscript and less speculative; at the

---

3   One of the best articles on the *Vita* to date, Christine Chism's "'Ain't gonna study war
no more": Geoffrey of Monmouth's *Historia Regum Britannie* and *Vita Merlini'*, *Chaucer Review*, 48 (2014), pp. 457–79 <https://doi.org/10.5325/chaucerrev.48.4.0458>,
also reads the *Vita Merlini* as a retreat, as Geoffrey's relinquishing the masculinist,
militaristic imperialism of the *Historia*. Her anti-colonial, ecocritical reading and my
poetological or epistemological take can coexist and complement each other, although
mine is admittedly more pessimistic.

end, when Merlin relinquishes his prophecy, the poet announces that he, too, will now fall silent. It has often been noted that the Merlin of Geoffrey's earlier *Historia Regum Britannie* is a natural stand-in for the historian-author: the seer who ranges freely across time, backward and forward; the sardonic adviser, impresario, and king-maker, at times coldly detached and at times overly involved in the events of the chronicle. Since the Merlin of the *Vita*, discontinuous though he may seem, is specifically said to be returned from the *Historia*, relating prophet and author would seem to be not only legitimate but invited. Hence, in some oddly abstract way, the *Vita* is also an autobiographical statement, with all the cautions this term requires here. That is, 'autobiography' should not be taken in the sense of furnishing biographical data about a writer of whom little is known, but in the sense that the text acknowledges, or actually creates, an 'I' that can be thought of as entering into a relationship with the character Merlin, to mirror him, identify with him, or distance him; and, since Merlin's story in the *Vita* is explicitly one of mental health and illness, an 'I' that can itself be thought of, in cautious and qualified ways, as having a mind and mental health. Celtologists will rightly point out that the 'madness' motif in the Celtic tradition cannot easily be equated with our ideas of mental illness. The Celtic prophet has shamanistic features, and his 'fury' is not always, or not exclusively, pathologized. But Merlin, his prophetic powers notwithstanding, is explicitly said to suffer in the *Vita*, to be ill and in need of a cure.[4] One should be cautious in extending this line of thought, this diagnosis, directly to the narrating voice or the author of the poem, in the sense of the Romantic notion of the hypersensitive poet who teeters on the brink of insanity. But the narrator clearly means to claim some of Merlin's shamanistic insight for himself, and to empathize with, perhaps even partake in his suffering. The project of the *Vita* could then be described as negotiating a way of knowing and a way of writing that is open but not too open, that admits the outside

---

4   For the complex connotations of 'wildness' or 'madness' in this cultural context, see Feargal Ó Béarra, 'Buile Shuibhne: Vox Insaniae from Medieval Ireland', in *Mental Health, Spirituality, and Religion in the Middle Ages and Early Modern Age*, ed. by Albrecht Classen (Berlin: De Gruyter, 2014), pp. 242–89; Jean-Michel Picard, 'Merlin, Suibhne et Lailoken: A propos d'un livre récent', *Revue belge de philologie et histoire* 80 (2002), pp. 1495–1503 (pp. 1500–02) <https://doi.org/10.3406/rbph.2002.4684>.

world and permits communication with it in ways that nonetheless do not leave the speaker overly exposed and vulnerable.

The 'house that is barely a house'[5] invites us to consider the mind as a building and the building as a mind.[6] It is about what comes in and what goes out: sensory data, knowledge, thought, writing, prophecy. Both directions are at issue. The prophetic mind, it seems, is both lucid and translucent, perspicacious but also alarmingly open to the outside and vulnerable to it. As a depiction of mental illness, the poem, despite some quite fantastical elements, still makes intuitive sense to us. One is continually tempted to relate it to our clinical and colloquial psychiatric terminology: is Merlin (or is his literary creator) 'bipolar', or 'on the spectrum'? Taken literally, questions of this sort are of course futile: one cannot diagnose an absent person, much less a fictional character, even less a fictional character created in a cultural setting so remote from ours. But the urge to ask these questions marks an important quality of the poem. We are confronted with a mind that is hidden and impenetrable, and at the same time open to enquiry and speculation.

Although it is hard to pinpoint written texts that can be securely dated earlier than the *Vita*, it seems uncontroversial that Geoffrey did not invent the story of Merlin the Wild Man; he was working from Celtic sources and traditions ('Merlin' being a Latinization of the Welsh 'Myrddin'). There are other texts, in the Black Book of Carmarthen and the Red Book of Hergest, that share his characters and similar motifs: 'Ymddiddan Myrddin a Thaliesin', in which the Welsh prophets lament the battle of Ardderyd (presumably identical with the unnamed battle of the *Vita Merlini*); a lament by Merlin alone, 'Afallenau' (Apple Trees); 'Cyvoesi Myrddin a Gwenddydd ei Chwaer', a dialogue between Merlin and his sister. There are parallels

---

5   Chism, 'Ain't gonna study', p. 466.
6   There is a venerable and varied tradition of seeing the mind as a container and/or an architectural structure. See e.g. the well-known work on memory palaces and theatres by Frances Yates, *The Art of Memory* (Chicago: University of Chicago Press, 1966), and Mary Carruthers, *The Book of Memory: A Study of Memory in Medieval Culture*, 2nd edn (Cambridge: Cambridge University Press, 2008); as well as Christiania Whitehead, 'Making a Cloister of the Soul in Medieval Religious Treatises', *Medium Aevum*, 67 (1998), pp. 1–29 <https://doi.org/10.2307/43629957>, and Britt Mize, 'The Representation of the Mind as an Enclosure in Old English Poetry', *Anglo-Saxon England*, 35 (2006), pp. 57–90 <https://doi.org/10.1017/S0263675106000044>.

in the Irish tradition (Suibhne Geilt) and in the Scottish-Cambrian region (Lailoken, who appears as a minor character in a twelfth-century saint's life by Jocelyn of Furness).[7] From all these narratives, it can be assumed that the strong dichotomy of court and forest, civilized and wild spaces, pre-exists Geoffrey; and that the figure of the 'wild' (*gwyllt/geilt*) warrior suffering from what we would call PTSD was a recognizable phenomenon in the Celtic world.[8] Geoffrey seems to have been instrumental in funnelling this motif from the Celtic to the courtly French and French-adjacent spheres, probably also anchored and reinforced by the biblical Nebuchadnezzar:[9] a person in crisis 'running wild' for a while before either returning to his old society or finding a place on its margins as a sage and visionary. In Chrétien's

---

7   Of the extensive literature investigating the connections between these sources, see
     for instance A. O. H. Jarman, 'Early Stages in the Development of the Myrddin
     Legend', in *Astudiathau ar yr hengerdd/Studies in Old Welsh Poetry*, ed. by Rachel
     Bromwich and R. B. Jones (Cardiff: University of Wales Press, 1978), pp. 326–49;
     A. O. H Jarman, 'The Merlin Legend and the Welsh Tradition of Prophecy', and
     Paul Zumthor, 'Merlin: Prophet and Magician', trans. by Victoria Guerin, in *Merlin:
     A Casebook*, ed. by Peter H. Goodrich and Raymond H. Thompson (New York:
     Routledge, 2003), pp. 103–28 and 129–59; Picard, 'Merlin, Suibhne et Lailoken'. On
     Taliesin, see Michael Aichmayr, 'Taliesin: Literarische Überlieferung der Taliesin-
     Figur', in *Verführer, Schurken, Magier*, ed. by Ulrich Müller and Werner Wunderlich
     (St Gall: UVK, 2001), pp. 903–14. The classic edition of the Welsh poems, in *The Four
     Ancient Books of Wales*, ed. and trans. by William F. Skene (Edinburgh: Edmonston
     and Douglas, 1968), is now conveniently available online at <https://www.sacred-
     texts.com/neu/celt/fab/index.htm> [accessed 30 July 2020]. An edition of the texts
     concerning Lailoken is in H. L. D. Ward, 'Lailoken (or Merlin Silvester)', *Romania*,
     22 (1893), pp. 504–26 <https://doi.org/10.3406/roma.1893.5789>. Translations of
     the Lailoken material as well as an excerpt from 'Afallenau' are also in an appendix to
     Clarke's edition of the *Vita Merlini* (pp. 226–35). None of the texts mentioned can
     be seen as Geoffrey's 'sources' in any uncomplicated way; the manuscripts postdate
     Geoffrey's work and seem quite aware of it, and while they may share common oral
     sources, there do appear to be influences in both directions. Even at the time, there
     was some confusion and considerable discussion on the relationship between the
     various prophet characters, whether there was one Merlin or several, or whether
     Lailoken (possibly a misunderstanding of a Welsh word for 'twin brother', by which
     Gwenddydd/Ganieda addresses him in 'Cyvoesi') is identical with Merlin. See Neil
     Thomas, 'The Celtic Wild Man Tradition and Geoffrey of Monmouth's *Vita Merlini*:
     Madness or Contemptus Mundi?', *Arthuriana*, 10 (2000), pp. 27–28 <https://doi.
     org/10.1353/art.2000.0017>; Ward, 'Lailoken', p. 512.

8   Thomas, 'Celtic Wild Man'; Ó Béarra, 'Buile Shuibhne'; Kenneth Jackson, 'The Motif
     of the Threefold Death in the Story of Suibhne Geilt', in *Féil-Sgríbhinn Eóin Mhic
     Néill/Essays and Studies Presented to Professor Eoin MacNeill*, ed. by John Ryan (1940;
     repr. Kill Lane: Four Courts Press, 1995), pp. 535–50 (p. 544).

9   Penelope Doob, *Nebuchadnezzar's Children: Conventions of Madness in Medieval Lit-
     erature* (New Haven, CT: Yale University Press, 1974).

Yvain and similar romances, the motif is shorn of its martial compo-
nent, the battle trauma, and reinterpreted as a lover's madness. The
house/not-house also has analogues in French and related traditions,
particularly in the matter of Tristan: the crystalline lovers' grotto in
Gottfried von Straßburg, where the crystal is very explicitly read as a
metaphor for thought, reading, and interpretation; and the glass palace
fantasized by a raving Tristan in the Oxford *Folie Tristan*.[10]

In all these traditional and courtly analogues, it is clear that the wilderness episodes and their enigmatic buildings represent an alternative
model of relating to one's society. In the well-known case of Chrétien's
Yvain, and other narratives influenced by it, the hero's madness is a
kind of reset button for a faulty socialization. Yvain retreats for a time
into an animal, 'bare-life' state, whence he can slowly rebuild towards
social embeddedness as he gradually reacquires the hallmarks of civilized life: hunting, cooked food, barter, human interaction, language.[11]
Other texts, including the *Tristan* romances and the *Vita Merlini*, are
not so optimistic about reintegration. In the *Tristan* texts, the rift with
the court is permanent and deadly. The *Vita Merlini* gives up on reintegration and attempts a workable compromise instead. It is heavily
predicated on a stark opposition of indoors and outdoors, civilized
and wild. The half-open, half-enclosed house is an obvious compromise, even introduced as a concession won through negotiation. What
Merlin, at least in his post-traumatic state, cannot bear is confinement
or close quarters. He experiences his stints at court as imprisonment
and negotiates for his 'freedom'. Nor can he bear the breaching of his
personal boundaries, his excessive openness to the solicitousness of his
loved ones. That is the problem the open-sided house is designed to address. People can join him there on his own terms, even and especially

---

10   Gottfried von Straßburg, *Tristan*, ed. and trans. [into modern German] by Rüdiger
     Krohn, 3rd edn, 3 vols (Stuttgart: Reclam, 1984), ii, pp. 408–41 (lines 16,679–
     17,274); in English as *Tristan*, trans. by Arthur Hatto (London: Penguin, 1967), pp.
     261–69. 'La Folie Tristan (Oxford)', ed. and trans. by Samuel N. Rosenberg, in *Early
     French Tristan Poems*, ed. by Norris J. Lacy, 2 vols (Cambridge: Brewer, 1998), i, pp.
     258–310 (lines 301–10). Discussed together in Jean-Charles Payen, 'Le palais de verre
     dans la Folie d'Oxford', *Tristania*, 5 (1981), pp. 17–28 (in English as 'The Glass Palace
     in the *Folie d'Oxford*: From Metaphorical to Literal Madness', trans. by Joan Tasker
     Grimbert, in *Tristan and Isolde: A Casebook*, ed. by Joan Tasker Grimbert (New York:
     Routledge, 2013), pp. 111–23).

11   This is a much-discussed episode. See, for instance, Anne Hunsaker Hawkins, 'Yvain's
     Madness', *Philological Quarterly*, 71 (1992), pp. 377–97.

his sister Ganieda (Latinized from Welsh 'Gwenddydd'), whose loving attentions he had been fleeing above all. The house does not cut him off from the wild outdoors he loves so much, and sensibly restructures his relationship with it. Where Gottfried's lovers' cave represents a radical, paradisiacal separation from society and is therefore unsustainable, Merlin's model is at least a comfortable, if emotionally subdued, long-term solution.

But the forest house, being an astronomical observatory, is also a machine for thinking and knowing, and finding a level thereof that will be sustainable, or even curative. During the period of his madness, Merlin's mind is both too open and too closed, and the semi-enclosed space is designed (by him) to correct this state of affairs. In the first place, the open-sided house filters, orders, and structures what comes to Merlin's attention, and regulates the temporal rhythms of his engagement with the world. In his madness, he was obsessed with the rapid cycle of the seasons, primarily for quite practical reasons, for seasonal changes helped or hindered his chances of survival in the wild, but also in an emotional way. His lengthy elegy on the beauties of the seasons is among the most lyrical passages in the poem, but the affect is mournful and aggrieved, as if the seasons were doing him a personal injustice:

> O qui cuncta regis, quid est cur contigit ut non
> tempora sint eadem numeris distincta quaternis?
> Nunc ver jure suo flores frondesque ministrat,
> dat fruges estas autumpnus micia poma.
> Consequitur glacialis yemps et cetera queque
> devorat et vastat pluviasque nivesque reportat.
> Singula queque suis arcet leditque procellis
> nec permittit humum varios producere flores
> aut quercus glandes aut malos punica mala.
> O utinam non esset hiems aut cana pruina!
> Ver foret aut estas, cuculusque canendo rediret
> et Philomela pio que tristia pectora cantu
> mitigat et turtur conservans federa casta
> frondibus inque novis concordi voce volucres
> cantarent alie que me modulando foverent,
> dum nova flore novo tellus spiraret odorem
> gramine sub viridi levi quoque murmure fontes
> diffluerent juxtaque daret sub fronde columba
> sompniferos gemitus irritaretque soporem. (146–64)

(O ruler of all, how happens it that all the seasons are not the same, distinguished only by their four numbers? As things are, the spring is bound by its own laws to provide the leaves and flowers; summer gives us the crops and autumn the ripe fruit. Then follows icy winter, which devours and lays waste all the others and brings again the rain and snow. It suppresses everything and causes damage with its storms. It will not let the earth produce its multi-coloured flowers, nor the oaks their acorns, nor the apple trees their russet apples. Would there were no winter, no white frost! Would it were spring or summer — and the cuckoo back in song, and the nightingale, who softens sadness with her tender air, and the turtle dove keeping her chaste devotion. Would that the other birds too, were singing their harmonies in the fresh foliage, while the earth refreshed, with flowers fresh, breathed out its scent from under the green turf, and springs ran babbling all around, and the pigeon among the leaves nearby kept up its drowsy cooing and brought sleep.)

The observatory seems to reset his mind to larger patterns, larger cycles, the motions of the planets and the sky, 'fire-breathing Phoebus with Venus and [...] the stars wheeling in the firmament', and this seems in some way to be beneficial to both his prophecy and his equanimity (563–64).

Second, the open-sided house appears to regulate, metaphorically, the degree to which his mind is opened to the outside, both actively and passively, in what he can see and in how transparent he is to others. Both things are of urgent concern in the first half of the poem; most of the tug of war between him and those who want what is best for him centres on these questions. Merlin goes to extraordinary lengths to thwart others' insight into him, his intentions, and his motivations. A central motif in the early part of the poem is the 'prophetic laugh' — not unique to this text but uncommonly central to it.[12] An uncom-

---

12 See J. A. Burrow, *Gestures and Looks in Medieval Narrative* (Cambridge: Cambridge University Press, 2002), pp. 80–81 <https://doi.org/10.1017/CBO9780511483240>; Lewis Thorpe, 'Merlin's Sardonic Laughter', in *Studies in Medieval Literature and Languages in Memory of Frederick Whitehead*, ed. by W. Rothwell and others (Manchester: Manchester University Press, 1973), pp. 323–39; Philippe Ménard, *Le rire et le sourire dans le roman courtois en France au Moyen Âge (1150–1250)* (Geneva: Droz, 1969), pp. 436–38. A pre-1100 analogue in an English (not Celtic) source is in the *Vita Aedwardi Regis*, ed. and trans. by Frank Barlow (Oxford: Oxford University Press, 1992), pp. 104–05. See Monika Otter, '1066: The Moment of Transition in Two Narratives of the

municative Merlin laughs suddenly, and when pressed to disclose the source of his merriment, drives a hard bargain to obtain concessions before agreeing to explain. All these episodes have to do with some sort of excessive openness, some missing boundary that would normally limit and perhaps protect the ordinary mind. Merlin's sudden insights are not funny in and of themselves, but I am reminded of Freud's contention that laughter stems from the sudden and unexpected conjunction of two things that are not ordinarily seen together. Merlin's mind skips temporal limits. He can see into the past: he knows of the extramarital fling his sister had just moments before (and she would rather he did not disclose that). He can see into the future: he knows the customer in the shoe shop will not live to wear the boots he is ordering. He can see through physical, spatial barriers: the beggar is sitting on top of a buried treasure without knowing it, and if only he had thought to dig a little he would have been set for life. Merlin can see through disguises and perceive personal identity, even across apparent gender lines: the boy who is brought before him in three different disguises, one of them female, in order to test his prophetic powers, does not throw him off at all. He can see the simultaneous truth of what appear to be mutually exclusive occurrences, as in the motif of the threefold death: he predicts the disguised boy will die of hanging *and* drowning *and* stabbing, and while that apparent impossibility is taken to discredit Merlin's prophetic gift, he later turns out to have been correct (246–346).[13] But this preternatural perspicacity is apparently only painful to him; it is not surprising that over the course of the poem he works to shed it and is eventually relieved at losing his prophetic gift.

Norman Conquest', *Speculum*, 74 (1999), pp. 565–86 (pp. 583–85) <http://doi.org/10.2307/2886761>.

13   Both the Lailoken and the Suibhne stories contain the same motif. See Jackson, 'Motive of the Threefold Death'. Predating Geoffrey, Hildebert of Lavardin (d. 1133) uses the same story in a riddling epigram, 'De Hermaphrodito', in which the impossibility of the three deaths is paralleled by the impossibility of being 'man, woman, and neither' all at once; this shows the wide availability of the motif beyond the immediate context of the Celtic prophet narratives (Hildebertus Cenomannensis Episcopus, *Carmina Minora*, ed. by A. B. Scott, 2nd edn (Munich: Sauer, 2001), epigram 23, pp. 15–16). Cf. Monika Otter, 'Neither/Neuter: Hildebert's Hermaphrodite and the Medieval Latin Epigram', *Studi medievali*, 3rd ser., 48 (2007), pp. 789–807. Perhaps the madly complicated constellation of conditions necessary to kill Lleu in the Fourth Branch of the Mabinogi is also related: Anne Lea, 'Lleu Wyllt: An Early British Prototype of the Legend of the Wild Man?', *Journal of Indo-European Studies*, 25 (1997), pp. 35–47 (pp. 37–39).

If we see Merlin's observatory as a thinking machine, as a means of and metaphor for regulating the attention, insight, and thought process of the prophet's mind, as well as its transparency to the outside, the glass houses of the Tristan texts can serve as a useful comparison. In both the Oxford *Folie* and Gottfried's *Tristan*, the glass has to do, unsurprisingly, with the crystal's proverbial clarity, with truth and transparency. In the *Folie*, the glass house is mentioned only in passing, as one of many outlandish pronouncements by Tristan as he feigns, or maybe not entirely feigns, madness. But the glass house seems to point to the perverse truth-telling his madman disguise has made possible: as a crazed beggar, he can stand right before the king and publicly disclose the entire story of his adulterous relationship with the queen. It is perfectly true, but will not be believed; the truth is completely disclosed yet remains completely hidden. The madman disguise radically resets the conditions of his communicative act and sets the entire discourse on a different plane. It makes the speaker's account both true and untrue, or, rather, brackets it off from any such consideration, shielding it from being taken as a literal account of events. Tristan, by adopting a fictional persona, has successfully fictionalized his account — even though it happens to be literally true.

Gottfried von Straßburg riffs on the crystal house more extensively than any other Tristan poet. (We do not know what Thomas, his source, had in this missing part of his poem, but probably nothing so elaborate.)[14] Gottfried's lovers' cave is carefully and teasingly set off as a not-quite-real event on the plot level, not really located in the story's chronotope: I have known this cave since I was ten years old, says the poet, although I have never been to Cornwall.[15] But the cave is, explicitly and overtly, a thinking machine. The abundant crystal, only one of the cave's miraculous qualities, enables an extravagant allegorization, where every physical detail is immediately and gloriously transparent

---

14   The Old Norse *Tristrams Saga*, a prose rendition of Thomas's romance and generally a good guide to its plot if not its poetry, has only a brief description of a cave in a *locus amoenus* (*The Saga of Tristram and Ísönd*, trans. by Paul Schach (Lincoln: University of Nebraska Press, 1973), p. 101). It also seems fair to assume that Gottfried incorporates into the lovers' cave features of Thomas's 'hall of statues' episode, which, in turn, is not preserved in Gottfried's unfinished retelling.

15   *Tristan*, lines 17,136–38.

onto its higher meaning.[16] There is plenty of irony in the account, of course: the absolute truthfulness of the paradisiacal lovers' cave is not only destined to be ruptured soon, but has been compromised from the start by the messiness of an adulterous relationship and the lying it necessitates. Yet the text seems earnest and sincere in its aspirational claim to crystalline clarity, its wistful desire for unobstructed passage from the literal to the allegorical senses.

That the *Vita Merlini* appears to do the exact opposite — it moves towards refusing any and all allegory — is in one way only an apparent contrast. Allegory appears to open up a text; an insistence on literal meaning appears to close it down. But in both cases, the aim is simplicity, univocity, and immediacy of meaning. Gottfried, in his ironic Neo-Platonic exuberance, locates this immediacy in the exceptional space of the lovers' cave, that elusive (non-)place and (non-)time of total transparency. But, like most Utopias, it is not actually achievable or sustainable in real life, and that is where Gottfried's deep social and epistemological pessimism is most visible.[17] Geoffrey's Merlin, by contrast, resolutely comes down on the side of the *sensus literalis*, nothing else. It is Taliesin who facilitates this solution. He sets a calm, scientific tone for the woodland observatory. Things are what they appear to be. Taliesin is given to lists and catalogues: weather phenomena; kinds of fish, their dangers, and their health benefits; islands (732–940). When asked about the healing spring that suddenly springs up in front of the forest house and has the power to cure Merlin's madness, he eschews the miraculous and instead gives a comprehensive listing of curative waters the world over:

> Sunt etenim fontes fluviique lacusque per orbem
> qui virtute sua multis et sepe mendentur.
> Albula namque rapax Rome fluit amne salubri,
> quem sanare ferunt certo medicamine vulnus.
> Manat in Italia fons alter qui Ciceronis
> dicitur. Hic oculos ex omni vulnere curat.

---

16 See, among many others, Volker Mertens, 'Bildersaal — Minnegrotte — Liebestrank: Zu Symbol, Allegorie und Mythos im Tristanroman', *Beiträge zur Geschichte der deutschen Sprache und Literatur*, 117 (1995), pp. 40–64 <https://doi-org/10.1515/bgsl.1995.1995.117.40>.

17 See Tomas Tomasek, *Die Utopie im 'Tristan' Gotfrids von Straßburg* (Tübingen: Niemeyer, 1985) <https://doi.org/10.1515/9783111350103>.

Ethiopes etiam stagnum perhibentur habere
quo velut ex oleo facies perfusa nitescit.
Affrica fert fontem qui vulgo Zema vocatur.
Potus dat voces subita virtute canoras. (1182–91)

(There are springs, rivers and lakes all over the world which
constantly provide relief for many through their special properties. The health-giving waters of the fast-flowing *Tiber* run
through Rome: men say they are a sure treatment to heal a
wound. Another Italian source is called *Cicero's Spring*. This
heals all kinds of damage to the eye. The *Ethiopians* are also
believed to have a pool which glistens like oil when poured over
the face. Africa has a spring usually known as *Zema*: drinking
from it gives the voice an immediate sweetness of tone.)

He lists, he names; he categorizes; he declines to interpret beyond the
most immediate literal meaning and practical application. His universe
is ordered, mapped, counted. One imagines him droning on, boringly
but reassuringly, and the music of his rational discourse soothes the
troubled minds of his associates.

Merlin now takes his cue from Taliesin's rationalism: he rebuffs a
request for prophecies, citing his advancing age (1264–69) and saying
that he has learned to be content with the small miracles of nature, such
as an acorn growing into an oak:

Hic illam crevisse sua jam sponte videbam
singula prospiciens, tunc et verebar in istis
saltibus atque locum memori cum mente notavi. (1276–78)

(Here I have seen that acorn grow unaided, observing every
detail. I felt a deep respect for its standing there in the clearing,
and I marked the spot in my memory.)

When asked about a strange formation of cranes flying overhead, Merlin responds not with prophecy but with natural history, explaining the
birds' behaviour in almost comically prosaic terms and then launching
into a Taliesin-like list of birds and avian behaviours (1311–83). It is
worth remembering that birds flying in formation were a *locus classicus*
for prognostication, one of the standard tools of Roman augury, but
Merlin pointedly passes up the opportunity:

Mox Merlinus eis, 'Volucres, ut cetera plura,
natura propria ditavit conditor orbis.
Sic didici multis silvis habitando diebus.
Est igitur natura gruum dum celsa pererrant,
si plures assint, ut earum sepe volatu
aut hanc aut aliam videamus inesse figuram.
Una modo clamando monet servare volando,
turbatus solitis ne discreperet ordo figuris.
cui dum raucescit subit altera deficienti.' (1298–1306)

(After a moment Merlin said to them, 'The Creator of the
universe assigned to birds, as to many other things, their own
special nature: this I have learnt during the many days of my
life in the woods. So, then, the nature of cranes is such that
if large numbers are present during their flight, they dispose
themselves, as we often see, in one or another arrangement. The
call of one among them serves to warn them to keep the order
of the flight and not to let the formation break up and disrupt
the traditional figure. When that bird grows hoarse and gives
up, another one takes its place.')

Despite this reassuring practicality, in the end Geoffrey is no more
optimistic about meaning and knowledge than Gottfried. Where Gottfried plunges us from heady possibilities into deadly catastrophe,
Geoffrey settles his Merlin into a tolerable, somewhat grey holding
pattern, where explanation coincides with the observable in almost
tautological fashion. There, he contemplates his approaching death in
a vague sort of monastic piety, in the select companionship of Taliesin,
Ganieda, and the late-arrived and newly cured fellow-warrior Maëldin.
'Quod erit per singula mecum, | ex hoc nunc commune tibi dum vivit
uterque' ('All I have I shall share with you from now on as long as
each of us may live', he greets the newcomer; 1450–51). In his initial
request for the woodland retreat, the passage quoted at the beginning
of this essay, Merlin seems to envision that it will lead to prophetic song
(*carmen*) and specifically political prophecy (the nation's future); and
both he and Taliesin deliver political orations at the beginning of their
seclusion. But as the poem progresses, he renounces prophecy too.

Towards the end, Geoffrey seems to strip away even the fiction
of the Merlin story. As the prophetic gift passes to Ganieda, to her
brother's delight, and she breaks into a prophetic rhapsody of the
sort Merlin used to utter, there is a subtle, telling, and (I think)

hitherto uncommented anachronism, a breakdown of the fiction: 'Ite Neustrenses', the newly minted prophetess exclaims, which Clark justifiably translates as 'Normans — go' (1511).[18] This is a deliberate breach of chronology. Whenever the dramatic date of the narrative is imagined to be (presumably the sixth century CE), Normans or *Neustrenses* were not the occupiers, not the issue that would trouble Ganieda or Merlin. Indeed, there were no Normans: we are several centuries before Scandinavians settled in northern France and became known by that name. Geoffrey does not take the anachronism quite so far as to call the invaders 'Normans', substituting the older term 'Neustrians'. But he has subtly, almost imperceptibly, moved his readers from the prophetess's distant past to their own, present, mid-twelfth-century world. In Geoffrey's first, highly successful work, the *Historia Regum Britanniae*, such connections between the mythical past and present politics are always invited, indeed inevitable; but there, readers were left to draw any such parallels themselves, the translations remain complex and uncertain, and the author never showed his hand or openly acknowledged any contemporary relevance. Here, Geoffrey is perhaps acknowledging that we have read his myth history in modern terms all along, in the *Historia* as well as in the *Vita*, even if we may not have been fully aware of doing so. That his apparent (but surely deliberate) chronological lapse goes down so smoothly, almost unnoticed, bears witness to this semi-conscious readerly operation.[19] Granted, there is no simple key to equating the peoples and powers in the *Historia* with those of Geoffrey's time, and Geoffrey's politics are far from clear. (I myself have always thought that he cynically or pragmatically plays all sides.)[20] And yet perhaps we have always

---

18   Chism reads this detail within the fiction, as Ganieda's prophecy reaching far into what to her is future ('Ain't gonna study', p. 477). Paul Zumthor, *Merlin le prophète* (Lausanne: Payot, 1943), pp. 37–38, notes that Ganieda's prophecy largely concerns Geoffrey's contemporary world, without remarking much on the anachronism.

19   On the 'palimpsestic' reading that takes the events as simultaneously historical and contemporary, see Siân Echard, 'Palimpsests of Place and Time in Geoffrey of Monmouth's *Historia Regum Britanniae*', in *Teaching and Learning in Medieval Europe: Essays in Honour of Gernot R. Wieland*, ed. by Greti Dinkova-Bruun and Tristan Major (Turnhout: Brepols, 2017), pp. 43–59 <https://doi.org/10.1484/M.PJML-EB.5.113253>.

20   Monika Otter, *Inventiones: Fiction and Referentiality in Twelfth-Century Historical Writing* (Chapel Hill: University of North Carolina Press, 1996), pp. 75–80. But before and since then, many scholars have seen a more definable political line in Geoffrey's

all known that Hengist's and Vortigern's 'Saxons' are the Normans of Geoffrey's time, and he no longer cares to disguise it. A bit earlier, he has, surprisingly, rejected the urgently awaited mythical return of King Arthur as a solution to his people's problems: surprisingly, because it was Geoffrey's *Historia* that so firmly tied Merlin to Arthurian myth history in the first place. When Taliesin recalls how Arthur was taken to Avalon to be cured, and suggests that now might be the time to send a ship and see if he is ready to return to help liberate the Britons and restore peace, Merlin demurs:

> 'Non,' Merlinus ait, 'non sic gens illa recedet
> ut semel in nostris ungues infixerit ortis.
> Regnum namque prius populusque jugabit et urbes
> viribus atque suis multis dominabitur annis.' (958–61)

> ('No,' Merlin replied. 'This is not the way the invader will leave,
> once he has fixed his talons in our land. Before that time comes,
> he will have conquered our kingdom and our people and our
> cities, and kept them under by force of arms for many years.')

It will take a succession of warlike leaders, who, however, 'will not complete their task' (non perficient); many generations down the line, kings will succeed in uniting 'Scotos Cambros et Cornubienses | Armoricosque' (the Scots, the Welsh, the Cornish and the men of Brittany) and bring the Celtic lands back to autonomy. When Taliesin objects that this will be well past the lifetime of those present, Merlin confirms: indeed, it will not be possible for a long time (962–81). This is possibly Geoffrey's most overt statement of his otherwise hard-to-read politics: he may be cheering on the Celts, and maybe also the English as opposed to the French-speaking newcomers; but he warns that the *Neustrenses* are here to stay and will not go anywhere any time soon. It is a tired, resigned statement, almost a renunciation of political prophecy and poetical fiction.

---

work, and several recent discussions have thrown further light on Geoffrey's possible politics. See for instance John Gillingham, 'The Context and Purposes of Geoffrey of Monmouth's *History of the Kings of Britain*', *Anglo-Norman Studies*, 13 (1990), pp. 99–118; Michael A. Faletra, 'Narrating the Matter of Britain: Geoffrey of Monmouth and the Norman Colonization of Wales', *Chaucer Review*, 35 (2000), pp. 60–85 <https:// doi.org/10.1353/cr.2000.0018>; Jennifer Farrell, 'History, Prophecy, and the Arthur of the Normans: The Question of Audience and Motivation in Geoffrey of Monmouth's *Historia Regum Britanniae*', *Anglo-Norman Studies*, 37 (2014), pp. 99–114.

The ending of the poem is sudden and dizzyingly quick; if you blink, you will miss it. Soon after Ganieda concludes her prophetic speech, Merlin gives her his blessing, and then instantly closes 'his mouth and his book': 'Spiritus osque meum compescuit atque libellum' (The spirit has silenced my mouth and my book; 1522). After this abrupt silencing, the poem's narrative voice returns to deliver a terse, five-line sign-off of its own, even naming itself:

> Duximus at metam carmen. Vos ergo, Britanni,
> laurea serta date Gaufrido de Monemuta.
> Est etenim vester, nam quondam prelia vestra
> vestrorumque ducum cecinit scripsitque libellum
> quem nunc Gesta vocant Britonum celebrata per orbem. (1525–29)

> (We have brought the song to an end. So, Britons, give a laurel wreath to Geoffrey of Monmouth. He is indeed your Geoffrey, for he once sang of your battles and those of your princes, and he wrote a book which is now known as the 'Deeds of the Britons' — and they are celebrated throughout the world.)

A proud advertisement of his magnum opus, to be sure, as well as an unambiguous salute to the Welsh and a declaration of belonging with them. But it is also, taken together with the opening lines, an 'Ille ego qui quondam' in reverse. Medieval and Renaissance readers were well acquainted with the (probably) spurious four-line tag that supposedly formed the original opening of the *Aeneid*, rapidly tracing what as early as late Antiquity had become a commonplace of literary criticism: that the great Virgil over his career progressed from pastoral to bucolic to epic, from small to great, from low to high, from oaten reeds to war trumpets, from a secluded rural idyll to a national and imperial stage.[21] Geoffrey, at the beginning and end of the *Vita*, traces the exact opposite course: from his 'quondam' epic ambition to the *musa iocosa*, from a celebration of *prelia* to the pastoral *calamus* of this poem (1–3). It is not an opening up, an unfolding of full poetic powers as the pseudo-Virgilian lines boast, but rather a retrenchment, a closing down, a going

---

21   See R. G. Austin, 'Ille Ego Qui Quondam', *Classical Quarterly*, n.s., 18 (1968), pp. 107–15 <https://doi.org/10.1017/S0009838800029153>; Severin Koster, *Ille Ego Qui: Dichter zwischen Wort und Macht* (Erlangen: Universitätsbibliothek Erlangen-Nürnberg, 1988); Luca Mondin, 'Ipotesi sopra il falso proemio dell'*Eneide*', *Cento-Pagine*, 1 (2007), pp. 64–78.

back on earlier promises. The narrative voice here clearly feels very close to Merlin; in fact, with the fiction crumbling in Ganieda's final speech, one could almost say that Merlin's and Geoffrey's voices merge here. We cannot say what wounds or discouragements the narrator (much less the historical person Geoffrey of Monmouth) has suffered, but to the extent that he lets the Merlin character speak for him, this is clearly not so much a proud conclusion to a successful career and a joyful passing of the baton, as it is a sad, disillusioned abdication. The poem's vatic voice, too, has apparently found the open poetic mind — perspicacious and transparent, private yet uniquely vulnerable to the outside world — too much of a strain, and like Merlin, he is relieved to relinquish his prophecy as rapidly as possible. Book closed.

Enclosure and Exposure

Locating the 'House without Walls'

ANNIE SUTHERLAND

Carried by the weight of long-standing tradition, we tend to visualize Christ as having been born in a stable. Turned away from an over-crowded inn, we imagine that Mary had no choice but to give birth in a rudimentary shelter, surrounded by animals. Like us, a multitude of influential patristic and medieval thinkers also associated the Nativity with this stable. John Cassian, for example, refers to the 'stabulum [...] in quo Christus Dominus noster natus est' (the stable in which Christ our Lord was born).[1] And Bernard of Clairvaux tells us that 'in stabulo nascitur Christus' (Christ was born in a stable), while Peter Abelard presents us with a Virgin who enters a *stabula* in place of a *camera* (room) in order to give birth.[2] The stable birthplace also, of course, features prominently in medieval visual iconography, where we often find it presented as a cave-like or ruined structure, open to the

---

1   John Cassian, *De Coenobiorum Institutis Libri Duodecim, Patrologia Latina* [hence-forth: *PL*], ed. by J.-P. Migne, 221 vols (Paris: Garnier, 1844–64), 49. 53–476 (192).

2   'Adhuc autem in stabulo nascitur Christus, et in praesepio reclinatur' (Thus, however, Christ was born in the stable and laid in the manger; Bernard of Clairvaux, *Sermones de tempore, PL* 183. 35–360 ('In Nativitate Domini', Sermo iii, 'De loco, tempore et aliis circumstantiis Nativitatis', 123D)); 'celi domina | Pro cameris intravit stabula' (the queen of heaven, instead of a room she entered the stable; Peter Abelard, 'Verbo Verbum Virgo Concipiens', in *Hymni, PL* 178. 1765–1816 (1789)).

elements.[3] And it is this condition of openness which lies at the heart of this chapter. Investigating exegetical and devotional responses to the circumstances of the Nativity, it suggests that the radical exposure endured by Christ at the moment of his birth was crucial to medieval understandings of the significance of the Incarnation. Exposure, in dialectical relationship with enclosure, lies at the heart of all of the Nativity accounts under consideration in the pages to come.

It is easy to see where the stable-birthplace tradition originated and how it gained traction. Luke's account of the Nativity tells us that the newborn Christ was laid in a *praesepium* (defined by the *Dictionary of Medieval Latin from British Sources* (*DMLBS*) as a 'stall for animals' or a 'receptacle for fodder').[4] And it is also from Luke that we learn that the Christ Child's first visitors were 'pastores [...] custodientes [...] super gregem suum' (shepherds [...] watching [...] over their flocks), advised by angelic hosts to visit the baby 'in praesepio'.[5] A child laid in a manger and visited by shepherds might logically be imagined to have been born in a stable.

Yet the stable is not mentioned in the Bible. The Gospel of Luke, which offers the most detailed narrative of the circumstances of Christ's birth, tells us only that Joseph and a heavily pregnant Mary travelled from Nazareth to Bethlehem in order to participate in a census initiated by Caesar Augustus and that, soon after their arrival, Mary 'peperit filium suum primogenitum, et pannis eum involvit, et reclinavit eum in praesepio: quia non erat eis locus in diversorio' (brought forth her firstborn son, and wrapped him up in swaddling clothes, and laid him in a manger; because there was no room for them in the inn; Luke 2. 7). In fact, far from telling us where Christ was born, Luke tells us only where Mary did *not* give birth ('non erat eis locus in diversorio').

The Douay–Rheims translation of the Bible, from which I quote in this chapter, renders the Vulgate's *diversorium*, from which Mary and

---

3   See e.g. 'The Nativity Group', in *The Grove Encyclopedia of Medieval Art and Architecture*, ed. by Colum P. Hourihane, 6 vols (Oxford: Oxford University Press, 2012), on-line version retrieved from <https://www.oxfordreference.com/view/10.1093/acref/9780195395365.001.0001/acref-9780195395365-e-1631> [accessed 27 July 2021].

4   *Dictionary of Medieval Latin from British Sources* <https://logeion.uchicago.edu/praesepe> [accessed 21 January 2022].

5   Luke 2. 7, 8, 12. All quotations are from the Douay–Rheims version of the Bible.

Joseph were turned away, as 'inn'. Most modern translations also tell us that there was no room for Mary and Joseph at the inn. Yet, while the *DMLBS* suggests that 'inn' is one of a number of legitimate translations of the Vulgate's *diversorium*, biblical scholars dispute its appropriateness as a rendition of the original Greek κατάλυμα (*kataluma*) which is used at this point in Luke's Gospel.[6] Although Strong's dictionary glosses *kataluma* as 'lodging place', 'guestchamber', and 'inn', others have pointed out that the more accurate Greek term for 'inn' is πανδοχεῖον (*pandocheion*), which is actually used with this precise meaning in Luke 10. 34 (the Parable of the Good Samaritan).[7]

That Luke does not use πανδοχεῖον in reference to the dwelling from which Mary and Joseph were turned away could be read as indicating that he did not have a public lodging place, such as an inn, in mind. Instead, it has been suggested, he was thinking of a space in a private home; such a space is, in fact, suggested by Strong's 'guestchamber', quoted above. Indeed, according to biblical scholar Stephen C. Carlson, the 'familiar translation' of κατάλυμα as 'inn' 'rests on a series of questionable exegetical assumptions'.[8] Admitting that the term has a broad semantic range and is, perhaps, most safely translated as nothing more specific than 'place to stay', he suggests that, in context, the entire clause in Luke

> should be rendered as 'because they did not have space in their accommodations' or 'because they did not have room in their place to stay'. This clause means that Jesus had to be born and laid in a manger because the place where Joseph and Mary were staying did not have space for him. Luke's point is not so much any inhospitality extended to Joseph and Mary but rather that their place to stay was too small to accommodate even a newborn.[9]

6   Definitions offered by *DMLBS* for *diversorium* (singular) are as follows: '1 inn, guest-house. b (private) apartment, compartment (esp. eccl. or mon.). c partition. d privy. e "day" (division of mullioned window)' (<https://logeion.uchicago.edu/diversorium> [accessed 17 January 2021]).

7   James Strong, *The New Strong's Concise Dictionary of the Words in the Greek Testament and the Hebrew Bible* (Washington: Faithlife, 2009).

8   Stephen C. Carlson, 'The Accommodations of Joseph and Mary in Bethlehem: κατάλυμα in Luke 2.7', *New Testament Studies*, 56 (2010), pp. 326–42 (p. 329).

9   Ibid., pp. 334–36.

And he goes on to point out that the fact that the baby was laid in a manger (*praesepio*) need not suggest that their small resting-place was a stable:

> This detail does not mean, as it would to Western Europeans, that Mary gave birth to Jesus in a stable or barn, because mangers were also found in the main rooms of first-century Judean village houses. Typically, the main room was divided into two sections at different elevations separated by about a meter. The animals were housed in the lower section, the people slept in the upper section, and mangers were located between them.[10]

According to such exegetical readings, then, the small space in which Mary gave birth need not have been a stable, and we need not imagine her and Joseph turned away from public lodgings. In a radical departure from traditional perceptions of the Nativity, it may be that we should visualize Christ's birth as having taken place at the heart of a (somewhat crowded) family home.

Such domestic circumstances are not generally entertained in medieval exegetical, homiletic, and meditative responses to the Nativity. While the smallness of Christ's birthplace is commonly remarked upon in both medieval and modern traditions (and this is something to which we will return), the public situation and exposed circumstances of his Nativity in the *diversorium* remain at the heart of medieval academic commentaries and affective meditations on the subject. That the persistent understanding of the Nativity's *diversorium* should be that it indicates a public (one might say 'open') space is interesting. The Greek *kataluma* (Vulgate *diversorium*) is not only used in Luke 2. 7, but also appears in Luke 22. 11, where it describes the upper room (or guest chamber) in which Christ and his disciples ate the Last Supper: 'Et dicetis patrifamilias domus: "Dicit tibi Magister, ubi est diversorium, ubi pascha cum discipulis meis manducem?"' (And you shall say to the goodman of the house: 'The master saith to thee, where is the guest chamber, where I may eat the pasch with my disciples?').[11] Yet medieval exegetes do not seem to have reflected on this *diversorium* in relation to that of Luke 2. 7, nor to have queried the common understanding of the term as referring to public lodgings in the narrative of

---

10 Ibid., p. 341.
11 *Diversorium* is also used in Mark's account of the Last Supper. Cf. Mark 14. 14.

the Nativity but to a private room in the Passion narrative. Indeed, the *DMLBS* suggests that contemporary interpretations of the word were sufficiently flexible to incorporate both; alongside the aforementioned translation of *diversorium* as 'inn' or 'guest-house', the *DMLBS* indicates that it could also be used to mean a '(private) apartment, compartment (esp. eccl. or mon.)'.[12] It seems, then, that while Luke 22's *diversorium* was understood to denote a domestic space, Luke 2's *diversorium* defined a more public location.

Another intriguing feature of medieval responses to the Nativity is that the crowded *diversorium* from which Luke tells us that Mary and Joseph were turned away appears to have been understood as the very space in which Christ was born. In fact, in many medieval accounts, it seems to have become elided with the stable to which (as we have seen) traditional readings of Luke's narrative suggest that the expectant parents retreated.[13] How, then, precisely was this *diversorium* conceptualized? What were its characteristics and why did it possess such imaginative potency as the supposed birthplace of Christ?

A particularly clear evocation of this space is provided by Peter Comestor (d. 1178), and it is to his account of the Nativity that we now turn. In his monumental *Historia Scholastica*, a profoundly influential biblical paraphrase and commentary, Comestor comments thus on the circumstances of Christ's birth:

> Difficile fuerat pauperibus, prae frequentia multorum, qui ob idipsum convenerant, vacuas invenire domos, et in communi transitu, qui erat inter duas domus, operimentum habens, quod diversorium dicitur, se receperunt, sub quo cives ad colloquendum, vel ad convisendum in diebus otii, vel pro aeris intemperie divertebant. Forte ibi Joseph praesepium fecerat bovi et asino, quos secum adduxerat, in quo repositus est Jesus.[14]

---

12 The Early Version of the Wycliffite Bible (a late fourteenth-century translation of the entire Bible from Latin into English) translates Luke 2's *diversorium* as 'comyn stable' and Luke 22's as 'herborgerie' (lodging place). The Late Version chooses the more neutral 'chaumbir' (room, chamber) for both.

13 For further discussion of the relationship between the *diversorium* and the stable, see Annie Sutherland, 'Þe Wohunge of Ure Lauerde and the House without Walls', in *Medieval and Early Modern Religious Cultures: Essays Honouring Vincent Gillespie on his Sixty-Fifth Birthday*, ed. by Laura Ashe and Ralph Hanna (Cambridge: Brewer, 2019), pp. 3–19.

14 Peter Comestor, *Historia Scholastica*, PL 198. 1045–1721 (1539–40).

(It was difficult for those who were poor, because of the huge crowds which gathered on account of this [i.e. the census], to find empty houses. And in the public thoroughfare, [in a space] with a roof which was between two houses, called an inn, they took them [i.e. Mary and Joseph] in, beneath which [roof] citizens gathered to chat, or to pass the time on days of leisure, or [to which] they turned during intemperate weather. As luck would have it, Joseph had made there a manger for the ox and the ass which he had brought with him, into which Jesus was placed.)

Central to Comestor's description is that the *diversorium* to which Mary and Joseph are directed is found in a busy road ('in communi transitu'), that it is a covered space ('operimentum habens') situated between two houses ('qui erat inter duas domus'), and that it is a public meeting-place ('sub quo cives ad colloquendum [...]').

All of these features of the *diversorium* are reproduced in Jacobus de Voragine's mid-thirteenth-century *Legenda Aurea*, which, like the *Historia*, circulated exceptionally widely in the European Middle Ages. Referring explicitly to Comestor as his authority, Voragine describes Mary and Joseph's arrival at Bethlehem thus:

Cum igitur ambo Betlehem aduenissent, et quia pauperes errant et quia omnia hospitia alii qui propter hoc ipsum venerant occupauerunt, nullum hospitium habere potuerunt. Deuerterunt ergo in communi transitu qui, ut dicitur in hystoriis scholasticis, erat inter duas domos operimentum habens. Qui deuersorium dicitur, sub quo ciues ad colloquendum uel ad conuescendum in diebus otii uel pro aeris intemperie deuertebant.[15]

(So, when they both arrived in Bethlehem, because they were poor and because all the other guest houses were occupied by those who had come there because of this [i.e. the census], they were not able to find lodgings. So, they turned into a public street which was, as is said in the *Historia Scholastica*, between two houses with a roof covering. [This covered space] is called a *diversorium*, beneath which citizens gathered to chat or to pass the time of day on days of leisure or [to which] they turned during intemperate weather.)

---

15   Iacopo da Varazze, *Legenda Aurea*, ed. by Giovannai P. Maggioni, 2nd edn, 2 vols (Florence: SISMEL, 1998), I, p. 65.

The etymology which Voragine supplies is derived from Isidore of Seville (d. 636), whose *Etymologies* emphasize the status of the *diversorium* as a civic location and gloss it thus:[16] '*Diversorium* dictum, eo quod ex diversis viis ibi conveniatur' (It is called a *diversorium* because there people gather from diverse roads).[17] But Bede (d. 735), writing a century after Isidore, makes no reference to this etymology, instead locating the *diversorium*'s diversity in its liminal situation and open structure: 'Diversorium est domus inter duos muros, duas ianuas habens. Figurat ecclesiam inter paradisum et mundum' (The *diversorium* is a house between two walls, with two doors. It represents the Church between paradise and the world).[18] What is interesting about this reading is that, although Bede anticipates Comestor and many others by situating the *diversorium* in a 'between' space ('inter duos muros', 'inter duas domos'), he also specifies that it therefore has 'duas ianuas' (i.e. two openings which constitute the 'sides' not provided by the two walls between which it stands). In other words, what Bede makes explicit is that it is a space which is entirely open on two sides (it is also worth noting that Bede's description makes no reference to the roof covering which features in Comestor's description). And he goes on to attribute an allegorical signification to these openings; they indicate that the *diversorium* prefigures the Church, situated between the realms of heaven and earth.[19] Such allegorical readings were not a priority for Comestor, whose primary focus at this point is the clarification of the historical circumstances of Christ's birth.

Yet, despite their different emphases, what all of these definitions might be said to have in common is an awareness of the *diversorium* as a public structure, characterized — on a number of levels — by multiplicity and openness. On the most basic level, of course, it has

---

16   Peter Comestor seems to signal his awareness of this etymological tradition when he
      tells us that 'cives [...] *divertebant*' (my italics) to the *diversorium*.

17   Isidore of Seville, *Etymologies*, Patrologia Latina 82. 73–760 (liber 15, caput III, 'De
      Habitaculis', 542C).

18   *Bibliorum Sacrorum cum Glossa Ordinaria*, 6 vols (Venice: [n. pub.], 1603), v, p. 707,
      accessed via the Lollard Society at <http://lollardsociety.org/> [accessed 27 July
      2021].

19   The *Patrologia Latina* attributes an identical reading to Pseudo-Jerome: '*Locus in
      diversio*, id est, domus inter duos muros, duas januas habet: figuram Ecclesie, inter
      paradisum, et mundum' (*Commentarii in novum testamentum*, Patrologia Latina 30.
      531–900 (569B)).

revealed itself to be a term open to diverse interpretation by diverse exegetes. But, in what follows, the focus will fall on the ways in which its diversity and openness were explored, nuanced, and understood in a variety of late medieval devotional texts. In other words, this chapter will consider the imaginative and affective potency of this open space.

For the Franciscan Bonaventure, writing an influential commentary on the Gospel of Luke in the thirteenth century, it is the openness and public situation of the *diversorium* which is most worthy of note. In discussing the birthplace of Christ, he alludes to Isidore's etymology, but pays more attention to Bede's reading of the space:

> For according to Isidore it is called a *diversorium* because diverse peoples might congregate there. And it is an open space. But according to Bede, it is called such because it has diverse openings. For it is an empty space between two districts of a town and has access to and egress from both.[20]

However, unlike Bede (but like Comestor), Bonaventure points out that this open space nonetheless offers shelter and protection: 'It is also covered because of inclement weather, so that the citizens could convene to talk among themselves.' This dialectic of enclosure and exposure is important to the imaginative functioning of the *diversorium* and is recognized by Bonaventure and others in the description of the space of the Nativity as at once intimate and public. Its provision of shelter is matched by its capacity to expose, and its smallness by its open, inclusive nature: 'And this space was constricted or even filled with others, so that she had only the tiniest of places among the brute animals.' The *diversorium* is, for Bonaventure, a paradoxical space at once both 'empty' and 'filled', both 'open' and 'covered'. And it is a space whose diverse occupants allow for the fulfilment of the prophecies of the Old Testament:

> Whence Christ would say what the Psalm has: 'I have become a beast among you, and I am always with you' (72:23). And this is verified in Jeremiah 14: 8–9: 'Why will you be as a wayfaring man, and as a stranger turning in to lodge? Why will you be as a

---

20 Bonaventure, *Commentary of the Gospel of Luke*, trans. by R. Karris, 3 vols (New York: Franciscan Institute Publications, 2001–04), I (2001), p. 147. Available from ProQuest Ebook Central at <https://ebookcentral.proquest.com/lib/oxford/detail.action?docID=3240049> [accessed 25 March 2021].

wandering man, as a mighty man that cannot save? But you, O Lord, are among us, and your name is invoked upon us,' etc.[21]

As suggested by Bonaventure's musings on the Nativity, reflections on Christ's birthplace found their way into the meditative literature of the late Middle Ages. For example, in the popular fourteenth-century pseudo-Bonaventuran *Meditationes Vite Christi*, often attributed to Johannes de Caulibus, the *diversorium* clearly informs the description of Christ's birthplace as 'quandam uiam coopertam, ubi homines tempore pluuie divertebant' (a certain covered street, into which men turned in time of rain). Here, we see again the foregrounding of a dialectical relationship between intimacy and exposure; within the communal space of the street, 'Ioseph, qui erat magister lignarius, forte aliqualiter se clausit' (Joseph, who was a master carpenter, in some way enclosed them). In this text, we are asked to gaze 'diligentissime' (with the greatest diligence) at the paradoxical space of the Nativity, at once private and public, sealed off yet open.[22]

Expanding on the pseudo-Bonaventuran *Meditationes*, the late fourteenth-century *Vite Christi* of Ludolph of Saxony describes the circumstances of Christ's birth thus:

> [E]t sic in communi transitu, in diversorium se receperunt, quod intra civitatem, in fine, juxta unam portarum sub rupe concave erat, non habens desuper tectum, ut hodie cernitur, nisi rupem de monte dependentem. Secundum *Bedam*, diversorium est spatiem inter duos vicos, ex utroque latere habens murum, et ex utraque parte portam, ut sit inde exitus in utrumque vicum, desuper coopertum propter aeris intemperiem, ut in festivis diebus possint ibi homines convenire ad colloquendum et solatiandum. Et figurat Ecclesiam inter paradisum et mundum existentem, in quam divertamus ab erroribus mundi hujus. Ibi etiam homines ad illam civitatem propter aeris intemperiem, locare consuererant: unde et diversorium dicebatur, quia illuc homines divertebant.[23]

---

21 Ibid., pp. 147–48.

22 Johannes de Caulibus, *Meditaciones Vite Christi*, ed. by C. Mary Stallings-Taney (Turnhout: Brepols, 1997), p. 31.

23 Ludolph of Saxony, *Vita Jesu Christi: Ex Evangelio et Approbatis ab Ecclesia Catholica Doctoribus Sedule Collecta*, ed. by Ludovic M. Rigollot, 4 vols (Paris: Palmé, 1878), I, pp. 68–69, pars 1, caput 9, 'De Nativitate Salvatoris Nostri'.

(They were finally received into a public accommodation in a communal passageway; this was inside the city, near one of the gates, under a concave cliff. There was no roof above it other than the overhanging rock, as can still be seen today. According to Bede, a *diversorium* is a passageway between two streets that has walls on two sides and doorways on each end opening onto the two streets, with a covering to provide protection in inclement weather; people gather here on festive occasions for conversation and comfort. This serves as an image of the Church, situated between paradise and this world, into which we turn from the deceptions of this world. People who had come to that city on business also sheltered their animals there from the elements, so it was also called a *diversorium* because people drove their animals in there.)

In this account, Christ's birthplace assumes characteristics of the cave, long associated with the Nativity in patristic writing and apocryphal tradition, yet it remains identified as the *diversorium*. Ludolph's emphasis falls on the space's protective capacities, both literal (it provides comfort in inclement weather) and figurative (as an image of the Church, it shields us from worldly deceit). But, as we have seen elsewhere, this emphasis is matched by an awareness of the space's liminality (it is close to the city edge and is situated 'inter' (between) other spaces) and of its openness to strangers. In fact, in Ludolph's text, its openness extends beyond its provision of a space for people to gather 'in festivis diebus' (on festive occasions). For he recognizes its capacity to encompass us all in its expansive reach; as a prefiguring of the Church, it is a space 'in quam *divertamus* ab erroribus mundi hujus' (into which *we turn* from the deceptions of this world; my italics).

In the early fifteenth century, Nicholas Love, an English Carthusian monk and prior of Mount Grace, produced a vernacular translation of the Pseudo-Bonaventuran *Meditationes*, not including any of Ludolph of Saxony's expansions. Entitled *Þe Mirour of þe blessede life of Jesu Criste*, Love's text remains close to its Latin original in recounting the circumstances of Christ's birth:

> And what tyme þei comen to Bethleem.' for þe gret multitude þat was þerinne þ[e] same tyme for þe self cause.' þei mi3t gete none herbere in none hous, bot in a comune place by twix tweyn houses, þat was hiled aboue, men fort stand þere for þe reyne, & was cleped a Diuersorie.' þei were nedet to rest inne, &

abide al þat tyme. In þe which place Joseph þat was a carpentary made hem a closere & a crach for hire bestes.[24]

(And at the time that they came to Bethlehem, because of the great multitude that was there at the same time, for the same reason, they were not able to get any lodging in any house, other than in a public place between two houses, covered above, in order for men to stand there when it was raining, called a *diversorie*. It was necessary for them to rest in there, and to remain all of that time. In which place, Joseph, who was a carpenter, made them an enclosure and a manger for their animals.)

Here, we see the characteristic emphasis on Christ's birthplace as both exposed ('comune') and enclosed ('hiled aboue') more clearly foregrounded. For where the Pseudo-Bonaventuran text had Joseph rather vaguely shielding his wife and child 'aliqualiter' (in some way), Love tells us that he built them a 'closere' (enclosure) within this public space. However, where the Latin *Meditationes* referred to the *diversorium* as a space 'inter duos vicos' (between two streets), Love places it 'by twix tweyn houses'. In so doing, he not only recalls Peter Comestor's terminology ('inter duos domos'), but also alerts us to a specifically English interest in Christ's birthplace as situated near — if not within — a house of some sort. With this in mind, the next part of this chapter will trace the origins and development of this insular reading of the *diversorium*. In order to do this, we have to go back to Peter Comestor and his influence on the devotional literature of thirteenth-century England.

We have seen that Comestor's explication of the circumstances of the Nativity exerted a considerable influence on meditative responses to the birth of Christ during the Middle Ages. While not alluding specifically to its multiple openings (Bede), or to the diversity of its occupants (Isidore), Comestor's account presents us with a space which is public and, despite its protective roof, to some degree exposed by virtue of the fact that it is not boundaried by its own four walls. Although it does not explicitly identify Christ's birthplace as a *diversorium*, the thirteenth-century *Speculum Religiosorum*

---

24   Nicholas Love, *The Mirror of the Blessed Life of Jesus Christ: A Reading Text*, ed. by Michael G. Sargent (Exeter: University of Exeter Press, 2004), capitulum 6m, 'Of þe Natiuite of oure lorde Jesu criste', p. 38, lines 6–13.

of Edmund of Abingdon (1174–1240) appears to have been inspired by Comestor in locating the Nativity to a 'casa sine pariete' (house without walls). Apparently intended initially for a religious audience, this early thirteenth-century text is a simple guide to the patterns of monastic prayer. Widely circulated in medieval England, its content includes fourteen short meditations on the life of Christ, appended to the seven canonical hours in the latter part of the treatise. Each hour has two meditations attached to it, one on the Passion and one on some other aspect of Christ's earthly life. The first of these meditations, to be undertaken before matins, involves consideration of the circumstances of Christ's birth, followed by consideration of the circumstances of his betrayal. The outline of the Nativity is much more comprehensive than that of the Passion, and begins thus:

> Ante matutinas sive nocte media cogitare debes de temporo, loco et hora in quibus Christus natus est. Tempus erat hiemale, quando maxima frigiditas solet dominari; hora noctis media, periculosior, durior seu gravior aliis horis, ideo dicitur intempestatum; *locus erat in via, in casa sine pariete.* Pannis involutus, instita ligatus, in praesepe positus ante bovem et asinum erat Iesus, quia non erat ei locus in diversorio.[25]

> (Before matins or in the middle of the night you must think about the season, place, and time in which Christ was born. The season was winter, when the greatest chill tends to dominate; the hour was midnight, more dangerous, harder, or more oppressive than other hours because it is said to be stormy; *the place was in the street, in a house without a wall.* Jesus was wrapped in cloths, wound in swaddling-bands, and placed in a manger before an ox and an ass, because there was no room for them in the inn.)

The ill-defined space which has featured in so many of the texts referenced in this chapter is here identified as a *casa* (house), albeit 'sine pariete' (without walls). The *casa*'s public location ('in via') obviously recalls Comestor's 'in communi transitu', and its wall-less-ness appears to be extrapolated from Comestor's description of the *diversorium* as situated between two houses, apparently possessing no walls of its own.

---

25   Edmund of Abingdon, *Speculum Religiosorum and Speculum Ecclesie*, ed. by Helen P. Forshaw (London: Oxford University Press for the British Academy, 1973), capitulum 18, 'De nativitate Christi et eius capcione in media nocte', pp. 82–84 (my italics).

This house without walls also appears in the Anglo-Norman *Mirour de Seinte Eglyse* ('le liu estoit enmi la voie, en une mesun sanz pareie'; the place was in the middle of the street, in a house without walls), a widely read translation of the Latin *Speculum Religiosorum*.[26] And, in expanded form, we also find it in the *Speculum Ecclesie*, which is generally accepted to be a back-translation into Latin from the Anglo-Norman *Mirour*. This translator, however, seems to have a more detailed familiarity with Comestor's account of the Nativity, and also includes an etymology of *diversorium*: '[L]ocus erat in media via, in una domo sine pariete, qui dicitur diversorium a divertendo: nam illic homines divertebantur pro pluvia et aliis tempestatibus' (The place was in the middle of the street, in a house without walls, which is called a *diversorium*, from the word meaning 'to turn off from the road': for men were diverted there because of rain or other bad weather).[27] In terms of their response to Peter Comestor, what all three of these versions of Edmund's Speculum have in common is their clear identification of the *diversorium* as a wall-less construction. In other words, they make Comestor's apparently two-walled structure much more radically and explicitly exposed. And all three also remove the *operimentum* (covering) which, in the *Historia Scholastica*, supplies a protective roof. While the *Speculum Ecclesie*'s account indicates the building's protective capacity, neither the *Speculum Religiosorum* nor the *Mirour* make reference to any provision of shelter. In the English tradition, then, Christ's birthplace becomes quintessentially open in the sense that it offers little or no protection to those in its space and remains unboundaried on all sides.

Of course, the very idea of a house without walls is logically and conceptually confounding. For how does one begin to imagine a space which lacks boundaries and delineation, a space which should be finite (after all, a house has four walls) but which resists closure? Yet such a space is precisely that which we see in Edmund's *Speculum*, and it is precisely that with which readers of the lyrical meditation *Þe Wohunge of ure Lauerd* (hereafter *Wohunge*) are faced. A thirteenth-century text apparently written, initially at least, for an audience of female anchor-

---

26   *Mirour de Seinte Egylse*, ed. by Alan D. Wilshere (London: Anglo-Norman Text Society, 1982), ch. 21 (xviii), 'De la [na]tivité Jhesu Crist e de la capciun a matines', p. 58.

27   Edmund of Abingdon, *Speculum Ecclesie*, capitulum 20, pp. 83–85.

ites, the *Wohunge* is a first-person reflection on Christ as lover and on aspects of his earthly life, most particularly his Nativity and his Passion. Roughly contemporary with Edmund's original *Speculum*, it also locates Christ's birth to a house without walls. It is impossible to say whether the *Wohunge* borrows from Edmund at this point or whether the anonymous author was directly familiar with the *Historia Scholastica*'s account of the Nativity. But, whatever its direct inspiration, its narration of Christ's birth follows in the same tradition as that of Peter Comestor and Edmund of Abingdon.

Occurring at roughly the mid-point of the text, following an extended meditation on Christ's attributes as ideal husband, the *Wohunge*'s account of Christ's birth takes the form of a direct address to him:

> Poure þu born was of þe meiden þi moder . for þenne iþi burð tid in al þe burh of belleem ne fant tu hus lewe þer þine nesche childes limes inne mihte reste . *Bot in a waheles hus imiddes þe strete* . poure þu wunden was irattes & i clutes & caldeliche dennet in a beastes cribbe.[28]

> (Poor you were born of the maiden your mother. For then, at the time of your birth, in all the city of Bethlehem you could not find any sheltering house in which you might rest your soft, childish limbs. But in a wall-less house in the middle of the street, poor, you were wrapped in rags and cloths and coldly laid in an animal's manger.)

Like the *Speculum Religiosorum* and the *Mirour*, the *Wohunge* makes no reference to this building's protective capacity, and neither does it mention Comestor's *operimentum*; like Edmund of Abingdon's wall-less structure, the *Wohunge*'s *hus* is a quintessentially exposed location, defined by the absence of what makes it what it is.[29]

I have written elsewhere on the *Wohunge*'s 'waheles hus' and its very particular resonances for an anchoritic audience whose walled

---

28 *Þe Wohunge of Ure Lauerd*, ed. by W. Meredith Thompson, EETS, orig. ser., 241 (London: Oxford University Press, 1958), p. 28, line 321–p. 29, line 329 (my italics).

29 *A Talkyng of þe Loue of God*, a prose meditation extant in two fourteenth-century manuscripts, includes an adaptation of the *Wohunge* in which the 'wouhless hous.amidde þe strete' is included. Unlike the *Wohunge* author, the *Talkyng* compiler comments that the house was 'a symple refuit.in so cold a tyme' (a humble refuge in such a cold time). *A Talkyng of þe Loue of God*, ed. by M. Salvina Westra (The Hague: Nijhoff, 1950), p. 42, lines 5–6.

and enclosed existence appears diametrically opposed to the un-walled and exposed circumstances of the Nativity.[30] I do not wish to repeat here what I have said elsewhere, but it is worth briefly revisiting my central contention, which is that the anchorite is intended to map the enclosed circumstances of her own life onto the exposed circumstances of Christ's earthly existence. Despite being shut off physically from her external surroundings, she is to cultivate a radical spiritual openness to the world around her, embracing and encompassing it in prayer and intercession. In other words, in her cell-bound existence she is to strive towards emulation of the incarnate Christ's radical vulnerability, seen most clearly at the moment of his birth in a 'waheles hus'. This mapping of the circumstances of the enclosed life onto those of the exposed Nativity is, in fact, articulated very clearly late in the *Wohunge*, when the anchoritic speaker thanks Christ for having 'broht [...] me fra þe world to bur of þi burðe . steked me i chaumbre' (brought me from the world to the bower of your birth, confined me in a chamber).[31] Here, the anchoritic cell and the 'wahelus hus' are elided, the former overtly identified as the 'bur' of Christ's 'burðe', the 'bower' of his 'birth'. Existence within both requires absolute vulnerability, an openness to all elements. The dialectical relationship between the conditions of exposure and enclosure that we have seen in so many of this chapter's Nativity scenes adopts new resonances in the context of anchoritic literature, revealing the two to be mutually reliant, if not — ideally — identical.

Although the *Wohunge* does not explicitly identify the 'waheles hus'/'bur of þi burðe' with the *diversorium* at any point, its author is clearly indebted to exegetical readings of that space. In this context, it is worth reminding ourselves that *DMLBS* records '(private) apartment, compartment (esp. eccl. or mon.)' as one of the definitions of *diversorium*, alongside 'inn, guest-house'. This association of the diversorium with a private religious space seems to have been influenced by the Vulgate's rendition of Jeremiah 9. 2: 'Quis dabit me in solitudine diversorium viatorum, et derelinquam populum meum et recedam ab eis?' (Who will give me in the wilderness a lodging place of wayfaring

---

30 See Sutherland, 'Þe Wohunge of Ure Lauerde'.
31 *Wohunge*, p. 35, lines 572–75.

men, and I will leave my people, and depart from them?). Here, we find the *diversorium* categorically associated with solitude, an association highlighted in the Glossa *Ordinaria's* marginal comment on this verse: 'Quasi dicat. Melius est habitare in solitudine, quam inter tanta scelera hominum commorari' (As if it said, it is better to live in solitude than to be detained among such sins of men).[32] Yet, that its position in 'solitudine' is countered by its sheltering of 'viatorum' (wayfaring men) encapsulates perfectly the curious liminality of this space, poised as it is between society and seclusion, between the conditions of openness and closedness. Such was the space into which Christ was born, and such was the space within which the anchorite was required to live.

In terms of the English tradition, the intriguing circumstances of Christ's birth do not, however, feature only in texts intended for those living lives of religious enclosure. On the contrary, we see them reflected on in devotional and homiletic literature intended for wide and diverse audiences. Sermons on the Nativity are, of course, an excellent repository of information in this context. The *Festial*, a popular late fourteenth-century collection of sermons composed by John Mirk, Augustinian canon and prior of Lilleshall, is particularly useful.[33] Like so much of the *Festial*, Mirk's Nativity sermon has been singled out as reliant on the *Legenda Aurea*; more specifically, its most recent editor, Susan Powell, comments that although his account of the arrival in Bethlehem is biblically inspired, it is more directly indebted to the *Legenda*.[34] Yet, while Mirk's narrative certainly borrows elements of the earlier account, it is by no means a straightforward imitation:

> But when þey comon into þe cyte, hyt was so ful of pepul þat
> þey myght[e] geton no herbor but turnet into a cave þat was
> bytwisse too houses, þeras men setton hore kapulus when þey
> comen to þe market, and þey fondun þer a crach wyth hey and
> setton þe oxe and þe asse þerto.[35]

> (But when they came to the city, it was so full of people that
> they were not able to get any lodging, but they turned into a

---

32   *Bibliorum Sacrorum cum Glossa Ordinaria*, IV, p. 653.

33   John Mirk, *Festial*, ed. by Susan Powell, EETS, orig. ser., 334–35, 2 vols (Oxford:
      Oxford University Press, 2009–11), I (2009), p. xix.

34   Ibid., II (2011), p. 284.

35   Ibid., I, p. 24, lines 49–54.

cave that was between two houses, where men put their horses
when they came to the market, and there they made a manger
with hay and placed the ox and the ass beside it.)

The space between two houses that we saw in the *Historia Scholastica*
and the *Legenda Aurea*, and the house without walls that we have
encountered in the English tradition, becomes, in Mirk's hands (rather
as it did in Ludolph of Saxony's) a 'cave [...] bytwisse too houses'.
The situation of the cave 'bytwisse' two houses is then taken as the
starting point for an extended reflection on the significance of Christ's
earthly life, in which the 'between-ness' of the Incarnation is singled
out as of central importance: '[He] ys prince of pees [who] was comyn
to make pees *bytwynne* God and mon, *bytwynne* angel and mon, and
bytwynne mon and mon' (The prince of peace who came to make
peace between God and man, between angel and man, and between
man and man).[36] The incarnate Christ, Mirk says, serves as a bridge
between heaven and earth, and between one man and another. It
makes sense, then, that he would be born in a liminal space which is
also defined by its position 'bytwisse' and 'bytwynne' (betwixt and
between). In fact, Mirk's cave recalls Bede's influential reading of the
diversorium as a space 'inter' (between) two walls, signifying 'ecclesiam
inter paradisum et mundum' (the Church between paradise and the
world). It is a space which facilitates movement and exchange, offering
protection against the elements yet crucially retaining a degree of
openness.[37]

  This open, liminal space also features — in a variety of forms —
in other Middle English homiletic and devotional texts which retell
the Gospel narrative. *La Estorie de Evangelie*, for example, is a metrical

36 Ibid., I, p. 23, lines 13–14 (my italics).
37 In William Caxton's late fifteenth-century *Gilte Legende*, Mary and Joseph's arrival
    at the *diversorium* is described in terms which reproduce almost exactly those of its
    source, the *Legenda Aurea*: 'And whanne thei come bothe into Bethlem thei myght gete
    hem no hous for thei were pore and multitude of other hadde all take up. Thanne thei
    turned hem to [a] comon place that was bitwene .ij. howses and was hilled aboue and
    called the diuersorie, wher men of the cite assembled togederis to speke and to dyne in
    idell dayes, or ellis for distemperaunce of the tyme, or ellis as som sayn that the churles
    of the contrey, whanne they come to the market, thei wolde teye thaire bestis, and for
    that cause was there a crache redie made' (*Gilte Legende*, ed. by R. Hamer, EETS, old
    ser., 327–28, 339, 3 vols (Oxford: Oxford University Press, 2006–12), I (2006), p. 33,
    line 48–p. 34, line 58).

life of Christ, reliant on a range of sources, first written in the late thirteenth century. Extant in incomplete form in seven geographically diverse manuscripts (including the compendious and significant Vernon) ranging from the thirteenth to the fifteenth centuries, it circulated widely throughout the late Middle Ages. Its account of the arrival in Bethlehem reads thus:

> In Bethlehem hous [Joseph] tok
> Luytel and pore, as seiþ þe bok
> In an old cote and al tofalle
> Nedden heo no betere halle.

> (In Bethlehem, [Joseph] took a house which was little and poor, as the book says, in an old, entirely ruined, hovel. They had no need of a better hall.)

The anonymous homilist goes on to tell us that, after Christ was born:

> Heo leyden him in bestes stalles
> Lloke bitwene two olde walles.
> [...]
> And Abacuc also haueþ iseyd,
> Bytwene two bestes he scholde be leyd.[38]

> (She laid him in the stalls of the animals — look between two old walls! [...] And Habakkuk has also said that he should be laid between two beasts.)

Here, while the *diversorium* does not feature quite as it has in the texts explored thus far, it is recognizable in the 'olde cote' which, being 'al tofalle', does not provide comprehensive shelter for its inhabitants. There is something of the English 'waheles hus' tradition in the evocation of a domestic space which does not function as it should. And the liminality that we have discerned as so characteristic of the Bethlehem birthplace is recognizable in the instruction to 'lloke' for Christ 'bitwene two olde walles' and in the recollection of Habakkuk 3. 2 ('[b]etween two animals thou art made manifest'), interpreted prophetically as an address to Christ. Once again, in the *Estorie*, we find the

---

38   *La Estorie del Evangelie: A Parallel Text Edition*, ed. by Celia M. Millward (Heidelberg: Winter, 1998), p. 123, lines 533–36; p. 123, line 547–p. 124, line 554.

Incarnation associated with an open space, poised between enclosure and exposure, situated in the middle of other spaces.[39]

The fourteenth-century *Stanzaic Life of Christ*, another metrical account of Christ's earthly existence, based on the Gospels, follows in the same tradition, narrating Mary and Joseph's arrival in Bethlehem thus:

> Quen þat Ioseph & Marie
> to Bethleem thus comen wer
> ffor thai wer pore & al nedie
> herber my3t thai non com ner
>
> forto leng in honestly,
> ffor taken was ich hous & maner
> to lords & men that were my3ty
> That non my3t they get þer ne her.
>
> But a hous woghles þer was,
> that sett was negh þe he3e-way,
> bitwene two houses hylyng it has,
> side al opone, soth to say,
>
> In quich hous men of that cite
> haden hor speche in wederes wete,
> vplondisch men þer, als rede we,
> ther setten hor horses in þat strete.[40]

(When Joseph and Mary had thus come to Bethlehem, because they were poor and very needy, they could not come near to any lodging in which they might honestly stay. For each house and manor was taken up by lords and mighty men so that they couldn't get [any accommodation] either here or there. But there was a wall-less house which was situated near the highway, between two houses. It had a roof but, to tell the truth, its sides were entirely open. In that house, men of the city gathered to converse when the weather was wet and, as we read, provincial men put their horses there, in that street.)

---

39 The *Cursor Mundi* (a compendious Middle English metrical history of the world) includes an account of the Nativity which does not make reference to the *diversorium* or the 'waheles hus'. It does, however, situate the Christ child in a liminal space: after Mary has given birth, 'bituix tua cribbes sco him laid' (she laid him between two mangers; *Cursor Mundi: A Northumbrian Poem of the Fourteenth Century in 4 Versions*, ed. by R. Morris, EETS, orig. ser., 57, 59, 62, 66, 68, 99, 101, 7 vols (Oxford: Oxford University Press, 1961–66), II (1966), p. 644, line 11,237).

40 *A Stanzaic Life of Christ*, ed. by Frances A. Foster, EETS, orig. ser., 166 (London: Oxford University Press, 1926), p. 13, lines 393–408.

Here, again, we see the *diversorium* replaced by the 'hous woghles' that we have noted as a particular feature of English Nativity narratives. And while, like Comestor and others, the *Stanzaic Life* emphasizes that this birthplace has a 'hylyng' (covering), it also depicts it as a space with 'side al opene', the emphatic 'al' indicating a condition of radical openness, recalling the spaces evoked in the anonymous *Wohunge* and the *Speculum* translations. Its capacity to provide shelter is compromised by its total lack of protective walls.

This wall-less space also features in the fourteenth-century North-ern Homily Cycle, perhaps the earliest collection of metrical homilies in Middle English. In this series, Christ's birth is located to a 'pendize [that] was wawles, | Als oft in borwis tounes es' (shed that was wall-less, such as is often in villages [and] towns).[41] The 'hous' here is replaced by the more makeshift structure of the 'pendize', its fragility compounded by its absent walls. And we see a similar edifice evoked in the mystery plays' retelling of the Nativity. In the York Cycle, for example, Joseph complains of Christ's birthplace: 'The walls are down on ilka side, | The roof is raved above our head' (The walls are down on each side, the roof is torn open above our head). They will, he says, be 'stormed in this stead' (exposed to storms in this place), which is no longer even protected by the *operimentum* (covering) present in so many of the continental evocations of the *diversorium*.[42] And in the Coventry Play of the Nativity, Joseph refers to Christ's birthplace as 'an hous that is desolat with-owty any wall' (a desolate house without any walls), the addition of 'desolat' reinforcing the abject circumstances of the Nativity.[43]

In the English tradition, then, we see the *diversorium* become a vividly imagined space which, while seeming to promise shelter (what, after all, is a house but a refuge?) fails in its provision, leaving its

---

41   *English Metrical Homilies from Manuscripts of the Fourteenth Century*, ed. by John Small (Edinburgh: Paterson, 1862), p. 63. For discussion of the current state of scholarship on this homily cycle, see Roger Ellis, 'The *Northern Homily Cycle*: A Work in Progress', *Medium Aevum*, 88 (2019), pp. 23–51.

42   *York Mystery Plays: A Selection in Modern Spelling*, ed. and trans. by Richard Beadle and Pamela King (Oxford: Oxford University Press, 1984), 'The Nativity', p. 60, lines 16–18.

43   *English Mystery Plays: A Selection*, ed. by Peter Happé (London: Penguin, 1975), 'The Nativity' (*Ludus Coventriae*, 15), p. 235, line 101.

inhabitants 'al opene' to the elements. Language of desolation and dilapidation (the 'old cote [...] al tofalle', the 'raved' roof) suggests that these texts are engaging fully with the human degradation willingly embraced by the incarnate Christ at the moment of his birth. But the Northern Homilist's linking of the 'wawles pendize' to structures which one encounters — in the present — in 'borwis tounes' (villages and towns) suggests that authors and audiences did not view the circumstances of the Nativity as unique to first-century Bethlehem, but were able to make connections between the biblical past and their own existence in fourteenth-century England. The openness of Christ's birthplace, described in terms so clearly redolent of everyday poverty, may have presented its medieval viewers with a means of understanding their own experience of earthly hardship, a way of situating their own privations within a redemptive context. But equally, Christ's 'wawles hus' may have challenged them to live as openly as he did. This is certainly how it appears to have functioned for anchoritic and religious readers, confronting them with a paradoxical requirement to live lives of spiritual vulnerability and generosity while physically isolated, if not enclosed; after all, the anchoritic 'chaumbre' *is* the 'bur' of Christ's birth, it *is* the 'wawles hus'. But it would be fair to say that if it poses that challenge to enclosed readers, it equally poses it to us all; as Ludolph of Saxony says, the *diversorium* is a space into which *we all* turn ('divertamus') to shelter 'from the deceptions of the world'. To invoke, once again, the mutually reliant categories of exposure and enclosure, it is an open space which — ideally — offers the promise of protection.

Viewed slightly differently, it is also tempting to speculate that the wall-less structure described in the English tradition (and, indeed, the space between two houses/walls evoked by Comestor and others) would have reminded medieval audiences of the architecture of the contemporary marketplace. Evidence supplied by surviving buildings in medieval market towns indicates that commerce was often conducted in open, colonnaded spaces found at ground-floor level beneath first-floor civic quarters.[44] Indeed, the insistence that we have seen

---

44 For discussion of the archaeology and architecture of the medieval marketplace, see James Davis, *Medieval Market Morality: Life, Law and Ethics in the English Marketplace, 1200–1500* (Cambridge: Cambridge University Press, 2012).

in many of these texts on the centrality of the birthplace ('negh þe
he3e-way', 'imiddes þe strete', 'in via', 'in communi transitu') further
encourages the association of the *diversorium/hus* with the marketplace, situated at the heart of civic life. To return to Jeremiah 9. 2's
evocation of the *diversorium*, although it can function as a place of solitude, it also offers shelter to *viatores*, to those who pass by on the road.
The association of Christ's birthplace with a bustling market may, in
fact, have been fruitful for medieval audiences in facilitating meditative
engagement with the significance of the Nativity. Firstly, it serves as a
reminder that humanity is purchased through the incarnate Christ's
redemptive sacrifice; the Crucifixion in particular was — and is —
often explained by recourse to the language of commerce. Second, the
birthplace-as-marketplace analogy provides us with a vivid manifestation of the *diversorium/hus* as a liminal ('inter'/'bytwene') space of
interaction and exchange. In situating itself in the 'bytwene', and in
facilitating contact between God and man, Christ's birthplace recalls
the marketplace as a place enabling communication between seller and
buyer, a liminal space in which one thing is exchanged for another.

We can also relate the liminality and openness of the Bethlehem birthplace to Christ's own nature as the revealed Word of God.
Medieval reflections on the Incarnation and on the New Testament
as a fulfilment of the Old are often interwoven with the language of
openness, as we see in the following example from the early thirteenth-
century *Ancrene Wisse* (Book of Guidance for Anchorites). Written for
an audience of enclosed women who may also have been early readers of the *Wohunge*, *Ancrene Wisse* includes a famous allegory likening
Christ to a chivalric lover-knight who has come to the rescue of a
besieged noblewoman, representative of humanity. His first move is to
send his messengers in advance of himself: 'Earst, as a mon þe woheð,
as a king þet luuede a gentil povre leafdi of feorrene londe, he sende
his sonden biuoren, þet weren þe patriarches ant te prophe[te]s of þe
Alde Testament, wið *leattres isealet*' (First, as a man who woos, as a
king who loved a poor gentlewoman from a foreign land, he sent his
messengers before him, who were the patriarchs and prophets of the
Old Testament, with *sealed letters*). But when the noblewoman refuses
to receive these Old Testament messengers, he decides to engage with
her directly: 'On ende he com him seoluen, ant brohte þe Godspel as

leattres iopenet; ant wrat wið his ahne blod saluz to his leofmon, luue gretunge, forte wohin hire wið ant hire luue wealden' (In the end he came himself, and brought the New Testament as *opened letters*; and wrote greetings to his beloved with his own blood, a love-letter, to woo her with and to gain her love).[45] As the fulfilment of messianic prophecies, the *Ancrene Wisse* author tells us that Christ 'opens' the closed books of the Old Testament, revealing an unambiguous offer of redemption. That he should have been born in a radically open space, therefore, makes absolute sense.

Indeed, Christ's open vulnerability remains crucial to his identity well beyond the moment of his birth; on the cross, the *Ancrene Wisse* author states, he 'open[s] his side, to schawin [us] his heorte' (opens his side, to show us his heart), revealing how 'openliche' (openly) he loves us.[46] Born in a quintessentially open location, he opens closed mysteries, and interacts openly with those who love him; as adjective, verb, and adverb, the category of 'the open' is indivisible from the incarnate Christ. But of course, as this chapter has argued, the condition of openness always relies for its existence on its dialectical relationship with that of closedness. The open birthplace that has been under consideration here invariably exists alongside ideas — and realities — of enclosure. The 'house without walls' is imaginable only by reference to the domestic space whose boundaries it negates. Equally, the *diversorium* not only invokes the walls and buildings which contain it on two sides, but is also a space which provides the shelter of a roof. And to return, finally, to Luke's Nativity narrative and to the very beginning of this essay, as a translation of the Greek κατάλυμα (*kataluma*), the *diversorium* always carries traces of a familial, domestic space, even as it evokes a public, peopled dwelling. The openness of Christ — and of his birthplace — is, ultimately, indistinguishable from the containment and protection that he — and it — offers.

---

45   *Ancrene Wisse: A Corrected Edition of the Text in Cambridge, Corpus Christi College, MS 402 with Variants from Other Manuscripts*, ed. by Bella Millett, EETS, orig. ser., 325–26, 2 vols (Oxford: Oxford University Press, 2005–06), I (2005), p. 146, lines 61–66 (my italics).

46   Ibid., I, p. 148, lines 126–27.

Unlikely Matter
The Open and the Nomad in *The Book of Margery Kempe* and the Middle English *Christina Mirabilis*

JOHANNES WOLF

> Where the Spirit of God is, there one can be free.
> That is why she flew effortlessly
> With her body straight through the air,
> Just like a bird that had no fear.
>
> Broeder Geraert on Christina Mirabilis

There is something deeply unstable, even unlikely, about being.[1] As postmodern humans we carefully navigate the tightrope strung between mind and body by René Descartes, increasingly unlikely — like our medieval ancestors — to draw clear and emphatic distinctions between these two poles.[2] An invitation to think about our selves as knit

---

[1] The epigraph is from *Sinte Kerstina heiligen leven*, lines 611–14, quoted following Anneke B. Mulder-Bakker, *Lives of the Anchoresses: The Rise of the Urban Recluse in Medieval Europe*, trans. by Myra Heerspink Scholz (Philadelphia: University of Pennsylvania Press, 2005), p. 12. Early gestures towards this chapter were presented at the 'Openness in Medieval Culture' symposium at the ICI Berlin in June 2019, and I wish to thank all attendees for a stimulating and truly interdisciplinary environment in which to think. I am also thankful for the readership, suggestions, and occasions of conversation provided by Annie Sutherland and Ruth Evans. Finally, I wish to thank Laura Varnam for introducing me to Margery Kempe nine years ago and for remaining a constant source of inspiration for new approaches to her strange and wonderful *Book*.

[2] Caroline Walker Bynum famously argues that this 'psychosomatic unity' is 'bequeathed by the Middle Ages to the modern world' (*The Resurrection of the Body in Western Christianity, 200–1336* (New York: Columbia University Press, 1995), p. 11).

together, as part of our bodies rather than fundamentally apart, evokes experiences of fragility as well as exultation. If our bodies *are* to some degree us, then we are always already bodies: matter projected into the world without our consent as a condition for existing at all. Despite everything, we are thrown into the world, opening and extending into it.

I am convinced that the illuminator of Merton College, MS. 269 knew this as they bent over the parchment to decorate this thirteenth-century copy of Ibn Rushd's commentary on Aristotle's *Metaphysics*.[3] The historiated initial on fol. 140^v, accompanying a discussion of being that opens with 'ens dicitur multis modis' ('being' can be expressed in many different ways), depicts a seated philosopher in contemplation, sheltered by a massive capital *E*. Stars constellate a deep blue sky; gold-leaved flowers burst from the background as if seeded somewhere beneath the page. His right hand is raised in an interrogative gesture directed towards the object pinched carefully between the fingers of the left. The object is a visual representation of the subject of the passage — of 'being', *ens*. It rises from the philosopher's fingers, a rounded mass of browns, greys, and greens within which channels and rivers bulge like the folds of the brain. Eight tendrils curl and reach out in all directions, as if testing, tasting, sensing the world. It bears little resemblance to *anything*, any thing, defying analytical distinctions and taxonomies. Its effect is to embarrass tendencies towards philosophical abstraction, insisting instead on the fundamentally fleshy and material core of *ens*. Being is protozoan, formless, explorative. Unrestrained, it spreads, suggesting the unlikely truths of matter.

This essay is not about Merton's MS. 269, nor is it about Aristotelian thinking in thirteenth-century Europe. It is, however, deeply invested in thinking about questions of identity and matter — questions that lead more than one medieval artist to launch *ens* into the world, unstable and occasionally unformed, and into contact with other entities and lives. The art I will consider here is textual rather than visual, and operates within markedly different cultural, historical, and intellectual contexts. It is late medieval, vernacular, and religious rather

---

3   The historiated initial discussed below was originally shared by Tuija Ainonen on Twitter, 29 October 2019 <https://twitter.com/AinonenT/status/ 1189094061493407744> [accessed 8 January 2020].

than high medieval, Latin, and technical. Yet it is my contention that a pair of Middle English women's holy lives from the fifteenth century can shed some further light on the problematics and tensions of being, thrown out and open into the world, in the Middle Ages. In their strangest and most trying of moments, the bodies of these religious women threaten to break down, break apart, and challenge fundamental distinctions that underwrite identity, agency, and species.

Witnessed by British Library, Additional MS. 61823 — identified only in 1934 — *The Book of Margery Kempe* describes the trials and tribulations of a fifteenth-century East Anglian laywoman of considerable means as she is driven by powerful devotional experiences into conflict with a world figured as deeply resistant to her performances.[4] Margery Kempe navigates relationships with her husband, goes on pilgrimages both within England and to the Continent and Holy Land, is slandered and reproved by both laypeople and religious, and is imprisoned and interrogated on suspicion of heresy. Even as she establishes important relationships with members of the Church, she remains unassimilable into the secure categories of late medieval devotional life, an indigestible element that frequently irritates the social order. The *Book's* textual journey mirrored the daring adventures of its subject: known only in an orthodox and heavily redacted printed recension until 1934, the single manuscript recovered from a cupboard in a Lancashire country home by Hope Emily Allen is commonly dated to the 1440s.[5] Despite Kempe's considerable aspirations to offer 'exempyl and instruccyon' (example and instruction) through her own experiences (*BMK*, p. 41), there is little to suggest that the *Book* was read or copied in any systematic or widespread manner in the decades following its composition and the death of its subject. Since its redis-

---

4   Quotations from the text will be taken from *The Book of Margery Kempe*, ed. by Barry Windeatt (Cambridge: Brewer, 2000), and will be accompanied by in-text parenthetical citations marked *BMK*.

5   Perhaps the most extensive treatment of the *Book's* textual history appears in Julie A. Chappell, *Perilous Passages: The Book of Margery Kempe, 1534–1934* (Basingstoke: Palgrave Macmillan, 2013); on the historical context of the discovery, see also David Wallace, *Strong Women: Life, Text, and Territory, 1347–1645* (Oxford: Oxford University Press, 2011), pp. 61–132. Anthony Bale has identified the likely scribe of Additional MS. 61823 as Richard Salthouse, a Benedictine monk at Norwich Cathedral ('Richard Salthouse of Norwich and the Scribe of *The Book of Margery Kempe*', *Chaucer Review*, 52.2 (2017), pp. 173–87).

covery it has by contrast become firmly situated in the canon of Middle English devotional literature.[6]

In her irreducibility to the strict roles of the medieval religious, Margery Kempe resembles the subject of my second case study, Christina Mirabilis (the Astonishing). Born in 1150 in Brustem in modern-day Belgium, Christina's life was recorded in a Latin *Vita* by the Dominican Thomas of Cantimpré and subsequently translated into both Middle Dutch and, later, Middle English — in which it is extant only in Bodleian Library, MS. Douce 114. A cowherd and the youngest of three sisters, the trajectory of Christina's life changes dramatically when, at the age of twenty-one, 'of inwarde exercise of contemplacyone she wex seek in bodily myghte and dyed' (due to the inward exercise of contemplation she grew weak in bodily strength and died).[7] Rather than allowing herself to be buried, however, she returns to life in spectacular fashion and engages in ever-increasing acts of contemplative and mortifying athletics in order to save the souls of her fellow Christians from Purgatory. Whilst it seems to have enjoyed some popularity during the medieval period, the *Life* of Christina Mirabilis has received far less critical attention than the *Book* of Margery Kempe, due in substantial part to scholarly embarrassment over the extremity of her miracles.[8] Despite their differences, in their insular

---

6   It has become so only through the hard work of generations of feminist medieval scholars, whose urgent correctives were and continue to be salutary to the field as a whole. Key interventions include Sarah Beckwith, 'A Very Material Mysticism: The Medieval Mysticism of Margery Kempe', in *Medieval Literature: Criticism, Ideology and History*, ed. by David Aers (Brighton: Harvester Press, 1986), pp. 34–57; Karma Lochrie, *Margery Kempe and the Translations of the Flesh* (Philadelphia: University of Pennsylvania Press, 1991); Lynn Staley, *Margery Kempe's Dissenting Fictions* (Philadelphia: University of Pennsylvania Press, 1994). Milestone essay collections are *Margery Kempe: A Book of Essays*, ed. by Sandra McEntire (London: Garland, 1992), and *A Companion to the Book of Margery Kempe*, ed. by John Arnold and Katherine J. Lewis (Woodbridge: Brewer, 2004); new approaches and perspectives are forthcoming in *Encountering the Book of Margery Kempe*, ed. by Laura Varnam and Laura Kalas Williams (Manchester: Manchester University Press, 2022).

7   'The Middle English Life of Christina Mirabilis by Thomas of Cantimpré', in *Three Women of Liège: A Critical Edition of and Commentary on the Middle English Lives of Elizabeth of Spalbeek, Christina Mirabilis, and Marie d'Oignies*, ed. by Jennifer N. Brown (Turnhout: Brepols, 2008), pp. 51–84 (p. 54). Subsequent quotations will be taken from this edition and accompanied by in-text parenthetical citations marked *CM*.

8   Modern critical unease is discussed in Alicia Spencer-Hall, 'The Horror of Orthodoxy: Christina Mirabilis, Thirteenth-Century "Zombie" Saint', *postmedieval: a journal of medieval cultural studies*, 8.3 (2017), pp. 352–75.

forms both texts, then, would have resonated with an increasingly literate and spiritually ambitious vernacular readership — one for whom being in the world remained an unavoidable fact of existence, and for whom religiosity entailed a committed openness to finding God in the wider world: in the streets of cities and in their fellow living beings. They offer models of an *ens* thrown into the world — unstable, fragile, and exploratory.

Margery Kempe's affective piety is marked by a pair of somatic responses to the images and echoes of Christ's life and Passion: 'krying and roryng' (crying and roaring; *BMK*, p. 163). Visual signs of God's grace working through her, these powerful and involuntary responses scandalize her companions, interrupt sermons, and prompt accusations of possession and mental illness (*BMK*, pp. 151, 288, 186). The effects of her devotional practice reject the outwardly demure trajectory of the enclosed contemplative, reaching out laterally into the social order in gestures of uncontrolled and uncontrollable openness to the world. The continued eruption of her self into the wider world is the key thread of the *Book*'s narrative, as the moment at which she gains the 'gift' of roaring makes clear. Whilst on pilgrimage in Jerusalem, Kempe ascends to Calvary and the site of Christ's execution. There,

> sche fel down that sche mygth not stondyn ne knelyn, but walwyd and wrestyd wyth hir body, spredyng hir armys abrode, and cryed wyth a lowde voys as thow hir hert schulde a brostyn asundyr, for in the cite of hir sowle sche saw veryly and freschly how owyr Lord was crucifyed. Beforn hir face sche herd and saw in hir gostly sygth the morning of owyr Lady. (*BMK*, p. 163)

> (she fell down so that she might not stand or kneel, but rolled and wrestled with her body, spreading her arms out wide, and cried with a loud voice as though her heart would break in half, because in the city of her soul she saw truly and vividly how our Lord was crucified. Before her face she heard and saw in her spiritual sight the mourning of our Lady.)

As it contorts into a cruciform symbol her body loses its coherence *as* a body, becoming an indistinct entity with which Kempe rolls and wrestles — although the proposition 'wyth', in Middle English as in Modern English, allows us to speculate whether she wrestles *against*

it or is in some sense *complicit* in it, embroiled in an intimate exploration of a being becoming un-stuck. *Walwen* — 'to roll' — is a verb
associated with the surge of the sea and the rising of the winds; there is
a storm brewing within the collapsing Kempe.[9] It is 'as if' her heart
would 'a brostyn asunder', an intensity of grief that plays out in the
breaking and shattering of her body, wracked by pain and wounding. As the passage shifts to the lexicon of the immaterial vision, the
material echoes of these experiences linger, stressing the tension at
the heart of 'the cite of hir sowle'. The standard defensive gestures of
contemplative writing — the text stresses that she sees 'veryly' (truly)
in her 'gostly syght' (spiritual sight) — are deployed to distance the
following clauses from the wild and unbounded *ens*, but it is too little
too late. What she sees '[b]iforn her face' (in front of her face) remains
'fresch' — vivid, sensory, and embodied. Kempe's heart contains cities,
multitudes of people, gathered to watch the death of God. It is no
wonder that it threatens to break under the pressure.

On her return from Palestine, Kempe finds affective triggers everywhere she turns. Her heart remains broken; in fact, it continues to
break in an ongoing experience of emotional trauma which cannot
even begin to settle and metamorphose into grief. Whilst overcome
simultaneously by anguish and love in Rome, she responds to the in-
quiries of concerned Italians with 'the Passyon of Christ sleyth me!'
(the Passion of Christ slays me!; *BMK*, p. 209), the insistently present
tense of her declaration suspending the normal trajectory of time in
an eternal present of desire and pain.[10] Later in the *Book*, a perplexed
priest at St Stephen's in Norwich responds to her cries with 'Damsel,
Jhesu is ded long sithyn' (Damsel, Jesus has been dead for a long time),
to which she responds — fiercely, doctrinally — 'Sir, hys deth is as
fresch to me as he had deyd this same day, and so me thynkyth it

---

9   *Middle English Dictionary*, ed. by Robert E. Lewis and others, online edition in *Middle
     English Compendium*, ed. by Frances McSparran and others (Ann Arbor: University of
     Michigan Library, 2000–18), s.v. 'walwen v.', sense 4a <https://quod.lib.umich.edu/
     m/middle-english-dictionary/dictionary/MED51618/> [accessed 21 March 2020].
     Jeffrey J. Cohen, *Medieval Identity Machines* (London: University of Minnesota Press,
     2003), pp. 154–87, discusses the 'becoming-liquid' of Kempe.

10   Kempe is, in Carolyn Dinshaw's words, 'a creature not merely in another time but rather
     with another time *in* her' (*How Soon Is Now? Medieval Texts, Amateur Readers, and the
     Queerness of Time* (Durham: Duke University Press, 2012), pp. 105–28 (p. 107)).

awt to be to yow and to alle Cristen pepil' (Sir, his death is as fresh to me as if he had died today, and I think it should be so to you and to all Christian people; *BMK*, p. 286). She does not, cannot, begin to process the Passion as loss, a process by which she might re-constitute her self. Reminders of the Passion are everywhere in her life, thorns that snag on her thin exterior and tear new wounds and openings into her, through which her interiority comes spilling out in cries and roars. Sermons, statues, children, dolls (*BMK*, pp. 286, 287, 191, 177): all of these trigger the storms of cries and tears that typify her performances. Margery Kempe is projected constantly into a world — both material and salvific — to which she is undeniably open, even porous; her exclamations and tears only further demonstrate the fluid nature of this subjectivity.

In other words: Kempe *fragments*. As she extends across times and places and sounds and tears, she stretches, pulls apart, threatens to disperse. She does not, however, break or cease to exist — rather, she seems to represent in her vertiginous openings to the world a version of what Rosi Braidotti refers to as 'nomadic becomings'. Braidotti describes this kind of becoming as an activation, a switch in perceptive mode:

> In those moments of floating awareness when rational control releases its hold, 'Life' rushes on towards the sensorial/perceptive apparatus with exceptional vigour and higher degrees of definition. This onrush of data, information and affectivity is the relational bond that simultaneously propels the self out of the black hole of its atomised isolation and disperses it into a myriad of bits and pieces of data imprinting or impressions.[11]

Margery Kempe reverberates with the energy of this sort of becoming. She is a self propelled outwards of herself into a world whose effects she experiences not merely differently to others but *more intensely*; her internal world balances on the precipice of affect and 'Life'. Braidotti goes on to argue that '[o]ne needs to be able to sustain the impact with the onrushing affectivity to "hold" it, without being completely

---

11   Rosi Braidotti, 'Intensive Genre and the Demise of Gender', *Angelaki: Journal of the Theoretical Humanities*, 13.2 (2008), pp. 45–57 (p. 46).

overwhelmed by it'.[12] For Kempe this 'holding' takes the form of a reverberation or forwarding of the experience, like the transmission of electric charge that must be released in order to avoid a short circuit, a blown affective fuse. What she sees and hears overwhelms by definition her subjective boundaries and so instead arcs out in cries and tears and forms that will not, *cannot* be controlled.[13] A world knit together by divine suffering is a world that disperses the subject that comes to know it back into the wilds, out of her own body and into the circuits of transmission, echo, and displacement that await.

Kempe's opponents wish most specifically for her to close the openings this gesture threatens to produce — through marriage, imprisonment, perhaps holy orders. These desires are summarized best by the irate Canterbury monk who tells Kempe: 'I wold thow wer closyd in an hows of ston, that ther schuld no man speke wyth the' (I wish you were enclosed in a house of stone, so that no man could speak with you there; *BMK*, p. 93). His specific desire is for her to be immured in stone, imprisoned or perhaps in a cell attached to a church as an anchoress, but the undertones of this declaration are more universal, reflecting a generalized anxiety about the movement and freedom of the female body — a body considered peculiarly physiologically open.[14] This Canterbury monk wishes Kempe's endlessly capacious extension into the world controlled and minimized, wishes that her body be rooted and literally closed to the multiple states and becomings it performs. *The Book of Margery Kempe* is, of course, a testament to the failure of this individual and the programme he represents — instead of allowing herself to be grounded, Kempe takes flight.

Immediately following her experiences at Calvary, the *Book* gives an overview of the typical trajectory of Kempe's affective responses. In the process of sketching out the general imprint of these events, however, the text offers a highly unusual and potentially destabilizing target for compassionate feeling. Whilst the Passion is one common trigger for 'the crying', there are others:

---

12   Ibid.

13   See also Julie Orlemanski, who describes Kempe's cries as a form of 'distributed expressivity' ('Margery's "Noyse" and Distributed Expressivity', in *Voice and Voicelessness in Medieval Europe*, ed. by Irit Ruth Kleiman (Houndmills: Palgrave Macmillan, 2015), pp. 123–38 (p. 130)).

14   See especially Lochrie, *Translations of the Flesh*.

And sumtyme, whan sche saw the crucyfyx, er yf sche sey a
man had a wownde er a best whethyr it wer, er yyf a man bett a
childe befor hir, er smet an hors er another best wyth a whippe,
yyf sche myth sen it er heryn it, hir thowt sche saw owyr Lord
be betyn er wowndyd, lyk as sche saw in the man er in the best,
as wel in the feld as in the town, and be hirselfe [a]lone as wel
as among the pepyl. (*BMK*, p. 164)

(And sometimes, when she saw the crucifix or if she saw a man
had a wound or if a beast had one, or if a man beat a child in
front of her, or struck a horse or another beast with a whip, if
she could see or hear it, she thought she saw our Lord be beaten
or wounded, just as she saw the man or the beast, in both the
field and the town, and by herself as well as in company.)

This description appears at first to chart the usual direction of Kempe's
visionary moments as recently charted by Julie Orlemanski: she moves
from the specific earthly situation — a confrontation with a crucifix,
or an image of a body in pain — to the divine realities it signifies.[15] Yet
here Kempe circles back almost immediately to the world; the image
of Christ in 'hir thowt' is traced back to the phenomena she 'myth sen
[...] er heryn' in her immediate surroundings. This structure complicates the movement of contemplative thought, which turns from
the mundane things and directs itself up towards the divine. Here the
structure of Kempe's own narrative draws us back almost immediately
into the sights and sounds of the world — and, in particular, to a recognition of *animal* suffering. Lisa J. Kiser has noted that this passage is
an unusual example of the 'animalisation' of Christ — the comparison
of the suffering son of God with the humility of suffering nonhumans,
a common motif in its own right — as it proceeds from the suffering
body *to* Christ, rather than using the animal body as a metaphor *for*
Christ.[16] This change of semiotic direction is important. Within the
narrative of the *Book* this animal suffering is emphatically real; it exists
in the texture of the story as a fact and a body every bit as weighty as
those of the humans with whom Kempe interacts. The *Book*'s fierce
insistence on the relevance of the material and domestic world is at the
centre of this moment, offering these injured animals a rare moment of

---

15   Orlemanski, 'Margery's "Noyse"', pp. 132–33.
16   Lisa J. Kiser, 'Margery Kempe and the Animalisation of Christ: Animal Cruelty in Late
      Medieval England', *Studies in Philology*, 106.3 (2009), pp. 299–315 (p. 314).

visibility as suffering, living things.[17] Kempe's unusual approach gives these animal bodies a weight and presence that is not contained or nullified by metaphor: they appear as suffering, bleeding entities that refuse to be assimilated entirely into the symbolic order.

The total effect of Kempe's visionary mode, which is tuned here to recognize and respond to the bare fact of suffering, is to reveal a network of violent acts that extends across species. In so doing it effect-ively suspends, at least for a moment, the gestures of distinction and categorization that regulate definitions of humanity and animality — distinctions that now run under the watchword 'species'.[18] Kempe sees only wounds, openings of the body which invite her compassionate devotional responses. The specifics of the body — age, gender, species — are secondary, becoming lost as she extends her list enthusiastically. These bodies lack 'organs' in the sense introduced by Gilles Deleuze and Félix Guattari:

> the body without organs is opposed less to organs as such than to organisation of the organs insofar as it composes an organism. The body without organs is not a dead body but a living body all the more alive and teeming once it has blown apart the organism and its organisation.[19]

Resisting the contained organizational structure of the 'organism' and the distinctions upon which it rests, this scene for a moment invites simply a procession of wounds and suffering whose investments refuse to be closed off, migrating instead across affective and species bound-aries. The nomadic *ens* (so explicitly without organs) becomes visible

---

17   David Lavinsky has provided an important caveat to readings of *The Book* as un-questioningly devoted to material mysticism ('"Speke to me be thowt": Affectivity, *Incendium Amoris*, and the *Book of Margery Kempe*', *Journal of English and Germanic Philology*, 112.3 (2013), pp. 340–64).

18   The study of animals and their representation in the Middle Ages is a growing field. See, for instance, Jeffrey J. Cohen, 'Inventing Animals in the Middle Ages', in *Engaging with Nature: Essays on the Natural World in Medieval and Early Modern Europe*, ed. by Barbara A. Hanawalt, Lisa J. Kiser, and Julie Berger Hochstrasser (Notre Dame: University of Notre Dame Press, 2009), pp. 39–64; Karl Steel, *How to Make a Human: Animals & Violence in the Middle Ages* (Columbus: Ohio State University Press, 2011); Bruce Holsinger, 'Of Pigs and Parchment: Medieval Studies and the Coming of the Animal', in *PMLA*, 124.2 (2009), pp. 616–23; Sarah Kay, 'Legible Skins: Animals and the Ethics of Medieval Reading', *postmedieval: a journal of medieval cultural studies*, 2.1 (2011), pp. 13–32.

19   Gilles Deleuze and Félix Guattari, *A Thousand Plateaus: Capitalism and Schizophrenia*, trans. by Brian Massumi (London: Bloomsbury Academic, 2012), p. 34.

here once again, reaching out irrepressibly for new connections and new associations. These bodies without species call us to attention, and demand access to an ethical order from which they are excluded at the very moment that they are constituted as animal — i.e. as *not human*.

If the *Book* proffers an invitation to this ethical order, it does not sustain it. Lisa J. Kiser ends her discussion of this passage optimistically, suggesting that it places animal suffering in 'a broader and more meaningful context' than is common in the medieval period.[20] Yet a wider exploration of the roles nonhuman animals perform in the *Book* offers little to suggest that the implications of this moment are activated in any lasting sense. Kempe's journeys and adventures are studded by animals whose presence, use, and subjugation is effortless. Horses are used for transportation from Leicester to Melton Mowbray (*BMK*, p. 240). Kempe rides a donkey on pilgrimage, nearly falling off her animal companion in a sudden devotional fervour; this time there is no indication that she recognizes the animal's state (*BMK*, p. 161). Even her oft-cited description of herself as a 'creature' serves only to reinforce the position of the nonhuman animal at the bottom of the species hierarchy. These passages indicate an entirely unexceptional relationship to nonhuman animals; their bodies are available as the unconsidered raw material for pilgrimage, narrative, and signification.

There is only one other sustained mention of animal cruelty in *The Book*. The contrast between these two moments, however, could not be starker. Restored by grace from the state of despair with which her text begins, Kempe at first refuses to 'leevyn hir pride' (leave her pride; *BMK*, p. 57), deciding instead to engage in a series of business ventures. One of them involves a horse mill.

> Sche gat hire tweyn good hors and a man to gryndyn mennys corne, and thus sche trostyd to getyn hir levyng. [...] Thys man [...] toke on of this hors and put hym in the mylle as he had don before, and this hors wold drawe no drawt in the mylle for nothing the man mygth do. The man was sory and asayd wyth al hys wyttys how he schuld don this hors drawyn. Sumtyme he led hym be the heed, sumtyme he beet hym, and sumtyme he chershyd hym, and alle avayled not, for her wold rather gon bakward than forward. Than this man sett a scharp peyr sporys

---

20   Kiser, 'Animalisation of Christ', p. 315.

on hys helys and rood on the hors bak for to don hym drawyn, and it was nevyr the bettyr. (*BMK*, pp. 59–60)

(She got herself two good horses and a man to grind corn for people, and thus she planned to make a living. [...] This man [...] took one of the horses and put him in the mill as he had done before, but this horse would not pull despite anything he tried. The man was vexed and applied all his wits to figuring out how to get this horse to pull. Sometimes he led him by the head, sometimes he beat him, and sometimes he treated him well, and none of these things helped, for he would rather go backward than forward. Then this man put a sharp pair of spurs on his heels and rode on the horse's back to make him pull, but nothing would improve the situation.)

This horse is nothing more than a prop. The violence mounted upon its body is described in a clarity whose claim to objectivism renders invisible the suffering to which Kempe will later find herself so surprisingly open. The beating of the animal passes by without remark, whilst the 'sharp peyr sporys' — which must have caused considerable damage — are simply listed as one of a number of failed attempts to get the horse moving. Any possibility of nonhuman agency is elided as this recalcitrant horse's rebellion is represented as a punishment from God — a 'merveyl' (marvel/miracle; *BMK*, p. 60) that robs this animal of its force. Pain, thick and sticky to Kempe in chapter 28, is invisible, denied the affective opportunities of sight and sound.

A more expansive interrogation of the *Book*, then, implies a rather bleak picture, which agrees with Karl Steel's argument that Kempe's compassion is 'not [...] for animals so much as it is for injuries in general, whether animals or human'.[21] For Steel, Kempe's momentary association with animals is enabled by the conceptual linkage of the female human body with the animal body through the medieval concept of the 'flesh'. Her rejection of meat and momentary association with animals is to be understood as a method of 'mastering the flesh by other means', an enactment of superiority through the 'elaborate management and refinement of the satisfactions of abstinence'.[22] Under

---

21   Karl Steel, 'Animals and Violence: Medieval Humanism, "Medieval Brutality", and the Carnivorous Vegetarianism of Margery Kempe', in *The Routledge Companion to Animal-Human History*, ed. by Hilda Kean (London: Routledge, 2018), pp. 1650–1716 (p. 1686) <https://doi.org/10.4324/9780429468933-21>

22   Ibid., pp. 1689, 1678.

this reading Kempe supplies '[a]ll the affective elements that we might think necessary for the development of animal rights [...] yet all they do is exacerbate the need to encounter suffering animals'.[23] Nonhuman pain is scripted into the devotional world as a side of perverse enjoyment and reflection; there is no shift towards a politicized compassion that argues for a minimizing of suffering or an assertion of anything that could be called animal rights. This reading suggests that in the *Book*, animal pain is understood only a useful canvas for human pain; its existence is helpful, *necessary* even, to the extent that it allows us to reflect on our own suffering. This is a paternalistic approach that dismisses the ethical validity of nonhuman suffering *as* suffering: it is the compassion of hierarchy.

My reading of *The Book of Margery Kempe* has to some extent confirmed the investments of this text in this hierarchy; it cannot be taken as formulating a clear argument for animal rights. Kempe is not unusual in this regard; in this capacity, at least, the *Book* is for once unexceptional. Yet I find myself unable — or unwilling — to commit entirely to this reading. Beyond the ideological account, the cause of this chapter I am writing still exists: chapter 28 of the *Book*, with its plainly suffering animals, waiting to stir. Kempe's compassionate gesture — gathering together children, men, and beasts — struck and moved me on first reading; it still does. It is a moment that transforms the *Book* and adds an unintentional new story to the varied tales it tells: a story of subjugation, exploitation, and pain to which animals are party *as themselves*. This is a story that would have remained invisible to me had Kempe not gestured, briefly, at a horizon she could not overcome — a horizon that is nonetheless breached, and remains open. Even if, this time, Kempe's body is 'closyd' off from others, the *text* is not, not fully. Turning now to Christina Mirabilis, I will situate this experience of flight and closure tentatively and provisionally in the textual body of the unenclosed female contemplative.

Unlike Kempe, Christina actually *flies*. She literalizes metaphor. She begins her life already entangled with animals; the third of three sisters, she is assigned 'to keep hir bestes on the felde that wente to pasture' (to keep her beasts that went to pasture on the field; *CM*, p. 53). Christina's

---

23   Ibid., p. 1687.

transformation begins after her death, brought on by 'inwarde exercise of contemplacyone' (inward contemplative exercise; *CM*, p. 54); once brought to the church and laid on the bier before her friends and sisters, the scene is set.

> And while the Masse was in doynge for hir soule, sodey[n]ly the body sterid and roos vp in the bere and anoon lifte vp, as a bridde, steigh into the beemes of the kyrke.
>   Then alle that were [there] fledde and hir eldist sister [alone] bode still with drede. And she abode in the kyrke roufe vnmoued tille the Messe was doon. (*CM*, pp. 54–55)

> (And whilst the Mass for her soul was in progress, the body suddenly stirred and rose up on the bier and then lifted up, like a bird, straight to the beams of the church.
>   Then all that were there fled, apart from her eldest sister, who remained there in dread. And she stayed still in the roof of the church until the Mass was done.)

Christina rises from the grave and keeps going — up into the rafters to join the grotesques and saints that people the eaves and corners of the church, whose petrification she seems to mirror. She has, it transpires, travelled through Purgatory to 'the trone of Goddes mageste' (the throne of God's majesty), where she has been offered the choice: stay with God in heaven, or 'turne ageyne to body' (return again to her body) to deliver through her own painful experiences souls from Purgatory and into heaven (*CM*, p. 56). Christina, of course, makes the saintly choice and is resuscitated by divine grace — to the surprise and fear of her community. She returns with a sanctified body, one equipped to resist the tortures of Purgatory which she will actualize in the world. She throws herself into ovens and is spun by the wheels of mills; she lies in graves and hangs herself with condemned criminals (*CM*, pp. 59, 60). Her body returns, unmarked, from these and other contortions, a living 'ensaumple [...] to stire men to repentauns and penauns' (example [...] to stir men to repentance and penance; *CM*, p. 56).

Beyond this exemplarity, however, lie other reverberations, other 'becomings'. For as Christina sheds her mortal body, she sheds her securely *human* status too. As she rises to the rafters of the church roof, she does so 'as a bridde' (like a bird), in the first of several gestures towards nonhuman existence. As Christina's new life unfolds, it becomes increasingly clear that 'the soteltee of hir spirite lothed the taste and sauoure of mennes bodyes' (the keenness of her spirit hated the taste and flavour of human bodies; CM, p. 55). As human society turns her stomach, she turns to a different mode of existence: 'Cristyn fledde the presens of folke with a wonder lothinge into wildernesse and into trees, into the coppys of tourys of chirches or of othere hye thinges' (with great disgust Christina fled the presence of people into the wilderness and into trees, into the turrets of church towers or into other high things; CM, p. 57). The text is at pains to demonstrate that such activities are not agential, or at least rational; the disgust Christina experiences as 'lothinge' is affective and overwhelming, whilst the very conditions of her new body seem to necessitate behaviour that launches her body from its humanity:

> Hire body was so sotil and lighte that she wente in hyghe thynges and, as a bredde, hengyd in ful smale twigges of trees. And whanne she wolde preye, she was constreyned to flee into tree coppys or touris or into othere summe hygh thinges that she, so beynge allone fro alle folke, myghte fynde riste of hire spirite. (CM, p. 61)

> (Her body was so subtle and light that she went into high things and, as a bird, hung in the tiny twigs of trees. And when she wished to pray she was forced to flee into treetops or towers or into other high things so that she, so being alone from all people, might find rest for her spirit.)

Christina's actions are determined by the 'sotil' and 'light' state of her new body, a finely tuned existence that has been rendered newly sensitive to the world around her. Her responses are not, strictly speaking, voluntary — she is 'constreyned', forced, to take literal flight and find the peace of wild things. These are necessary reactions to a newly tuned existence, a body opened to the horror and potential of the world: generative and disgusting in the same breath, a teeming intensity of life unveiled when Christina consumes alms presented to her by sinners: 'hit semyd to hir that she yeet the bowellis of paddokes or of todes or the guttis of neddirs' (it seemed to her that she ate the bowels of frogs or toads or the guts of snakes; CM, p. 66). Like Kempe, Christina is an open body, presented to a world whose effects she experiences as a headlong rush — Braidotti's (Woolf's) 'Life'.[24]

Where Kempe's boundlessly compassionate gaze momentarily renders human and animals confused, Christina's experience engulfs her in a continuous mode of becoming that flitters between species. In a *Life* that runs to just over seven hundred lines, she is compared to a bird on five occasions. Occasionally she becomes aquatic, once staying 'vndir the water of the flode of Moyse [...] sex dayes or more' (under the water of the Meuse river [...] for six days or longer) — 'as a fyshe' (as a fish), as the text later stresses (*CM*, pp. 60, 64). She fixes her own clothes with shreds of the natural world, using 'noon othere threde but [...] the barke of a tree that is called *Tilia* or with wykers of salow or with prickes of wode' (with no other thread but [...] the bark of a tree called the *lime tree* or with willow branches or with thorns of wood; *CM*, p. 67). At midnight she stirs up the dogs of St Trond and runs 'fast byfore hem as a best' (fast before them as a beast), and is driven by them 'thurgh buskes and brerys and thikke thornes' (through bushes and briars and thick thorns; *CM*, p. 61). Christina has become something other — but never completely so, never entirely abjected or contained by a single position, an unfinished process that 'is neither the swinging of the pendulum of dialectical opposition, nor [...] the unfolding of an essence in a teleologically ordained process', but rather 'the process of affirmation of the unalterably positive structure of difference, unhinged from the binary'.[25] This unhinged, open, endlessly possible *ens* is made most visible by Christina during periods of deep devotional activity:

> And efte soone whan she prayed and Goddes grace of contemplacyone come to hir [...] alle hir membrys were closed togedir on a lumpe, nor there myghte nothinge be perceyued of hir but allonly a rownde gobet. And after that spirituel felynge, whan the actuel felynges come to her kynde ageyne, in the maner of an vrychyn, the lumped body yode to the owne shappe and strekyd oute the membrys that were firste stoken vnder an vnlikely mater and forme. (*CM*, pp. 61–62)

---

24   Braidotti, 'Intensive Genre', p. 46.
25   Ibid.

(And as soon as she prayed and God's grace of contemplation
came to her [...] all her limbs shrunk together into a lump,
and nothing might be seen of her apart from a round gobbet.
And after that spiritual experience, when the material feelings
returned to their natural disposition again, in the manner of
a hedgehog, the rounded body transformed to its own shape
and stretched out the limbs that were before hidden under an
unlikely matter and form.)

Affected by the force and power of God's grace, Christina's body shifts
and changes into a single 'gobbet', an indistinct rounded shape — the
'vnlikely mater and forme' of a self transforming under the pressure of
the divine. She comes to mirror the protozoan entity of Merton College, MS. 269, a star of purely living flesh without organs. Christina's
'kynde' — her essential nature, the properties essential to her as *ens* —
is placed at the centre of this passage as the fulcrum around which it
turns. Grace transforms her, and only the return of 'actuel felynges' to
her 'kynde' prompts a return to her normal shape. Even as she extends
out into the world again, however, she does so 'in the maner of an
vrychyn': in the manner of a hedgehog, a becoming-animal at exactly
the moment that her 'kynde' offers an opportunity for normalcy and
stability.

Christina's contemporaries, like Kempe's, respond with discom-
fort — but they are notably more enthusiastic in their persecutions.
They become her hunters and jailors, and she is 'soghte, founden, and
taken of hir freendys and tyed with yren chaynes' (sought, found, and
taken by her friends and bound in iron chains) on a variety of occasions
(*CM*, p. 58); at their most desperate, her community even employ
a 'ful wicked and ful strange man' (a very wicked and cruel man),
who promptly chases her down and breaks her leg (*CM*, p. 63). It is
only once Christina's breasts miraculously produce a healing oil whilst
imprisoned that her captors recognize the error of their ways and 'leet
hire go' (let her go; *CM*, p. 64). Her freedom is, however, short-lived.
Her continued performances and acts of generalized penance result in
a growing reputation and, in turn, in ever-growing crowds that travel
from afar to 'see miracles and meruales of God in Cristyne' (to see the
miracles and marvels of God in Christine; *CM*, p. 64). The religious
of St Trond respond with considerable anxiety to this development,
praying to God to intervene lest the marvellous eruptions of Christina

'turne beestly myndes of men into wikkyd wirkynge' (turn the bestial minds of humans to wickedness; *CM*, p. 64). Their prayers reflect a widespread medieval concern with the veracity and potentially demonic sources of the disturbing phenomena described as 'meruales' in Middle English, but the text also suggests a fear that the unstable, 'nomadic' resonances of Christina's *ens* — which reverberate on the frequency of animality — might harmonize with the 'beestly' within us all.[26] It seems that God agrees and, in chapter 14 — titled 'How hire lyfe was temperid to men' (How her life was moderated for humans) — acts.

> And so it fel vpon a daye that she, stirid of spirite ful hougely, ranne to a chirche in a towne that is callid Wellen and, fyndynge the fonte stoon open, she plonged hirselfe alle therein. And with that, as it is seyde, she gate there that fro then forthe the menere of hire lyfe was more tempyrde to men. (*CM*, p. 65)

> (And so it happened one day that she, greatly stirred in her spirit, ran to church in a town called Wellen and, finding the font open, plunged herself entirely into it. And with that, as it is said, she did that so that from then on the manner of her life was more moderated for humans.)

Driven by God and the demands of her community, Christina immerses herself in the font at Wellen, effectively re-enacting her baptism as a symbolic re-entry to a society conditioned by limits and closure. The dynamics of this shift are wrapped up in the Middle English verb *tempren*, translated here (following Brown) as 'moderated'. It is a verb connected intimately with ameliorative or regulative behaviour, bringing together a wide variety of technical, scientific, and normative interventions, including the mixture of substances and solutions; the balancing of water temperature, airflow, and the humours; the punishment of ethical deviants; the adjustment of pathological or unsociable behaviour; and the appropriate tuning of instruments.[27] Folded at the centre of these proliferating meanings is a newly curbed and finely

---

26   On the culture of miracles, see Stephen Justice, 'Did the Middle Ages Believe in their Miracles?', *Representations*, 103 (2008), pp. 1–30.

27   *Middle English Dictionary*, s.v. 'tempren v.', senses 1a, 1b, 2a, 4a, 5a, 6a, 7a, 8a, 8b, 10b <https://quod.lib.umich.edu/m/middle-english-dictionary/dictionary/MED44748/> [accessed 21 March 2020].

tuned Christina, a wild and nomadic *ens* that has been restrained, softened, balanced, regulated, and ultimately 'disciplined': brought into better harmony with the closed and violent world of humans.

The closure demonstrated so clearly by the *Life* of Christina Mirabilis allows for a clearer reading of the reassertion of species lines in *The Book of Margery Kempe*. Both texts hold the slowly germinating seeds of another way of becoming. Neither text can actualize these dormancies, generative and viral as they are. Yet this does not mean that they do not exist — nor that the contexts that produce them are not important. In *The Posthuman*, Rosi Braidotti writes that

> [t]hese rebellious concepts [of posthuman association] for me are related to the feminist consciousness of what it means to be female. As such, I am a she-wolf, a breeder that multiplies cells in all directions; I am incubator and a carrier of vital and lethal viruses; I am mother-earth, the generator of the future. [...] The becoming-posthuman speaks to my feminist self, partly because my sex, historically speaking, never quite made it into full humanity, so my allegiance to that category is at best negotiable and never to be taken for granted.[28]

As medieval women, both Margery Kempe and Christina Mirabilis are ancestors of Braidotti's, bodies and selves for whom membership of the category of 'full humanity' involved an endless labour of assertion, doomed to result only in fragile and temporary acceptance at the edge of a phallogocentric hierarchy. Perched on the edge of full being, however, both Kempe and Christina change. Their toes lengthen to talons and feathers sprout from their skin. Braidotti's point shines through in both Kempe's *Book* and Christina's *Life*: as controlled, subjugated, and dehumanized selves, these women find themselves flickering on the edge of animality.[29] As holy women in the world, they frustrate their contemporaries and worry institutional structures. As bodies thrown out into a world whose vital onrush only they can feel, both Kempe and Christina gesture to a form of openness and becoming utterly unavailable to a ratiocinative order premised on control, limit, and barrier: the vulnerable and exploratory *ens*, being qua being. Their

---

28   Rosi Braidotti, *The Posthuman* (Cambridge: Polity Press, 2013), pp. 80–81.
29   Steel, 'Animals and Violence', p. 1686, makes a similar argument about Kempe, al-
       though as we have seen his conclusions are rather different.

texts, themselves a composite and gendered play of clerical control and contemplative authority, trend towards orthodoxy and closure — but recuperation remains a constant, verdant possibility.

Writing on the narratives of Douce 114, Vincent Gillespie has re-marked that they represent 'a shift of genre [...]. Narrative is winning out over theology: the text will not engage in theological evaluation; religious actions speak louder than theological words.'[30] This structure is nowhere more obvious than in the tense dynamics I have explored here; the narrative thrust of passages and moments in both books threatens to run, expand, and burst from their orthodox containers. Both texts are explicitly designed to be exemplary: Kempe's *Book* au-thorizes itself with the claim that '[a]lle the werkys of ower Saviowr ben for ower exempyl and instruccyon, and what grace that he werkyth in any creatur is ower profyth' (all the works of our Saviour are ex-amples for us and for our instruction, and the grace that he works in any creature is our profit; *BMK*, p. 41); Thomas of Cantimpré ends his text with a purgatorial charge: 'Take heed therfore, thou reder, how mykel wee be bounden that see Cristyn haue suffryd so many turmentys [...]. And we dreed to do penauns for oure selfe and for oure synnes' (Take heed, therefore, you reader, how many people we may be indebted to, having seen Christina suffer so many torments [...]. And we dread to do penance for ourselves and our sins; *CM*, p. 83). Orlemanski has astutely observed that part of the function of exempla is 'to show the aesthetics of emplotment acting on bodies as personae are made to suffer and embody ideological imperatives'; they are ideology acting on the narrative plane.[31] Yet if Kempe and Christina are representa-tions of ideology, channelling lessons about Christ's Passion and the doctrine of Purgatory, then their very existence *in* and *as* narrative complicates their reception. Their stories, episodic and daring, hold special velocities that escape their intended use. Where an effective exemplum might be short and efficient, these texts dilate, reach out, extend in unusual directions to make unstable connections and strange

---

30   Vincent Gillespie, 'Religious Writing', in *The Oxford History of Literary Translation in English: To 1550*, ed. by Roger Ellis (Oxford: Oxford University Press, 2008), pp. 234–83.

31   Julie Orlemanski, *Symptomatic Subjects: Bodies, Medicine, and Causation in the Litera-ture of Late Medieval England* (Philadelphia: University of Pennsylvania Press, 2019), p. 139.

associations. They demonstrate a deeply textual *ens*, generous and distributed and vital. Their reach is unstoppable. We, as readers, may choose to take Christina's own practice as a metaphor for the act of interpretation itself, as an invitation to seize trembling and unlikely affinities, to run with wolves, and to fly:

> Then hire spirite felynge that she was closed and stoken in the celar, she toke a stoon of the celare flore and in an houge spirite she made the walle thurgh. And as an arowe that euere the faster it is streyned in the bow, the strenger it fleeth, euen so hir spirit artyd abouen right with the selfe body of verrey fleshe, as hit is seide, flowe forth as a briddge in the eyre. (*CM*, p. 63)

> (Then, her spirit recognizing that she was enclosed and restrained in the cellar, she took a stone from the cellar floor and with mighty strength she threw it through the wall. And like the arrow that flies more forcefully the stronger it is pulled by the bow, just so her spirit, pulling upward her own fleshly body, as it is said, flew forth as a bird in the air.)

Including the Excluded
Strategies of Opening Up in Late Medieval Religious Writing
ALMUT SUERBAUM

OBSCURITY

The literary works which this essay considers have often been neglected. Before turning to the texts themselves, it may therefore be
worth considering modern scholarly approaches to them, since those
provide the lens through which we perceive medieval culture. In the
case of literary works, there are a number of often unspoken assumptions which shape critical analysis and condition what is considered
to be 'inside' the scholarly frame. Concepts of a canon presuppose
a closed circle of authors or works who belong and are recognized,
excluding those who do not fit the preconceptions. Often, these acts
of exclusion may be based on non-literary criteria — works made by
or for women, for example, can be invisible when the dominant model
is male authorship. Nevertheless, exclusion is most commonly justified
on aesthetic grounds. Because the works excluded do not conform to
established aesthetic norms, they are considered to be of lower quality and therefore relegated to the margins. Assumptions about textual
qualities can work in the same way: the norm is considered to be a
stable text created by a single author — despite the fact that many

medieval texts are unstable, changed and adapted by every new generation of readers and copyists, brought into contact with new texts in compilations, abbreviated, or rewritten in a process of creative reading and rereading, but also writing and rewriting, in which there is no single stable hierarchy between a controlling single author and passive recipients of the authentic text, but instead a creative interaction.

Medieval religious songs have often been neglected by modern scholars because they do not fit the categories defined in the nineteenth century as markers of literary status: religious songs are mostly anonymous; their transmission is unstable, so that often, there are multiple variants instead of a single authorial and authorized version; finally, they defy normative poetics in using loose forms rather than the highly regulated strophic forms of the secular love lyric requiring pure rhyme and metrically identical repetitions.[1] As a result, these more open, less regulated forms were often marginalized by modern scholars, because they defy the desire for stable authoritative texts attributable to a single, known author to whom poetic greatness can be attributed. This also means that many of these texts have not been edited, and because they mostly lack author-attributions, even the ones edited are largely invisible to anyone searching for names of well-known authors.

In the context of this volume, religious songs are interesting, however, precisely because of their porousness, because they give evidence of the ways in which complex concepts from speculative theology, which were by many considered the prerogative of experts and best kept away from novices and laypeople, nevertheless found their way to audiences beyond the closed circles of university disputations or monastic discourse. The songs are evidence for the circulation of ideas beyond tightly controlled sites of knowledge, which in the period are also the seats of textual production — since monastic scriptoria as well as university circles are responsible for the larger part of manuscript production in Latin well into the late Middle Ages.

---

1   For details, see Almut Suerbaum, '*Es kommt ein schiff, geladen*: Mouvance in mystischen Liedern aus Straßburg', in *Schreiben und Lesen in der Stadt: Literaturbetrieb im spätmittelalterlichen Straßburg*, ed. by Stephen Mossman, Nigel F. Palmer, and Felix Heinzer (Berlin: De Gruyter, 2012), pp. 99–116.

An example will illustrate such differences in transmission as well as literary form. In 1841, Philipp Wackernagel, a nineteenth-century Swiss-German schoolteacher and elder brother of the philologist and editor Wilhelm Wackernagel, published a collection of 850 German hymns from Martin Luther to the seventeenth century, expanded into a five-volume collection between 1864 and 1877 in order to capture both Latin hymn traditions and vernacular religious song from the beginnings to the post-Reformation period.[2] The preface of the first volume paints a picture of familiar Protestant myth-making: Latin religious hymns flourished in the early Christian period of Ambrosius and Gregory the Great, spread across Europe, and sparked adaptations. Some of these are of great power and beauty, though Wackernagel considers most of the later, that is medieval, hymns to be of little aesthetic value and often bordering on the heretical ('von schwächlichem oder gar das Wort Gottes verläugnendem abgöttischem Wesen').[3] Wackernagel sees this period of decline reversed during the Reformation, when the works of Luther and his followers Melanchthon, Stigelius, and others return to the true origins of the early Latin hymns with texts of their own, characterized by simplicity and purity ('wie in unmittelbarem Anschluss an die Hymnen von Ambrosius und Gregorius zu ihrer ersten Einfachheit und Reinheit zurückgeführt').[4] He highlights the methodological difficulties facing anyone attempting to collect material transmitted with a degree of textual licence and variance: while he considers it therefore methodologically desirable to go back to the manuscript tradition, he acknowledges the scale of the task were it to involve searching every monastic or cathedral library — and notes that it would by definition have to be an international enterprise.[5] While he therefore considers a complete critical edition of all hymns and sequences (roughly 4000) an impossibility, he offers an anthology of 850, building on the work of two earlier collections by Mone and David, but abandoning their thematic ordering in favour of a chrono-

---

2   Philipp Wackernagel, *Das deutsche Kirchenlied von M. Luther bis auf N. Herman und A. Blaurer* (Stuttgart: Liesching, 1841) and *Das deutsche Kirchenlied von der ältesten Zeit bis zum Anfang des XVII. Jahrhunderts*, 5 vols (Leipzig: Teubner, 1864–77).

3   Ibid., I (1864), p. vii.

4   Ibid.

5   Ibid., p. viii

logical one. He highlights his own contribution in adding material from the fourteenth century and onwards, especially such vernacular songs which use strophic forms familiar from vernacular folk song, or using refrain forms:

> Vom vierzehnten Jahrhundert an habe ich Vieles selbständig gesammelt, besonders auch in Beziehung auf die eigentümlichen Lieder, welche in der Form der Auffassung wie der Verse und der Melodien nicht den Hymnen, sondern dem deutschen Volksliede gleiche und auch wiederkehrende Zusätze an den Strophen lieben, welche jene nicht kennen.[6]

> (Starting with the fourteenth century, I have added much which I had collected myself, especially with reference to those unique songs which in their form, themes, verse-structure, and tunes resemble German folk songs rather than Latin hymns, especially in their preference for refrains, unknown in the hymn repertoire.)

Amongst his selection of fourteenth-century hymns, he includes a group of eleven songs which he attributes to Johannes Tauler (nos. 457–68), the thirteenth-century preacher and pupil of Eckhart. These attributions rely either on the judgement of the sixteenth-century reformer Daniel Sudermann, who transcribed them from the manuscripts of the convent 'St Nikolaus in undis' in Strasbourg which had ended up in the Berlin library, or on the fact that they were included in the 1543 Cologne print of Tauler's collected works. The second of the cantilenae from the Cologne print may serve as an example. It is prefaced by a rubric which sets out its place in the sequence of songs and the state of mind of its putative author:[7]

> 'Ein ander lietlin.
> Der das dichte, dem was also zu mut.'

> Min geist hat sich ergangen
> in eine wueste stil,
> da noch wort noch wise in stet.
> Din wesen hat mich vmbfangen,
> das ist kein wunder inne.

---

6   Ibid., II (1867), p. ix.

7   Cf. Almut Suerbaum, 'The Pseudo-Tauler *Cantilenae*', *Ons Geestelijk Eerf*, 84 (2013), pp. 41–54.

Min geist hat sich ergangen,
vernunft kan das nit erlangen
es ist oben aller sinnen,
und des wil ich mich suchen lan.

Min geist hat sich ergangen
zu einer stunt:
Sink in den grunt,
Die ungeschaffenen selicheit die wirt dir kunt.

Scheid dich von nit,
du finds das nit
das die zunge leüget und blibt doch yet,
das der geist aleine verstet
der keines urteils pflegt.[8]

('Another song. He who composed it felt like this.' || My spirit
has found succour in a silent desert without word or tune.
Your nature has embraced me; that is no wonder. || My spirit
has found succour; reason may not attain that, it is beyond all
senses, and therefore I will allow myself to be sought out. ||
My spirit has found succour at one time: sink into the abyss;
you will find uncreated blessedness. || Separate yourself from
nothing, you will not find that which the tongue denies and yet
remains, that which only the spirit understands who does not
judge.)

The song uses diction which is familiar from mystical theology as developed by Eckhart and transmitted in vernacular sermons by Eckhart's
pupils, including Johannes Tauler. In particular, it draws on images
and conceits of negative theology such as the concept of approaching
God not through a process of acquiring virtues, but rather through
stripping the soul of everything which is earthly, so that the desert can
become the place of closest proximity to God precisely because it lacks
all attributes. Similarly, an approximation to God is achieved not by
soaring to great heights but by sinking into an abyss ('grunt'), and not
through sophisticated reason but rather in the stripping away of sound
and words as well as reason.

The song thus evokes complex and indeed contested religious
concepts such as the union between the human soul and the divine.
At the same time, it uses a literary form which is neither the artful

---

8   Wackernagel, *Das deutsche Kirchenlied*, ii, pp. 306–07.

prose that was common for vernacular as well as Latin sermons, nor the highly regulated strophic forms of French-inspired secular love songs with their sophisticated use of literary technique and their aura of literary exclusivity. Instead, as the variants of this song demonstrate, it creates a ruminative process that circles the central concepts.[9] At the same time, the Cologne print manifests the unease of early modern readers with such open forms of textual tradition, because it firmly reinserts the song into conventional structures by assigning it to an ordered sequence — it is 'another' song, preceded by a similar one — and an author who has experienced what the song articulates. By thus attributing the song to Johannes Tauler, the Cologne print exemplifies early modern unease with late medieval collaborative and collective modes of writing.[10]

COURTLY EXCLUSIVITY: THE NOBLE HEARTS

In order to understand how such processes of literary rather than social inclusion or exclusion work, it may be helpful to contrast the seemingly artless songs which baffled nineteenth-century collectors with some of the secular forms against which both contemporary audiences and nineteenth-century scholarly editors may have measured them.

Like the religious lyric moving between the spheres of liturgical and theological Latin on the one hand and the vernacular on the other, the courtly world is inherently multilingual. Throughout much of the high Middle Ages, the dominant relationship for texts in German is that between the two vernaculars, French and German, with French often providing the pre-text which a German poet adapts and appropriates. The choice of the vernacular, addressed at secular aristocratic audiences, is programmatic and differentiates these texts for lay readers from the sphere of theological Latin learning. Nevertheless, Latin and theological allusions are often present at one remove. As Gottfried's *Tristan* highlights, this act of cultural appropriation is a complex one, in which Latin theological discourse is often alluded to, even if secular readers may be much less familiar with it than the learned author.

---

9   For a record of the transmission, see Judith Theben, *Die mystische Lyrik des 14. und 15. Jahrhunderts: Untersuchungen — Texte — Repertorium* (Berlin: De Gruyter, 2010).

10 Cf. Suerbaum, 'Pseudo-Tauler *Cantilenae*'.

Within the prologue of Gottfried's *Tristan*, the author-persona situates himself within both traditions:

> Tribe ich die zît vegebene hin,
> so zîtic ich ze lebene bin,
> sô'n var ich in der werlt sus hin
> niht sô gewerldet, alse ich bin.
>
> Ich hân mir ein unmüezekeit
> Der werlt ze liebe für geleit
> Und edelen herzen z'einer hage,
> Den herzen, den ich herzen trage,
> Der werlde, in die mïn herze siht,
> Ine meine ir aller werlde niht
> Als die, von der ich hoere sagen,
> Die keine swaere enmüge getragen
> Und niuwan in vröuden welle sweben:
> Die lâze ouch got mit vröuden leben.[11]

(Were I to waste my time while I am still alive, I would not move in this world in as worldly a manner as I actually do. ‖ I have chosen a pastime — for the sake of the world, and to please noble hearts, those hearts who are dear to my heart, and that world which sees into my heart; I do not mean the world of those many who (as I hear it said) cannot bear hardship and only want to experience joy: may God let them live in that joy.)

As the prolific wordplay underlines, Gottfried's narrator plays a sophisticated game of exclusion and inclusion with his listeners: by drawing attention to the limited time on earth remaining to him, he sets himself apart from the youthfulness of his implied audience, yet in doing so, evokes the privilege of age and experience. The court, a sphere of love associated with youth, is both desirable and distant. In a stance familiar from other courtly writers, it is the desire to please his audience which motivates his writing, suggesting that writer and audience inhabit the same world. Yet at the same time, Gottfried's narrator draws sharp distinctions: the noble hearts to whom he wishes to appeal are not in fact identical with the courtly, aristocratic audience, because the narrator insinuates that most of those listeners are driven by the desire to attain joy without suffering — a desire which the narrator devalues as worldly

---

11   Gottfried von Straßburg, *Tristan und Isold*, ed. and trans. by Walter Haug and Manfred
      Scholz, 2 vols (Frankfurt a.M.: Deutscher Klassiker Verlag, 2011), lines 41–54.

and ignoble. Like the truly noble hearts in his audience, he knows that true love cannot but involve suffering.

In addressing the so-called 'noble hearts', Gottfried revels in paradox, since the term is intended to denote exclusivity. Courtly society, composed of aristocratic ladies and gentlemen, was self-aware of the fact that only a small minority could belong to this circle. Yet in Gottfried's use, the term no longer refers to a social reality, because it dismisses many of the potential members of this exclusive circle as too worldly, in other words, too focused on pleasure. Nor is it used here as an aesthetic category, because it excludes only those who desire pleasure, insisting on the fact that true discernment knows that joy and suffering are inextricably linked, and that desire therefore needs to include the willingness to suffer.

The literary strategies employed by Gottfried's narrator are thus twofold: rhetorically, he employs forms of exclusion, separating those who truly discern the nature of love and joy from the mundane, who cannot accept true paradox. At the same time, this strategy of redefining nobility as discernment is inclusive, because it allows every member of the audience to accept the position of the narrator. Potentially, it is thus open to all listeners, drawing them into the world and the aesthetic and ethical judgement of the narrator. Yet this seemingly open invitation deliberately retains an air of exclusivity through a mode of polarizing choices and a simultaneous rejection of those who make the wrong choice. It is this strategy of exclusive inclusion which generates the fascination and pull of Gottfried's narrative, requiring readers to suspend judgement and the value-systems of their everyday world, because that is the only way to for them be included in a world in which an adulterous relationship can be the only true form of love.

Gottfried's play with the rhetorical impact of a *captatio benevolentiae* is exceptional in its artifice, yet it draws on the paradoxical tension between exclusion and inclusion which underpins courtly literature, in that courtly culture is representative, based on figures who can be inhabited by all potential listeners and open to all, while at the same time developing that inclusiveness through strategies of exclusion, defining true courtliness through its exclusivity. This is overt where courtliness is still recognizable as a social category — we know that historically, both writers and audiences of secular courtly texts are aristocratic, members of a relatively small and closed group. Yet Gottfried's text is an extreme example of allowing terms like *edel* (noble) to shade from being a simple marker of social class into an internalized category, where it is conceivable that those who are externally noble lack true nobility because they are incapable of discerning aesthetic quality. It is this sense of exclusivity which makes Gottfried appear modern to contemporary readers, because it is achieved through a strong sense of authorial presence behind an ironically unreliable narrator.

The sense of openness in Gottfried is thus ultimately dependent on an author who is in control of his material as much as his audience. Art and artificiality are a mark of exclusive expertise which, while flattering the audience into believing they can emulate the author's discrimination and taste, manipulates them into suspending value judgements in order to gain acceptance into an exclusive circle. As a result, this author persona comes closest to modern notions of authorship centred around intention and individuality. It represents an influential, though by no means universal model of thirteenth-century writing, and is the dominant frame of reference for contemporary pre-Foucauldian readings. It therefore serves as a useful contrast to the very different modes of reading and writing explored in religious writing which is more or less contemporary with Gottfried.

Gottfried's story of exclusive if destructive love draws on biblical imagery, though critics are divided over whether it does so in order to appropriate or to subvert Christian ideals. This is perhaps most evident in the spaces inhabited by the protagonists. Tristan and Isolde are each introduced with a royal backstory featuring their lineage, allowing us to see their ancestry, inserting them into a network of social ties and obligations: Tristan, orphaned at birth, is first publicly recognized in all his exceptional talents at the court of his maternal uncle Marke; Isolde, the beautiful princess, emulates the medical skills of her mother both in healing Tristan and in recognizing in him the killer of her own maternal uncle, for whose death she had sworn vengeance. Compared to his sources, Gottfried heightens the paradoxical parallels: both lovers are drawn to one another, because each excels within their own group; at the same time their familial obligations mean that each is loath to engage with the other. While both therefore establish an identity which relies on the respect of others around them, an identity which therefore rests on being accepted as a member of a group, their love makes them outcasts. Again, Gottfried highlights this through the spaces in which they are able to live their identity as lovers: at sea, on the ship crossing to Ireland; in an orchard; finally, in exile from the court. All other versions frame this space of their exile from the court as a desert, because they are deprived of all courtly status, but also of all marks of civilization. Gottfried, by contrast, turns their exile into a form of paradise in which they are sustained by song, requiring no food. They are alone, in total seclusion — and yet this state is no exile, since nature allegorically turns into their court: the babbling brook is their cup-bearer, the birds provide music. What earlier versions had configured as a place of exclusion turns, in Gottfried's version, into a space in which the lovers are at the same time remote, removed from the prying eyes of the court, and yet reminded of the fact that their existence is inherently social, part of a network of social relations. This remote *locus amoenus*, like the liminal space of the ship conveying them towards Ireland, is the only place in which they can consummate their love without having to hide it from outside observers, the only place where they can openly be what the prologue had suggested was their nature and destiny: lovers whose devotion to one another is absolute. Nevertheless, this is no state of untroubled openness — their seclusion is broken when the court searches for them, and the moment at which they are exposed to the eyes of King Marke and the court is marked by a charade of separation, when Tristan places his sword between himself and Isolde before King Marke sets eyes on them. This is an act of dissimulation — Tristan and Isolde pretend to be chastely separated, but that open display of distance is in itself a deception. King Marke is only too willing to believe what he sees publicly, because it allows him to uphold the pretence that Isolde is his loyal wife. The scene is also an invitation to the reader to accept that what is out in the open and visible in plain sight may be more complex than it appears. Yet the scene also underlines the precariousness of the lovers: the spaces in which they consummate their love are remote, so that not everyone can reach them — yet none of them offer seclusion to the lovers, who are always surrounded by jealous watchers whom they have to deceive in order to avoid public shame. In Gottfried's version, this tension ultimately leads to the destruction of both lovers — not simply their death, but also their loss of integrity and identity. Love, at least love as experienced by Tristan and Isolde in their particular setting, is destructive. Whether there can ever be a state where absolute love for a beloved is compatible with a social existence as one amongst a group is something the text leaves open.

RELIGIOUS EXCLUSIVITY: SPIRITUAL NAKEDNESS

While Gottfried's secular love story revels in aesthetic exclusivity in which the ideal of love is possible only in isolation, yet obtainable only for those who excel in the refinement by which courts define themselves, religious writing of the period usually invokes a concept of common humanity in which all human beings are equal. Eckhart, the fourteenth-century Dominican theologian and mystic, explores this notion:

> Ez sprechent die meister gemeinlich, daz alle menschen sint glich edele in der nature. Aber ich spriche waerlîche: alles das guot, das alle heiligen besezzen hânt und Maria, gotes muoter, und Kristus nâch sîner menscheit, daz ist mir eigen in dirre natûre.[12]

> (The masters all agree that all human beings are equally noble in their nature. Yet I say, in truth all goodness which the saints and Mary, the mother of God, and Christ according to his humanity possess, is mine by nature.)

In a characteristic syntactic and intellectual structure, Eckhart refers to the received wisdom of the masters, which means Aquinas and the accepted theological teachings: they all hold that human beings are not distinguished from one another but are all noble by their nature. Their emphasis is on inclusive levelling of differences. Eckhart, by contrast, reconfigures this theological dogma not by questioning its validity, but by changing its rhetorical force: in his version, the emphasis is no longer on the indistinguishable equality of all human beings, but on the exceptional nature of the speaking 'I', who compares himself not to

---

12   Meister Eckhart, *Werke*, 2 vols (Frankfurt a.M.: Deutscher Klassiker Verlag, 2008), I, ed. and trans. by Josef Quint, ed. by Niklaus Largier, Sermon Q5b, 'In hoc apparuit caritas dei in nobis', p. 66, lines 23–27.

other non-descript human beings, but to an ascending triad of exceptional figures: the saints, who by common belief excel in their virtue;
Mary, who as the mother of God is unique amongst human beings;
finally Christ, who is both human and divine. By claiming the same
virtue as Christ, the speaker thus undercuts the radical differentiation
between God and man, focusing instead on the uniqueness of his own
status as good by nature.

Nevertheless, this claim to exclusivity is not a social one, and it
is in principle open to all those who listen to the sermons, because
the speaker is both exceptional in his boldness and representative, in
that he is human and shares human nature with all listeners who are
discerning and courageous enough to accept these premises.

Such statements are at the heart of Eckhart's theology, which
argues for the undifferentiated unity of the human soul and God, or, as
in this sermon, the fact that God assumes human nature, even though
not a human person: 'Disiu natûre ist ein und einvaltic' (This nature is
one and undivided).[13] The sermon is clear about the difficulties which
accepting this can cause, and requires anyone who desires to attain this
state of oneness with God to forego individuality:

> alsô daz er dem menschen, der jensît mers ist, den er mit ou-
> gen nie gesach, daz er dem alsô wol, guotes günne als dem
> menschen, der bî im ist und sîn heimlich vriunt ist. Also die
> wîle dû dîner persônen mêr guotes ganst dan dem menschen,
> den dû nie gesaehe, sô ist dir waerliche unreht noch dû gelou-
> getest nie in desen einvaltigen grunt ein ougenblick.[14]

> (such that he is as well disposed to someone who is across the
> sea and whom he has never set eyes on, as to someone who
> is close and an intimate friend. For as long as you are better
> disposed to your own person than to someone whom you have
> never seen, things are not right with you, and you have never
> for a single moment gazed into that undivided depth.)

As a result, the state of nakedness or being-without (blôzheit) requires
those who want to achieve it to leave all aspects of their created humanity behind. Ultimately, therefore, this exclusive state of being at one

---

13   Ibid., Q5b, p. 68, lines 3–4.
14   Ibid., lines 7–14.

with God is achievable for all, in a strategy which mirrors Gottfried's paradoxical invitation to all listeners to become part of an exclusive group.

Like Gottfried, Eckhart uses paradox as the linguistic and philosophical form of expressing this invitation. Whereas in Gottfried's text, addressed to a social elite of listeners, this paradox of the noble hearts as exclusive yet potentially open to all members of the exclusive audience may be a form of literary play for the cognoscenti, its theological and political provocation is evident in Eckhart, against whom the archbishop of Cologne, Heinrich von Virneburg, opened an inquisitorial process in 1326. Concern focused on the vernacular sermons, though some of the Latin texts were also suspect, and in particular on statements which argued for the unmediated birth of God in the human soul, which would set aside the fundamental distinction between the uncreated creator in eternity and his creation living in time. After several rounds of hearings, claims, and counter-claims, Eckhart was interrogated by a papal commission in Avignon, which in 1328, after Eckhart's death, concluded that a series of twenty-eight statements from his sermons were either heretical or evil-sounding, rash, or suspect of heresy. The papal bull *In agro dominico* of 27 March 1329 confirmed fifteen statements as heretical and another eleven as evil-sounding or suspect.[15] While this bull and its condemnation may only have circulated in Cologne, it affected the transmission of Eckhart's writings, even if it did not supress them, and resulted in a transmission which was widespread, indicating that the sermons were known and read widely, but largely anonymous. Notably, it directed attention to the status of the vernacular, since the incriminated statements were largely those made in the vernacular sermons. The concern about vernacular heterodox statements or formulations indicates the anxiety around the more open status of the vernacular, in which terms are less clearly terminologically defined than in Latin, the language of the universities, and therefore open to a range of interpretations or readings. Such linguistic openness is therefore seen as a risk within a context of theological and doctrinal fixity; yet the use of the vernacular and the

---

15   Eckhart, *Werke*, I, pp. 725–26 (commentary); cf. Bernard McGinn, 'Eckhart's Condemnation Revisited', *The Thomist*, 44 (1980), pp. 390–414.

proliferation of these sermons in the vernacular, albeit without Eckhart's name, also indicate that the opportunities which the vernacular opens up are welcomed by readers and drive the later transmission. While Gottfried's artful and artificial literary text is addressed to a social elite, Eckhart's vernacular sermons may have been delivered behind convent walls to the small groups of nuns whose pastoral care was in the hands of the Dominicans, and yet they circulated in much wider spheres. They are informed by Eckhart's training as a Dominican at the *studium generale* in Cologne, probably under Albertus Magnus, and the University of Paris, where he was granted the *licentia docendi* (licence to teach) in the academic year 1302–03. Yet they very clearly also draw on vernacular traditions of speaking about God as used by religious women in the second half of the thirteenth century, from Marguerite Porete in Paris to Mechthild of Magdeburg, whose *Flowing Light of the Godhead* he may have known. These vernacular texts by women reflect the greater openness of a language which, because it is not that of the universities or of doctrinal statements, is less terminologically fixed and therefore open towards new ways of thinking about God, even if these were then deemed heterodox in certain cases.[16]

OPENING UP: RELIGIOUS SONG

While Eckart's vernacular writings are the best-known example of heterodox thinking within the established world of the universities and convents, the thinking reflected in them proliferated beyond those initial audiences to much wider readerships, often through intermediary adaptations. Some of this reception can be traced through a series of authors and texts, most prominently in the next generation of Upper German Dominicans, Heinrich Seuse and Johannes Tauler, but also in the Low Countries in the works of Ruusbroec and Nicolaus Cusanus.

---

16   Mechthild of Magdeburg, *Das fließende Licht der Gottheit*, ed. by Gisela Vollmann-Profe (Frankfurt a.M.: Deutscher Klassiker Verlag, 2003); the near-contemporary translation into Latin is available now in a new edition, *Lux Divinitatis*, ed. by Ernst Hellgardt, Balázs Nemes, and Elke Senne (Berlin: De Gruyter, 2019). It reflects the fact that certain of the potentially heterodox statements from the vernacular version were redacted in the Latin version; cf. Gisela Vollmann-Profe, 'Mechthild von Magdeburg — deutsch und lateinisch', in *Deutsche Mystik im abendländischen Zusammenhang*, ed. by Walter Haug and Wolfram Schneider-Lastin (Tübingen: Niemeyer, 2000), pp. 144–58.

But the indirect adaptation of Eckhart's thought, especially on the birth of God within the human soul, is tangible much more widely and includes Luther, whose thinking on the Trinity and the Eucharist was informed much more strongly by late medieval adaptations of Eckhart and Tauler than his self-staging of a radical break with the Middle Ages suggests.[17]

Eckhart's thoughts were developed in sermons and treatises directed at listeners in specific convents (albeit clearly disseminated more widely beyond these in later redactions, even reaching urban lay readers). Later generations, by contrast, adapted his theology in literary forms which are more open in their transmission. One of the most interesting of these formats is religious song, which may in some cases originate from the bilingual culture of south-west German Dominican convents, where Latin and the vernacular coexist, but also extends beyond that closed circle of convents. As discussed in the earlier sections of this paper, they represent a textuality and literary culture which is very different from the author-centred and tightly controlled textuality of the courtly love lyric and romance produced at and for the aristocratic courts. The Dominican convents are no less closely interconnected with one another than the secular courts, and as Eckhart's role in the spiritual care of the Dominican sisters demonstrates, they are very much part of emerging theological speculation. But within these convents, writing is a process seen as important in itself, as an act of worship, not the necessary route towards a fixed object.

The final section of this paper is devoted to one such example of religious song, the so-called *Granum sinapis* (Mustard Seed), attributed to Eckhart in the later tradition, though not necessarily by him. The song employs vocabulary and concepts which clearly resonate with Eckhart's vernacular sermons and may have been informed by them, even if Eckhart is not the author. In strophe 5, it develops a characteristically paradoxical space:[18]

---

17 Cf. Eckhart, *Werke*, I, pp. 715–42 (commentary).

18 Edition in Kurt Ruh, 'Textkritk zum Mystikerlied *Granum sinapis*', in *Festschrift Josef Quint*, ed. by Hugo Moser and others (Bonn: Bouvier, 1964), pp. 169–84; cf. Theben, *Die mystische Lyrik des 14. und 15. Jahrhunderts*, pp. 186–93.

Das wüste gût
ni vûz durch wût,
geschaffen sin
quam nî dâ hin:
us ist und weis doch niemant was,
us hî, us dâ
us tîf, us hô
us ist alsô,
das us ist weder diz noch daz.

(No foot has ever crossed this desert; created reason has never
penetrated there. It is, and yet no one knows what; it here, it
there, it far, it near, it low, it high, it is just so that it is neither
this nor that.)

Unlike the pseudo-Tauler cantilena, the *Granum sinapis* uses pure
rhyme and a fixed, if simple strophic form of couplet and embracing
rhyme. The use of antithetical structures to construct paradoxes is
equally striking. Yet whereas Gottfried's use of paradox highlighted the
hermeneutic exclusivity of operations intelligible only to a small group
of insiders, its function here is, I would like to argue, the opposite:
where no one can know the nature of the desert which represents
Divine nothingness and un-createdness, the paradoxical phrases open
up the relationship to all who are willing to experience this tension,
drawing listeners into the space opening up between the two po-
lar opposites. The contradictions therefore point to a sphere beyond
antithesis of the 'neither here nor there', 'neither low nor high'. Gram-
matically, the negations employed evoke the positive concept while
abstracting from it: that which cannot be seen is invisible, yet of course
the act of speaking about it in this form makes it visible to us conceptually. At the same time, the use of paradox is inclusive, in that the desert
is both high and low, both here and there, which implies it cannot be
captured by either of the antithetical attributes alone. Yet theologically,
in the tradition of pseudo-Dionysian thought, this move beyond the
antithetical oppositions is a path towards the Divine, who stands above
and beyond creation in pure nothingness — or, as Eckhart had phrased
it, *blozheit* (nakedness). Letting go of created categories is thus the
only possible path towards the Divine. Yet this state of abstraction,
which Eckhart calls *gelazenheit*, which has overtones of both 'abnegation' and 'being at peace', is not just the subject of a theological or

philosophical treatise but created through the language of the song. Its musical form of circular movement performs the movement of opening up to God in a world beyond that of the created oppositions. While drawing on exclusive, contested, and at times risky theological statements, the song moves away from conventional learned forms of lyric poetry addressed to an exclusive audience and returns Eckhart's speculative theology to the more loosely constituted and therefore more open circles of laypeople from whom he may have drawn some of his inspiration.

CONCLUSIONS

As has become clear, the spiritual movement amongst women in the fourteenth century played an important role in opening up forms of discourse which had been the exclusive prerogative of those within monastic communities. By appropriating concepts of speculative theology, especially those of abnegation of the world and union with the divine, they suspend the fundamental difference between creator God and creation, opening up a space in which the human participates in the divine. At the same time, they do so in forms which move away from the closely controlled metrical forms of courtly lyric poetry, preferring loosely strophic forms in formats which are textually unstable, because each new version of a song can add new strophes or rearrange existing ones, adapted by different users to their own spiritual needs and preferences. Finally, many of these lyric forms are open in their preference for an indeterminate first-person singular, which encourages the imaginative inhabiting of a lyric 'I', drawing on techniques of thirteenth-century aristocratic role poetry, but merging them with liturgical practices of inhabiting the first-person speaker of the Psalms.[19]

Such opening up to new audiences, new forms, and new ways of transmission is not a linear process, and it is notable how both the reform movement of the fifteenth century and the Protestant rediscovery of some of these texts in the fifteenth century reinsert forms of

---

19   Annie Sutherland, 'Performing the Penitential Psalms: Maidstone and Bampton', in *Aspects of the Performative in Medieval Culture*, ed. by Manuele Gragnolati and Almut Suerbaum (Berlin: De Gruyter, 2014), pp. 15–38.

control. Where the fifteenth-century observant reform highlights the role of obedience, especially for religious women, seventeenth-century collectors such as Daniel Sudermann reinsert conceptions of male authorship by attributing songs such as 'Min geist hat sich ergangen' to Johannes Tauler. By reinserting the anonymous song into an authorial *oeuvre*, Sudermann's collection closes down the open semi-liturgical form by incorporating it into a closed, proprietorial biography: the songs are no longer the fluid results of a process of engaging imaginatively with Eckhart's processes of abnegation, but attributed to a specific period in Johannes Tauler's life, when the rubric claims he composed the song while staying with his sister during his final illness. None of this is historically attested, but the individualized reading deliberately narrows the scope of the song. In contrast with these biographical readings, familiar to us from the nineteenth century, the actual and lived openness of the fourteenth-century versions becomes all the more striking, and they attest to a different, more collective form of premodern textuality.

While these songs have often been neglected because they do not conform to aesthetic norms informed by modern notions of individual authorship, closed textuality, and subjective experience, they present us with a culture of openness in which these irregular, obscure, aesthetically 'wild' songs allow us a glimpse of poetic practices which are both collective and inclusive.

Openness and Intensity
Petrarch's Becoming Laurel in *Rerum vulgarium fragmenta* 23 and 228

MANUELE GRAGNOLATI AND FRANCESCA SOUTHERDEN

THE PLANT WORLD

This chapter explores the relationship between Petrarch, poet of the *Rerum vulgarium fragmenta* (henceforth *Rvf*), and the laurel tree, a symbol that usually stands for the poet's beloved Laura but in the two poems we will look at comes to be connected also with the lyric 'I'.[1] In other words, while the laurel is a pervasive symbol in Petrarch's *Rvf*, in keeping with the Ovidian myth of Apollo and Daphne, it is the *beloved* who is usually transformed into the laurel, frustrating the poet's desire to possess her and making that frustration the root of poetry. This scenario corresponds to Freud's idea of sublimation as the diversion of libidinal energies towards nonsexual aims — like artistic creation, intellectual pursuits, or, in general, objects of higher social value. The

---

1   This article has also appeared in Manuele Gragnolati and Francesca Southerden, *Possibilities of Lyric: Reading Petrarch in Dialogue; With an Epilogue by Antonella Anedda Angioy* (Berlin: ICI Berlin Press, 2020), pp. 45–63. We refer to Petrarch's collection — also known as the *Canzoniere* or *Rime sparse* — using the authorial Latin title.

body of Laura/Daphne that her lover fails to possess is 'transferred' into the poetic sign, and desire is 'sublimated' into verse.[2]

In keeping with Leo Bersani's concept of aesthetics and the way in which we have thought of Petrarch elsewhere, our approach here is to read Petrarch's lyric textuality not as transcending or 'taming' eros but as replicating the movement of desire, extending it to text, and allowing the reader to experience it.[3] In particular, we have looked at one of the poems we will analyse here, *canzone* 23, the so-called 'canzone delle metamorfosi' (*canzone* of the metamorphoses), and have argued that its textuality shapes a subjectivity that combines metamorphosis and hybridity and is centred on the poet's impossibility, or unwillingness, to relinquish sensual desire.[4]

In this chapter, we return to *Rvf* 23 and look at it together with another poem from Petrarch's collection, sonnet 228, and consider both from the perspective of the poet's fusion with the laurel. The 'becoming laurel' of our title is to be taken literally, since in these texts the Petrarchan subject *becomes* the laurel tree in *Rvf* 23 and has the laurel implanted into him in *Rvf* 228, then proceeding to beautify it with his tears and sighs. In looking at *Rvf* 23 and 228, we are interested in the kind of subjectivity and desire — or even sexuality — that might correspond to Petrarch's 'becoming' a laurel tree and that we might locate in relation to the plant world more broadly. Our sense is that

---

2   On this dynamic in Petrarch, see Lynn Enterline, 'Embodied Voices: Petrarch Reading Himself Reading Ovid', in *Desire in the Renaissance: Psychoanalysis and Literature*, ed. by Valeria Finucci and Regina Schwartz (Princeton: Princeton University Press, 1994), pp. 120–45; on Freudian sublimation, see Jean Laplanche and Jean-Bertrand Pontalis, *The Language of Psycho-Analysis*, trans. by Donald Nicholson-Smith (London: Hogarth Press, 1973), pp. 431–33.

3   See Leo Bersani, *The Freudian Body: Psychoanalysis and Art* (New York: Columbia University Press, 1986), esp. pp. 47–50.

4   See Gragnolati and Southerden, *Possibilities of Lyric*, pp. 17–44. On *Rvf* 23, see John Brenkman, 'Writing, Desire, Dialectic in Petrarch's *Rime* 23', *Pacific Coast Philology*, 9 (April 1974), pp. 12–19; Annalisa Cipollone, '"Né per nova figura il primo alloro ...": La chiusa di *Rvf* XXIII, Il *Canzoniere* e Dante', *Rassegna europea di letteratura italiana*, 11 (1998), pp. 29–46; Durling in his introduction to *Petrarch's Lyric Poems: The 'Rime Sparse' and Other Lyrics*, ed. and trans. by Robert M. Durling (Cambridge, MA: Harvard University Press, 1976), pp. 26–33; Giovanna Rabitti, '*Nel dolce tempo*: Sintesi o nuovo cominciamento?', in *Petrarca volgare e la sua fortuna sino al Cinquecento*, ed. by Bruno Porcelli (= *Italianistica*, 33.2 (May/August 2004)), pp. 95–108; Sara Sturm-Maddox, *Petrarch's Metamorphoses: Text and Subtext in the 'Rime Sparse'* (Columbia: University of Missouri Press, 1985), pp. 9–38; Gur Zak, *Petrarch's Humanism and the Care of the Self* (Cambridge: Cambridge University Press, 2010), pp. 35–37.

the 'becoming tree' entails a loss of self, a kind of dispossession and opening to the outside, that conveys a sense of desire not as lack but as intensity.

Our reading is shaped in dialogue with writers who have thought about plants and their modes of existence and have thereby suggested new ways to think about subjectivity — ways that we propose to connect with the concept of openness in the work of Rosi Braidotti. Specifically, we want to relate these ways of thinking about plants to Braidotti's concept of 'polymorphous vitalism', a means of experiencing desire not as a state of lack but as intensity and excess, which she has developed through Gilles Deleuze and Félix Guattari's notion of 'becoming'[5] — and that is the reason why the title of our chapter includes the idea of 'becoming'. For Braidotti, '[b]ecoming has to do with emptying out the self, opening it out to possible encounters with the "outside"', thereby expanding the possibilities of subjectivity and envisioning a self that can be 'joyfully discontinuous, as opposed to being mournfully consistent'.[6] In other words, becoming entails a loss of autonomy that is 'non-unitary' but not destructive. Insofar as 'the firm boundaries between self and other' dissolve, there is 'an enlargement of one's fields of perspective and capacity to experience', and this enlargement entails a space of becoming which does not limit love to the human subject but instead opens to a 'whole territory' around it.[7]

Some of the philosophers and theorists who have thought about plants have envisioned a similar kind of openness to the outside, like for instance Emanuele Coccia in his 2016 book *La vie des plantes: Une métaphysique du mélange* and Hélène Cixous in her novels *La* and *Illa*, especially as studied by Sarah-Anaïs Crevier Goulet.[8] The main idea here is the interconnectedness of plants, that is, the idea that they are

5   See Rosi Braidotti, 'Intensive Genre and the Demise of Gender', *Angelaki: Journal of the Theoretical Humanities*, 13.2 (2008), pp. 45–57, where she engages in depth with Gilles Deleuze and Félix Guattari, *A Thousand Plateaus: Capitalism and Schizophrenia*, trans. by Brian Massumi (Minneapolis: University of Minnesota Press, 1987).

6   Braidotti, 'Intensive Genre', p. 47.

7   Ibid., esp. pp. 55–56.

8   See Emanuele Coccia, *La Vie des plantes: Une métaphysique du mélange* (Paris: Éditions Payot & Rivages, 2016), in English as *The Life of Plants: A Metaphysics of Mixture*, trans. by Dylan J. Montanari (Cambridge: Polity Press, 2019), from which quotations are taken; Hélène Cixous, *La* (Paris: Gallimard, 1976) and *Illa* (Paris: Des Femmes, 1980), both discussed in detail by Sarah-Anaïs Crevier Goulet, 'Du jardin d'essai/*esse* à l'hortus conclusus: Figures de la naissance et du végétal dans l'oeuvre de Hélène

porous organisms, and that there is a fluid boundary between inside and outside such that the two become hard to differentiate. Plants' natural tendency is to spread: in *La*, Cixous's narrator describes how when she is in a garden to which she feels connected 'vegetally' ('J'ai toujours eu la certitude que j'étais liée à un vrai jardin par ... Parenté archivégétale?'), her body fuses with the earth and surrounding flora such that it is 'étendu partout', as stretched out and vast as the earth itself.[9] And plants are related to each other through an interconnectivity that is also evident in their spreading *across* the earth. According to Coccia, this spreading connotes an ultimate form of openness in the sense that the borders are undone between what we think of as 'the subject' and the milieu: 'One cannot separate the plant — *neither physically nor metaphysically* — from the world that accommodates it. It is the most intense, radical, and paradigmatic form of being in the world.'[10] This sort of 'being together', this coexisting, of plants is, as the title of Coccia's study indicates, a 'métaphysique du mélange' (metaphysics of mixture). In an even more open sense, this state of coexistence of plants is also a 'jumble' of things, for they are conjoined and yet still distinct from one another, in the way that things in an ecosystem are fundamentally entwined, but their particularity and distinctions are nonetheless maintained.[11]

Thinking about the sort of subjectivity to which this kind of 'mélange' might correspond, we find suggestive the following lines from Braidotti's essay on Virginia Woolf's relationship with Vita Sackville-West: a 'field [...] of perpetual becomings' in which '[w]hat happens is vitalist erotics, which includes intensive deterritorializations, unhealthy alliances, hybrid cross-fertilizations, productive anomalies and generative encounters — allowing 'the unfolding of ever-intensified affects'.[12] In Braidotti and in some other works that consider plants in relation to *eros*, this sort of openness and becoming relates to sexuality and not just desire. For example,

Cixous', in *Des jardins autres*, ed. by Paolo Alexandre Néné and Sarah Carmo (Paris: Archives Karéline, 2015), pp. 257–80.

9   Cixous, *La*, pp. 57–58.

10   Coccia, *Life of Plants*, p. 5 (emphasis ours).

11   As Coccia writes: 'In order for a climate to exist, all the elements within a given space must be at once mixed and identifiable' (ibid., p. 27).

12   Braidotti, 'Intensive Genre', p. 55.

Natania Meeker and Antónia Szabari have analysed the treatment of plants as modes for human sexuality in the seventeenth-century writings of Guy de la Brosse and Cyrano de Bergerac. Within those works, Meeker and Szabari have traced what they term 'a scene of queer animacy [a term they take from Mel Chen], in which affects and sensations are mobilized across different kinds of bodies and diverse modes of being'. This phenomenon is all the more surprising given that plants are usually considered asexual and yet become an (imagined) site of 'flexible and formally inventive pleasures', 'multiplying pleasures at the limit of what we might recognize as subjectivity itself'. Meeker and Szabari also cite Timothy Morton on tree-hugging as a form of eroticism, which suggests that '[t]o contemplate ecology's unfathomable intimacies is to imagine pleasures that are not hetero-normative, not genital, not geared towards where the body stops and starts'.[13]

This line of thought has been suggestive for our thinking about the Petrarchan subject's 'becoming laurel' in *Rvf* 23 and 228, where that opening to the *végétal* seems intimately bound to the question of pleasure for him.[14] In particular we would like to develop the connec-tion between Braidotti's concept of the 'di-vidual' or open subject, the vegetal, and the idea that it represents an intensification of desire.[15] In this sense, passivity is the possibility of 'an affective, de-personalized, highly receptive subject',[16] which is the closest Petrarch's 'I' gets to a form of dispossession (which the ego usually resists) and corresponds,

---

13   Natania Meeker and Antónia Szabari, 'Libertine Botany: Vegetal Sexuality and Vegetal Forms', *postmedieval: a journal of medieval cultural studies*, 9.4 (2018), pp. 478–89. The quotation from Morton is taken from his 'Guest Column: Queer Ecology', *PMLA*, 125.2 (2010), pp. 273–82 (p. 280).

14   On the concept of *végétal*, see Crevier Goulet, 'Du jardin d'essai/*esse*'; and for the way in which becoming-plant has been theorized in Deleuze and Guattari's *Mille plateaux*, see Hannah Stark, 'Deleuze and Critical Plant Studies', in *Deleuze and the Non/Human*, ed. by Jon Roffe and Hannah Stark (London: Palgrave Macmillan, 2015), pp. 180–96. See also Luce Irigaray and Michael Marder, *Through Vegetal Being: Two Philosophical Perspectives* (New York: Columbia University Press, 2016); Michael Marder, *Plant-Thinking: A Philosophy of Vegetal Life* (New York: Columbia University Press, 2013) and *The Philosopher's Plant: An Intellectual Herbarium*, with illustrations by Mathilde Roussel (New York: Columbia University Press, 2014).

15   See Rosi Braidotti, 'Writing as a Nomadic Subject', *Comparative Critical Studies*, 11.2–3 (2014), pp. 163–84, where she defines the 'di-vidual' as 'a singularity bounded by its own powers to endure intensities and relations to others' (p. 183 n. 9).

16   Braidotti, 'Intensive Genre', p. 46.

as we have begun to suggest, to an experience of desire not so much as lack but as intensity, or as Braidotti has called it, the 'intensive multipli[cation] of affects'.[17]

OPENING TO LOVE

Our analysis begins with *canzone* 23, where the poetic subject undergoes a series of transformations explicitly modelled on Ovid. The poem is a blueprint of Petrarch's early poetry, one centred on the unrequited love of the troubadour and the Ovidian traditions. In view of the latter, the poem focuses on the transformations of the 'I' through the effects of love — first into a laurel and then into swan, stone, fountain, flint, voice, and stag, evoking respectively the Ovidian myths of Daphne, Cygnus, Battus, Byblis, Echo, and Actaeon. All these are imposed on a helpless subject who has no choice but to yield to the force of sensual desire.

We are interested in the first three stanzas, which articulate the first metamorphosis of the 'I' — the one into a laurel — and situate it as the turning point in the subject's affective history. In particular, the poem opens with the idea that in his youth, a time defined in terms of freedom, or 'libertade', the poet was not subject to love. What is significant is that this state of not being touched by love is described in terms of enclosure and of a stone-like protection which was tearless and unbending:

> Nel dolce tempo de la prima etade,
> che nascer vide et anchor quasi in herba
> la fera voglia che per mio mal crebbe,
> perché cantando il duol si disacerba,
> canterò com'*io vissi in libertade,*
> *mentre Amor nel mio albergo a sdegno s'ebbe.*
> [...]
> I' dico che dal dí che 'l primo assalto
> mi diede Amor, molt'anni eran passati,
> sí ch'io cangiava il giovenil aspetto;
> e *d'intorno al mio cor pensier' gelati*
> *facto avean quasi adamantino smalto*
> *ch'allentar non lassava il duro affetto.* (1–6; 21–26)

---

17   Ibid., p. 48.

(In the sweet season of my first youth, | which saw the birth and budding growth | of the wild desire that grew to torment me, | I will sing, because singing renders grief | less bitter, *of how I lived in freedom then,* | *while Love was still scorned in my heart.* | [...] | I say, then, that many years had passed | since the day of Love's first assault, | so that my youthful aspect was changing; | and *icy thoughts around my heart* | *had made it almost as hard as diamond,* | *giving no rein to my obstinate desire.*)[18]

It is in this context that Love intervenes, and with the help of a 'powerful lady', Amor turns the subject into the laurel:

Lagrima anchor non mi bagnava il petto
né rompea il sonno, et quel che in me non era,
mi pareva un miracolo in altrui.
[...]
Ché sentendo il crudel di ch'io ragiono
infin allor percossa di suo strale
non essermi passato oltra la gonna,
prese in sua scorta una possente donna,
ver' cui poco già mai mi valse o vale
ingegno, o forza, o dimandar perdono;
e i duo mi trasformaro in quel ch'i' sono,
facendomi d'uom vivo un lauro verde,
che per fredda stagion foglia non perde. (27–29; 32–40)

(No tear yet stained my breast | or woke me from my sleep, and what I lacked | seemed miraculous in others. | [...] | For that pitiless foe of whom I speak, | seeing that none of his darts had yet | pierced beneath my clothing, | took into his service a powerful lady, | against whom neither cunning, nor force, | nor begging for mercy ever was (or is) much use; | and these two transformed me into what I am, | making of me, a living man, a laurel tree, | which, though winter come, never sheds a leaf.)

This first metamorphosis is thus set up as loss of autonomy, yet strangely it is not something merely negative but rather a softening. In other words, there is a twist in this part of the poem, and this twist with respect to the idea of wounding, penetrability, and porosity is seen as more positive. In *Rvf* 23, therefore, the idea of *libertade*

---

18   All quotations are from Francesco Petrarca, *Canzoniere*, ed. by Marco Santagata, rev. edn (Milan: Mondadori, 2010). Unless otherwise stated, English translations of Petrarch's lyric poems are by Caroline Dormor and Lachlan Hughes. All emphasis is ours.

and autonomy appears as something more limiting and resonates with Braidotti's stress on the open subject and what she calls the 'di-vidual': a 'subject-in-becoming' whose processes are 'collective, intersubjective and not individual or isolated'.[19] In other words, becoming the laurel really means an opening up to affect. Following Braidotti, who herself is in dialogue with Baruch Spinoza's *Ethics*, we can say that relinquishing *potestas* — the forms of restrictive and institutionalized power — allows for finding one's *potentia*, a state of creative potentiality and possibility that is the foundation of vitalist erotics.[20]

The actual metamorphosis is described in detail in stanza 3 of Petrarch's poem, in which the poet rewrites Ovid's description of Daphne turning into the laurel as his own transformation:

> Qual mi fec'io quando primier m'accorsi
> de la trasfigurata mia persona,
> e i capei vidi far di quella fronde
> di che sperato avea già lor corona,
> e i piedi in ch'io mi stetti, et mossi, et corsi,
> com'ogni membro a l'anima risponde,
> diventar due radici sovra l'onde
> non di Peneo, ma d'un più altero fiume,
> e n' duo rami mutarsi ambe le braccia! (41–49)

> (Imagine my surprise when first I took note | of my transfigured person, | and saw my hair become the very leaves | with which I had hoped to be crowned, | and my feet, with which I stood and walked and ran, | become two roots (since every member | answers to the soul) beside the rippling waters, | not of Peneus, but of a nobler river, | and both my arms transform into two branches!)

Critics have pointed out that the poet's transformation into the laurel in lines 38–40 (beautifully illustrated in a 1470 Venetian incunable now in the Biblioteca Queriniana in Brescia)[21] is connected to a passage from the *Triumphus Cupidinis* that describes love as complete loss

---

19   Braidotti, 'Writing as a Nomadic Subject', p. 173.

20   Ibid., pp. 171, 174–75.

21   The Petrarca Queriniano incunable is one of the most richly decorated examples of Petrarch's works produced in the fifteenth century. It can be viewed digitally at <http://www.misinta.it/biblioteca-digitale-misinta-2/1400-2/1470-petrarca-canzoniere-e-trionfi-miniato> [accessed 20 August 2020]. For further details on this incunable, see Francesco Petrarca, *Canzoniere, Trionfi: L'incunabolo veneziano di*

of control and autonomy and as all-consuming: 'e so in qual guisa | l'amante nell'amato si transforme' (and I know in what way | the lover turns into the beloved; III. 161–62).[22] Love is an experience of dispossession: for instance, Santagata talks of the poet being 'dispossessed of his own identity' (spossessato dalla propria identità) to the degree that he 'loses consciousness of himself' (perde coscienza di sé). The experience is a form of 'ecstatic forgetfulness' (smemoramento estatico).[23] Moreover, the concept of the lover's transformation into the beloved seems to displace into a lyric context the theological concept of 'compassion', that is, the idea that Mary's love for Christ during his Passion transformed her into an image of her son because, as Bonaventure writes, 'the power of love transforms the lover into an image of the beloved' (vis amoris amantem in amati similitudinem transformat).[24]

If we want to understand better what it means to 'become laurel' in Rvf 23, we could look at the metamorphoses that follow, but actually reading the poem it becomes clear that all that matters is the first metamorphosis: the following ones are either temporary or a fantasy and did not actually happen.[25] What this means is that the poet never got out of being a laurel, and indeed line 38 states: 'i duo mi trasformaro in quel ch'i' sono' (and these two transformed me into what I am), so it is clear that the actual permanent condition of the lyric 'I' is the one described in lines 17–20:

> et un penser che solo angoscia dàlle,
> tal ch'ad ogni altro fa voltar le spalle,
> e mi face obliar me stesso a forza:
> che tèn di me quel d'entro e io la scorza. (17–20)

Vindelino da Spira del 1470 nell'esemplare della Biblioteca civica Queriniana di Brescia con figure dipinte da Antonio Grifo, INC. G V 15, ed. by Giuseppe Frasso, Giordana Mariani, and Ennio Sandal (Rome: Salerno, 2016).

22   The Triumphi are quoted from Francesco Petrarca, Trionfi, Rime estravaganti, Codice degli abbozzi, ed. by Vinicio Pacca and Laura Paolino (Milan: Mondadori, 1996). Translations are ours.

23   See Santagata's note in Petrarca, Canzoniere, p. 105.

24   Bonaventure, De assumptione B. Virginis Mariae, sermo 2, in Bonaventurae opera omnia, ed. by PP. Collegii S. Bonaventurae, 10 vols (Quaracchi: Collegium S. Bonaventurae, 1882–1902), IX (1901), p. 161; see also Otto G. von Simpson, 'Compassio and Co-redemptio in Roger van der Weyden's Descent from the Cross', Art Bulletin, 25 (1953), pp. 9–16.

25   On this dynamic, see Gragnolati and Southerden, Possibilities of Lyric, pp. 17–44.

(and a single thought which causes only anguish, | and makes me deaf to all other thoughts, | and forces me to forget myself entirely: | for it governs all that is in me, and I only the shell.)

The image of the 'scorza' (literally the bark of the tree) makes it clear that here the poetic subject really *is a* tree: he is only thinking of Laura, and that thought alienates him from himself as a sense of fusion into the beloved that dispossesses the lover of his identity. *That* seems to be the state of being turned into Laura. That condition, after all, is the result of a violent transformation — but at the end of the poem it is also revealed to be a pleasurable one:

né per nova figura il primo alloro
seppi lassar, ché pur la sua dolce ombra
ogni men bel piacer del cor mi sgombra. (167–69)

(nor could I ever leave the first laurel behind | for a new form, for its sweet shade | expels all lesser pleasure from my heart.)

In these lines, too, there is a striking combination of identity and alterity in the relationship between the poetic subject and the laurel tree. On the one hand, as Carla Freccero has argued, there seems to be an irreducible 'masculinized identification' between the poet and the 'alloro', which reiterates the initial dynamic of the transformation into the 'lauro verde'.[26] On the other hand, with the 'nova figura', the gender of the subject shifts between masculine and feminine, and as Marguerite Waller has noted, the 'ombra' itself is both double and a locus of instability: 'The shadow of the laurel is his shadow and he is, in some sense, its shadow [...], but his awareness of that fact prevents reification of himself in the image of some seemingly more substantial counter.'[27] Santagata glosses the final line, on the effects of this shadow, as: 'it chases from my heart all other passion as less beautiful' (mi scaccia dal cuore ogni altra passione, come meno bella), where passion

---

26 See Carla Freccero, 'Ovidian Subjectivities in Early Modern Lyric: Identification and Desire in Petrarch and Louise Labé', in *Ovid and the Renaissance Body*, ed. by Goran Stanivukovic (Toronto: University of Toronto Press, 2001), pp. 21–37 (esp. pp. 27–30).

27 See Marguerite Waller, *Petrarch's Poetics and Literary History* (Amherst: University of Massachusetts Press, 1980), p. 104.

is pleasure and carries this paradoxical tone that for us is a cipher of Petrarchan desire and pleasure.[28]

MÉLANGE

While *canzone* 23 stages the poet's transformation into the laurel, in *Rvf* 228 Love opens the left side of the lyric subject and plants the laurel tree in the middle of his heart. In this poem we find an opening and a wound, which is followed by an act of nurturing, and indeed critics such as Nicholas Mann have spoken of Petrarch as a 'gardener' in relation to this sonnet, one who 'cultivates' the laurel in the double sense of the Latin *cultus*, meaning both to 'cultivate' and to 'worship':[29]

> Amor co la man dextra il lato manco
> m'aperse, e piantòvi entro in mezzo 'l core
> un lauro verde sí che di colore
> ogni smeraldo avria ben vinto et stanco.
>
> Vomer di pena, con sospir' del fianco,
> e 'l piover giú dagli occhi un dolce humore
> l'addornâr sì, ch'al ciel n'andò l'odore,
> qual non so già se d'altre frondi unquanco.
>
> Fama, Honor et Vertute et Leggiadria,
> casta bellezza in habito celeste
> son le radici de la nobil pianta.
>
> Tal la mi trovo al petto, ove ch'i' sia,
> felice incarco; et con preghiere honeste
> l'adoro e 'nchino come cosa santa.
>
> (Love opened my left side with his right hand | and planted, in the middle of my heart, | a laurel tree so green in colour | that it would far outshine any emerald. || The ploughshare of pain, the sighs of my heart, | and the raining down of sweet tears from my eyes | have so embellished it that its fragrance wafted heavenward; | I do not think that other leaves have ever equalled it. || Fame, honour, virtue, grace, | chaste beauty with

---

28   See Santagata's note in Petrarch, *Canzoniere*, p. 123.

29   Nicholas Mann, 'Petrarca giardiniere (a proposito del sonetto ccxxviii)', *Letture Petrarce*, 12 (1992), pp. 235–56. On the broader topic of Petrarch and gardens, see also William Tronzo, *Petrarch's Two Gardens: Landscape and the Image of Movement* (New York: Italica Press, 2014), pp. 1–23. This image of Love as 'gardener' is also present in *Rvf* 64. 6–7: 'del petto ove dal primo lauro innesta | Amor più rami'.

celestial demeanour: | these are the roots of the noble plant. ||
Wherever I am, I find it a happy burden | on my chest; and with
honest prayers | I adore and bow to it as a sacred thing.)

A wound that is opened by Love is a common image in the lyric
tradition, but here it also alludes to the Christian trope of receiving the
stigmata. Yet with Coccia's earlier suggestion in mind, it is impossible
to read the poem and consider the plant as separate from the world
that accommodates it. So, while the 'I' does not *become* the laurel in
this poem (as it did in *Rvf* 23), there is a mixing of the 'I' with the tree.
In the case of the Petrarchan sonnet, the 'I' is the 'world that receives'
the plant, and as in *Rvf* 23 we find an 'impossible separation' between
the subject and the laurel. In *Rvf* 23 it is a result of transformation, and
in *Rvf* 228 it is in Coccia's sense of *mélange*.

Sonnet 228 opens by reiterating the beginning of *Rvf* 23 and
describes the origin of the poet's love for Laura: Love, Amor, takes
hold of the subject and literally opens ('m'aperse') his left side and
implants the laurel into the very centre of his heart ('in mezzo al
core'). Then the poet cultivates the plant with his suffering and by
watering it with tears, which in a very Petrarchan way are defined
oxymoronically as 'dolce humore' (sweet water). This bodily act of
nurturing the plant makes it special and unique, and the word 'odore',
relating to the fragrance of the tree, indicates the sensual character of
the poet's desire. Yet 'odore' also evokes the 'arbor odorifera' (fragrant
tree) of Petrarch's *Coronation Oration* (Collatio laureationis), where
the laurel is the symbol of poetic fame and glory, as well as the *dolce
lignum* of the cross and the sweet fragrance linked to God.[30] Indeed,
as Manuela Boccignone has shown, if the beloved's presence in the

---

30 On these intertexts see Rosanna Bettarini's commentary on line 7 of the poem in
Petrarca, *Canzoniere*, p. 1056. The reference to the sweet fragrance of the Lord comes
in Genesis 8. 21, 'Odoratusque est Dominus odorem suavitatis', as Castelvetro notes in
his commentary (also cited in Bettarini). On *dulcedo* and *suavitas* as characteristics of
God, see also Mary Carruthers, *The Experience of Beauty in the Middle Ages* (Oxford:
Oxford University Press, 2013), pp. 80–107. Petrarch's *Collatio laureationis* is available
in English as 'Petrarch's Coronation Oration', trans. by Ernest Hatch Wilkins, *PMLA*,
68.5 (December 1953), pp. 1241–50. The Latin text is in *Opere latine di Francesco
Petrarca*, ed. by Antonietta Bufano, 2 vols (Turin: Unione tipografico-Editrice Torinese, 1975), II, pp. 1255–83. According to Mann, 'Petrarca giardiniere', pp. 244–45,
the perfume of the tree can also be connected to the fame and immortality the poet
seeks to bestow on Laura; he cites Song of Songs 1. 3 ('unguentum effusionis nomen
tuum') and Catullus VI. 16–17 as possible sources.

poet's heart is a common, well-established motif of the lyric tradition, the image of the tree implanted in the heart corresponds to the cross and has a strong Christological connotation in medieval allegorical tradition, which we might also perceive in poems in which Petrarch consciously sets the laurel tree, associated with Laura, against the tree of the cross (see especially *Rvf* 142).[31]

The following tercet describes the laurel, that is, the beloved Laura, as a 'nobil pianta', suggesting that the beloved is a noble and even pure being, and it is therefore different from the way in which Laura is often described as incompatible with God and even as his enemy. Laura would seem to be not an evil distraction but rather depicted in the lyric mode associated with the divinization of the *donna*, more in line with a certain *stilnovo* mode that runs from Guinizzelli to Dante. At this point it would seem that there is nothing problematic in this love — and indeed critics have even read the poem as signalling 'the protagonist's progress on the arc of his spiritual journey' insofar as it stages 'the ordering of the inchoate matter of the passions into a new textual body of the virtues'.[32] Instead, we argue that a real turn takes place in the following and final tercet, actually in the last line and its vertiginous twist: up to 'preghiere oneste', the reader expects the sonnet to culminate with a sort of moral climax, but instead suddenly we are presented with an image of idolatry: 'l'adoro e inchino come cosa santa' (I adore and bow to it as a sacred thing). The verb 'adoro' signals the conflation, since it means both to show devotion to a divinity and, in courtly lyric, to worship the beloved lady as though she were divine. (It is, for example, found in Giacomo da Lentini, Chiaro Davanzati, and Cino da Pistoia.)

A suggestive antecedent for this conflation may be found in the final stanza of Guido Cavalcanti's *ballata* 'Perch'i' no spero di tonar giammai':

---

31   Manuela Boccignone, 'Un albero piantato nel cuore (Petrarca e Iacopone)', *Lettere italiane*, 52.2 (April–June 2000), pp. 225–64. On the image of the tree in Petrarch and Jacopone, see Lina Bolzoni, *La rete delle immagini: Predicazione in volgare dalle origini a Bernardino da Siena* (Turin: Einaudi, 2002), pp. 103–44.

32   See most recently Thomas E. Peterson, '"Amor co la man dextra il lato manco" (*Rvf* 228) as Allegory of Religious Veneration', *MLN*, 135.1 (January 2020), pp. 17–33 (pp. 31–32).

Tu, voce sbigottita e deboletta
ch'esci piangendo de lo cor dolente,
coll'anima e con questa ballatetta
va' ragionando della strutta mente.
Voi troverete una donna piacente,
di sì dolce intelletto
che vi sarà diletto
starle davanti ognora.
Anim', e tu l'adora
sempre, nel su' valore. (37–46)

(Bewildered and frail voice, | you who weeping leave my griev-
ing heart, | with my soul and this little ballata | tell her of my
fractured mind. | You will find a dazzling lady, | with such sweet
intellection | that it will delight you | to remain eternally in
her presence. | Then, my soul, adore her | always, in all her
valour.)[33]

As Claudio Giunta has observed, Cavalcanti's poem is constructed
upon the model of contemporary wills and testament and, in particular, reproduces the motif of the *commendatio anime*, that is, the
recommendation of one's soul to God with the hope that after death
it may succeed in enjoying the beatific vision. Significantly, though,
Cavalcanti's text replaces God with the lady and concludes by making
the wish that the poet's soul dwell in an eternal contemplation of his
beloved, where the verb 'adora', which resonates with the biblical line
'quia ipse est dominus tuus et adora eum' (Psalm 44. 12), suggests a
love that is experienced with the intensity of faith.[34]

Petrarch's sonnet undertakes a similar operation and concludes by
staging what in Augustinian terms can be understood as a form of idolatry, that is, the act of turning the creature into the Creator and thereby
perverting the *ordo amoris*, according to which worldly, mortal things
are not to be desired or enjoyed per se but used as instruments (objects
of use, *uti*) that move the soul towards God, who alone represents the

---

33   The quotation from Cavalcanti is taken from Guido Cavalcanti, *Rime*, ed. by Roberto
      Rea and Giorgio Inglese (Rome: Carocci, 2011). Translation by Caroline Dormor and
      Lachlan Hughes.

34   Claudio Giunta, *Codici: Saggi sulla poesia del Medioevo* (Bologna: il Mulino, 2005),
      pp. 45–61. The biblical reference is noted by Roberto Rea in his commentary to the
      poem in Cavalcanti, *Rime*, p. 199. On Cavalcanti's ironic use of biblical intertexts, see
      Paola Nasti, 'Nozze e vedovanza: Dinamiche dell'appropriazione biblica in Cavalcanti
      e Dante', *Tenzone*, 7 (2006), pp. 71–110.

ultimate object of desire and the only object of enjoyment (*frui*).[35] In John Freccero's reading, this kind of idolatry, which is a recurrent feature of Petrarch's *Rvf*, corresponds to a reification of the sign and of desire, both of which are emblematized in the figure of the laurel, which Petrarch makes into a self-sufficient symbol of poetic autonomy: 'a poetry whose real subject matter is its own act and whose creation is its own author' with no reference to the world beyond the one the *Rvf* itself creates. For Freccero, this project risks stripping both the poet's beloved (Laura) and desire of their vitality in order to arrive at immortality and the illusion of substance, when really the object the poet pursues is a mirage, and the sign, in the absence of an external referent, remains opaque and unknowable.[36] In contrast, while our reading of the two poems acknowledges the presence of the idea of desire as non-progression as well as the presentation of the poet's fidelity to love as wrong in Augustinian terms, we contend that ultimately the poems do not present the steadfastness of the poet's desire for Laura as mere reification or fixation, but rather as a paradoxical openness to passion and the susceptibility to being moved.

The proposition with which we would like to conclude this chapter is that the connection between the poet and the laurel, which is unusual not in terms of frequency but in terms of modality, is a sign of a profound intimacy between *canzone* 23 and sonnet 228 — an intimacy that is certainly related to the poet's unwavering sensual desire but that also helps us to appreciate an aspect that is usually less perceived in Petrarch's poetry: the paradoxical pleasure deriving from dispossession and softening the boundaries with the other.[37] Sonnet 228 may even convey a sense of commingling at the level of sound, in the linguistic texture of the words, since according to Mann we might see in the 'core' (heart) of line 2 a fusion of 'or' and 'co' sounds, the first

---

35   See Augustine, *De doctrina christiana*, *Patrologia Latina*, ed. by J.-P. Migne, 221 vols (Paris: Garnier, 1844–64), 34. 15–122 (liber I, caput 4). On this distinction, see also Elena Lombardi, *The Syntax of Desire: Language and Love in Augustine, the Modistae, Dante* (Toronto: University of Toronto Press, 2007), p. 15.

36   John Freccero, 'The Fig Tree and the Laurel: Petrarch's Poetics', *Diacritics*, 5.1 (spring 1975), pp. 34–40 (esp. pp. 38–39). On petrified immobility as the hallmark of *canzone* 23, see also Teodolinda Barolini, 'The Making of a Lyric Sequence: Time and Narrative in Petrarch's *Rerum vulgarium fragmenta*', *MLN*, 104.1 (January 1989), pp. 1–38 (p. 30).

37   On paradoxical pleasure, see Gragnolati and Southerden, *Possibilities of Lyric*, pp. 17–44.

of which runs from 'Amor' (line 1) through to 'adoro' (line 14) and the last of which is especially prominent in the final line, 'l'adoro e 'nchino come cosa santa'.[38] In the case of both poems, this pleasure comes from the subject's passivity, which enables it to be penetrated and affected from the outside and after to remain in that state as one of unparalleled 'sweetness' (dolcezza; Rvf, 23) and 'happy burden' (felice incarco; Rvf, 228). Our hypothesis is that this paradoxical pleasure is connected to the plant imagery informing the two poems, and that if read with the works that have recently focused on the plants' mode of existence, our two texts vibrate with a desire that makes the subject boundless and expands it into the experience of intensity.

---

38   See Mann, 'Petrarca giardiniere', p. 252.

III. COMMUNITY

Highest Openness
On Agamben's Promise
DAMIANO SACCO

The question of the promise, be that in philosophy or in any general-ized field of critical enquiry, is perhaps always completely reducible to the promise of the question itself. That is to say, the question of the stakes of the promise — the promise of thinking, of philosophy, of lit-erature — is to be traced to the promise of the question itself, i.e. to the promise of the question that thinking is expected to deliver. It is then only natural, given this notion of promise — of promise as a certain openness to the question — to ask whether there might be a highest promise to attend to, a most urgent one, as it were. As such, the highest promise would stand for the utmost openness to the question. In the following, the three guidelines of openness, promise, and question are traced back to the one self-constituting and self-promising openness that serves as a common ground for all three guidelines: the openness and promise of language.

*

The occasion for the present discussion of the question of openness and promise is provided by the conjuncture of these themes in two of Giorgio Agamben's seminal works, namely *The Open: Man and*

Animal and *The Highest Poverty: Monastic Rules and Form-of-Life*.[1] In these two works, the themes of openness and promise are unfolded in thirteenth-century settings instantiated, firstly, by the discussion of a messianic miniature depicting a form of reconciliation between animal and human natures, and, secondly, by the analysis of the vow or promise pledged by the Franciscans upon entering monastic life. The question to be addressed here will be the extent to which the notion of openness put forth in *The Open* can be connected to the question of the promise, precisely through the messianic element introduced by the miniature, and, vice versa, the extent to which the question of the promise or vow addressed in *The Highest Poverty* can be set in dialogue, in spite or by virtue of the cloistered nature of the cenoby, with a certain notion of openness.

The first section of this essay introduces the notion of openness developed by Agamben in *The Open*, and positions it with respect to Agamben's broader philosophical project. *The Open* confronts the *locus classicus* of the relation between man and animal by means of a reading of Martin Heidegger's seminal 1929–30 lecture course. Through a discussion of the different forms of openness that, according to Heidegger, distinguish man from the animal, Agamben presents his own notion of openness as that of a constitutive element of the concept of life itself. Openness will stand in this instance for a certain void of representation that articulates the very separation between human life and animal life. The discussion of the messianic miniature found in *The Open* will introduce the promise, and at the same time the danger, that this notion of openness constitutes for the Western philosophical and political traditions. The second section, 'Promise I', effects a transition between this notion of openness and that of a certain structure of the promise, namely a certain horizon of messianicity that cannot be reduced to any particular messianism. The third section presents that which, according to Agamben's *The Highest Poverty*, has been one of the most successful attempts in the Western tradition at constituting a life that inhabits this openness and this promise, namely the *experimentum vitae* of the Franciscans. Through the unique form of their vow and of

---

1   Giorgio Agamben, *The Open: Man and Animal*, trans. by Kevin Attell (Stanford: Stanford University Press, 2003); Giorgio Agamben, *The Highest Poverty: Monastic Rules and Form-of-Life*, trans. by Adam Kotsko (Stanford: Stanford University Press, 2013).

their promise, the Franciscans are claimed to come closest to inhabiting that openness that in the miniature of *The Open* has been set as the
very horizon of messianicity. The last section, 'Promise II', points to
the common ground that underlies the two instances of openness and
promise presented in *The Open* and in *The Highest Poverty*, namely the
openness and promise of language itself.

THE OPEN

Agamben introduces the question of man and animal, the question of
'the open' according to the title of his book, through the discussion
of a miniature found in a Jewish Bible of the thirteenth century. The
miniature depicts the messianic banquet in which 'the just ones' will
take part at the end of time. The righteous ones — the 'rest' who will
be there when the Messiah arrives — are depicted in the miniature
as having human bodies and animal heads: more precisely, as having
the heads of the four eschatological animals (the cock, the eagle, the
ox, and the lion). To all appearances, Agamben seems to open his
book on the question of man and animal by means of a miniature
that depicts the very becoming redundant of this question: at the end
of time, the question of man and animal will no longer be a relevant
one — there will be no animal nature that is disavowed to erect the
dignity of the human, and there will be no intrinsic essence of man
that is founded through the exclusion of the animal. The righteous
ones appear to be, at least in Agamben's reading, completely indifferent
to the question of man and animal, and therefore to what we should
trust to be the question of the open. After a brief appearance, the
miniature is left behind; the book then turns to the discussion of a
number of philosophical references, ranging from Bataille and Kojève
to Benjamin and Heidegger.

The theoretical backbone of Agamben's argument is indeed developed through a reading of Heidegger's 1929–30 lecture course
entitled *The Fundamental Concepts of Metaphysics: World, Finitude, Solitude*, which was not published until 1983, in German (in Italian in
1992 and in English in 1995).[2] The question of man and animal is

---

2   Martin Heidegger, *The Fundamental Concepts of Metaphysics: World, Finitude, Solitude*,
     trans. by William McNeill and Nicholas Walker (Bloomington: Indiana University
     Press, 1995).

then confronted by Agamben through a reading of Heidegger's own confrontation. It is by now apparent, however, that it is in no way immediately clear what the question itself of man and animal could be. Is the question at stake 'what is the difference between man and animal?' Or perhaps 'what is the relation between them — what is proper to man that the animal lacks and what is proper to the animal that man supplements with a specific capacity, perhaps of being the animal that speaks, the political animal, and so forth?' From the start, both Agamben and Heidegger make it clear that the question cannot be approached in this way. All these standpoints, Heidegger argues, end up anthropomorphizing the animal or 'animalizing' man. On the contrary, the claim is that the question is to be approached only by following a directive provided by a certain notion of openness. The animal, Heidegger will conclude, is not 'open' to the entity (*das Seiende*, a particular being) — which is to say, the animal is not 'open' to any being that can be said to be or to exist (this flower, this stone, the sun). And yet, at the same time, one cannot quite deduce from this that the animal is instead closed off from the entity. For if the animal cannot be said to have access to the entity, to be open to it, this access cannot be said to be refused to the animal either — for that would imply the very possibility for this access to be either granted or refused in the first place. That is to say, according to Heidegger, the animal has no access to the play of openness and closedness, the concealment and unconcealment of entities and of something like a 'world.' Building on Uexküll's work,[3] Heidegger will argue that the animal consists — at least from the human standpoint — of a set of instinctual relations that are dis-inhibited or activated by a certain entity. For example, a tick consists of nothing but a few of these relations or drives: the one activated by the smell of an animal that makes the insect drop onto it, the one that compels the tick to ascertain the temperature of the body and confirm that the landing has been successful, and finally the one that drives the tick to find the least hairy spot to start feeding.[4] Beyond these privileged channels of experience of its surroundings, however,

---

3   Jakob von Uexküll, *A Foray into the Worlds of Animals and Men: With a Theory of Meaning*, trans. by Joseph D. O'Neil (Minneapolis: University of Minnesota Press, 2010).

4   Ibid., pp. 44–45.

the animal is claimed to have no relation to the world. To support his claim, Heidegger will refer to an experiment performed on bees in which they dis-inhibit the drive to suck honey. Once the experimenter cuts the bee's abdomen open, Heidegger reports, the bee simply keeps sucking and dis-inhibiting its drive, unconcerned with the fact that the honey flows right out of its abdomen.

On the other hand, if the animal is neither quite open to nor quite closed off from the existent, the latter is not just open (*offen*) to man but is in fact manifest (*offenbar*), literally open-able.[5] In other words, man is open to the existent not only as to a dis-inhibitor to a drive, but is open to the very possibility (*-bar*) of suspending the relation to the entity — that is, through this suspension, man is open to the very domain of possibility (once again, *-bar*, '-able') of either being open to or closed off from the existent (with the *-bar* barring a simple openness to the entity, and, at the same time, enabling a different 'openness' to, or possibility for, openness and closed-off-ness). A certain notion of 'difference' between man and animal, then, starts to emerge: a difference that nevertheless does not quite qualify as one between two entities, for at stake is precisely a notion of openness to the world — a notion of openness to difference itself. The difficulty encountered in posing the question of man and animal as a question of difference between two entities is then traced to the allegedly more fundamental 'difference' that obtains between these two entities insofar as *their very relation to difference itself,* their very openness to the world, is at stake.

The key point to be taken in order to return to Agamben and, eventually, to the messianic miniature is the following: Heidegger traces the issue of the distinction between man and animal back to a prior notion of openness, an openness that grants man access to the existent while refusing the animal not only this access, but the very

---

5   'Beings are *not manifest* [*offenbar*] to the behaviour of the animal in its captivation, they are not disclosed to it and for that very reason are *not closed off* from it either. Captivation stands outside this possibility. As far as the animal is concerned we cannot say that beings are closed off from it. Beings could only be closed off if there were some possibility of disclosure at all, however slight that might be. But the captivation of the animal places the animal essentially outside of the possibility that beings could be either disclosed to it or closed off from it. To say that captivation is the essence of animality means: *The animal as such does not stand within a manifestness* [*Offenbarkeit*] *of beings. Neither its so-called environment nor the animal itself are manifest as beings'* (Heidegger, *Fundamental Concepts of Metaphysics*, p. 248).

possibility for this access to be either granted or denied. If the animal can be considered to be neither open to the existent nor closed off from it, man appears to be characterized not simply by a structural openness to the world but by the very possibility of a play between openness and closedness, concealment and unconcealment. It is, then, in the very possibility of *not* having access to the existent that man and animal seem to show their closest connection *and*, at the same time, their most conspicuous difference. Heidegger will provide in this respect a lengthy phenomenological description of the experience of profound boredom in order to present the possibility of the complete suspension of man's access to entities and to the world. Profound boredom (*tiefe Langeweile*) constitutes — like its better-known counterpart in *Being and Time*, Angst — one of the *existentialia* through which the structure and possibilities of existence can come to appear in existence itself. In profound boredom, it is the very domain of the possibilities of entities — the possibility for this book to entertain, to disappoint, for the train to arrive, and so on — it is these very possibilities that come to be at stake by refusing themselves completely, leaving man in a state of impotence with respect to the sheer indifference of the world (with the *-bar* of *offenbar* functioning only as a closure rather than also as an access to the domain of possibility). It is, then, in the deactivation of the possibilities of entities, in the disappearance of the possibilities of possibilities themselves, that man's relation to the world — man's relation to a world that refuses itself — lies closest to that of the animal. For when the existent appears to refuse itself completely to us, how is one still to make a case for a fully constituted difference between man's closure and the animal's structural impossibility of having access to the very play between openness and closure to the world? How is one to tell apart, in the space opened by the very refusal of the existent, man's actual and effective closure from the animal's allegedly constitutive *fore*closure? Agamben writes:

> The man who becomes bored finds himself in the 'closest prox-imity' — even if it is only apparent — to animal captivation. Both are, in their most proper gesture, *open to a closedness*; they are totally delivered over to something that obstinately refuses itself.[6]

---

6   Agamben, *The Open*, p. 65.

It appears that the very possibility of being closed off from entities delineates a space in which man and animal might be as close as they can be, a space in which it becomes impossible to determine whether a tangency or a lack of contact between the two realms is at stake.

*

Agamben's own gesture lies in zooming in on this particular space — on the space between man and animal, a space that precedes the *difference* between man and animal, for at stake in this space is precisely difference itself. The title of Agamben's book, *The Open*, does not signal simply the open of the world or of the disclosure of entities, but also the open of this space, the open of a void of representation that simultaneously joins and disjoins man and animal. The void of this space can, in fact, be approached only asymptotically: either from the animal side — but man cannot fully translate the experience of the animal into conceptual terms — or from man's side, but again at that point at which the world refuses itself completely to us and every possibility of conceptualization fails. On the one hand, the animal is open to a closure, or better to a *fore*closure, in that it can neither be said to be open to the entity nor to be closed off from it; proper to man, on the other hand, is instead the possibility to suspend, in certain existential states, his relation to the world — and, through this suspension, to be open, paradoxically, to the (fore)closure that is proper to the animal.

The question of this void, of the open of this void of representation, is for Agamben not only a theoretical question, but also eminently *the* political question, a question that concerns precisely the threshold that makes possible the articulation between man and animal. Agamben claims that the articulation between man and animal takes place through the suspension of one domain, that of the animal, its exclusion, and the foundation of man through the capture of what has been suspended and excluded. The articulation of man and animal functions, then, according to a logic of the exception (*ex-capere*), namely by means of a capture (*capere*) or inclusion *by way of* an exclusion (*ex*). According to Agamben, the anthropogenic machine, i.e. the metaphysical apparatus (*dispositivo*) that engenders our concept of 'man', affords the production of the human always by excluding something akin to the 'animal', and by constantly redefining the limit at which a life can properly be called human. Agamben's notion of 'bare life' is precisely that of a threshold at which life enters the political domain — once again, a void of representation that articulates the boundary between animal life (ζωή) and politically qualified life (βίος):

> Like every space of exception, this zone is, in truth, perfectly empty, and the truly human being who should occur there is only the place of a ceaselessly updated decision in which the caesurae and their rearticulation are always dislocated and displaced anew. What would thus be obtained, however, is neither an animal life nor a human life, but only a life that is separated and excluded from itself — only a *bare life*.[7]

Power, that as such is always bio-power, decides, i.e. according to the etymology of the word 'separates', which lives are worthy of the political domain and which lives are to be excluded from it — which lives can be killed and which lives are worth being saved.

Once the space of the political has been identified with the decision, the separation and the articulation that take place in and through the anthropogenic apparatus, the question, and in fact the task come to be located in a certain halting of this metaphysical machine — that is, the task comes to be that of thinking, and therefore enabling, a life that is not separated from its bare life, a life that is not grounded by the exclusion of a 'bare' hypostasis. For Agamben, the exhibiting of this void of representation coincides with disclosing the possibility of its interruption, a possibility that is coextensive with a promise. The miniature with which the book opens can then be read as the presentation of a messianic setting in which the anthropogenic machine would be interrupted, in which it would no longer be possible to decide and separate what is human from what is animal. In this framework, messianicity would be coextensive with a deactivation of the mechanism by which life is articulated through the separation and exclusion of a certain kind of life itself. Animal life and properly human life, *zoe* and *bios*, would not be raised and reconciled in a higher form of life, but their opposition would rather precipitate by means of an interruption

---

7   Ibid., p. 38.

of gravity itself: as Agamben has it, the two terms of the opposition would 'coincide' in the etymological signification of falling together. The open, the void that served to articulate the anthropogenic machine, would come to be deactivated, and would thus provide the living being with the possibility of inhabiting it in a new mode. To install oneself in this space of indifference to the human and to the animal, in this space of profound boredom, in which it is undecidable whether one has suspended the human relation to the world or whether one has achieved the animal foreclosure to entities — to inhabit the form of life of the righteous ones in the messianic miniature — would imply accessing that which Agamben calls a state of happiness.

PROMISE I

One could then venture to postulate a link between this notion of openness to the world or to the existent — of openness to the other, of openness as the transcendence of always being (*sein*) in the open of a there (*da*), i.e. the Heideggerian notion of the transcendence of *Dasein* — *and* a particular structure of 'messianicity', a dimension of the messianic opened by the promise. Crucially, however, the messianicity instituted by this promise or openness would not be reducible to any of the historical messianisms of the Judaeo-Christian tradition, but would rather first provide the very ground for their possibility. It is through this link that we are to understand the appearance of the messianic miniature that opens Agamben's book. The depiction of the righteous ones does not merely display the end of time or the end of violence, exclusion, and injustice by means of a realized transcendence — i.e. by means of the transcendence of a future that would bring about a final reconciliation or appeasement of the constitutive scission that marks profane time. On the contrary, the righteous ones make manifest, that is, *offenbar*, the very structure of promise or messianicity *as such*. That is to say, they *live*, as indicated by their having the heads of the eschatological animals, a notion of eschatology that is equivalent to the transcendence or openness of life: they live this transcendence not as a supplemental attribute or hidden power, but as the matter of life itself. It is in this sense that that the structure of eschatology displayed in the miniature cannot be traced back to any notion of teleology, but rather provides a space to think the difference itself between telos and eschaton, namely the difference between the end of time and the time of the end. It is then a priority to dissociate as firmly as possible this structure of messianicity or openness from the teleology of any messianism. The following are four indicative pointers to this irreducibility.[8]

1. Messianicity as openness to the other is not exclusively directed at the future. In this regard, we, and most of all Agamben himself, owe to Benjamin the thinking of the claim that the past makes upon us, a claim that constitutes us in our openness towards an other that is neither present nor to come, and that is therefore not reducible to the possibility of the coming of any messiah. 'We', as Benjamin says, have been entrusted with a promise: that of redeeming not our future, but the future of the past; that is to say, we have been entrusted with the task of redeeming the possibilities that have never taken place, the possibilities that in not being actualized have been missed.[9] We have been promised: that is, *we* have been set as the transitive object of a promise — a promise that lays with us the impossible task of redeeming the missed possibilities of the past. A redemption that would not simply be a recuperation, but a setting free of these missed possibilities: a setting free of the past, of the future of the past, and of the future that lies ahead of this present or future setting free — a redemption of time itself.[10] We constitute the messianicity of the past that entrusts us with this task, and, at the same time, we are ourselves constituted by this very messianicity as if by an openness to

---

8   The following reflections are based on a somewhat peculiar Derridean reading of Agamben and Benjamin. For the notions of 'impossible mourning', 'messianicity without messianism', and the speculative difference between eschaton and telos, see e.g. Jacques Derrida, *Specters of Marx: The State of the Debt and the New International*, trans. by Peggy Kamuf (New York: Routledge, 1994), as well as Jacques Derrida, *Memoires for Paul de Man*, trans. by Cecile Lindsay and others (New York: Columbia University Press, 1989).

9   See thesis II in Walter Benjamin, 'On the Concept of History', trans. by Harry Zohn, in *Selected Writings*, 4 vols (Cambridge, MA: Harvard University Press, 2004–06), IV: *1938–1940*, ed. by Michael W. Jennings (2006), pp. 389–400 (pp. 389–90).

10   Giorgio Agamben, *Potentialities*, trans. by Daniel Heller-Roazen (Stanford: Stanford University Press, 1999), p. 158, writes: 'In the paradoxical figure of this memory, which remembers what was never seen, the redemption of the past is accomplished.' For the relationship between memory and redemption, see also Giorgio Agamben, *The Time That Remains: A Commentary on the Letter to the Romans*, trans. by Patricia Dailey (Stanford: Stanford University Press, 2005).

this promise: *we ourselves*, by opening to the claim of the past, come to display our eschatological heads.

Our own constitutive messianicity marks the impossible task of a work of mourning directed at the past, at the missed possibilities of the past, at time itself. The mourning of these missed possibilities is, however, irreducible to any notion of a working through of a loss, i.e. it is irreducible to any detachment from or incorporation of a lost object. The mourning of possibilities — and one could advance the claim that the mourning of every lost object is always a mourning of its possibilities — can only set itself up as a task: the task of redeeming these possibilities, of reactivating the very possibilities of these possibilities. A task that, however, constitutes itself as an impossible one, for to take even a moment longer to fulfil it would infinitely increase the measure of the task itself, i.e. the measure of the missed possibilities to be mourned. A task that, in any case, is insurmountable not only because infinite, but rather because the very notion of its success would be self-contradictory and self-defeating. Succeeding in laying the claim of the other to rest would entail having conceived the other as a lost object to be incorporated or to be separated from, without considering that the success of either of these operations would precisely entail fixing the destiny of the missed possibilities that the work of mourning has set out to redeem. It is to the extent that the work of mourning is inherently bound to fail that it can be said that we are constituted by nothing but the failure — or *weakness* as Benjamin has it — of our own messianicity.[11]

Coextensively with the claim we receive from the 'past', we ourselves make a claim directed to what we indicate as the 'future'. Our promise institutes the possibility of futurity as the site of the possibility of either fulfilling or missing what we envisage to be the possibilities of our own time. Once again, 'we' are constituted by an openness to a future that cannot be reduced to any present presence, for doing so would precisely entail extinguishing the very possibility of futurity, the potentiality of potentiality. Derrida's celebrated formula of a 'messianic without messianism' points to this notion of openness — an openness out of which the very possibility of historical messianisms

---

11   Benjamin, 'On the Concept of History', p. 390.

is drawn, but that is nevertheless irreducible to this possibility, for the actual coming of a messiah would deactivate the very openness of this promise. Once again, we are constituted by the failure or weakness of our messianicity, by the failure to mourn for those possibilities of ours that will inevitably be missed. We pledge a claim for our own possibilities, we swear by the name of their own possibilities, and we swear by the lack of a name for the potentiality for potentiality. Our openness is the double failure of mourning for our past and for our future, our failure of mourning for time.

2. Messianicity cannot be reduced to any messianism, for what we indicate by 'past' and 'future' as the possible loci for the coming of the messiah are invariably reconfigured *by virtue of* the very openness of messianicity. That is, the sites of the past and of the future are constituted *by* the very operations of mourning the past and 'mourning' the future. The future that we envisage is at each turn reconfigured by the missed possibilities of the past and by the claim they lay upon us; accordingly, the past, and the future of the past (its possibilities), are in turn reconfigured by our practice of mourning the future.

3. Were the coming of the messiah to respect the profane or linear structure of time, could one still call this coming by the name of justice? Could one still call by this name a certain 'per-version' of the messiah, namely the very turning away from the injustice that has been allowed to hold sway throughout secular time? How could one trust or find any solace in a messiah that had let injustice have its course, only then to claim the glory of its redemption? In this respect, Quentin Meillassoux has recently proposed what could be called a certain 'speculative dignity', namely a certain injunction to reject as perverse any messiah that would come after having let even just one death or suffering take place.[12]

4. Were, on the contrary, the coming of the messiah to alter the very structure of profane time, this alteration, this coming, would not be liable to be represented *in* time. The notions of messiah and of coming, of the coming of the coming, would themselves be altered by the coming itself: for, indeed, the coming, by coming, by altering the structure of profane time, would therefore alter also the very notion

---

12   See Quentin Meillassoux, 'Spectral Dilemma', *Collapse*, 4 (2008), pp. 261–76.

of coming, of coming in time. Messianicity, as openness to this utmost 'possibility', would then constitute the 'possibility' of the alteration of possibility itself; it would constitute the possibility of the alteration or even the erasure of the messiah and messianism themselves, and would therefore never be reducible to them.[13]

Having outlined the connection between openness and a certain notion of messianicity that cannot be reduced to any messiah or messianism, let us turn to a different attempt by Agamben to think this promise, namely to think the promise of a vow — not quite a vow to openness, but rather what appears at first to be a vow to seclusion. The singular structure of the promise taken by the Franciscans upon entering monastic life will be seen to delineate a notion of openness that most closely approximates the one presented by the righteous ones in the messianic miniature discussed by Agamben in *The Open*. The two notions of openness will be seen to make contact precisely to the extent that the righteous ones and the Franciscans promise to live a life that can only be constituted by the dimension of the promise itself — a life that is indistinguishable from the very openness of their promise.

THE HIGHEST POVERTY

The Highest Poverty is the penultimate volume of Agamben's *Homo Sacer* project, the twenty-year-long investigation into the Western tradition developed in terms of the historical unfolding of the *dispositif* of *sacertas*, namely the unfolding of the metaphysical machine of exception that has been seen at work in the instance of life and 'bare life'. *Sacer*, indeed, according to Roman law, qualifies someone who can be killed — albeit not sacrificed — without committing a crime; someone, therefore, for whom the law is suspended and does not apply — or, rather, an instance to which the law applies as to an exception, i.e. by dis-applying itself. *Highest Poverty* constitutes the turning point

---

13   This is a 'possibility' that is, if not coincident with, at least contiguous with that of negative theology. In the context of theology, it was advanced by Peter Damian in the eleventh century; see John D. Caputo, *The Weakness of God: A Theology of the Event* (Bloomington: Indiana University Press, 2006), pp. 182–207. See also the discussion of this 'anarchic' possibility in Quentin Meillassoux, 'L'Inexistence Divine' (unpublished doctoral thesis, University of Paris, 1997).

at which the *Homo Sacer* project initiates the unfolding of its own
gesture and operation on the tradition whose workings it has carefully
exposed. As mentioned above, throughout the Western political and
philosophical experience, the notion of life, which in this respect is
always the notion of a life worthy of the political domain, has been
constituted by means of a scission that has always separated it from a
'bare' hypostasis. The exclusion of this hypostasis has been coextensive
with the founding of sovereign power, i.e. of that power that according
to the Schmittian framework can decide on the exception, of what
has been included by way of an exclusion (*ex-capere*). Sovereignty,
as per Schmitt's definition, is instituted precisely by the possibility of
deciding what constitutes a state of emergency or a state of exception
(*Ausnahmezustand*), namely by the possibility of suspending the law
in order to secure precisely the continued existence of the law itself.[14]
The history of the *dispositif* of *sacertas* (*sacertà*), i.e. of the logic of
exception that excludes/includes 'bare' or *sacer* life, unfolds, according
to Agamben, along an axis that points towards the creation of a space
in which the domains of bare life and politically qualified life can no
longer be distinguished (*una soglia* (threshold) *di indistinzione*). That
is to say, this history follows a trajectory directed at the creation and
maximal extension of a space in which the law can apply as it would to
an exception, namely by suspending its own validity: a space in which
the law is both within and without itself. The proposal of the *Homo
Sacer* project consists, then, in a certain operation on the tradition it
has itself exposed: having uncovered the metaphysical functioning of
the anthropogenic machine, the task of the politics to come lies in
thinking and realizing a life from which, as in the case of the righteous
ones depicted in the messianic miniature, something like a bare life
could never be separated and excluded.

Agamben finds in the theoretical formulations developed by the
Franciscans the pointer to a speculative notion of form-of-life (*forma
vitae, forma vivendi, vita vel regula, regula et vita*) that would not be
susceptible to any excluding/including scission. In *Highest Poverty* the
speculative notions of 'form-of-life' and 'use' are reclaimed from the

---

14   Carl Schmitt, *Political Theology: Four Chapters on the Concept of Sovereignty*, trans. by
      George Schwab (Chicago: University of Chicago Press, 2005).

context of the Franciscan experience and receive their full elaboration in the last volume of the *Homo Sacer* project, *The Use of Bodies*. Crucial in this respect is, then, the Franciscans' attempt at constituting a life outside the bounds of property and of law by means of the declarations of highest poverty (*altissima paupertas*) and the abdication of every right (*abdicatio omnis iuris*). As such, Agamben writes, theirs stands as 'perhaps the most extreme and rigorous attempt to achieve the Christian's *forma vitae* and define the figure of the practice in which it is worked out'.[15] Most relevant for the present discussion is the fact that the *experimentum vitae* of the Franciscans takes place by means of a promise, by means of a vow or an oath.

Crucially, we are to understand this promise not simply as a factual vow to relinquish all possessions for the sake of the cenoby (that is, as a vow to sacrifice the worldly life in order to live according to a certain norm) — but rather, we are once again to understand this promise in terms of a certain openness. For the Franciscans, in pledging their vows, do not merely constitute a life through the factual sacrifice of their material properties; that is, they do not merely constitute a life by making themselves *sacer*, i.e. by excluding themselves from the world and therefore constituting an included exception (sacrifice as *sacrum facere*). To constitute themselves by means of a sacrifice would still entail belonging to and depending on what they wish to deactivate insofar as they would come to be included in the law by a merely subtractive act, i.e. through a logic of exception. Sovereign power would then be able to decide on them as on exceptions outside the law — and therefore the law itself would apply to them by dis-applying itself: their sacrifice would include them in the *dispositif* of *sacertas*. The openness of the Franciscans lies in their promise: a promise that can be constituted neither by a transitive object nor by a lack thereof, but is rather to remain constitutively an openness for openness itself. All that can be promised by the Franciscans is, therefore, only the structure of the promise itself: all they can be open to is only openness itself. Agamben writes that the vow

> does not obligate one, like the law, simply to fulfil determinate acts and keep away from others, but produces in the will a

---

15   Agamben, *The Highest Poverty*, p. 86.

'permanent and, as it were, habitual bond' (*vinculum permanens et quasi in habitu* [...]). Here the vow is a 'vow of the vow' (*habet pro obiecto votum*), in the sense that it does not refer immediately to a certain action or a certain series of acts, but first of all to the bond that is itself to be produced in the will [...]. [This] is the paradox of an obligation whose primary content is not a certain behaviour, but the very form of the will of the one who, by promising the vow, has been bound to God.[16]

It is by deactivating the fulfilment of the promise and openness that the Franciscan way of living constitutes itself as a form-of-life, as a space of incessant practice and self-constitution, an aesthetics of existence that promises its own promise and that is open to its own openness. But why is it the case that the promise needs to turn upon itself to open a space to which the logic of exception would neither apply nor, in the case of an exception, dis-apply?

The structure of the promise or of the oath is indissociable from that of *sacertas*, for to pronounce a vow or a *sacramentum*, Agamben argues, always means to give oneself over to the gods one swears by — to con-secrate oneself to the gods should the promise be broken (*sacratio*). As Agamben writes,

the one who pronounces the vow, more than being obligated or condemned to execution, becomes [...] a *homo sacer*. His life, insofar as it belongs to the infernal gods, is no longer such, but rather he dwells in the threshold between life and death and can therefore be killed by anyone with impunity.[17]

More specifically, to take a vow or an oath marks *the very possibility* of the dimension of *sacertas*, the possibility of losing every right before the gods and before the *polis*. Agamben relies on Benveniste in order to connect the oath and the condition of being *sacer* through the metaphysical operator of possibility: 'The *sacramentum* is properly the action or object by which one anathematises one's own person

---

16   Ibid., pp. 56–57; embedded quotes are from Francisco Suárez, 'De voto', in *Opera omnia*, 28 vols (Paris: Vives, 1856–78), xiv (1869), pp. 750–1179 (p. 804). Agamben also relies on Suárez's claim ('De voto', p. 804) 'that the vow properly so-called, insofar as it signifies that act by means of which a person obliges himself with respect to God, cannot have for its object any human act other than the obligation itself, that is the bond that is realized through the act of vowing oneself'.

17   Agamben, *The Highest Poverty*, p. 38.

in advance [...]. Once the words are spoken in the set forms, one is *potentially* in the state of being *sacer*.'[18] It is from this standpoint that the Franciscan *experimentum* (i.e. experiment and experience) can be assessed in its full potential: precisely as that of a promise that, in not having a direct object, in being a promise *of the promise itself*, subtracts itself from the very possibility of *sacertas*. For if the condition of *sacertas* is enacted or deactivated by the being broken or being kept of the promise, by promising the promise itself the Franciscans subtract themselves from the dimension of *sacertas* altogether, for to break their promise — the promise of taking the promise — would entail precisely *not* making a promise, and therefore *not* being liable to the condition of *sacertas*. Through their singular promise they succeed in situating themselves outside the very possibility of *sacertas*, for a promise of a promise can neither be kept nor broken — it can only be promised. If a *sacramentum*, i.e. an oath or a vow, is to be taken as a potentiality for *sacertas*, the vow to keep pledging the vow and the promise of promising the promise stand for the unfolding of a potentiality of potentiality itself, for the deactivation of the possibility of *sacertas* by means of a potentializing of potentiality.

It is in this respect that the unique openness set forth by the Franciscans is to be taken: namely, as an openness to openness itself, as an openness to potentiality and as a potentiality for openness. By living their promise, by making their lives indistinguishable from the openness of their promise, the Franciscan *experimentum* stands as close as possible to the openness depicted in the messianic miniature discussed by Agamben in *The Open*. The righteous ones are then the ones who live their own eschaton and their own promise: they *are* promised (as the content of messianic time) insofar as they *are*, precisely, *the promise*, the openness constituted by a life that is its own eschaton. They not only *display* their eschaton by means of their animal heads, but rather they are able to live it — they are messianic to the extent that they come to live their eschaton and to the extent that their form-of-life is constituted by the promise of their own openness. In the figure

---

18   Émile Benveniste, *Dictionary of Indo-European Concepts and Society*, trans. by Elizabeth Palmer (Chicago: Hau Books, 2016), p. 447 (my emphasis). See also Giorgio Agamben, *The Sacrament of Language: An Archaeology of the Oath*, trans. by Adam Kotsko (Stanford: Stanford University Press 2011), p. 30.

of the righteous, life and promise, life and eschaton can no longer be separated. In other words, a life that cannot be distinguished from its form, a form-of-life, is one that neither constitutes its form nor is constituted by it, but rather promises itself as an incessant practice *of* the promise itself — a practice out of which both form and life come to emerge. It is to this extent that Agamben can argue that life and form can be said to constitute each other only so long as they enter a threshold (*soglia*) in which they can no longer be distinguished. In this space of indifference, life and form are not simply sublated into a higher form-of-life, but rather their very opposition is deactivated and they fall together: they *coincide*. The Franciscans succeed in rendering inoperative the dialectic of life and form precisely by situating themselves in the potentiality of the promise and in the promise as potentiality — in a *sacramentum* that precisely by always reconfiguring the possibility of *sacertas* situates them beyond the dimension of *sacertas* itself.

It is beyond the present discussion to verify why this *experimentum* might have taken place in the setting provided by the Franciscan experience. One can refer to Agamben's discussion of how the pressing relations between liturgy, the office, and the various orders within the Church provided a space for a different *modus vivendi* precisely when liturgy itself threatened to have the firmest grip on life.[19] It is relevant to the present analysis, however, to note that the attempt of the Franciscans might have not been successful due to their inability to locate the site that first affords the structure of their promise and of their vows — namely, their attempt might have failed because they did not link the promise of their promise with the only other self-referentially constituting and self-promising potentiality that institutes something like a form-of-life: the promise of language, its *sacramentum*.

PROMISE II

Where does that leave us — leave us in the sense of a rest that remains? We have seen that 'the rest' is not constituted by those who will have remained at the time of the messiah's arrival, but is rather comprised of

---

19   For an in-depth discussion of the relationship between liturgy and life, see Giorgio Agamben, *Opus Dei: An Archaeology of Duty*, trans. by Adam Kotsko (Stanford: Stanford University Press, 2013).

those who will have remained in the openness of a certain messianicity: that is to say, of those who, by living their openness as their own eschaton, deactivate the wait for the messiah in realizing that they are themselves messianic — or, rather, that there can be something like a 'themselves' only by virtue of a messianicity that cannot be reduced to any messianism. The claim is that one of the most exemplary attempts at living this openness, that of the Franciscans, had to fail precisely because language could still afford a hope for a messiah — or, more specifically, because the history of the Western experience of language had not yet come to its own end. That is to say, language still preserved the possibility for a final word, a word capable of grounding the whole of language and of providing an anchoring point for all signification. The final word would have marked the name of God, the name of the messiah — but also, crucially, the name of language itself, the name of the name. That is to say, insofar as the possibility of the coming of a messiah persists, so does the possibility of the appearance of a word that would structure the whole of meaning and signification. The meaning of 'profane' words would no longer take place *only* by virtue of their mutual relations and differential play — i.e. simply by their inhabiting the openness of language — but, rather, the meaning of all words would be determined *conclusively* by their relations to one autonomous and transparently self-signifying word, which would, as such, *close* the differential system of signification. The name of the messiah or the name of God, as this very word, would then not be the name of any one thing in particular, but would rather be the name of meaning itself — the name of language. It is to this extent that the death of God, the death of the name of language, marks the coming to terms of the Western tradition with the lack of a final word.[20] In preserving the possibility for a final word, and therefore the possibility for a coming of the messiah, language conceals its constitutive structure of messianicity — namely, the structure of openness or promise that can never be reduced to the actuality of any final messianic word. That the structure of openness or messianicity should be at the core of the constitution of something like a form-of-life is, then, not an

---

20   See Giorgio Agamben, 'La parola e il sapere', *aut-aut*, September–December 1980, pp. 155–66 (p. 157).

accidental or contingent event of history, but is rather coextensive with the very structure of messianicity inherent to language (a structure of messianicity that, once again, cannot be reduced to the coming of any messianic word). Accordingly, the lack of a final word reveals that there is no such 'thing' as language itself, that there is no autonomous and independent set of relations between words that would constitute a complete and finished whole. Every speech act, in taking place, points retroactively to the fiction of a fully constituted autonomous language; every instance of discourse (*parole*), in taking place, points to the fiction of an independent language (*langue*). Every event of language appears to shape and form language in the same way a gesture shapes a sculpture — but the presupposition of a statue or a monument of language is only the retroactive fantasy produced by events of language that are each time utterly singular, events of language whose gestures cannot be accounted for and subtracted to reach a prior independent language. The highest openness, the openness of messianicity, is, then, the openness to and for language, for a language that is always to-come; which is to say that the highest openness is an openness to nothing, for language is no-thing at all: strictly speaking, one can never assert, within language, that something like language 'is' (or, for that matter, that it 'is not').

Once again, where does that leave us? According to Agamben, the end of the trajectory that has directed the Western experience of language leaves us all as part of a rest:

> What is proper to this time — to our time — is that, at a certain point, *everyone* — all the peoples and all the humans on earth — has found themselves in a position of *rest*. That entails, upon a closer look, an unprecedented generalization of the messianic condition.[21]

We are all part of the rest because we all partake of the last experience of language, a last experience that is an experience of the end. And yet, even granting that we might all have remained to live the last experience of language, the experience marked by the impossibility of the coming of a final word, we do not appear to be feasting like the

---

21   Giorgio Agamben, 'Postilla 2001', in *La comunità che viene* (Turin: Bollati Boringhieri, 2001), pp. 89–93 (p. 92; my translation).

righteous ones of the messianic miniature. It is as if, Agamben claims, the community of the rest *were* to all extents the community of the righteous ones, *and yet* it did not quite know it, and believed itself still separated from the order of the messianic — somewhat akin to Hegel's unhappy consciousness. But, truly, there is no difference between the community of the rest and the community of the righteous ones, i.e. the community of those who live their eschaton *as* their openness and their promise of language. The coming community, the community which has already and always already come, is neither a community of different men nor a community of men speaking a different language: the coming community is, in fact, neither a community of men nor a community grounded in any language. The failure in completing the deconstruction of the human rests with the persistence of the presupposition of some-thing like language, the persistence of a presupposition that would unify the humans by providing a common element shared by everyone — and therefore qualifying those who do not possess 'human' language as either animals or savages.[22] It is only by dispossessing man of the only possession that inheres to its concept, namely language — so that the 'human' may come to speak not by disposing of a possession, but rather by being deposed by what cannot be possessed — that the very notion of the human (as that of the animal having language, *zoon logon echon*) can be unhinged at the very site of the articulation that separates it and at the same time joins it to the animal — so that the very notion of human as nothing but that which possesses (*echein*) could eventually come to pass. That there is no such thing as language would mean that there is no such thing as the human. The singularity of the event of language, irreducible to any substance that would precede it and that would be common to all instances of discourse, points to the singularity of the constituent of the coming community, a singularity irreducible to any substance that would make the unique or the singular commensurate with anything else.

---

22   The structure of presupposition produces the aporia in which the notion of the 'human' both precedes and follows its origin in language: the human arises with language, but something like 'human language' relies on an autonomous notion of the human to set it apart from other languages.

*

The highest openness is that experience of the promise that constitutes a singularity out of an unrepeatable mourning of the past and of the future, i.e. out of an always singular mourning of time. In other words, the highest openness is the experience of an always singular mourning of language, namely the experience that confronts every instance of discourse with the irredeemable truth that there is no-thing like language — that we have always been abandoned by language and that language has always abandoned itself. We mourn the loss of language, or rather, language mourns its own loss. The community of the just ones, the community of justice, would then only be the community born out of the experience of this mourning, the community that would have turned this mourning into its glory — the glory of not being a community of humans or a community grounded in any language. The highest openness — i.e. the openness of language, of the promise, and of the question — is a universally singular openness to nothing, a universally singular openness to the potentiality of potentiality.

The Monastic Enclosure

BENJAMIN THOMPSON

Of the many forms of openness discussed in this book, monasticism touches on a good number: physical, spiritual, intellectual, individual, and institutional. Physical openness, and its antithesis or complement, closedness, is embodied not only in celibacy, but also movement: the freedom of religious to leave the precinct, and the liberty afforded to others to enter it. The founding text of Western monasticism, the Rule of Benedict, prohibited these freedoms; but they varied between different monastic rules, orders, and cultures, and they changed over time, in principle and practice. Spiritual openness was naturally fundamental to monastic culture. The human responds to God opening himself to humanity in the Incarnation with an open soul, the ordinary Christian in the routine of prayer and confession, the mystic by a complete emptying out of self to allow the divine to fill it. Between these extremes, the monastic practice of obedience, which at first sight seems restricted and closed, sought to train the will to be open to the will of God and ultimately to conform to it.

Religious houses have not traditionally been identified with intellectual openness. Their early medieval learning is held to have been challenged by the high medieval secular scholars who advocated rational questioning of inherited truth and opening texts up to interpretation. Apart from the injustice this does to monastic thinkers, monasteries also played a role in preserving texts and keeping them available, or open, especially in the early period, and they continued to disseminate them through society, for instance in preaching or reproducing devotional books, right through to the printing press. Internal monastic practice centred around the inculcation of liturgical, biblical, and regulatory texts and their elucidation, or opening up, for the religious. And the external history of monasticism can be seen as a contest over the interpretation of its key texts, above all the Rule, both between and within orders.

Individuals are both closed and open, both unique and part of a larger continuum. They have their own identity distinct from all others, defined by the boundaries of the self; but they are interdependent and formed through interaction with other people and the societies they inhabit. The relationship between the individual and the community is a key feature of monasticism. We may view monasteries institutionally in the same way. Each was unique, and the Rule prescribed independence for each house; but increasingly most were part of orders or provinces, and members of Church, kingdom, and Christendom. Competition between houses and orders and with other parts of the Church helped to define identities. The boundary between the monastery and its immediate local society will be of particular interest here: how far could the enclosure prescribed by the Rule be maintained and isolate a house from external influences?

Monastic history can be written both from the inside and the outside.[1] Internal evidence is plentiful for the liturgy, for regimes of regulation and governance, and for texts written and copied by monks attesting to their learning, culture, and sometimes spirituality.[2] Visit-

---

[1]   For a general introduction (including the matters discussed above): C. H. Lawrence, *Medieval Monasticism: Forms of Religious Life in Western Europe in the Middle Ages*, 2nd edn (London: Longman, 1989); and now much more fully, *The Cambridge History of Medieval Monasticism in the Latin West*, ed. by Alison I. Beach and Isabelle Cochelin, 2 vols (Cambridge: Cambridge University Press, 2020), and, less comprehensively, *The Oxford Handbook of Christian Monasticism*, ed. by Bernice M. Kaczynski (Oxford: Oxford University Press, 2020); for England, still, David Knowles, *The Monastic Order in England*, 2nd edn (Cambridge: Cambridge University Press, 1963) and *The Religious Orders in England*, 3 vols (Cambridge: Cambridge University Press, 1948–59). Only a tiny proportion of the vast literature on monasticism can be cited here. For a thoughtful essay, see Ludo J. R. Milis, *Angelic Monks and Earthly Men: Monasticism and its Meaning to Medieval Society* (Woodbridge: Boydell, 1992), although I offer a different interpretation.

[2]   See e.g. Knowles, *Monastic Order*, chs 23–31.

ations and financial accounts can give us a more mundane glimpse into a house's experience.[3] Equally plentiful are records of the acquisition, tenure, and exploitation of property, which locate a religious house in its economy and local society, its nexus of patrons and benefactors, tenants and servants, supporters and competitors.[4] Wider evidence sees the monastery as an object of the jurisdiction of Crown, episcopate, and religious orders. I first came across monasticism through the Cistercian reforms and images of the isolation of Fountains and Rievaulx, and later stayed at the Trappist Caldey Island; but my doctoral work was very much from the outside, on the role of religious houses in local society.[5] Knitting together these two perspectives is the core challenge for the monastic historian.

In principle they are complementary: sealing off monks and nuns from society was intended to open them up to God. Selected monastic officials engaged with the external world so as to ensure the house's material viability and allow others the necessary isolation. But this balance could be easily upset, in practice by the pull of the world beyond what was strictly necessary, or in principle by monastic idealism to change it and pressures on religious to demonstrate their utility in it. The internal/external dichotomy might therefore be experienced as tension rather than complement, whether for the individual — St Bernard oscillating between seeking union with God in his bare cell and participating in the great affairs of Europe — or the institution (we will observe tensions between enclosed religious and worldly officials), or in competing ideals about how far religious should contribute to society. Whether enclosure and openness were complementary or in conflict is in itself a matter of interest.

Openness can therefore be approached, a little paradoxically, through the monastic enclosure. The Benedictine Rule prescribed a near-impermeable barrier around the monastery in order to restrict interaction with society outside, to prevent both religious leaving the precinct, and others entering it. But the enclosure was also a metaphor

---

3   See the final section below.

4   See e.g., from a large literature, Barbara F. Harvey, *Westminster Abbey and its Estates in the Middle Ages* (Oxford: Clarendon Press, 1977).

5   My original approach was much influenced by Richard W. Southern, *Western Society and the Church in the Middle Ages* (Harmondsworth: Penguin, 1970), ch. 6. See various articles of my own cited here.

for spirituality, and was contrasted with external secularity, whose most striking manifestations were money, sex, and time. Time, so crucial to the rhythm of the monastic day, was to be used for God and the community, for the divine office and manual labour; but it was all too easily diverted towards secular busy-ness, even under the cover of necessary administration. Sex was the most egregious transgression of a code of personal behaviour requiring dedication to God and resistance or closure to the wiles of the world, for which it also functioned as a metaphor; it was also connected to meat-eating. Third, since goods were to be held in common, private property detracted from the common life and closed members off from each other individualistically; money functioned as a metaphor for the failure of community. Enclosure thus constituted both a set of literal rules for religious, and an analogue for the secularity which they might encounter outside, or which might enter the monastery.

This far-from-comprehensive three-part survey will proceed by scrutinizing a selection of texts from nearly a millennium of monastic history. First, the Rule itself, Lanfranc's Cluniac-influenced customs for post-Conquest English monasticism, and the early Cistercian statutes are considered. Second, the papal reform proposals of the 1330s provide a focus for the state of the enclosure at that point. While all these texts were normative, they were also increasingly informed by practice. Finally, the later Middle Ages are analysed through late medieval visitations: these might *prima facie* seem to depict actual practice, but turn out to be at least as valuable for the discourses and assumptions they recorded and perpetuated — openly or not, as we shall see.

RULES AND CUSTOMS

The Rule of Benedict was clear that the monastery was an enclosed space in which the brothers were trained in the Lord's service, and which should not be unnecessarily breached by dealings with the outside world.[6] The whole text is very internalized in its tone and

---

6   Many editions and translations are available, including online. *RB 1980: The Rule of St Benedict in Latin and English with Notes,* ed. and trans. by Timothy Fry (Collegeville, MN: The Liturgical Press, 1981), is the most frequently cited modern scholarly edition. Privileging the Rule is of course problematic: Albrecht Diem and

coverage; it is almost entirely devoted, after a statement of monastic ideals, to detailed prescriptions for the liturgy, monastic discipline, and the regulation of the monastery's daily life. Ideally, the house is to be constituted so that all necessities such as water, the mill, and the garden are placed inside the precinct and various crafts ('artes diversas') can be conducted there, with no need for monks to wander outside to the detriment of their souls (c. 66). There is hardly any comment on the world beyond the monastery, and the monks' contact with it is tightly controlled: they will be punished if they leave the enclosure ('claustra monasterii'), even for a small thing, without the abbot's permission (c. 67). Equally, there is very little reference to outsiders coming into the house, except as recruits or guests; there are no references to servants, except in the spiritual sense and to the monks serving each other (c. 35). Even the procedures for receiving postulants make no reference to their external origins, except that wandering monks from far away ('de longiquis') might ask to stay (c. 61). All such applicants are quickly incorporated into the monastery, and into the text of the Rule.

Nevertheless, it is briefly acknowledged that some brothers will be working too far away to come frequently to the oratory, and that others might need to go on business (c. 50). Moreover, hospitality and almsgiving are fundamental duties of the religious. Guests attract a detailed and careful account of their reception and provision: accommodation and food are always to be ready for them, they eat with the abbot at his table, and two monks by annual turns staff their kitchen (c. 53). Relief of the poor is the fourth of the seventy-three instruments of God's works (c. 4), although thereafter they are mentioned rather in passing: the cellarer is to provide for them (c. 31), great care is to be taken with the reception of the poor and travellers (c. 53), they might knock on the door of the house (c. 66), and worn-out clothes and those of novices may be given to them (cc. 55, 58). Even in this very internally focused rule, therefore, which does not comment at all on society outside, the world cannot be entirely kept out. The tension between the enclosure and the need for some contact cannot be avoided altogether.

Philip Rousseau, 'Monastic Rules (Fourth to Ninth Century)', in *Cambridge History of Medieval Monasticism*, ed. by Beach and Cochelin, I, pp. 162–94.

Nevertheless, there is a series of safeguards. The guestmaster is to handle guests, who not only eat separately with the abbot, but have a separate kitchen and accommodation so that they do not disturb the monks (cc. 31, 53, 56). Moreover no monk is to address them unless ordered to do so by the abbot. There are strict rules for monks working outside the monastery or sent on journeys: they must say the offices wherever they find themselves (c. 50); they must not eat outside if on a journey of less than a day, even if pressed, on pain of excommunication (c. 51); and they must not relate what they have seen or heard in the world, which is very destructive ('quia plurima destructio est'; c. 67). The porter was to act as the intermediary between the monastery and the world, in a no-man's-land which enabled him to control the interface (c. 66). Letters and gifts sent from outside were carefully regulated: nothing was to be received but through the abbot, who could decide to give anything to another brother even if sent by family (c. 54). Nobles bringing oblates must promise not to give them anything (c. 59), just as new monks divest themselves of all their property and clothes (c. 58). Private property is to be completely forbidden, because monks should not even control their own bodies and wills; everything is to be distributed only by the abbot (cc. 33–34, 55). Thus the Rule exerts careful control not only over contact with the world but also over worldliness. Indeed, while there are plentiful emphasis on the use of time and strict injunctions against property, women are simply not mentioned at all in the text.

Western monasticism's subsequent evolution through the Anianic and Cluniac reforms informed Archbishop Lanfranc's *Constitutiones,* written in the 1070s both specifically for his cathedral priory at Canterbury and more generally to remould conquered English monasticism.[7] Although the sense of interiority remains strong in a document that is still primarily internally focused, the world outside is slightly more present than in the Rule. The rules for monks going on journeys are more detailed and elaborate, with instructions for their blessing when departing and returning and for saying the offices, as well as the injunction to avoid 'curiositatem, scurrilitatem, otiositatem' (c. 97).

---

7   *The Monastic Constitutions of Lanfranc*, ed. and trans. by David Knowles, rev. by C. N. L. Brooke (Oxford: Clarendon Press, 2002), pp. xvi–xx, xxviiii–xlii; the edition tracks the synergies with the Cluniac customs.

Obedientiaries returning with their servants were to be checked by the guestmaster for correct behaviour (c. 90). A brother might die when away from the house and need to be brought back on a horse (c. 114). The almoner was to go round the locality to find the poor and relieve their wants (c. 91), a Cluniac practice that in fact did not catch on in England.[8] Indeed, the poor are much more present than in the Rule, not only on major festivals such as Maundy Thursday (when they were led into the cloister and personally given tuppence by each monk; cc. 28–32), but also in the distributions of food in memory of deceased abbots (three poor men daily for a year) or monks (one pauper for a month, at the abbot's discretion; cc. 82, 113).[9] There are many more details about the reception of guests, whether layperson, cleric, or monk (c. 90). Visitors might be shown round the buildings, although not in riding-boots or barefoot. Laity might be admitted to adore the cross on Good Friday (cc. 40–45). Nobles brought in their sons to be oblates (c. 105), and might also come to ask for confraternity with the house, when they would sit beside the abbot (c. 108); laypeople could also be buried in the precinct (c. 87). There are now several mentions of servants around the monastery, although monks were not to talk to them unnecessarily (cc. 85, 90, 91). Moreover, women appear in the text: the almoner should be careful not to enter a house where a sick woman was lying but only to send necessaries with servants (c. 91); and women could apparently seek confraternity in person, presumably if they were noble enough (c. 108).[10] If these signs are occasional, it is hard to avoid the sense of the world edging its way into the cloister.

It was these and other incursions that provoked the semi-eremitical reaction that we associate above all with the Cistercians.[11] Monasteries were not to be constructed in cities, castles, or towns,

---

8   *Constitutions of Lanfranc*, p. 132 n. 334.

9   Regular daily distributions may be simply assumed; they are very present at Cluny: 'Antiquiores Consuetudines Cluniacensis Monasterii Collectore Udalrico Monacho Benedictino', *Patrologia Latina* [PL], ed. by J.-P. Migne, 221 vols (Paris: Garnier, 1844–64), 149. 635–778 (henceforth 'Ulrich'), III. 24; 'Ordo Cluniacensis per Bernardum Saeculi XI. Scriptorem', in *Vetus Disciplina Monastica*, ed. by Marquard Herrgott (Paris: Caroli Osmont, 1726), pp. 134–364 (henceforth 'Bernard'), I. 3, 9, 13.

10 Such must be the meaning of the exception 'si mulier non sit' attached to the kissing of the brothers.

11 *Narrative and Legislative Texts from Early Cîteaux*, ed. by Chrysogonus Waddell (Cîteaux: Commentarii cistercienses, 1999), pp. 458–68.

'but in places removed from contact with people' (sed in locis a conversatione hominum semotis; c. 1). Monks were not to stay outside the cloister (c. 6), and women were absolutely forbidden to enter it, or monastic granges, whatever the necessity (c. 7). The emphasis on basic simplicity replicated these injunctions metaphorically: the Rule was to be followed closely in questions of food, clothing, and *mores* (c. 2). Clothing was to be 'simplex et vilis', without cloaks, shirts, or wool (c. 4); vestments must not have silk, gold, or gems (c. 10). There was to be no white bread (c. 14), nor meat or even fat or lard in abbeys or granges, unless for the sick (c. 24). But the Cistercian insistence on self-sufficiency required some reconfiguration of the monastery's relationship with the world. Refusing external revenues (rents, churches, altars, burial fees, tithes, manors, serfs, taxes on lands, dues from ovens or mills), which were hostile to monastic purity (c. 9), monks were instead to cultivate land, far from the habitations of seculars, by the labour of their own hands (c. 5). But such monks would struggle to attend the offices eight times a day, and the expansion of a house's estates might require external pernoctation. Circumventing the ban on serfs or hired servants, therefore, the order created a labour force of *conversi* or lay brothers to cultivate the monastic granges: they took vows for a modified form of monastic life without the liturgical obligations or rigorous discipline of a choir monk, as the monks' partners in temporal and spiritual things (c. 8). This arrangement was partly an exercise in relabelling, and raised questions of supervision which are hinted at in the statutes: monks might be sent to a grange, but must not stay long (c. 6). Thus the Cistercian attempt to remove the monastery from the world still required negotiation with it, and compromises which were not to have an entirely successful future.[12]

The relationship between the individual and the community within the monastery was configured in different ways in these texts. Closure to the world aimed to maximize, within the community, openness of the religious to each other. The Rule prescribed, for the parts of the day not occupied in communal liturgy, manual labour and spiritual

---

12   Janet Burton and Julie Kerr, *The Cistercians in the Middle Ages* (Woodbridge: Boydell, 2011), pp. 155–56.

reading (c. 48), which the Cistercians interpreted to require a threefold balance that they set out to restore.[13] But the Rule actually said rather little about labour and reading, and devoted most of its space to collective activities in church, chapter, and refectory; the overall emphasis is on the life lived in common. In fact, Benedictine practice between the seventh and eleventh centuries saw public liturgy expand to occupy most of the day, above all at Cluny.[14] Nevertheless, Lanfranc, following Cluniac texts, enjoined frequent saying of individual 'psalmi familiares' through the day: as each monk prayed for their family, friends, and benefactors, they maintained at least an imaginative connection to the world they had left.[15] The Cistercians went further in carving out individual spiritual space: they cut centuries of liturgical accretion back to the precise provisions of the Rule so as to restore not only manual labour but also private prayer and spiritual reading (c. 2).[16] Monks could cultivate a more direct connection with God individually, rather than with and through fellow-monks.

Flight from the world did not mean it could be ignored: the necessity of survival, the need for recruits, and the demands of hospitality and almsgiving all required some negotiation with it. And the complexities of relationships within the monastery opened up more dimensions of monastic openness.

REFORM IN THE 1330s

The Cistercians were only one manifestation of the high medieval ferment of religious movements seeking to configure their relationship to the world in increasingly different ways.[17] Some were even more ascetic, such as the Carthusian monks who lived in individual cells and spent very little time in communal activity. Others lived more in the world so as to minister to it, while still living under vows and by different standards; the friars, recalling earlier movements of wandering

---

13   Knowles, *Monastic Order*, pp. 211–12.
14   Lawrence, *Medieval Monasticism*, pp. 80–81, 100–01.
15   *Constitutions of Lanfranc*, pp. xxii–xxv, 6, 10, 12, 20, 26, 32, 74, 124, 136.
16   See n. 13 above; Cistercian statutes, cc. 22, 47 (in *Narrative and Legislative Texts from Early Cîteaux*).
17   For the general developments in this paragraph, Lawrence, *Medieval Monasticism*, chs 8, 10–12.

hermits, went further than the canons in rejecting landed property and living by mendicancy. Hospitals, military orders, increasing space for women, and other developments all testified to a diversification of the ways in which people sought to live a religious life with different forms and degrees of (un)worldliness. If there had ever been a 'Benedictine monopoly', it was firmly ended in the long twelfth century.

The Cistercians also exemplify the corollary of these multiple inspirations: their channelling into institutions and religious orders. The Rule itself had been one of many late antique attempts to institutionalize world-rejecting asceticism into a cenobitic or collective form of life. As 'a little rule for a beginning' for 'a school in the Lord's service', it acknowledged the need to train recruits in the ascetic life and to perpetuate spiritual inspiration beyond a single generation within institutional structures.[18] Rules, constitutions, general chapters, and visitation — typically thought to have been perfected by the Cistercians — were designed to preserve ascetic standards and prevent inevitable decline. But institutionalization also involved compromise and itself risked diluting original fervour. Thus both the ever-present possibility of actual decline in standards and the institutionalization which was designed to prevent it made current reality vulnerable to criticism in the light of a primitive ideal.[19] Calls for correction and reform were endemic to monastic orders, as they were throughout the Church as a whole.[20]

The Benedictines caught up with the better-structured new orders in 1215 with their organization by Innocent III into provincial chapters.[21] This generated systematic evidence of provincial legislation, along with sporadic records of visitation.[22] But by the early fourteenth

---

18 'Minimam inchoationis regulam', 'dominici scola servitii' (*Rule of Benedict*, prologue, c. 73); see also Lawrence, Medieval Monasticism, pp. 11–25.

19 I have no space here to discuss a further pressure that shaped the development of religious houses and orders, the demands of society on them; for some earlier thoughts, see my 'Introduction: Monasteries and Medieval Society', in *Monasteries and Society in Medieval England: Proceedings of the 1994 Harlaxton Symposium*, ed. by Benjamin Thompson (Stamford: Watkins, 1999), pp. 1–33.

20 Benjamin Thompson, 'The Polemic of Reform in the Later Medieval English Church', in *Polemic: Language as Violence in Medieval and Early Modern Discourse*, ed. by Almut Suerbaum, George Southcombe, and Benjamin Thompson (Aldershot: Ashgate, 2015), pp. 183–222.

21 Lateran IV, c. 12.

22 *Documents Illustrating the Activities of the General and Provincial Chapters of the English Black Monks, 1215–1540*, ed. by William A. Pantin, Camden Society, 3rd ser., 45, 47,

century there was felt to be a more urgent need for a general reform, which the Avignon Pope Benedict XII (formerly the heresy-hunter of Montaillou fame, Jacques Fournier) supplied between 1335 and 1339 for his own Cistercians, as well as the Augustinians and Benedictines.[23] His 1336 *Summi magistri* for the latter attempted to restore many key features of the Rule, especially the enclosure.[24] Women were to be absolutely excluded from wherever the monks went, even their mothers and sisters (c. 20). Nor were monks to consort in such places with seculars, or indeed animals. Their interaction with servants was to be limited to necessary conversation, and was not to include eating and drinking with them (c. 21). Everyone was to sleep together in one room, not in private (c. 27). Brothers were to attend all the hours and the major Mass, and priests were to say Mass regularly (c. 28). The licence of the superior was required to leave the monastery, and only for reasonable cause (c. 25). Monks were to maintain traditional dress and were not to be given money for food or clothes (cc. 18, 24). Various other clauses forbade monks to own their own property or engage in private commerce (e.g. c. 17), including the temptation to keep items outside the monastery, on its estates, or with relatives and friends (c. 16). Thus the main elements of the Rule's vision of separation from the world and from worldliness were firmly and clearly restated.

Several indications show, however, that this attempt to uphold the original standard was to some extent hopeless. In the first place, the reiteration of these prohibitions in provincial legislation and visitations cannot be regarded as purely formulaic.[25] Second, Benedict XII had to compromise explicitly on one of the most basic regular provisions of all, meat-eating. While emphasizing 'moderatio, sobrietas et modestia' (c. 27), he accepted what had become common practice, that meat could be eaten on four days of the week by rotating monks to eat in

54, 3 vols (London: Camden Society, 1931–37); Christopher R. Cheney, *Episcopal Visitation of Monasteries in the Thirteenth Century*, 2nd edn (Manchester: Manchester University Press, 1983 [1st edn, 1931]).

23   Peter McDonald, 'The Papacy and Monastic Observance in the Later Middle Ages: The *Benedictina* in England', *Journal of Religious History*, 14.2 (1986), pp. 117–32 (p. 118).

24   *Concilia Magnae Britanniae et Hiberniae, a Synodo Verolamiensi A.D. CCCC XLVI. ad Londinensem A.D. M DCCXVII*, ed. by David Wilkins, 4 vols (London: R. Gosling), II, pp. 585–651.

25   Cheney, *Episcopal Visitation*; *English Black Monks*, passim (e.g. the first set of statutes of 1218–19, I, 8–14); and see the final section below.

the infirmary. His self-consciousness about making this concession is shown in the accompanying ban on seculars being present to observe the practice, to prevent them denigrating the religious life, an attempt to enclose the monastery from public knowledge. And third, the whole programme was soon undermined both by his successor and by local action.[26] Clement VI suspended all the penalties enforcing *Summi magistri*, leaving it to visitors armed largely with exhortation. Then the English Benedictines watered them down by various quasi-legal fixes, such as creative accounting with the numbers on which the permitted proportion of meat-eaters was calculated, and other little exceptions: private use of a house's property and alms was acceptable for pious purposes, as was possession of small personal items; silence in the refectory was only to be observed while the president was eating, after which quiet chat was permitted.

Summi magistri also shows that monks lived in a more complex world, especially with respect to the monastic economy and the interconnections between houses. The splitting of monasteries' sometimes widely scattered estates between different obedientiaries combined with the insistence on the direct management of manors (a feature of the English economy from *c.* 1200) required increasing numbers of monastic officials to engage in business, handle goods and money, and leave the precinct. To ensure that monasteries were not defrauded by private interest, Benedict XII banned inessential leases and the delegation of the food-administration to non-monks (cc. 15, 19). It was accepted that obedientiaries out on business would not attend the hours (c. 28), and that monks might have to be absent overnight, in which case they must have cowl and breviary with them (c. 25). Thus the insistence on retaining monastic control of the economy required brothers to be out in the world far more than the Rule had envisaged.[27] The many connections between houses had the same effect. They were now either members of monastic orders or collected into provincial chapters; and larger houses also had dependent priories, cells, and granges, as well as parochial and other benefices sometimes staffed

---

26   McDonald, '*Benedictina* in England', pp. 124–25.
27   See common legislation around monks visiting other monasteries: Ulrich, III. 22; Bernard, I. 9; *Constitutions of Lanfranc*, p. 130; *English Black Monks*, I, 82 (also 11, 17–18, 39, 83, etc.).

by monks. *Summi magistri* legislated for brothers posted to a house's manors, parishes, benefices, or dependent priories: they must live in pairs (at least), follow all the rules, say the hours, live in common, and not go out on the town to eat or drink, and so on (c. 26). Discipline in cells was a long-standing problem, exacerbated in the English case by the number of priories and properties owned by French abbeys, many of them run by a monk or two sent across the Channel: often the cells produced little economic benefit for the mother-house, which was intent rather on maintaining established, if far-flung rights.[28] Thus the ways in which religious houses were distributed and interconnected diluted the absolute enclosure and autonomy depicted in the Rule and required a number of compromises with its principles. The text of *Summi magistri* shows us, therefore, against its will, a much more complex pattern of Benedictine interaction with the world than the internally focused Rule had suggested.

Benedict XII's own positive agenda for the monastic orders exacerbated this tension. He famously sought to modernize the monastic orders with respect to education, where the secular Church and the friars had overtaken them. Knowledge of theology and law would feed back into the monastery a better understanding of both divine excellence and human justice (c. 7). Thus each house was to have a master to teach the trivium (c. 7), and if it had twenty brethren or more it was to send a monk to the university (c. 8). This meant that some monks would be permanently out in the schools, for whom the prohibitions on receiving stipends and on private chambers were suspended (c. 9). A monk-schoolmaster would also have his own money for books and other necessaries; and in the absence of a suitable monk the stipendiary schoolmaster was to be a resident secular, another incursion into the precinct. The Benedictines (and other orders) could not be autonomous in a world in which they had to compete and which made demands on them.

Late medieval monasticism was faced with a series of paradoxical challenges. The enclosure was breaking down not just (presumably)

---

28 *English Black Monks*, iii, index, s.v. 'monks': not to live alone, sent to cells, e.g. i, pp. 17, 267–68, ii, pp. 51–52, iii, pp. 115–16; Cheney, *Episcopal Visitation*, pp. 160, 170; Marjorie Morgan, *The English Lands of the Abbey of Bec* (Oxford: Clarendon Press, 1946), pp. 14–20, 33–37.

because of the laxity of humanity, but also because a more diverse and complex world had grown around it and threatened its distinctiveness: other ecclesiastical bodies could now perform all the functions which had once been the preserve of the Benedictines. *Summi magistri* contains contradictory responses to these predicaments. One was to reaffirm the enclosure: yet both the compromises in the text and its hobbling in the aftermath made clear that this was impossible. The other was to accept that monks needed to compete in the world and prove their social utility.[29] But, as well as itself breaking down the enclosure, this threatened to raise the question whether religious were necessary at all, a contradiction that ran through the remaining two monastic centuries to the Reformation.

LATER MIDDLE AGES: INTEGRATION AND OPENNESS

Prima facie, we can get close to late medieval monasteries through visitation records, which seem to 'open up' what was actually happening in them to external (and modern scholarly) scrutiny.[30] Prosecuting counsel can easily compile a collection of lurid images in order to condemn late medieval monasticism: the dogs thronging the cloister; monks out hunting or drinking; high-level commercial activity such as the prior with his own thousand sheep; the fancy 'frokkes' and linen underwear; the dancing in the guesthouse at Norwich; sodomy, pregnant nuns, and monks who had suspect access to women; the 'lunaticus' and violent prior of Wymondham who (quite apart from only

---

29　Benjamin Thompson, 'Monasteries, Society and Reform in Late Medieval England', in *The Religious Orders in Pre-Reformation England*, ed. by James G. Clark (Woodbridge: Boydell, 2002), pp. 165–95 (pp. 182–84).

30　Below, I use mainly *Visitations of the Diocese of Norwich, AD 1492–1532*, ed. by Augustus Jessopp, Camden Society, new ser., 43 (London: Camden Society, 1888; henceforth *Norwich*); but similar examples can usually be found not only in *English Black Monks*, but also in *Visitations of Religious Houses in the Diocese of Lincoln*, ed. by A. Hamilton Thompson, Canterbury and York Society, 7, 14, 21, 3 vols (London: Canterbury and York Society, 1915–27; henceforth *Lincoln*); *Visitations in the Diocese of Lincoln, 1517–1531*, ed. by A. Hamilton Thompson, Lincoln Record Society, 33, 35, 37, 3 vols (Lincoln: Lincoln Record Society, 1940–47; henceforth *Lincoln, 1517–1531*); *Collectanea Anglo-Premonstratensia*, ed. by Francis A. Gasquet, Camden Society, 3rd ser., 6, 10, 12, 3 vols (London: Camden Society, 1904–06); see Knowles, *Religious Orders*, I, pp. 78–112, II, pp. 204–18, III, pp. 39–51, 62–86. I am unable here to notice differences between male and female houses, but hope to do so elsewhere. Some houses visited were Augustinian as well as Benedictine.

attending matins once a month) inter alia drew a sword, struck two brothers with a stone in the cloister, and maliciously broke a brother's claricord, a kind of harp.[31] The point of visitations was to reveal and correct excesses, and the fact that we know about these and other enormities shows that they too were not tolerated by either religious or visitors.

Nevertheless, the assumptions which the parties brought to visitations reveal the weakening of the enclosure, partly because of the emphasis on regulating rather than preventing irregular practice. There were plenty of legitimate reasons for monks to be outside the precinct. Apart from business and benefices, holidays to friends or relatives were acceptable, albeit at only one per year, and walks beyond the precinct were normal but should not go too far.[32] Similarly, seculars were no longer to be excluded from religious houses, but their presence was to be monitored; friends were to come to the parlour in the infirmary, not to monks' chambers; the movements of female servants were to be confined to certain areas.[33] The number of horses kept by monasteries and their frequency of use by monks were to be limited.[34] The same mindset applied to the forms of worldliness entrenched in the cloister, such as the regulation of dress or meat-eating. The privatization of both space and property was now routine, as we have seen with respect to individual chambers; concern focused on their number, the equity of distribution, who went into them, what they did in them (for instance, sleeping), and what was kept in them; one monk was found to have stolen a cookery book 'furtive'.[35] Wages distributed on anniversaries or in lieu of pittances allowed monks to save or spend their own money, but this was to be regulated: cash was to be kept by an official until applied for, and it was to be spent only on necessaries, not 'voluptuose'

---

31 See e.g. Norwich, pp. 191, 213, 215, 279 (dogs); 21, 121, 280–83 (hunting); 99, 116–17, 122, 162 (drinking); 21, 114 (commerce); 74, 77–78, 97, 201, 274, 279–82 (clothes); 75 (dancing); 109 (pregnancy), 204, 250 (sodomy), 72–78, 86–89, 96–100, 102–03, 184, etc. (suspect women); 96–99 (lunatic prior).

32 English Black Monks, II, pp. 114, 123, I, 67, III, p. 84; Lincoln, I, p. 80, III, p. 379.

33 Norwich, pp. 77, 79, 142; Lincoln, I, p. 74; Christopher R. Cheney, 'Norwich Cathedral Priory in the Fourteenth Century', Bulletin of the John Rylands Library, 20 (1936), pp. 3–30 (art. xxi).

34 English Black Monks, II, p. 111.

35 See the suspect women, n. 31 above; Norwich, pp. 54, 97, 199, 201, 204–05.

on food, drink, and worse.[36] The visitations reveal in time-and-place detail how the large principles of monastic texts up to even 1336 had been largely abandoned in favour of regulating excesses.

There is in fact a revealing converse strain in visitation-complaint about the failure to maintain acceptable living standards. The buildings were not kept repaired and had become ruinous; windows were broken and draughty.[37] Pittances and wages were not paid properly or fully; the wine was sour, meals were sparse, the meat was poor, it was too salty, there were no spices.[38] The habits were in poor shape; monks did not have enough firewood in winter; there were no seats in the cloister and no light in the dormitory.[39] Such complaints disclose at least middling expectations of material comfort, as against the poverty of the Rule. They also extend to the rigour of life. Monks were not being permitted their accustomed recreations; the rotation of duties and relaxations, whether saying the Mass and offices or eating meat in the infirmary, was not drawn up fairly; they were not permitted horses for journeys; they were forced to celebrate or attend even when ill; officials were over-zealous in correction.[40] These sensitivities around the distribution of favours and penalties underpin what seem to be frequent reports of divisions within communities. Sometimes the juniors thought that the obedientiaries and seniors were running things in their own interests: older monks were keeping the young in ignorance of the finances, or the seniors made the juniors perform all the divine offices in their own absence.[41] On the other hand some superiors favoured the younger monks as companions and officers, sidelining the seniors' influence.[42] This competition for the fruits of both comfort and leisure is revealing of a set of expectations almost opposite to that of the Rule.

---

36 Cheney, 'Norwich Cathedral Priory', arts xvi–xvii.

37 *Norwich, passim* (e.g. pp. 18, 71–79, 85–87, 95–101, 101–06, 198).

38 *Norwich*, pp. 61, 96, 101, 106, 198, 280–82 (wages); 16, 26, 86, 96, 121, 139, 145, 283, 286–87, 290–91 (food and wine); *Lincoln*, iii, p. 376 (spices).

39 *Norwich*, pp. 4, 23, 102, 105, 128, 185.

40 *Norwich*, pp. 61, 73, 74, 76, 108, 118, 139, 211, 249 (recreations); 26, 53, 138–40, 193, 216, 250, 253 (correction); *Lincoln*, i, pp. 37, 105–06, ii, pp. 55–59, 305, 309, 316 (horses).

41 *Norwich*, pp. 73, 197–98, 203, 205, 253, 281–83, 290.

42 *Norwich*, pp. 74, 77, 143, 165; and for general tensions with unruly juniors, e.g. pp. 109, 202.

These tensions even had an effect on the core monastic function of collective liturgy. Houses that were struggling for material viability were likely to underperform. Debt was frequently reported, and the failure of officials to account or make inventories was common. Thus not enough monks were maintained, or enough boys in the almonry (who sang at some hours); or enough monks at the university or schooling in the house.[43] The vestments were in a poor state, and the books, especially liturgical ones, were not kept in good order (in one case doves were said to be befowling them); the bells needed repair, there was no clock.[44] Perhaps more insidiously, the elaboration of offices and obediences had broken the community down into different departments and groups. Obedientiaries might form a strong majority of the strength of a smaller monastery, and one third of a large one.[45] There was therefore a perennial concern over the religious' attendance at the divine office, which both sloth and legitimate business precluded.[46]

What visitation records reveal depends on the tension between their open- and closed-ness. The visitors' aim was to prise open the hidden secrets and defects of the house.[47] They did this, after an 'opening' ceremony, firstly through secret, one-to-one interviews which disclosed *detecta* only to the visitor and his staff. Then the *comperta* were revealed and injunctions published. How keen were visitors to find anything? That some were less intent than others is suggested by series of routine records depicting what may have been routine occasions; visitors' main object might be to assert jurisdiction and collect procurations rather than finding fault, exposing scandal, and putting themselves to the trouble of correction.[48] But, equally, zealous visitors like Bishop Alnwick of Lincoln were deeply concerned for the state of the houses, as witnessed by the detailed nature of the records they generated and their care in preserving them.[49]

---

43   *Norwich*, pp. 7, 96, 107, 161–64, 165, 192, 253.

44   *Norwich, passim*, e.g. pp. 77, 161–62 (incl. doves); 61, 98, 163, 209 (clocks).

45   See the officers named in the visitations as a proportion of all the religious, e.g. Walsingham, 1532, *Norwich*, pp. 314–15.

46   A frequent complaint throughout visitations; see nn. 41–42 above.

47   For procedure see Hamilton Thompson's introductions in *Lincoln*, I, pp. ix–xii, II, pp. xliv–lxii.

48   See many of the 1532 visitations in *Norwich*, pp. 270–319.

49   *Lincoln*, II–III; cf. the often lighter *Lincoln, 1517–1531*, II–III.

Although the religious were obliged to open up about their house's faults, those in lax institutions might have a common incentive to close ranks and keep them hidden. The more open to the world they were, the greater the premium on keeping this close. We have explicit reports of brothers agreeing not to report anything.[50] In fact, the visitations where some or all report 'omnia bene' raise suspicion.[51] Apart from a possible desire to conceal enormities, they may suggest lax expectations which did not see anything much wrong in behaviour which would have horrified the founding fathers, or was reported by others. Sometimes in such cases it is evident that everything was far from good.[52] Deponents occasionally revealed that their superior had told them to keep quiet.[53] Corrupt heads had an evident incentive to go down this path: correcting the abbot of St Benet's misdeeds would cost him two hundred marks.[54] We know of these instances, of course, because brethren did not comply and opened up. This was often a result of a house divided by rivalries and resentments; monks out of favour with the ruling clique had the opposite incentive to blab to the visitors, often motivated by the unequal distribution of the fruits of monastic living. Hence the sense of querulousness and division that seems to pervade all-too-many religious houses, with resentments boiling over into reports of bad language and insults, quarrels and dissensions, and occasionally violence.[55] One visitor anticipated further trouble around his own injunctions and enjoined the brothers not to quarrel (openly?) about the *comperta* but to live peacefully thereafter.[56] Thus the impression these reports give may itself be distorted, precisely because the visitation process encouraged mutual complaint, covered by the relative anonymity of the individual interview. Perhaps these apparently dramatic snapshots of internal dissensions may paint too lurid a picture of houses which in practice exhibit merely a few containable

---

50   *Norwich*, p. 126.

51   See n. 48 above; and *Norwich, Lincoln* and *Lincoln, 1517–1531, passim.*

52   Also *Lincoln, 1517–1531*, I, pp. lxxiv–lxxv, lxxxi.

53   *Norwich*, p. 114; *Lincoln*, II, p. 193.

54   Ibid., p. 126.

55   *Passim* and above; and for divided houses, e.g. *Norwich*, pp. xix, 71–79, 113–23, 196–206; *Lincoln, 1517–1531*, II, pp. lxxv–vi.

56   *Norwich*, p. 7; see also p. 123, where the visitor warned the prior (see n. 53 above) not to punish any of his canons for their conduct during the visitation.

rivalries. These records may therefore open up more than was really warranted — or the apparent openness of 'omnia bene' may in fact close down all sorts of hidden problems.

We may ask, finally, how were the *comperta* and injunctions published, or made open? Did these texts have active agency in the world to change future behaviour? Efficient bishops filed a copy in their chancery, and presumably deployed them in the scandalous cases where they planned to return in a few months.[57] But with the usual interval of several years or more, the chances are that such records languished, closed in the archives.[58] Indeed, summonses to visitations might include a demand for previous injunctions; but equally they might not.[59] The present injunctions were addressed to the house, and at Ramsey in 1432 Bishop Gray enjoined that they be put up in the dortor so that all the monks could see them.[60] But visitors explicitly did not want them published beyond the house, to save the honour and fame of the house.[61] Ultimately, once the visitation had been dissolved, the head recovered his jurisdiction: the prior of Walsingham had explicitly reminded — rather, threatened — his canons, 'I will rule again'.[62] We have few visitation records in monastic archives: it was all too easy for heads and/or their monks to bury these texts and remove them from the consciousness of their fellows.[63] In closing them down, these documents were thus deprived of any power.

CONCLUSION

Our view of late medieval monasticism is revealed in a kaleidoscopic dynamic of the openness and enclosure of the visitation procedure and the documents which recorded it. Monastic orders were as capable as individual religious houses at closing down attempts at reform, as we have seen with the *Benedictina* in England. Henry V, mindful of

---

57 See n. 47 above; *Lincoln*, II, pp. lv–lvi; *Norwich*, p. 7.
58 I have not found evidence of bishops bringing injunctions with them to ordinary visitations.
59 *Lincoln*, II, p. lxiii; *Norwich*, p. 21.
60 *Lincoln*, II, pp. 106–07.
61 *Lincoln*, II, pp. liv–lv, lix–lx.
62 *Norwich*, p. 114: 'ego iterum regnabo'.
63 Cheney, *Episcopal Visitation*, pp. 13–15; *Lincoln*, II; *Lincoln, 1517–1531*, I, p. civ.

the comfort that memory of the monks' prayers brought him on the morning of Agincourt, aimed to return to 'pristine religion': greater monastic efficiency and the removal of distractions would produce unceasing prayer for the estate of realm and Church.[64] The thirteen articles he presented to the English Benedictines in 1421 propounded good administration but also addressed the key laxities of monastic life: horses, meat-eating, clothes, attendance at choir, private property, private chambers, and egress from the enclosure, the last two explicitly linked to access to women. The provincial chapter was obliged to engage openly with each article; but by skilful argument they closed them down to seven, with most of the loose practices essentially preserved. Their Tudor successors were more brazen when faced by Wolsey's demands for a return to 1336: they argued that religious did not want to be austere like the Carthusians or Observants, and that most would leave, denuding the monasteries and making them unable to keep up any kind of regular observance and divine service.[65] This was a straightforward admission that it was no longer possible for many to follow the Rule; if you wanted the monks' prayers, you would have to abandon asceticism.

It was this disjunction which Cromwell was finally able to exploit by putting monasteries into a double-bind. He exacerbated the tension between the monks' practical openness to society and their statutory enclosure. In his injunctions stability in the precinct headed the articles relating to the monastic life, followed by the exclusion of women and having only one entrance to the house.[66] Enforcing the enclosure flew in the face of centuries of monastic custom, but was firmly rooted in the authority of the Rule. He was thus able to create a crisis which enabled him to close down these too-open institutions. He succeeded in passing the 1536 Suppression Act in Parliament partly by manipulating an open book, in the form of the findings ('*comperta*') of his recent monastic visitation.[67] At a glance these appeared to show that large

---

64   *English Black Monks*, II, pp. 98–134.

65   Ibid., III, pp. 123–24.

66   *Concilia*, III, pp. 789–91.

67   Anthony N. Shaw, 'The *Compendium Compertorum* and the Making of the Suppression Act of 1536' (unpublished doctoral thesis, University of Warwick, 2003), pp. 335–54, 391–406.

numbers of monks had admitted to sexual immorality: in fact, a minority had admitted privately to self-abuse, but the book was laid out to give a visual illusion of mass confession, exploiting the openness of the visible page. Nor was this the last paradoxical conjunction of openness and enclosure in the Henrician Reformation. The genuinely enclosed and austere religious of the time, the Carthusians, who might have been able to argue for the survival of their end of the monastic spectrum on the grounds that they were still observing the old codes, and indeed might have supported Wolsey's programme, in fact opposed reform because it had become bound up with the rejection of the Pope and the enforcement of the royal supremacy and the succession.[68] In this final act of engagement with and openness to the world of politics, these enclosed orders guaranteed their own destruction.

---

68   Knowles, *Religious Orders*, III, pp. 229–36.

The Openness of the Enclosed Convent
Evidence from the Lüne Letter Collection
EDMUND WAREHAM

In an undated letter from the late fifteenth or early sixteenth century, a nun in the northern German Benedictine convent of Lüne greets another nun from the nearby Benedictine convent of Ebstorf in the name of Jesus, the living water. The letter is one of almost 1800 letters which survive from Lüne between *c.* 1460 and 1555.[1] The writer informs the recipient that she is well and hopes the same for her fellow-nun. She is thankful that the Ebstorf nun has found comfort in her letters and recognized the constancy of their bond. Even if the Lüne nun knew that her writings were childish and unpolished, she notes that she would not cease from sending material. In the hope that the Ebstorf nun will recognize the intention behind the letter, the Lüne nun, switching back and forth between Latin and German, writes:

> Karissima, ik sende juw nunc pro presenti Jesum Christum, probaticam piscinam, dat gy dar pro deductione temporis et ob dulcedinem consolationis tho ghan, quando et quam sepe vobis libet. Habet enim quinque porticus, de alle tyd open stad omnibus langwidis aridis et tribulatione pressis motionem

1   'Netzwerke der Nonnen: Edition und Erschließung der Briefsammlung aus Kloster Lüne (ca. 1460–1555)', ed. by Eva Schlotheuber and others with Philipp Stenzig and others <http://diglib.hab.de/edoc/ed000248/start.htm> [accessed 26 October 2020].

aque gratie et pietatis salutem et sanitatem anime et corporis
largiter fundentibus, unde den aqueductum konne gy ubique
myd juw hebben, tam diebus quam noctibus, in omnibus locis
et angulis, wor gy trostes unde vrolicheyt behoven.[2]

(Dearest, I send you now for the time being in the present Jesus
Christ, the sheep pool, so that you can approach it to while
away the time and for the sweetness of consolation whenever
and however often it pleases you. For it has five porches, which
at all times stand open for all those who are weak, withered,
and subdued by tribulation, pouring out in abundance the
movement of water of mercy and piety, giving salvation and
health to the soul and body. And you can have this aqueduct
with you wherever you are, at day and night, in every place and
corner, when you are in need of comfort and gladness.)

The letter concludes with the writer passing on greetings to the prioress
of Ebstorf, as well as the subprioress (referred to by the initials 'EL'),
and with a commendation in the name of Christ, in the hope that he
may open a fountain of water for them.[3]

The letter draws on a passage in the Gospel of John:

Now there is at Jerusalem by the sheep market a pool, which
is called in the Hebrew tongue Bethesda, having five porches.
In these lay a great multitude of impotent folk, of blind, halt,
withered, waiting for the moving of the water. For an angel
went down at a certain season into the pool, and troubled the
water: whosoever then first after the troubling of the water
stepped in was made whole of whatsoever disease he had.[4]

Medieval commentaries on the passage noted the significance of the
number five. Aquinas, for example, drawing on John Chrysostom, observed how the five porches signified in the mystical sense the five
wounds on the body of Christ.[5] Other authors established a connection between the pool and the cross. For the twelfth-century anchorite

---

2   Kloster Lüne, Hs. 15, quire 24, fols 6^v–7^r.

3   Kloster Lüne, Hs. 15, quire 24, fol. 7^v: 'E cum hoc valeatis in salute ac sanitate
     hominis, virtusque in Christo Jesu sponso nostro, qui vobis fontis venas aperiat'.
     See the antiphon for the Feast of St Clement: 'Oremus omnes ad dominum Jesum
     Christum dixit beatus Clemens ut confessoribus suis fontis venas aperiat' (Cantus ID
     004191).

4   John 5. 2–4 (King James Version).

5   St Thomas Aquinas, *Commentary on the Gospel of John: Chapters 1–5*, trans. by Fabian
     Larcher and James A. Weisheipl (Washington: Catholic University of America Press,
     2010), p. xxiv.

Frau Ava from Melk, the wood for the cross of Christ lay waiting in the well before its eventual construction. In the iconographical tradition, such as a book of hours made for Catherine of Cleves between 1442 and 1445 depicting the Legend of the Wood of the Cross, the 'Piscina Probatica' appeared as a small round pool.[6] When the Lüne nun writes that she is sending the nun in Ebstorf 'Jesus Christ, the sheep pool', we can assume, based on other evidence from the Lüne letter collection, that she may well have been sending a depiction of the scene or of Christ's wounds.

Berndt Hamm has emphasized an impulse in the later Middle Ages to make the treasures of the mercy of Christ, Mary, and the saints open to as many people as possible and to make them more easily accessible. This impulse was not new but given a fresh accent in the fifteenth and early sixteenth centuries, as a newfound emphasis on Christ's humanity went hand in hand with his approachability.[7] The letter from Lüne in many respects confirms such a trend. The nun evokes a language of fluidity, emphasizing that 'the movement of the water of mercy and piety' pours out 'in abundance'. The recipient can turn to the image at any time and at any place whenever she is in need, for the porches 'at all times stand open for all'. In her study of spiritual practice in late medieval northern Germany, Caroline Walker Bynum argues, similarly to Hamm, that the question of how to access God's mercy was a leading concern of the fifteenth century. 'How', Bynum asks, 'if Christ has gone away in resurrection and ascension [...] do Christians find him present here on earth?'[8] Answers to that question resulted in a proliferation of visual material in the period, in particular imagery connected to Christ's wounds, which Bynum interprets less in terms of violence and violation, and more 'as doorway and access, refuge

6   Barbara Baert, 'The Pool of Bethsaïda: The Cultural History of a Holy Place in Jerusa-
     lem', *Viator*, 36 (2005), pp. 1–22 (pp. 7, 11–15).

7   Berndt Hamm, 'Die "nahe Gnade" — innovative Züge der spätmittelalterlichen Theo-
     logie und Frömmigkeit', in *'Herbst des Mittelalters'? Fragen zur Bewertung des 14. und
     15. Jahrhunderts*, ed. by Jan A. Aertsen and Martin Pickavé (Berlin: De Gruyter, 2004),
     pp. 541–57 (pp. 545, 555).

8   Caroline Walker Bynum, *Wonderful Blood: Theology and Practice in Late Medieval North-
     ern Germany and Beyond* (Philadelphia: University of Pennsylvania Press, 2007), p. 7;
     Caroline Walker Bynum, 'Violent Imagery in Late Medieval Piety: Fifteenth Annual
     Lecture of the GHI, November 8, 2001', *GHI Bulletin*, 30 (2002), pp. 3–36 (p. 23).

and consolation.[9] The imagery of the open, flowing wounds was not new and was common in thirteenth-century women's writing.[10] What seems to have changed in the fifteenth century was the frequency in its use, in both textual and visual sources.[11] In the Cistercian convent of Medingen, for example, twenty-five kilometres south-east of Lüne, the nuns produced a tapestry in the fifteenth century, the *Wichmannsburg Antependium*, where a woman climbs up a ladder to reach the side wound of Christ.[12]

This article reflects on what openness meant for a group of enclosed nuns by examining an exceptionally large corpus of letters which survive from the convent of Lüne. Older studies on convents had a tendency to look at these institutions from the outside in, often on the basis of male-authored sources such as rules or visitation protocols.[13] A major shift in the historiography has been to reverse this by looking at the convents from the inside out, by turning to sources produced by the nuns themselves, such as chronicles, notebooks, or letters.[14] Much writing in these pragmatic forms was often written for the community itself and not intended for a wider readership.[15]

9   Bynum, *Wonderful Blood*, p. 14. See also Caroline Walker Bynum, *Dissimilar Similitudes: Devotional Objects in Late Medieval Europe* (New York: Zone Books, 2020).

10 Bernard McGinn, *The Flowering of Mysticism: Men and Women in the New Mysticism (1200–1350)* (New York: Crossroad Herder, 1998), pp. 270–71.

11 Racha Kirakosian, *From the Material to the Mystical in Late Medieval Piety: The Vernacular Transmission of Gertrude of Helfta's Visions* (Cambridge: Cambridge University Press, 2020); Rosalynn Voaden, 'All Girls Together: Community, Gender and Vision at Helfta', in *Medieval Women in their Communities*, ed. by Diane Watt (Toronto: University of Toronto Press, 1997), pp. 72–91.

12 Henrike Lähnemann, '"An dessen bom wil ik stigen": Die Ikonographie des Wichmannsburger Antependiums im Kontext der Medinger Handschriften', *Oxford German Studies*, 34 (2005), pp. 19–46.

13 Heike Uffmann, 'Inside and Outside the Convent Walls: The Norm and Practice of Enclosure in the Reformed Nunneries of Late Medieval Germany', *Medieval History Journal*, 4 (2001), pp. 83–108 (p. 86); Eva Schlotheuber, 'Gelehrte Bräute Christi': *Geistliche Frauen in der mittelalterlichen Gesellschaft* (Tübingen: Mohr Siebeck, 2018), p. 2.

14 Heike Uffmann, *Wie in einem Rosengarten: Monastische Reformen des späten Mittelalters in den Vorstellungen von Klosterfrauen* (Bielefeld: Verlag für Regionalgeschichte, 2008); Anne Winston-Allen, *Convent Chronicles: Women Writing about Women and Reform in the Late Middle Ages* (University Park: Pennsylvania State University Press, 2004); Eva Schlotheuber, *Klostereintritt und Bildung: Die Lebenswelt der Nonnen im späten Mittelalter; Mit einer Edition des 'Konventstagebuchs' einer Zisterzienserin von Heilig-Kreuz bei Braunschweig (1484–1507)* (Tübingen: Mohr Siebeck, 2004).

15 Schlotheuber, *Klostereintritt*, pp. 321–27.

By contrast, convent letter writing acted as a bridge with the outside world, one of the many ways in which the convent wall could become permeable and pervious and for nuns to be part of a wider network of exchange.[16] For nuns, like monks, used correspondence for all manner of reasons, from defending their interests to organizing economic affairs. In particular they sought to maintain contact with friends and family in other convents or lay society. In so doing they often reminded them of their function, especially their prayers.[17] It is this latter point which forms the focus of this article, which considers the specific textual and visual practices by which these brides of Christ sought to make their bridegroom's mercy open and accessible to those beyond the convent wall. The Lüne letter collection sheds new light on the practice of enclosure, on the nature of both practical and symbolic communication from and to an enclosed community, and on the nuns' own perspective and reflections of their enclosed status and role in society. Convent letters were a way of creating and sustaining enclosure, as the nuns sought to close themselves both externally and internally from the influence of the outside world whilst simultaneously opening themselves and others up to Christ's grace and mercy.[18]

*

No original letters survive, but copies are preserved in three letter books in the convent archive, two of which (Kloster Lüne, Hss. 15 and 31) were most likely compiled in the 1530s, when the convent was threatened with closure by attempts to introduce the Lutheran

---

16   Claire Walker, '"Doe not supose ma well mortifyed Nun dead to the world": Letter-Writing in Early Modern English Convents', in *Early Modern Women's Letter Writing, 1450–1700*, ed. by James Daybell (Basingstoke: Palgrave, 2001), pp. 159–76; Bronagh Ann McShane, 'Visualising the Reception and Circulation of Early Modern Nuns' Letters', *Journal of Historical Network Research*, 2 (2018), pp. 1–25.

17   Lena Vosding, 'Klösterliche Briefkunst: Die ars dictaminis im Kloster', in *Ars dictaminis: Handbuch der mittelalterlichen Briefstillehre*, ed. by Florian Hartmann and Benoît Grévin (Stuttgart: Hiersemann, 2019), pp. 493–517 (p. 496).

18   Lena Vosding, 'Die Überwindung der Klausur: Briefkultur der Frauenklöster im Spätmittelalter', in *Zwischen Klausur und Welt: Autonomie und Interaktion spätmittelalterlicher Frauengemeinschaften*, ed. by Sigrid Hirbodian and Eva Schlotheuber (Ostfildern: Thorbecke, in press); Felix Heinzer, '*Claustrum non manufactum* — Innenräume normativer Schriftlichkeit', in *Schriftkultur und religiöse Zentren im norddeutschen Raum*, ed. by Patrizia Carmassi, Eva Schlotheuber, and Almut Breitenbach (Wiesbaden: Harrassowitz, 2014), pp. 141–65 (p. 142).

Reformation, and the final book (Hs. 30) in the 1550s. Hs. 15, which this article will draw evidence from, contains material largely from the pre-Reformation period and seems to have acted primarily as a model-letter collection. Comprised of thirty-four quires and written by a number of hands, the manuscript is marked by a high frequency of undated and anonymized letters or letters which use only initials. Hs. 15 contains both outgoing and incoming correspondence and was not as systematically organized as the two other letter books. Nevertheless, certain quires were thematically structured, such as a group of condolence letters (quire 14) or a series of congratulatory letters to relatives on marriage (quires 20 and 27). It is important to be constantly aware of the two possible levels of analysis: the information imparted by the letter at, first, the point of transmission and, second, the moment of collection. The character of an individual letter reflected and was to a degree dependent on the collection as a whole.[19]

The corpus is significant for a number of reasons. In terms of extent, the number of letters from Lüne is far greater than collections from other German convents, such as the fifty-four German letters from the Poor Clares of Söflingen near Ulm,[20] the fifty-three German letters which Katerina Lemmel wrote in the Birgittine convent of Maihingen at the start of the sixteenth century,[21] the forty-one original Low German letters from the Westphalian canonical foundation of Langenhorst written between 1470 and 1495,[22] the twenty-one letters from the Benedictine convent of Oberwerth,[23] or the letters which

---

19   Lena Vosding, 'Gifts from the Convent: The Letters of the Benedictine Nuns at Lüne as the Material Manifestation of Spiritual Care', in *Was ist ein Brief? Aufsätze zu epistolarer Theorie und Kultur/What Is a Letter? Essays on Epistolary Theory and Culture*, ed. by Marie Isabel Matthews-Schlinzig and Caroline Socha (Würzburg: Königshausen & Neumann, 2018), pp. 211–33 (p. 214); Giles Constable, *Letters and Letter-Collections* (Turnhout: Brepols, 1976), p. 60.

20   Max Miller, *Die Söflinger Briefe und das Klarissenkloster Söflingen bei Ulm a.D. im Spätmittelalter* (Würzburg-Aumühle: Triltsch, 1940).

21   *Pepper for Prayer: The Correspondence of the Birgittine Nun Katerina Lemmel (1516–1525); Edition and Translation*, ed. and trans. by Volker Schier, Corine Schleif, and Anne Simon (Stockholm: Runica & Mediaevalia, 2019).

22   Albert Wormstall, 'Eine westfälische Briefsammlung des ausgehenden Mittelalters', *Zeitschrift für vaterländische Geschichte und Altertumskunde*, 53 (1895), pp. 149–81.

23   Anja Ostrowitzki, 'Klösterliche Lebenswelt im Spiegel von Briefen des 16. Jahrhunderts aus dem Benediktinerinnenkloster Oberwerth bei Koblenz', *Studien und Mitteilungen zur Geschichte des Benediktinerordens und seiner Zweige*, 124 (2013), pp. 167–206.

members of the Pirckheimer family sent to their brother Willibald from various convents.[24] The sheer number of letters from Lüne reflects the diversity of interactions which a convent would engage in, from the organization of benefices to managing orders of cement. In contrast to other convent letter collections, it does not simply include correspondence of officeholders, such as the abbess or prioress, but ordinary nuns as well, writings both individually and in groups.[25]

A further significance of the letter collection lies in the nuns' use of language. Just over 250 letters which were recorded were written in Latin, around 650 in Low German, and just shy of 900 in a hybrid mixture of the two languages, as in the example at the beginning of this article. The letters demonstrate the importance of language in processes of inclusion and exclusion. A defining feature of the Lüne letter collection as a whole is that nuns wrote in different languages depending on the recipient: the hybrid mixture of the two languages for communication with female convents of the region; German for communication with layfolk, notably family members and the Lüneburg town council; and Latin for male clerics and the provosts, secular officials who held jurisdiction over the convents. The linguistic, verbal, and rhetorical dexterity and creativity of the nuns was marked by high standards of education in Latin, a key feature of the northern German convent landscape when compared to the south.[26] The application of this knowledge allowed the nuns to develop different communication strategies for different audiences.

---

24 *Caritas Pirckheimer — Quellensammlung*, ed. by Josef Pfanner, 4 vols (Landshut: Caritas Pirckheimer Forschung, 1966–67), II: *Briefe von, an und über Caritas Pirckheimer (aus den Jahren 1498–1530)* (1966); Eva Schlotheuber, 'Willibald und die Klosterfrauen von Sankt Klara — eine wechselhafte Beziehung', *Pirckheimer Jahrbuch für Renaissance und Humanismusforschung*, 28 (2014), pp. 57–75.

25 Vosding, 'Gifts', p. 212.

26 Eva Schlotheuber, 'Intellectual Horizons: Letters from a Northern German Convent', in *Mysticism and Devotion in Northern Germany in the Late Middle Ages*, ed. by Elizabeth Andersen, Henrike Lähnemann, and Anne Simon (Leiden: Brill, 2013), pp. 343–72; Henrike Lähnemann, 'Bilingual Devotion: The Relationship of Latin and Low German in Prayer Books from the Lüneburg Convents', in *Mysticism and Devotion in Northern Germany*, ed. by Andersen, Lähnemann, and Simon, pp. 317–41; Jeffrey F. Hamburger, Eva Schlotheuber, and Susan Marti, *Liturgical Life and Latin Learning at Paradies bei Soest, 1300–1425: Inscription and Illumination in the Choir Books of a North German Dominican Convent*, 2 vols (Münster: Aschendorff, 2016), I, pp. 67–75.

Finally, the timespan of the correspondence covers two significant episodes and processes in the history of the convent, namely the introduction of a monastic reform in 1481 and the onset of the Protestant Reformation in the 1520s and beyond. The letters offer a unique insight into the first-hand reaction of a group of women to the often quite dramatic changes which the convent experienced as a result of these attempts at reform.[27] In 1481 a group of seven nuns from Ebstorf came to Lüne in order to enact a reform, referred to by the nuns as the 'reformatio'. Bertha Hoyer, the prioress of Lüne from 1468, was forced to resign her office and was replaced by one of the Ebstorf sisters, Sophia von Bodenteich. The reform movement sought a return to the idealized state of the monastic life by encouraging strict observation of the rules, the abolition of private property, the reintroduction of the common life, and a tightening of enclosure. This resulted in a number of changes to the convent, including an increase in the number of sisters, changes in the social makeup, and alterations and additions to the convent's buildings.[28] Many of these changes were recorded in a convent chronicle which was begun at this time, part of an expanding body of internal sources from this period which, alongside the letter books, included a new copy of the statutes and instructions on the election of the provost.[29]

*

Silvia Evangelisti has remarked how 'enclosure, when enforced, did not necessarily imply the isolation of convents or the breaking-off of all contact with the world'.[30] The Lüne letters offer a particularly rich example of this process in action: many letters written after the introduction of the reform are an expression of the nuns' discipline and commitment to the religious life. Indeed, the term 'open convent'

---

27 Johannes Meyer, 'Zur Reformationsgeschichte des Klosters Lüne', *Zeitschrift der Gesellschaft für niedersächsische Kirchengeschichte*, 14 (1909), pp. 162–221.

28 June L. Mecham, *Sacred Communities, Sacred Devotions: Gender, Material Culture, and Monasticism in Late Medieval Germany* (Turnhout: Brepols, 2014), pp. 5–6.

29 *Die Chronik des Klosters Lüne über die Jahre 1481–1530: Hs. Lüne 13*, ed. by Philipp Stenzig (Tübingen: Mohr Siebeck, 2019). The statutes and instructions for the election of the provost are currently being edited by Philipp Stenzig and Philipp Trettin.

30 Silvia Evangelisti, *Nuns: A History of Convent Life, 1450–1700* (Oxford: Oxford University Press, 2007), p. 7.

(*ein offens closter*) was employed to refer to a convent's state before its reform and when enclosure was not strictly observed.[31] This had parallels to the situation in Italy, where the designations 'open' and 'closed' were adopted in lists of female communities in Rome, whereby 'closed' meant that members observed rules of enclosure and 'open' referred to houses which did not follow a widely recognized rule.[32] Such open monasteries (*monasteri aperti*) included a wide variety of female communities, including groups of nuns who had sworn solemn vows but did not observe strict enclosure, or houses of tertiaries.[33]

In their letters the nuns showed a high degree of self-awareness of their enclosed status. Whilst in southern Germany the heart was employed as a popular metaphor of the enclosed convent, in northern Germany the nuns drew on the allegory of the vineyard to describe their existence.[34] In an original piece of Latin verse composition addressed to Provost Nikolaus Graurock on the Feast of Palm Sunday, for example, two young Lüne nuns refer to 'the vineyard of this enclosed paradise'.[35] Nuns were one of the few groups in the Middle Ages who could not participate in the *Präsenzkultur*, a culture of presence, which influenced political and social communication. Visibility was of vital importance for this *Präsenzkultur* and was played out in ritual settings such as the diet or Church festivals.[36] By contrast, nuns sought to create another form of presence, in which they simultaneously employed

---

31   Uffmann, 'Inside and Outside', p. 105. See, for example, an open letter from Geiler of Kayserberg to the Penitential Sisters of the Magdalena convent in Freiburg in 1499: *Die aeltesten Schriften Geilers von Kaysersberg: XXI Artikel — Briefe — Todtenbüchlein — Beichtspiegel — Seelenheil — Sendtbrieff — Bilger*, ed. by Léon Dacheux (Freiburg i.Br.: Herder, 1882), pp. 216–17: 'Ich kâme darhinder das ich meyn / das wolche vnware Obseruantzen / die auff eüsserlichen glitz / vnd eüsserliche übungen vnd verderblicher feind weder die offnen clôster / vrsach ist / wann in die offnen clôster kumpt niemands der seiner seele heil sûcht / er sicht offentlich dz es ein verfârlicher stadt ist / darumb so verfart da kein gûtwilliger mensch / wann er wag sich nit darein / aber in einem glastcloster / da der schein der Obseruantz ist / da ernert manich gût frumm menschen.'

32   Katherine Gill, 'Open Monasteries for Women in Late Medieval and Early Modern Italy: Two Roman Examples', in *The Crannied Wall: Women, Religion, and the Arts in Early Modern Europe*, ed. by Craig A. Monson (Ann Arbor: University of Michigan Press, 1992), pp. 15–47 (pp. 35–36).

33   Gill, 'Open Monasteries', p. 16.

34   Schlotheuber, 'Intellectual Horizons', p. 359.

35   Kloster Lüne, Hs. 15, quire 2, fol. 10ʳ: 'in vinea paradisi claustralis'.

36   Gerd Althoff, *Spielregeln der Politik im Mittelalter: Kommunikation in Frieden und Fehde* (Darmstadt: Primus, 1997), pp. 229–57.

their letters in order to break down the spatial and temporal distance between writer and recipient, whilst at the same time using their special access and openness to Christ to make him known and present to recipients beyond the convent wall.[37] This is more in line with Hans Ulrich Gumbrecht's use of the term, in which pre-Reformation eucharistic piety as practised by the nuns can be regarded emphatically as participation in a culture of presence.[38] In a particularly striking example, a nun in Lüne congratulates a nun in another convent on her coronation, the final stage in the entry process into a convent, at which she was handed a consecrated veil, ring, and crown. Quoting the words of Christ in the Gospel of Matthew, the recipient is encouraged to lift the eyes of her heart and her body to the mountains of Christ's wounds and the rivers of his blood. Even if Christ is not physically present, he is united with them in the consumption of the Eucharist, when she will gaze upon him with joyful eyes and without her veil:

> 'Ecce ego vobiscum sum, etc.' [Matthew 28. 20] und wol dat we des nicht sen konnet foris per presentiam corporalem, so love we doch indubitanter, dat he sik omni tempore mit us uniert per sumptionem sacramentalem, unde denjennen, den we nu entfanget cum omni desiderio in venerabili sacramento, den scolle we sine fine seen gaudentibus oculis absque velamente.[39]

> ('Lo, I am with you always, etc.' And even if we cannot see this by his physical presence, we still believe beyond all doubt that he is united with us at all times in the consumption of the Eucharist. And we should see him, whom we now receive with all our desire in the venerable sacrament, without end with joyful eyes and our veils removed.)

The choice of language in each letter acted as a marker of a particular relationship, and in this instance the use of code-switching was characteristic of correspondence between nuns and a further way of facilitating presence. In another letter to a nun in Ebstorf from Lüne, for example, written after 1484, the writer notes in a mixture of both Latin and German that although 'we are physically separated, we are

---

37   Vosding, 'Gifts', p. 217; Constable, *Letters*, pp. 13–14.

38   Hans Ulrich Gumbrecht, *Production of Presence: What Meaning Cannot Convey* (Stanford: Stanford University Press, 2004).

39   Kloster Lüne, Hs. 15, quire 19, fol. 5ᵛ.

all bound together inseparably in the bond of sisterly love.[40] The combination of the two languages signalled, reinforced, and verbalized the
unity between these two women, bound together as sisters in Christ
who had vowed to live chaste, secluded lives.[41] It created a language
of intimacy between nuns which could only work for those who had
the same frames of reference as each other, including biblical allusions,
monastic terminology, and neologisms, such as the word 'uniert'. In
contrast, in letters to relatives, such as those to celebrate family mar-
riages, the nuns would write only in German. Nuns would note that
as relatives they would expect to be invited to the marriage celebration but, because of their commitment to enclosure, they could not
attend.[42] Instead, they sent a letter and a whole host of saints to stand
in for them, including, in one instance from the nun 'GT' to her brother
Melchior, 'all the inhabitants of the heavenly city of Jerusalem'.[43] In
employing the language of sisterhood, the nuns were making clear that
they understood the convent as another family, one that superseded
their previous family relationships.

A further means of helping to create this sense of presence was
achieved by the nuns attaching devotional images (*Andachtsbilder*) to
their letters. With the letter to Ebstorf the Lüne nun sends a 'small
painted sheet as a sign of sisterly love', without specifying what is
depicted.[44] More detail is provided in the letter sent to the nun to
celebrate her coronation. In this instance the Lüne nun, as a sign of her
affection, sends the newly crowned nun a devotional image depicting
the Holy Face of Jesus in the hope she will receive it with as much
love as it was sent. She hopes that, whenever the recipient gazes upon
the depiction of the Veil of Veronica with her physical eyes, she will

---

40   Kloster Lüne, Hs. 15, quire 26, fol. 12^v: 'wente wy allen samen verbunden synt in
     vinculo sororie karitatis indissolubiliter, wol dat we corporaliter separati sint'.
41   Kat Hill, 'Brotherhood, Sisterhood, and the Language of Gender in the German
     Reformation', *Reformation & Renaissance Review*, 17 (2015), pp. 181–95 (p. 182).
42   See e.g. Kloster Lüne, Hs. 15, quire 20, fol. 2^v: 'nu borde my wol van susterke leve
     weghen, dat ik ok scholde jedghenwardich wesen to dyner koste na dem male, dat ik
     dyn ynege suster byn; doch so westu wol, dat dat nicht wesen kan efte mach'.
43   Kloster Lüne, Hs. 15, quire 20, fol. 3^r: 'Wy senden dy in unse stede alle de inwoner der
     hemmelschen stat Jerusalem, de wy ghebeden hebben to unsen kerkmissen.'
44   Kloster Lüne, Hs. 15, quire 26, fols 15^{r-v}: 'Item honoranda domina nostra S[ophia]
     B[odenteich] et ego transmittimus dilectionis vestre unaqueque parvum depictum
     folium insignum sororie karitatis.'

be enlightened both internally and externally.[45] This desire for a face-to-face meeting with Christ was embodied by Veronica, a witness to his Passion, and depictions of the sudarium 'lent life to a face the viewer longed to see, but had in fact never seen'.[46] In 1953 a number of devotional images were discovered when the floorboards of the choir of the Cistercian convent of Wienhausen, one hundred kilometres south of Lüne, were literally opened up. This included eight parchment miniatures depicting the Holy Face painted in two rows, which could have been cut apart and are presumed to have been produced by the Wienhausen nuns themselves to aid their devotion and to be sent as gifts to other nuns.[47]

As Gumbrecht suggests, 'something that is present is supposed to be tangible for human hands',[48] and the value of such images for private devotion lay not just in their visual qualities, but their tactile ones as well. In the desire to make Christ's presence manifest and open to all, medieval artists, including nuns, 'created images for those who wanted above all to touch, who wanted to have the scenes of their salvation tangibly present before them'.[49] The Apostle Thomas proved particularly popular in the northern German convents as a figure who represented this impulse towards the tangibility of the divine, as he was the only person after Christ's resurrection to be allowed to touch his body.[50] On 4 June 1489, for example, a Lüne nun sent Mechthild von Ingersleve in Ebstorf, soon to be crowned a

---

45   Kloster Lüne, Hs. 15, quire 19, fols 5^{r-v}: 'so sende we juk amabilem et sanctissimam faciem eiusdem sponsi nostri depictam in folio in signum vere dilectionis, et licet pulcheritudo illius sit inscrutabilis et inscriptibilis ac omni creature incomprehensibilis, so sint we doch begherende dat willen tali amore entfanghen, quali affectu we juk dat sendet, et ipse, qui ob signum amoris reliquit nobis hanc effigiem in panniculo veronice, de mote juk lumine gratie sue illustreren intus ac foris, quotiens oculis corporalibus hanc intuetis.'

46   Jeffrey F. Hamburger, *The Visual and the Visionary: Art and Female Spirituality in Late Medieval Germany* (New York: Zone Books, 1998), p. 320.

47   Ibid., pp. 323–26.

48   Gumbrecht, *Production*, p. xiii.

49   Henk van Os, 'The Monastery as a Centre of Devotion', in *The Art of Devotion in the Late Middle Ages in Europe 1300–1500*, ed. by Henk van Os, trans. by Michael Hoyle (London: Merrell Holberton, 1994), pp. 50–59 (p. 54).

50   Henrike Lähnemann, '*Saluta apostolum tuum*: Apostelvereherung im Kloster Medingen', in *Weltbild und Lebenswirklichkeit in den Lüneburger Klöstern: IX. Ebstorfer Kolloquium vom 23. bis 26. März 2011*, ed. by Wolfgang Brandis and Hans-Walter Stork (Berlin: Lukas Verlag, 2015), pp. 41–64 (pp. 52–55).

nun, an image of the Holy Face. In the letter the Lüne nun hopes that Christ will look upon Mechthild with the same eyes of mercy as he did with his Apostle Thomas when he commanded him to place his fingers in his side, and that her heart will be filled with the same light of mercy as when Christ enlightened and touched Thomas's heart.[51] The link between presence and openness becomes even clearer in a devotional image which survives from Wienhausen, depicting the doubting apostle placing his fingers into Christ's open side wounds.[52] Written and drawn by their own hands, the letters and the images which the nuns produced were a visible and tactile sign of the nuns' devotion and their desire to be both physically absent yet spiritually present.

*

The letters from Lüne and the surviving images from Wienhausen formed just one part of a much wider trend to seek closer access to Christ's grace and mercy through the commemoration of his Passion.[53] Christ's open, flowing heart proved particularly attractive in this regard, including for the Lüne nuns, and verbal and adjectival forms of 'open' in both Middle Low German (*open*) and Latin (*aperire*) occur most frequently in relation to this image. The attractiveness of devotion to Christ's heart and his open wounds lay to some extent in the flexibility of the image. On the one hand, influenced by Bernard of Clairvaux, it could encourage internal, mystical devotion by using the heart to find spiritual unity with Christ. On the other hand, it could allow less mystical and more popular forms of piety to develop around it, by seeing in the wounds the sacrificial, saving, and protecting power of Christ's Passion.[54] The

---

51 Kloster Lüne, Hs. 15, quire 16, fols 2^{r–v}: 'et idcirco pro inditio intime dilectionis erga vos transmittimus vobis unum folium depictum et licet sit parvum in materia, tamen continet in se effigiatam faciem nostri salvatoris, qui magnitudine splendoris sui replet altitudinem celi ac latitudinem terre, unde de mote oculo pietatis sue juk so lefliken ansen alze he ansach beatissimum discipulum Thomam, dilectum apostulum vestrum, do he to eme sprak: "Infer digitum tuum huc et vide", unde ok in juwe herteken schinen laten illud lumen gratie et cognitionis, dar he ene mede vorluchtede do he sprak unde syn herte berorde, dum dixit: "Dominus meus et deus meus."'

52 Inv. Nr. Wie Kc 020. See Bynum, *Dissimilar Similitudes*, inside front cover.

53 Hamm, 'Die "nahe Gnade"', p. 542.

54 Ibid., p. 551.

Lüne letters bear witness to the variety of different communicative contexts in which verbal and visual depictions of the heart could be employed and above all how the devotional practices of the nuns flowed out beyond the convent walls into wider society.

Letters evoking the flowing honey from Christ's heart and the blood from his wounds, often sent with an image attached to them, were used in particular to provide consolation about a sorrow and condolence after a death. In 1500, for example, a nun from Lüne wrote in Latin to Prioress Walburga Grawerock of the convent of Walsrode, eighty-five kilometres south-west of Lüne, after news had reached her that the prioress had had to resign her office because of an illness. She mourns the illness which afflicts Walburga but rejoices more strongly as the former prioress is now free from the burden of office. Employing a similar allegory about Walsrode's enclosed status, the Lüne nun remarks how Walburga truly laboured in the vineyard of the Lord during the heat of day, leading by example through word and deed, and living life according to the rule. As a sign of her affection, the Lüne nun sends an image of Christ, which shows the father of mercy with a bowed head, open veins, and flowing wounds, adding that Walburga can run to him when afflicted by tribulation.[55] Both letter and image became a visible and tangible sign of the shared participation in Christ's mercy.

That is also the case in a letter sent to a maternal relative and her children whose husband and father had recently died, but in this case the Lüne nun draws on similar imagery but writes in German. She sends a painted image of Christ's heart which the relative should gaze upon when she is sad. Quoting Matthew 11. 28 in German ('Komet to my alle, de gy bedrouet unde beswaret synt, ik wil juk sulven trosten'; Come unto me, all ye that labour and are heavy laden, and I will give you rest), the Lüne nun sends a 'small, holy little sheet' with an image of the sweet, honey-flowing heart which 'stands wide open for us all'. From this heart 'all holiness, goodness, and mildness has flowed out,

---

55   Hs. 15, quire 22, fol. 9ᵛ: 'Pro inditio ergo dilectionis translego vestre reverentie ymaginem nostri salvatoris, qui quasi pater misericordiarum inclinato capite, apertis venis et effluentibus vulneribus prestolatur adventum sue dilecte sponse, quam paratus est in tribulatione recipere, ad quem in omnibus tribulationibus vestris recurrere debetis'.

and for our sake he had himself wounded and through this opened up
the paradise of delight, the apothecary of all kinds of herbs and the
treasure-chamber of divine wisdom and eternal sweetness'.[56] It was a
common rhetorical strategy for the nuns to contrast the smallness of
the image with the expansiveness and openness of the multisensorial
space which it evoked.

The letters and images which were sent at moments of distress
or sadness served at the same time as a sign of the nuns' spiritual
discipline and commitment, particularly within the context of the
monastic reform and the tighter enclosure which this entailed. The
links between the reform, writing, and visual material connected to
the heart can be vividly seen in a letter written around 1484 by two
young nuns in Lüne to Elisabeth Bockes. Elisabeth had been one of
the original seven Ebstorf sisters who came to Lüne in 1481 to enact
its reform, and she returned three years later. In their letter, sent to
mark the New Year and, like the majority of letters between convents,
switching between Latin and German, the nuns express their thanks
for Elisabeth's efforts during the reform:

> [W]e danket juwer leve lefliken unde fruntliken vor alle
> woldath, truwe unde leve, de gy vaken vnde vele by us
> heft bewiset van usen junghen iaren wente an dessen dach,
> sunderken de wile, de gy hir myd us weren pro reformatione,
> do gy mannighen swaren arbeyt myd us hadden.[57]

> (We thank you lovingly and friendlily for all your help, loyalty,
> and love which you often and very much showed to us from our
> young years to the present day, especially during the time you
> were with us for the reform, when you had much hard work to
> do with us.)

As a sign of their thanks, the two Lüne nuns send Elisabeth an image:

> Alderleveste, sende we juk an rechter leve en luttik hilgen-
> bladeken, dar vynde gy inne ghemalet dat benediede, sote,
> gotlike herte uses leven salichmakeres, dat he umme user leue

---

56   Kloster Lüne, Hs. 15, quire 27, fol. 14^r: 'dar us alle salicheyt ghude unde myldicheyt
     utherverloten ist unde dar he umme user leve willen heft ghewundet laten unde heft
     us gheopent den paradys der wollust, de aptheken allerleye krude unde de trezekamer
     der gotliken wisheit unde der ewighen soticheyt'.

57   Kloster Lüne, Hs. 15, quire 19, fol. 7^r.

willen openen led myd dem scharpen spere; unde bynnen
in dessem herteken syd dat alderschoneste begherlikeste kyn-
deken Jesus, dat mote juk gheuen dor syne hilgen mynscheyt
en nye, vrolick, sunt, salich iar.[58]

(Most dearest, we send you with true love a small devotional
image, in which you will find painted the blessed, sweet, divine
heart of our dear Saviour which he for our sake had opened
with the sharp spear; and inside this little heart sits the most
beautiful, beloved child Jesus, who through his holy humanity
may grant you a new, happy, healthy, and blessed year.)

The two young nuns continue by expanding on the significance of the
image:

[U]nde allent, wes gy begherende synt, beyde an dem
lyve unde an der sele, dat gy sughen moten ute synem
honnichvletenden herten den hemmelschen invlote syner
gotliken gnade unde soticheyt so vullenkomelken, dat gy dar
ghansliken moten inne vordrunken werden.[59]

(And everything which you desire, both in body and in soul, so
that you might suck from his honey-flowing heart the heavenly
flow of his divine mercy and sweetness in such a complete way
that you may get completely drunk by it.)

A pen drawing on parchment of the infant Jesus in a heart, measur-
ing 7.1 × 6.8 cm, survives in Wienhausen, depicting him carrying the
rod and cross in his hand.[60] The Lüne letter offers direct evidence of
the context in which such an image would have been sent and how
its meaning could have been expounded. As Peter Schmidt has observed regarding the exchange of such small-scale images in the context
of the reformed Dominican nuns of Nuremberg, the communicative
aspects could be multifaceted.[61] In Lüne the text and image served

---

58   Ibid.
59   Ibid.
60   Horst Appuhn and Christian von Heusinger, 'Der Fund kleiner Andachtsbilder des
      13. bis 17. Jahrhunderts im Kloster Wienhausen', *Niederdeutsche Beiträge zur Kunstge-
      schichte*, 4 (1965), pp. 157–238 (p. 195).
61   Peter Schmidt, 'Die Rolle der Bilder in der Kommunikation zwischen Frauen und
      Männern, Kloster und Welt: Schenken und Tauschen bei den Nürnberger Domini-
      kanerinnen', in *Femmes, art et religion au Moyen Âge*, ed. by Jean-Claude Schmitt
      (Strasbourg: Presses Universitaires de Strasbourg, 2004), pp. 34–61 (p. 34).

two purposes. First, both at the moment of writing and later at the moment of compilation the letter strengthened the communal bonds between Lüne and Ebstorf which had been reinforced and renewed by the reform. Second, it took a highly common motif, that of the flowing heart, but made it more personalized as the nuns painted it with their own hands and in so doing cemented the strong sense of feeling which existed between the two young Lüne nuns and Elisabeth, whom they evidently looked up to. The emphasis on Christ's humanity was closely linked with the language of fluidity, as Christ's mercy flowed between the nuns in an act which constituted both communal and personal elements.

*

In keeping with the model-letter character of Hs. 15 as a whole, the letters which employed the language of openness present a highly idealized picture of convent life. The nuns drew in particular on a common stock of imagery surrounding Christ's heart and his wounds which they could then deploy, in Latin, German, or a mixture of both. The letters were compiled in the 1530s at a time when the convent was under direct threat of closure and the nuns sought to create an archive of correspondence which illustrated their rights, freedoms, and sincere commitment to the common, enclosed life. Indeed, across Germany, there was often a direct parallel between the nuns' reformed status and their levels of resistance to the introduction of the Protestant Reformation, as the view of the convent as an open garden of paradise gave way to new metaphors of the convent as closed-off prison.[62]

A more in-depth study is required of the language of openness in Hss. 30 and 31, which comprise letters from the post-Reformation period, but one letter which survives from Hs. 15 illustrates the new situation vividly. On 26 September 1525 Abbess Margarete Stöterogge of the Cistercian convent of Medingen provided Prioress Mechthild Wilde of Lüne with an account about the recent visit of Duke Ernest I of Brunswick-Lüneburg to Medingen. The territory was under severe financial pressure at this time, and Ernest saw in the convents

---

62 Barbara Steinke, *Paradiesgarten oder Gefängnis? Das Nürnberger Katharinenkloster zwischen Klosterreform und Reformation* (Tübingen: Mohr Siebeck, 2006).

a potential source of income. Despite an interrogation which lasted several hours, the nuns of Medingen refused to hand over any goods to Ernest but ultimately had to accept that an inventory of goods be given to him. Abbess Margarete wrote in great fear to Mechthild that the community would face repercussions and the potential confiscation of convent property. Margarete sought consolation from Mechthild in her time of need, quoting Thomas à Kempis in Latin that 'in times of necessity friendships prove themselves'.[63] In her distress, she turned to familiar language and imagery and expressed hope that the most pious consoler would open up the treasures of his wounded heart and protect both Medingen and Lüne from all evil during these dark times.[64] The appeal to Christ to open up his wounded heart in this letter was far from idealized; it was made at a time of genuine fear when the nuns were faced with direct threats of violence and closure. As convents sought to collaborate and work together in their resistance to the duke, appeals to the openness and accessibility of Christ's mercy had never been more important.

---

63   Kloster Lüne, Hs. 15, quire 2, fol. 3ᵛ: 'Et vulgariter: in necessitatibus amici sunt probandi'; the source is chapter 16 of Thomas's *Vallis liliorum*.

64   Kloster Lüne, Hs. 15, quire 2, fol. 3ᵛ: 'Ille, qui tribulatorum exstat, consolator piissimus, aperiet vobis theasaurum sui vulnerati cordis et dignetur reddere pro vice consolationem suam divinam, ac ipse hoc tempore malo tuetur vos simul et nos sub alis sue misericordie ab omnibus malis.'

The Book Half Open
Humanist Friendship in Holbein's Portrait of Hermann von Wedigh III

OREN MARGOLIS

Amongst the most notable features of Renaissance portraiture in the decades after the year 1500 is the abundance of books. Again and again, in lay portraits and pictures of clerics, in paintings of men and of women, in Italy and in the North, we find a bound volume — sometimes in the hand, sometimes on a desk, shelf, or parapet, sometimes one of many — as the sitter's frequent and often solitary companion. There are multiple explanations for this development: the legacy of religious painting, such as the depiction of the Virgin reading or the iconographic representation of saints with attributes; the impact of Renaissance humanism and the scholarly self-assertion it entailed (often by direct appeal in the composition of these portraits to saintly representations); and, perhaps most importantly, the proliferation and the growing prestige of the printed book and specifically of printed literature as a mark of good breeding, elite education, cultural and intellectual sophistication, and lettered *otium*. These causes are, of course, not unrelated to each other, and certainly all inform a tradition such as the portrait with the *Petrarchino* or other small book of poetry that became so prevalent in Italian and Italianate art (Figure 1).[1] I do not propose to inquire further about causes, origins, or developments here, or even to talk in general. In fact, this essay will be

---

1   For example, see Novella Macola, 'I ritratti col Petrarca', in *Le lingue del Petrarca*, ed. by Antonio Daniele (Udine: Forum, 2005), pp. 135–57; Giuseppe Patota, 'Petrarchino',

extremely specific, focusing on one portrait with a book painted in
1532 by Hans Holbein the Younger (*c.* 1497–1543). I do, however,
wish to consider the significance of inviting into the portrait another
entity that, like the sitter him- or herself, was distinguished by a unique
and individual skin — though admittedly one that did not of necessity
or inherently belong to what it contained (most books in this period
were sold unbound).[2] These facts, when they intersected with the intellectual and artistic agenda of a painter such as Holbein, made the
book a particularly rich place of metaphor and simile.[3] According to
the maxim of Erasmus of Rotterdam (*c.* 1466–1536), inscribed on his
two most widely disseminated portraits — a 1519 medal by Quentin
Metsys (1466–1530) and a 1526 engraving by Albrecht Dürer (1471–
1528) — his better picture could be found in his books.[4] But what are
the implications of placing that better picture not only alongside the

---

    Bollettino di italianistica, n.s., 13.1 (2016), pp. 53–69; Kate Heard and others, *The
    Northern Renaissance: Dürer to Holbein* (London: Royal Collection Publications, in
    association with Scala Publishers, 2011), pp. 203–05 (no. 93); more generally, Novella
    Macola, *Sguardi e scritture: Figure con libro nella ritrattistica italiana della prima metà
    del Cinquecento* (Venice: Istituto Veneto di Scienze, Lettere ed Arti, 2007), and Marco
    Paoli, '*Galeotto fu il libro e chi lo dipinse*: Ritratti di letterati e scienziati cinquecenteschi
    raffigurati con un libro. Primo censimento', *Rara volumina*, 22 (2015), pp. 5–28.

2   Indeed, bindings were more likely to reveal to whom books belonged. On binding:
    Lucien Febvre and Henri-Jean Martin, *The Coming of the Book: The Impact of Printing
    1450-1800*, trans. by David Gerard (London: Verso, 1997 [1957]), pp. 104–08;
    Anthony Hobson, *Humanists and Bookbinders: The Origins and Diffusion of Humanistic
    Bookbinding 1459-1559* (Cambridge: Cambridge University Press, 1989). On the
    unbound book in manuscript publication before the print era and its various aesthetic
    and affectual possibilities, see Nicolò Crisafi in this volume.

3   I derive my distinction between these terms in the following discussion partly from
    Mark Roskill and Craig Harbison, 'On the Nature of Holbein's Portraits', *Word &
    Image*, 3 (1987), pp. 1–26 (esp. pp. 2–6). I prefer to speak of the book as meta-
    phor/simile than of a 'double portrait' precisely because a straightforwardly natural-
    istic depiction of a bound book gives no clue necessarily as to its identity or its inner
    character; it is therefore quite unlike a portrait of a person (as understood). Cf. Macola,
    Sguardi e scritture, p. 20: 'compagni di vita e dotati di vita, i libri trasformano spesso il
    ritratto in un doppio ritratto'. Even a naturalistic depiction of an open book may be an
    illusion of representation: Nicholas Herman, *Le Livre enluminé, entre représentation et
    illusion* (Paris: BnF Éditions, 2018), pp. 11–58 (esp. pp. 31–32).

4   ΤΗΝ ΚΡΕΙΤΤΩ ΤΑ ΣΥΓΓΡΑΜΜΑΤΑ ΔΕΙΞΕΙ. While the Greek συγγράμματα can
    mean 'writings' more broadly, in this context it is a translation of *libri*, which Erasmus
    used when he first wrote this phrase in a Latin letter to Johann Werder, 19 October
    1518, in *Opus epistolarum Des. Erasmi Roterodami*, ed. by Percy S. Allen and others,
    12 vols (Oxford: Clarendon Press, 1906-58) (= Allen), III, p. 413 (ep. 875); see
    Oren Margolis, 'Hercules in Venice: Aldus Manutius and the Making of Erasmian
    Humanism', *Journal of the Warburg and Courtauld Institutes*, 81 (2018), pp. 97–126
    (esp. pp. 98–102, 121–22; though with the correct date here). Images of the Metsys

Figure 1. Jean Clouet, *L'Homme au Pétrarque* (*c.* 1530–35), oil on panel,
38.4 × 33 cm. Royal Collection Trust/© Her Majesty
Queen Elizabeth II 2020.

painted *effigies* or likeness, but in a medium that can be opened and
closed?

Holbein's portrait of Hermann von Wedigh III, now on display at
the Metropolitan Museum of Art in New York, is in a beautiful state
of preservation, allowing the viewer to appreciate the great economy
with which the artist produced his compelling effect (Figure 2).[5] The

medal and the Dürer engraving are available on the website of the Victoria and Albert
Museum (inv. 4613-1858, E.4621-1910).

5   Maryan W. Ainsworth and Joshua P. Waterman, *German Paintings in the Metropolitan
Museum of Art, 1350–1600* (New Haven, CT: Metropolitan Museum of Art, distributed
by Yale University Press, 2013), pp. 133–37, 301–02 (no. 30, ill. and figs 114, 116–17).
Extensive (but not complete) bibliography is available on the Metropolitan Museum
website. Relevant works include Hildegard Krummacher, 'Zu Holbeins Bildnissen
rheinischer Stahlhofkaufleute', *Wallraf-Richartz-Jahrbuch*, 25 (1963), pp. 181–92 (pp.
185–87); Thomas S. Holman, 'Holbein's Portraits of the Steelyard Merchants: An
Investigation', *Metropolitan Museum Journal*, 14 (1980), pp. 139–58 (p. 145); Stefan

Figure 2. Hans Holbein the Younger, *Hermann von Wedigh III* (1532),
oil and gold on oak panel, 42.2 × 32.4 cm, with added strip of 1.3 cm at
bottom. Metropolitan Museum of Art, New York; bequest of
Edward S. Harkness, 1940.

sitter is a young man, dressed in a fur-trimmed black velvet cloak
with luminous pile-on-pile sleeves. He holds a pair of kid gloves in
his left hand, on which he wears a ring bearing a coat of arms, and
rests his right hand on a table covered in green baize. The body's
torsion is reminiscent of female portraits by Leonardo da Vinci, to
whose work Holbein had been exposed (certainly in France, likely in
Milan).[6] With pink flesh emerging from his embroidered whitework

Gronert, *Bild-Individualität: Die 'Erasmus'-Bildnisse von Hans Holbein dem Jüngeren*
(Basel: Schwabe, 1996), pp. 42–47; Katrin Petter-Wahnschaffe, *Hans Holbein und der
Stalhof in London* (Berlin: Deutscher Kunstverlag, 2010), pp. 79–92, 347–48.

6   Krummacher, 'Zu Holbeins Bildnissen', p. 186; Oskar Bätschmann and Pascal Griener,
Hans Holbein (Princeton: Princeton University Press, 1997), pp. 120–48.

shirt and lace collar, held together by fine ties, Wedigh's youthful face nevertheless shows a hint of stubble along the jawline and beneath the chin. The light growth suggests the passage of time, and indeed time plays an important role in this picture. Gold letters on the blue background indicate the year in which it was painted and that the sitter was then twenty-nine years of age: a message of transience delivered in monumental form. Wedigh's eyes draw the viewer towards the book that hangs over the table's front edge, casting a shadow on the green baize (Figure 2a). The book has two clasps: one open, one closed. A slip of paper emerges from the top of the book, in the space left free by the open clasp; the text on the slip reads *Veritas odiu(m) parit* — truth breeds hatred. Unlike the text on the slip, which faces the sitter, the inscriptions on the book itself face the viewer. The brown blind-tooled calfskin cover bears the letters 'H. H.', identifying the artist (in the vernacular); while the abbreviation 'HER WID' and a device with the letter *W* in a shield on the gilt fore edge identify the sitter by name and as a patrician of Cologne.[7]

The portrait was in Cologne by no later than 1539, when it served as a model for another portrait of a young man by Barthel Bruyn the Elder (1493–1555); and it appears to have been one of two portraits by Holbein of members of the Wedigh family. Because of its compositional similarities and its date, it has often been classed as one of the so-called 'Steelyard portraits' of the German merchants resident at the Hanseatic trading base in London, which Holbein produced, alongside other public projects for the Steelyard, in the years immediately following his return to England for a second sojourn in 1532: a time at which other possibly expected sources of patronage — such as that of Thomas More (1478–1535), who had resigned the Lord Chancellorship mere months before his arrival — had dried up.[8] The

---

7   Elsewhere Holbein identified himself as Iohannes Holbein or Holpenius. He was
     Holbenius to Beatus Rhenanus; Erasmus called him Olpeius.

8   The monumental *Triumph of Riches* and *Triumph of Poverty* painted for the Steelyard
     merchants' hall no longer survive, though colour drawings of them by Lucas Vorster-
     man the Elder (*c.* 1595–1675) exist, divided between Oxford (Ashmolean Museum,
     WA 1970.93) and London (British Museum, 1894-7-21.2). Holbein was also engaged
     by the merchants to design an ephemeral *Apollo and the Muses on Parnassus* for the
     entry of Anne Boleyn into London in 1533. See Susan Foister, *Holbein in England*
     (London: Abrams, 2007), pp. 68, 70–71 (nos. 65, 68, 69).

Figure 2a. Hans Holbein, *Hermann von Wedigh III*, detail.

fact of the Wedigh portrait's presence in the sitter's home town has
been seen as evidence for the Steelyard portraits' intended destination,
and a resultant understanding of these works (as a class) as tokens of
memory and meditations on distance and death has therefore influenced interpretations of this painting — even though, beyond the most
basic generic conventions and with the exception of memorializing the
sitter's appearance at a given age, such concerns are largely extraneous
to anything, textual or otherwise, contained within it.[9] The research
of Katrin Petter-Wahnschaffe, which casts doubt on the idea that Hermann von Wedigh was ever a Hanseatic merchant or even in London,
and leads to the proposal that Holbein therefore painted his portrait
en route in Cologne for display in an 'ancestor gallery', is therefore

---

9　　See e.g. Holman, 'Holbein's Portraits', pp. 142–43; Roskill and Harbison, 'On the
　　Nature', pp. 16, 23; Susan Foister, *Holbein and England* (New Haven, CT: Yale Univer-
　　sity Press, 2004), pp. 206–14 (esp. p. 214: 'Holbein's Hanseatic portraits are presented
　　as explicit injunctions for the sitters to be remembered. The preoccupation with mor-
　　tality is overwhelming').

highly compelling, even if it may reopen the separate question of the Steelyard portraits' purpose.[10] Indeed, the inscription on the slip in the book makes little sense in a merchant portrait.[11] And, in contrast to the other, certifiable Steelyard portraits, which invariably show the sitter with letters, bills, or other accoutrements of trade, the Wedigh portrait depicts the sitter with a book.[12]

That book is of critical importance to understanding the painting. Attempting to make sense of its prominent presence and the text on the slip, a number of scholars have identified it as a Lutheran book, perhaps Luther's Bible, and the text as a pugnacious reference to the truth of Lutheran religion.[13] This historicizing interpretation is predicated on the work having been painted in London on the eve of the break with Rome, where and when German merchants might indeed be conveyors of Lutheran literature. Yet quite apart from the question of location, there are other, more essential reasons for doubting this interpretation of book and text. Cologne and its patriciate were and remained deeply Catholic.[14] Moreover, as already identified by Fritz Saxl, a rejection of the coarseness and pugnaciousness associated with Luther was evident in Holbein even in his Reformation prints of the 1520s, which led Luther's most devoted supporters to reject him and his works in turn as essentially Erasmian.[15] In *The Ambassadors* (1533), a picture of two

---

10 Petter-Wahnschaffe, *Hans Holbein*, pp. 88–92.

11 In contrast to the Virgilian citation in Holbein's Derick Berck portrait (1536), also at the Metropolitan Museum: Petter-Wahnschaffe, *Hans Holbein*, pp. 69–74.

12 Cf. Roskill and Harbison, 'On the Nature', pp. 23–24, misidentifying the gloves as 'bills or invoices', and thus understanding the inscription on the slip as a commentary on the 'truthful and forthright representation', which functioned as a response to 'the animosity and belligerence which German merchants had experienced in London'.

13 First proposed by Alfred Woltmann, *Holbein und seine Zeit*, 2 vols (Leipzig: Seemann, 1866–68), II (1868), pp. 230–31, with the understanding that the sitter was English; Quentin Buvelot in Stephanie Buck and others, *Hans Holbein the Younger, 1497/98–1543: Portraitist of the Renaissance* (The Hague: Royal Cabinet of Paintings Mauritshuis, 2003), pp. 80–83 (no. 12); Foister, *Holbein and England*, p. 208.

14 Robert W. Scribner, 'Why Was There No Reformation in Cologne?', *Historical Research*, 49 (1976), pp. 217–41.

15 Fritz Saxl, 'Holbein and the Reformation' [originally delivered in 1925], in *Lectures*, 2 vols (London: Warburg Institute, 1957), I, pp. 277–85. So too Erwin Panofsky, *The Life and Art of Albrecht Dürer* (Princeton: Princeton University Press, 1943), p. 239: '[Erasmus] belonged, not to Dürer but to Holbein.' See also Theophil Burckhardt-Biedermann, 'Über Zeit und Anlaß des Flugblattes: Luther als Herkules Germanicus', *Basler Zeitschrift für Geschichte und Altertumskunde*, 4 (1905), pp. 38–44; Edgar Wind, '"Hercules" and "Orpheus": Two Mock-Heroic Designs by Dürer', *Journal of the*

orthodox Catholics (one a bishop), the presence, among other objects, of a Lutheran hymnal represents not truth but division.[16]

A different, more humanistic direction is suggested instead by the appearance of Holbein's initials on the cover. This feature links the portrait to a debate in which Holbein's art had previously engaged. In a portrait of Erasmus with a Renaissance pilaster painted in Basel in 1523, a book in the foreground displayed the sitter's name as a mark of his authorship, while an inscription with Holbein's name on a book in the background asserted an equality of *auctoritas* between the scholar and the painter.[17] The conceit is sophisticated but clear: Erasmus's book is like a painting, showing his reader his better picture; Holbein's painting, the product of an author in his own right, is like a book. In the Wedigh portrait, Holbein's initials make a claim to authorship of the painting by being placed on a book that also bears the name of the sitter: the viewer is therefore encouraged to view the volume as a simile for the work as a whole. Fundamentally, then, this is a Holbein painting that — leaving aside for now the question of its destination — we can in the first instance view *as a Holbein painting*: as a picture about art, sharing in the intellectual engagements that distinguish the artist's wider oeuvre.

Warburg Institute, 2 (1939), pp. 206–18 (pp. 217–18, pl. 40b); Thomas Kaufmann, *Der Anfang der Reformation: Studien zur Kontextualität der Theologie, Publizistik und Inszenierung Luthers und der reformatorischen Bewegung* (Tübingen: Mohr Siebeck, 2018), pp. 301–11; cf. Robert W. Scribner, *For the Sake of Simple Folk: Popular Propaganda for the German Reformation* (Oxford: Clarendon Press, 1994), pp. 32–34. On the importance of Holbein's Bible images across confessional boundaries, see David H. Price, 'Hans Holbein the Younger and Reformation Bible Production', *Church History*, 86 (2017), pp. 998–1040.

16 Mary F. S. Hervey, *Holbein's 'Ambassadors': The Picture and the Men* (London: Bell and Sons, 1900), pp. 219–23, emphasizing the deep desire of Georges de Selve, bishop of Lauvar (right-hand figure) for Christian reconciliation and unity; Foister, *Holbein and England*, pp. 217–19; Kate Bomford, 'Friendship and Immortality: Holbein's *Ambassadors* Revisited', *Renaissance Studies*, 18 (2004), pp. 544–81 (pp. 558–59). Cf. the openly evangelical interpretation of Jennifer Nelson, *Disharmony of the Spheres: The Europe of Holbein's Ambassadors* (University Park: Pennsylvania State University Press, 2019), pp. 111–23, linking the painting to the marriage and coronation of Anne Boleyn and seeing it as 'a nervous commemoration of a new, disharmonious but notionally liberated Europe': a difference of emphasis, perhaps, though harder to reconcile to the actual sitters.

17 As discussed in Margolis, 'Hercules in Venice', pp. 97–98, 120, 124; Bätschmann and Griener, *Hans Holbein*, p. 30.

Seen in this light, not only is the inscription on the slip important, but so too is the condition of the book, which is in fact really quite unusual. Why is one clasp open and the other closed? An explanation that seeks to explain away by recourse to narrative — i.e. that we are looking at an unfolding scene, and the book is about to be *either* fully opened *or* fully clasped — is unsatisfying because this is not evidently a narrative painting. Along similar lines, a previous scholar has suggested that the single closed clasp represents interrupted reading.[18] Interrupted reading is not infrequently depicted in Italian portraiture of the period, often indicated by the sitter-reader's finger slipped into a volume of poetry; and there are examples in northern painting too. But if that were the case and the clasp did have such a significance, one would have to believe that an interrupted Hermann von Wedigh nevertheless carefully placed a piece of paper in the book and partially clasped it before (following narrative logic) assuming this strange pose. Surely it does not depict interrupted reading as such: a single closed clasp is sufficient to preclude that option.

The most legible piece of evidence pertaining to the book is obviously the text we have read on the slip. Around this time, these words — *Veritas odium parit* — were adopted as a motto by Pietro Aretino (1492–1556), in which form they first appeared beneath a portrait bust engraving by Giovanni Jacopo Caraglio (*c.* 1500–65), where Aretino is depicted wearing the gold chain he received from King Francis I of France (r. 1515–47) in 1533: a fitting device for a man described around the frame of the portrait as *flagellum principum* (scourge of princes), and one regularly reproduced in his publications, with or without the image (Figures 3 and 4).[19] Aretino's motto is a proud and

---

18   Gronert, *Bild-Individualität*, p. 46.

19   The engraving must date from after November 1533, when Aretino acknowledged
      receipt of the chain from the king, and before November 1535, when it served as model
      for the woodcut frontispiece to an edition of *La cortigiana*: see *Ceremonies, Costumes,
      Portraits and Genre*, ed. by Mark McDonald, The Paper Museum of Cassiano dal Pozzo:
      A Catalogue Raisonné: Series C, 1, 3 vols (London: Royal Collection Trust, in asso-
      ciation with Harvey Miller, 2017), I, p. 880 (no. 1575); Pietro Aretino, *Cortigiana*
      (Venice: Francesco Marcolini, 1535), sig. A1ʳ. Aretino also employed the phrase in
      his comedy *Il marescalco*, first drafted in 1526–27 but revised and only published in
      1533. The character of the Pedant attributes it (said in praise of Alfonso d'Avalos)
      to 'lo *acerrimus virtutum ac vitiorum demonstrator*' — evidently Aretino, who would
      use this descriptor for himself: Pietro Aretino, *Il marescalco*, ed. by Giovanna Rabitti,
      in *Edizione nazionale delle opere di Pietro Aretino*, 10 vols (Rome: Salerno Editrice,

Figure 3. Giovanni Jacopo Caraglio, *Pietro Aretino* (*c.* 1533), engraving,
19.0 × 15.3 cm (sheet of paper). Royal Collection Trust/© Her Majesty
Queen Elizabeth II 2020.

defiant statement of the satirist's social function, far removed from anything that could be seen to support the *pedantissimo* Martin Luther.[20]

1992–), v/2 (2010), p. 87 (v. 3); 1536 edition (Venice: Francesco Marcolini) fronted
by woodcut after Caraglio with motto, sig. A1^r; motto, descriptor, and woodcut portrait by or after Titian in 1538 edition of his letters (see Figure 4). See also Raymond B.
Waddington, *Aretino's Satyr: Sexuality, Satire, and Self-Projection in Sixteenth-Century
Literature and Art* (Toronto: University of Toronto Press, 2004), pp. 63–64, 96–103;
David Rosand and Michelangelo Muraro, *Titian and the Venetian Woodcut* (Washington, DC: International Exhibitions Foundation, 1976), p. 270 (no. 82).

20　So called in a letter of Aretino to Benedetto Accolti, Venice, 29 August 1537 (published
1538), in *Lettere*, ed. by Paolo Procaccioli, in *Edizione nazionale delle opere di Pietro
Aretino*, IV/1 (1997), p. 261; see also the dedication of *La cortigiana* to Cardinal
Bernardo Clesio (1485–1539), prince-bishop of Trent, which immediately follows the
woodcut portrait in the 1535 edition (sig. A2^r): 'Et cosi tanti gentil'huomini che vi
serveno, tanti Vertuosi che vi celebrano, et tanti Cavalieri che vi corteggiano finirano
di conoscere […] di che qualita sia lo huomo che essi adorano, non altrimenti che vi
habbia finito di conoscere il diabolico Luthero'.

DIVVS P. ARETINVS
ACERRIMVS
VIRTVTVM ET
VITIORVM
DEMONSTRATOR

VERITAS ODIVM PARI.

Figure 4. *De le Lettere di M. Pietro Aretino: Libro primo* (Venice: Francesco Marcolini, 1538), ♠2ᵛ: workshop of/after Titian (?), portrait of Aretino, woodcut. Munich, Bayerische Staatsbibliothek, 2 Epist. 2, urn:nbn:de:bvb:12-bsb10142585-8.

But, as an evidently combative usage, it is worth noting nonetheless that his publication of it postdates Holbein's picture.

The words, however, originate in Terence, appearing in the Roman playwright's *Andria* (The Woman of Andros) as one half of a proverbial expression. This comes at the beginning of the play, in the freedman Sosia's response to his master Simo's account of the way his son has lived:

SIMO: sic vita erat: facile omnis perferre ac pati;
cum quibus erat quomque una is sese dedere,
eorum obsequi studiis, adversus nemini,
numquam praeponens se illis; ita ut facillume
sine invidia laudem invenias et amicos pares.

SOSIA: sapienter vitam instituit; namque hoc tempore
obsequium amicos, veritas odium parit.

(SIMO: Such was his life: he easily went along and put up with
everyone; gave himself up to his company; complied with their
pursuits. An enemy to none, never did he put himself before
them. That's what without causing jealousy best earns praise
and breeds friends.

SOSIA: He has made wise provisions for life; for nowadays,
complaisance breeds friends, truth breeds hatred.)[21]

The line recurs in Cicero's dialogue *De amicitia* (On Friendship), where
it is credited explicitly to Terence. The speaker is Laelius, and the
subject is the importance and difficulty of well-intentioned rebuke
amongst friends:

Sed nescio quo modo verum est, quod in Andria familiaris
meus dicit:
  Obsequium amicos, veritas odium parit.
Molesta veritas, siquidem ex ea nascitur odium, quod est
venenum amicitiae, sed obsequium multo molestius, quod
peccatis indulgens praecipitem amicum ferri sinit; maxima
autem culpa in eo, qui et veritatem aspernatur et in fraudem
obsequio impellitur.[22]

(But somehow what my friend says in the *Andria* is true:
  Complaisance breeds friends, truth breeds hatred.
Truth is troublesome if indeed from it is born hatred, which
is the poison of friendship; but much more troublesome is

---

21   Terence, *Andria*, 62–68 (I. 1), in *P. Terenti Afri Comoediae*, ed. by Robert Kauer and
      Wallace M. Lindsay (Oxford: Oxford University Press, 1963), p. 5. Unless otherwise
      noted, all translations are mine. I prefer 'complaisance' to 'flattery', with which the
      phrase is sometimes rendered, in light of Terence's usage (note *obsequi* in line 64)
      and of the evidence of subsequent classical and Renaissance readings, including those
      discussed below and that of Machiavelli in his version of *Andria*, in *Edizione nazionale
      delle opere di Niccolò Machiavelli*, 6 parts (Rome: Salerno Editrice, 2001–), III/1, ed.
      by Pasquale Stoppelli (2017), p. 21: 'chi sa ire a' versi acquista amici e chi dice il vero
      acquista odio'.

22   Cicero, *De amicitia*, 89.

complaisance, which, by indulging his transgressions, allows a friend to be borne headlong away. And yet the greatest fault is in him who both scorns truth and is driven by complaisance into error.)

Cicero's solution to this problem is to reclaim and repurpose Terence's word *obsequium*, moving it out of opposition to *veritas* and contrasting the latter instead with *assentatio*, flattery and adulation:

> Omni igitur hac in re habenda ratio et diligentia est, primum ut monitio acerbitate, deinde ut obiurgatio contumelia careat; in obsequio autem, quoniam Terentiano verbo libenter utimur, comitas adsit, assentatio, vitiorum adiutrix, procul amoveatur, quae non modo amico, sed ne libero quidem digna est; aliter enim cum tyranno, aliter cum amico vivitur.

> (In this entire matter reason and care must therefore be used: first, that advice is free of harshness; second, that rebuke is free of insult. Yet in complaisance — since I gladly adopt Terence's word — have courtesy at hand, and put away flattery, hand-maiden to the vices, which is unworthy not only of a friend but even of a free man. We live in one way with a tyrant, in another with a friend.)

Freedom to rebuke with the truth is held to be essential to friendship — indeed, to be at the heart of what ennobles it, distinguishing it for only those who are free. And instead of condemning *obsequium*, or associating it with *assertatio*, Cicero claims for it the possibility of containing the right manner in which, given human nature, it is best to address a friend with the advice he needs. In this rereading of Terence — a re-rereading that takes place within the dialogue, openly against the grain — the two halves of the proverb are no longer at odds. This is certainly the background for its deployment by Petrarch (1304–74) in the second of his two letters to Cicero — a conciliatory affair after the previous epistle, which upbraided his revered ancient correspondent's shockingly unphilosophical way of life. Petrarch's description of the author of the adage as *familiaris tuus* is probably a lapse — Terence, *familiaris meus*, was a friend of the historical Laelius, not of Cicero — rather than a conscious association of the primary interlocutor with Cicero himself, but is regardless a usage that reveals his source.[23]

---

23   *Epistolae familiares*, xxiv. 4, in Pétrarque, *Lettres familières*, 6 vols (Paris: Les Belles Lettres, 2002–15), vi, ed. by Vittorio Rossi (2015), pp. 579, 581: 'ut ipse soles dicere,

I do not believe that the volume in the Wedigh portrait is intended to represent a copy of Terence. *Andria* is the first play in a corpus that survives from Antiquity *in toto*, and it invariably appears first in all early printed editions.[24] The slip, meanwhile, is inserted towards the back of the book. Just as visual evidence was lacking for the identification as a Lutheran Bible, so too is there none here to support such a literal interpretation. But our enquiry can bring us closer to Holbein: to the most important humanist in his career and in his world. Erasmus included the full proverb in his *Adagiorum collectanea* of 1500 and then, in 1508, in the much-expanded Aldine edition of *Adagiorum chiliades* (or the *Adagia*). After this, it featured, with still further commentary, in each successive edition of the famous and popular compendium. The evidence of their correspondence shows that the proverb, often explicitly associated with 'the comic', gained currency in the circle of intellectuals around Erasmus in Basel in the 1520s: the humanist Bonifacius Amerbach (1495–1562), the printer Andreas Cratander (d. *c.* 1540), the physician Paracelsus (1493–1541), and Gilbert Cousin (1506–72), Erasmus's amanuensis.[25] This was the very circle with and to which Holbein, his 1526–28 sojourn in England excepted, collaborated and belonged. Amerbach sat for Holbein in 1519 and likely introduced him to Erasmus.[26]

The dual classical inheritance is evident in Erasmus's treatment. While in the *Collectanea* he merely calls it 'a very famous aphorism', in the *Adagia* he attributes the words to Terence.[27] Like Cicero, how-

---

quod ait familiaris tuus in Andria: *Obsequium amicos, veritas odium parit'* (with editor's quotation marks around 'familiaris' removed).

24 Catalogue of editions until 1600 in Harold Walter Lawton, *Térence en France au XVIe siècle: Editions et traductions* (Paris: Jouve, 1926), pp. 63–251, 263–78, noting 461 editions of the complete Terence and only 15 of the *Andria* alone.

25 Bonifacius Amerbach to Andreas Cratander, Avignon, *c.* 27 November 1520, in *Die Amerbachkorrespondenz*, ed. by Alfred Hartmann and others, 11 vols (Basel: Verlag der Universitätsbibliothek, 1942–2010), II (1943), pp. 271–72 (ep. 756): 'Novisti comici illud, obsequium amicos, veritatem odium parere'; Paracelsus to Bonifacius Amerbach, Colmar, 4 March 1528, ibid., III (1947), p. 309: '[...] nisi quod id demum verissimum esse comperio, veritatem parere odium?'; Gilbert Cousin to Erasmus, Nozeroy?, end May 1536, in Allen, XI, pp. 326–30: 'Nam etiamnum comici verbum, quo veritatem odium parere dixit [...].'

26 Portrait at Kunstmuseum Basel (Amerbach-Kabinett 1662, inv. 314).

27 Erasmus, *Collectanea*, 224, in *Opera omnia Desiderii Erasmi Roterodami* (Amsterdam: North-Holland Publishing; Leiden: Brill, 1969–) (= *ASD*), II/9, p. 118: 'celebratissima sententia'. The preceding adage, 'Davus sum, non Oedipus', is attributed to *Andria*

ever, he uses the proverb to make his own distinctive argument about friendship:

> Senarius est proverbialis apud Terentium in Andria, non admonens, quid oporteat fieri, sed ostendens quid vulgo fiat. Vulgaris enim amicitia constat obsequiis; nam invicem connivere ad familiarium vitia, *Haec res et iungit iunctos et servat amicos*. At inter veros amicos nihil est veritate iucundius, modo absit *asperitas agrestis et inconcinna gravisque*. Porro qui vulgo plurimis studet amicus esse, moribus alienis obsecundet [...]. Non probari vero sententiam hanc poetae, satis indicat, cum ait: *Nanque hoc tempore*, id est his corruptis moribus.[28]

> (This senarius is a proverb in Terence's *Andria*, not so much suggesting what ought to happen as saying what commonly does. Indeed, common friendship consists in complaisances: for each in turn to look aside from the vices of friends, 'This is what joins friends and keeps them joined together' [Horace, *Satires*, i. 3. 54]. On the other hand, among true friends nothing is more pleasing than the truth, provided there is no 'boorish asperity, uncultivated and disagreeable' [Horace, *Epistles*, i. 18. 6]. But he who wishes to be the friend of as many as possible amongst common people must comply with the fashions of others [...]. It is clear enough that this aphorism does not in fact meet with the poet's approval, since he says, 'for nowadays', that is, according to the corrupt fashions of our time.)

Erasmus goes on to cite Cicero, and, in later editions, adds other examples of related usages.[29] The need occasionally to cloak, obscure, or soften the truth from the motive of *pietas* and in the interest of harmony indeed became one of his great preoccupations — as well as points of conflict with erstwhile followers — in the early 1520s, precisely when the case of Luther, who stood in Erasmus's mind for a radically different ethos of non-concealment, was beginning to envelop him.[30]

(line 194), however. From *De copia* (1512) it appears Erasmus understood Cicero to have attributed the invention of the word *obsequium* to Terence; in this he was following Quintilian and Donatus: *ASD*, I/6, pp. 52, 53 n.

28 Erasmus, *Adagia*, II. 9. 53, in *ASD*, II/4, p. 248.

29 A reference to Pindar, *Nemeans*, v. 16–18, was added in 1526; one to Agathon, quoted in Athenaeus, *Deipnosophistae*, v. 47, in 1528.

30 As discussed in Silvana Seidel Menchi's profound introduction to *Iulius exclusus e coelis*, in *ASD*, I/8, pp. 5–131 (esp. pp. 107–10), also abridged in Erasmo da Rotterdam, *Giulio*, ed. and trans. [into Italian] by Silvana Seidel Menchi (Turin: Einaudi, 2014), pp. xcvi–c.

Erasmus's two citations of Horace are no less important for being unattributed — explicitly at any rate, as they are well known and would both be cited again in *The Praise of Folly*.[31] In its original, Horatian context, the latter belongs to the poet's advice to a young *amicus* on how to comport himself as the *amicus* of a patron. Even worse than being a *scurra* (parasite) — held to be as different to a friend as a *matrona* (honourable married woman) is to a *meretrix* (whore) — is to be one who presents his boorish behaviour as virtue and frankness. Virtue, instead, is the mean between the vices, far from either extreme.[32] In *The Praise of Folly*, Erasmus follows this passage quite closely: though he eschews the poet's demeaning term for the flatterer, Horace is cited by name, and the type of well-meaning flattery that belongs to Folly and is not intended to mislead is judged closer to virtue. Friendship is not especially the focus, which is rather a recommendation of the amiable middle ground between obsequious and unpleasant dispositions familiar from Aristotle's *Nicomachean Ethics*.[33] In the commentary on the Terentian adage, however, Erasmus is instead concerned with what is proper to 'true friends'. The reader who appreciates the Horatian reference may likewise appreciate the importance to that source text of the distinction between different classes of friend. Erasmus's citation from the *Satires* makes this point even more strongly. There, what is a passage intended by its author as a plea for tolerance of others' faults — and what in the *Moriae encomium* will be attributed to Folly herself — is repurposed to impugn a type of friendship deemed 'common'.

Indeed, in his commentary on the adage Erasmus refers to what is 'common' — the words are *vulgaris* and *vulgo* (from *vulgus*) — no fewer than three times: common friendship, common behaviour, in the presence of common people. This is as many times as he uses words that refer to truth. This sense of common, *vulgaris*, is that which is associated with the multitude, the masses, and the mob, and often has pejorative connotations. It was also, of course, associated with the rejected vernacular:

---

31   *Moriae encomium*, in *ASD*, IV/3, p. 92: 'Age, connivere, labi caecutire, hallucinari in
      amicorum vitiis [...] atqui haec una stulticia et iungit, iunctos et servat amicos'; ibid.,
      p. 130: 'asperitas, ac morositas inconcinna, ut ait Horatius, gravisque'. The Horatian
      source of the latter is not noted in the critical edition of the *Adagia*.

32   Horace, *Epistulae*, I. 18. 3–9: 'Virtus est medium vitiorum et utrimque reductum.'

33   Aristotle, 1126b–1127a (*Ethica Nicomachea*, IV. 6. 1–9).

He acted in an unfriendly way [*non amice*] indeed — he who turned the hateful passages plucked from my books into German and disseminated them among the people [*evulgavit*]. I had not written them for the *vulgus*, nor had I wished for them to be read bare.³⁴

People and things to be extolled or endorsed, meanwhile, were distinguished by their distance from it. In a letter of 1520, Erasmus praised Quentin Metsys as an uncommon craftsman (*artifex non vulgaris*); while, defending his *Colloquies* in print against his critics among the Paris theologians, he asserted their *non vulgarem utilitatem* (uncommon utility) for the education of boys not only in style but also in morals.³⁵ That this word stood out to later readers of the *Adagia* and could colour their reading of the Terentian proverb can be seen from a letter of Cardinal Jean du Bellay (1492–1560), patron and protector of Rabelais, in which he reminds Cardinal Charles de Guise (1524–74) of *illud vulgatissimum* [...] *comici*.³⁶ Now it is the proverb itself that is *vulgatissimum*: very well known, common, and notorious.

Yet there is another meaning of 'common' too, which is covered in Latin by the adjective *communis*. This word refers to what is public, shared, universal, and accessible, rather than merely widespread, and is without the pejorative and divisive connotations of *vulgaris*. Perhaps the opposition between these Latin words seems starker to the English-speaker, whose language translates them the same way; but I think the ontological distinction is clear, and is nevertheless raised by

---

34 Erasmus, *Spongia adversus aspergines Hutteni* (1523), in *ASD*, ɪx/1, p. 194: 'Quam vero non amice fecit, qui decerpta ex libris meis odiosa loca vertit in linguam Germanicam et evulgavit. At ego illa vulgo non scripseram neque volebam nuda legi'; see also Seidel Menchi, in *ASD*, ɪ/8, p. 130.

35 Letter to Nicolaus Everardi, 17 April 1520, in Allen, ɪv, p. 237 (ep. 1092); 'De utilitate colloquiorum' (1526), in *ASD*, ɪ/3, pp. 741–52 (p. 742).

36 Jean du Bellay to Charles de Guise (later Lorraine), Rome, [7] May 1548, in *Correspondance du Cardinal Jean du Bellay*, ed. by Rémy Scheurer and others, 7 vols (Paris: Klincksieck; Société de l'histoire de France, 1969–2017), ɪv (2011), pp. 168–70 (ep. 841): 'Vous me pardonnerez, Monseigneur, si la foy, devotion et observance que j'ay envers le Roy et envers vous-mesmes me transportent a vous dire ce que dessuz. L'ung et l'autre trouverez assez de gens qui vous flatteront; de ceulx qui vous disent les veritez, je ne sçay si en trouverez beaucoup nam illud vulgatissimum est comici veritatem odium parere.' Du Bellay employs another Terentian proverb found in the *Adagia* in the same letter: 'in te enim maxime haec faba cuditur'; cf. *Adagia*, ɪ. 1. 84, 'In me haec cudetur faba', in *ASD*, ɪɪ/1, p. 192: 'Terentius in Eunucho [line 381]: At enim isthaec in me cudetur faba'.

Erasmus's repeated insistence on the proverb's vulgarity. A distinction
between what is vulgar and what truly belongs to all moreover seems
to me to be the problem (in the sense of the crux of the matter) at
the heart of the Erasmian humanist project more broadly — a project
that sought to make accessible to and for the benefit of Latin Christendom the shared inheritance of literature and eloquence, but feared
its comorbidities: the cacophony, dissonance, and social, political, and
religious fracture that unguarded reading, writing, and publishing for
the masses could bring. This is the delicate balance — or productive
contradiction? — between openness and concealment that animates
the project; and these are the priorities that, despite the general adoption of the educational and rhetorical components of its programme
across the growing confessional divide, cannot but lead it to a rejection
of Luther. In what may be its most explicit manifesto, the essay on the
adage *Festina lente* (make haste slowly), Erasmus blamed for disorder
the profit motive that drove *sordidi typographi* and *vulgares excusores*,
squalid and vulgar printers.[37] The contrast between *vulgaris* and *communis* is especially clear in the context of the *Adagia*, not least because
the entire collection begins with the proverb *Amicorum communia omnia* — among friends all is common.[38] Erasmus claimed this for a good
omen: originating with Pythagoras and preached by Plato, it embodied
more than anything else what Christ wanted for his followers. Both
in the volume and then also outside it, in the famous catalogue of his
works addressed to Johannes von Botzheim, Erasmus presented his
compiling and writing of the *Adagia*, inaugurated with this proverb,
as motivated by his feelings of friendship for his dedicatee William
Blount, Lord Mountjoy (1478–1534).[39] Thanks to the ambiguous
power of the printed book, however, Erasmus and Mountjoy's friend-

37 *Adagia*, ii. 1. 1, in *ASD*, ii/3, pp. 7–28 (p. 18).

38 *Adagia*, i. 1. 1, in *ASD*, ii/1, pp. 84–86; also in the *prolegomena* to the *Adagia*, in *ASD*,
    ii/1, pp. 60–61; already proverbial in Terence, *Adelphoe*, 803–04. See Kathy Eden,
    *Friends Hold All Things in Common: Tradition, Intellectual Property, and the Adages
    of Erasmus* (New Haven, CT: Yale University Press, 2001), pp. 25–27; Kathy Eden,
    '"Between Friends All Is Common": The Erasmian Adage and Tradition', *Journal of the
    History of Ideas*, 59 (1998), pp. 405–19.

39 In *Adagia*, iii. 1. 1, 'Herculei labores', in *ASD*, ii/5, pp. 23–41 (pp. 36–37), with
    Mountjoy named from 1523 edition onward, but already indicated by the title 'Moece-
    nas ille meus', understood to be the dedicatee; Allen, i, pp. 16–17 (ep. 1341A); Eden,
    Friends, pp. 1–5.

ship, based on the sharing of the commonplaces of Antiquity, can be shared with all lovers of good letters. And because they now (literally) hold this heritage in common, the readers are linked to Erasmus in a humanist friendship that reaches back through the ages to include the Ancients themselves. The antidote to the commonness and vulgarity of the masses is in Erasmus's readers' own hands.

Is this what these followers and readers of Erasmus were dramatizing when they incorporated the Terentian adage into their own letters? In the letters of Paracelsus and Gilbert Cousin mentioned above, as well as that of Jean du Bellay previously cited, it is notable that the first half of the proverb, *obsequium amicos*, is missing. In each of these cases, the letter writer is remarking upon the problem of truth-telling, not necessarily of friendship — though du Bellay, who uses it to warn Charles de Guise against all of those who will 'flatter' him rather than give him their honesty as his own 'devotion and obedience' demand, seems to be referring to the full proverb and specifically to Cicero's gloss of it (which Erasmus also provided).[40] Yet the genre of the personal letter, and the fact of quoting an adage (itself a kind of shared speech) on the topic of friendship, which moreover came from a collection that was *about* friendship — that between Erasmus and Mountjoy, as well as that ideal one among the Erasmian republic of letters — make friendship a subject regardless. Employing the adage becomes, in that sense, a phatic usage, one which establishes and affirms contact on given terms. The practice among Erasmus's readers of quoting only one half of the adage may be read as an allusion to the fact that the reader with whom it is shared essentially already shares in it: he also knows the saying of the comic, and can provide it himself.

---

40   In a similar vein, see Baldesar Castiglione, *Il libro del cortegiano*, ed. by Vittorio Cian (Florence: Sansoni, 1947), p. 111 [I. 44]: '[Conte Ludovico:] [...] si è ritrovato tra gli antichi sapienti chi ha scritto libri, in qual modo posso l'omo conoscere il vero amico dall'adulatore. Ma questo che giova? se molti, anzi infiniti son quelli che manifestamente comprendono esser adulati, e pur amano chi gli adula, ed hanno in odio chi dice lor il vero?'; responding almost certainly to Plutarch, *Moralia*, I. 48e–74e, translated by Erasmus as 'Quo pacto possis adulatorem ab amico dignoscere', in *ASD*, II/4, pp. 117–63, but, given the suggestion of multiple ancient sources and the critical comment, likely also to Cicero and possibly to the Erasmian essay itself. See also Jorge Ledo, 'Erasmus' Translations of Plutarch's *Moralia* and the Ascensian *editio princeps* of ca. 1513', *Humanistica Lovaniensia*, 68 (2019), pp. 257–96, and, on Castiglione's engagement with Erasmus, Guido Rebecchini, 'Castiglione and Erasmus: Towards a Reconciliation?', *Journal of the Warburg and Courtauld Institutes*, 61 (1998), pp. 258–60.

This pattern of usage tells us at least two important things about how we should interpret the Holbein painting. In the first place, it tells us quite simply that this is a humanist picture: that is to say, it is a picture embedded in textual relationships — those between texts, and in texts between people. To the extent that it is also *about* humanism, meanwhile, it suggests to us that this painting's subject is humanist friendship.[41] Hermann von Wedigh is fashioned as learned and sophisticated precisely because he is fashioned as a friend with a share in a republic of letters. Led by the inscription, the painting (on behalf of its sitter) not only exploits this discourse, but also (on behalf of its artist) offers a new contribution to it. The half-adage about friendship incites the active involvement of the reader-viewer, creating a friendship centred on literature and an intimacy based on part-concealment, as it does in the letters of the readers of Erasmus.

But there is another question that this picture raises in a way that is distinct from those in the adage's previous textual history, and that is the question of authorship. Certainly, the adage itself is iterative, weaving around multiple compatible, but not identical or fully reconcilable authorities on friendship of different sorts — the common sort, friendship-as-clientage, and the truer sort — themselves often interlocking textually. The common nature of adages (in both senses: their ubiquity and their non-proprietary quality) challenges ideas about authorship that the presence of the book in the painting's foreground inscribed with both Holbein's and the sitter's names implies. At the same time, and from a very different perspective, Holbein's painted book challenges textual notions of authorship (shared or individual) and the primacy of the written word in giving an authoritative representation. Here one must again recall Erasmus's famous warning that his true self and 'better picture' were found not in his image — executed and propagated by Metsys and Dürer, as well as by Holbein — but in his *libri*, his συγγράμματα. In contrast, and just as it did in his Erasmus portrait, Holbein's name on the painted book asserts an equality between artistic and literary authorship. Wedigh's name asserts a similar equality between the textual and the visual representation of the self.

---

41   Cf. Gronert, *Bild-Individualität*, pp. 46–47.

At this point, however, any further interpretation along these lines must split in two directions, both of which look back to the *Adagia*. On the one hand, Holbein's verisimilistic representation of Wedigh invests the book, which Holbein's claim to authorship has rendered as a simile for the portrait, with the sitter's selfhood. The function of the adage, meanwhile, is dramatized by the projection of the slip from the book towards the viewer, transgressing the picture plane. Its shared nature and the discourse on friendship in which the portrait itself engages likewise encourage the viewer to recall the second adage in Erasmus's collection, *Amicitia aequalitas. Amicus alter ipse* (Friendship is equality; a friend is a second self).[42] Viewing Holbein's portrait thus becomes akin to the sharing of the self that, according to the Erasmian maxim, could only truly be accomplished by reading. Although Wedigh is not fashioned as an author in the way Erasmus would have been, he does receive an identity as a friend by his relationship to these texts. On the other hand, Holbein's assertion of his own pictorial author-ship presents a contrast to the shared authorship and ownership of adages (though not of the *Adagia*), which is brought into the painting by means of the text on the slip. Thus exacerbating the ambivalence already present in the potential disconnect between cover and con-tents, the slip makes the book a zone of instability which threatens to undermine the notion of representing textual and pictorial authorship altogether, and even the possibility of fully representing a legitimized, authorial truth. This openness to further interpretation and ultimate irresolvability are, to my mind, the underside of Erasmian philological optimism and absolutely characteristic of the movement.[43]

It is time to return to the clasps. Our turn away from a narrative or iconographic interpretation of the painting towards a textually and socially situated one — that is, as a painting that figures its own role within literary and social relationships — argues against an identi-fication of the clasps as a sign of interrupted reading. But they may be identifiable with shared reading. In a fine earlier example of the

42   *Adagia*, I. 1. 2, in *ASD*, II/1, p. 86.
43   See Thomas M. Greene, 'Erasmus' "Festina lente": Vulnerabilities of the Humanist Text', in *The Vulnerable Text: Essays on Renaissance Literature* (New York: Columbia University Press, 1986), pp. 1–17; Barbara C. Bowen, *The Age of Bluff: Paradox and Ambiguity in Rabelais and Montaigne* (Urbana: University of Illinois Press, 1972), pp. 7–17.

Erasmian friendship portrait, Metsys's diptych of Erasmus and Pieter Gillis, desks covered in green baize and wooden shelving in the background containing the two humanists' books visually join the two panels.[44] The shared library, entirely of works written or edited by Erasmus, is only made whole by the union of the paintings, depicting the Pythagorean principle and humanist adage of friends holding all things in common. The Gillis panel also contains a clasped book on the green baize. Holding a letter from their mutual friend Thomas More, the painting's intended recipient, Gillis points at a book that is oriented towards the viewer, in this case also ideally understood as More.[45] A friendship portrait, certainly — but a closed one, speaking to the friendship between these three men (and perhaps the artist whose achievement this was too). Holbein's Wedigh portrait appears to have no pendant, and a book is not a library: it is neither enclosed by specific relationships nor by specific spaces. Unlike that of Metsys, Holbein's subject is not a particular humanist friendship, but humanist friendship in general. I would suggest, then, that the half-adage on the slip — to be completed by the literate friend, thus furthering intimacy over distance — is in a metaphoric relationship with the half-unclasped book. The adage can be completed, the book fully opened, and the sitter's selfhood shared with the friend who sees it.

---

44   On the Metsys diptych, see Lorne Campbell and others, 'Quentin Matsys, Desiderius Erasmus, Pieter Gillis and Thomas More', *Burlington Magazine*, 120 (1978), pp. 716–25; Larry Silver, *The Paintings of Quinten Massys, with Catalogue Raisonné* (Oxford: Phaidon, 1984), pp. 105–33, 235–37.

45   An identification of the book with *Antibarbari*, as the inscription on the cover indicates, is problematic: though written largely by 1495, it was only published in 1520, three years after the diptych was painted. The inscription is probably a later addition.

References

PRIMARY SOURCES

Abelard, Peter, *Collationes*, ed. and trans. by J. Marenbon and G. Orlandi (Oxford: Clarendon Press, 2001)
—— *Expositio in Hexameron*, ed. by Mary Romig (Turnhout: Brepols, 2004)
—— *Sic et non*, ed. by Blanche B. Boyer and Richard McKeon (Chicago: University of Chicago Press, 1976–77)
—— 'Verbo Verbum Virgo Concipiens', in *Hymni*, PL 178. 1765–1816 (1789)
Alan of Lille, *Distinctiones*, Patrologia Latina 210. 685–1012
Alighieri, Dante, *La Commedia secondo l'antica vulgata*, ed. by Giorgio Petrocchi, 4 vols, 2nd edn (Florence: Le Lettere, 1994)
—— *The Divine Comedy*, trans. by Mark Musa, 3 vols (Harmondsworth: Penguin, 1984–86), I: *Inferno* (1984)
—— *Inferno*, trans. by Robert Hollander and Jean Hollander (New York: Anchor, 2000)
—— *Monarchia*, ed. and trans. by Prue Shaw (Cambridge: Cambridge University Press, 1995)
—— *Paradiso*, trans. by Robert Hollander and Jean Hollander (New York: Doubleday, 2007)
—— *Purgatorio*, trans. by Robert Hollander and Jean Hollander (New York: Anchor, 2003)
Die Amerbachkorrespondenz, ed. by Alfred Hartmann and others, 11 vols (Basel: Verlag der Universitätsbibliothek, 1942–2010)
Ancrene Wisse: A Corrected Edition of the Text in Cambridge, Corpus Christi College, MS 402 with Variants from Other Manuscripts, ed. by Bella Millett, EETS, orig. ser., 325–26, 2 vols (Oxford: Oxford University Press, 2005–06)
Aretino, Pietro, *Cortigiana* (Venice: Francesco Marcolini, 1535)
—— *De le Lettere di M. Pietro Aretino: Libro primo* (Venice: Francesco Marcolini, 1538)
—— *Edizione nazionale delle opere di Pietro Aretino*, 10 vols (Rome: Salerno Editrice, 1992–)
Augustine, *Confessions*, ed. by James J. O'Donnell, 3 vols (Oxford: Clarendon Press, 1992)
—— *Confessions*, trans. by Francis J. Sheed, ed. by Michael P. Foley, intro. by Peter Brown, 2nd edn (Indianapolis: Hackett, 2006)
—— *Confessions*, trans. by William Watts, Loeb Classical Library, 26–27, 2 vols (Cambridge, MA: Harvard University Press, 1912)

—— *De doctrina christiana, Patrologia Latina* 34. 15–122

Bede, *In Cantica canticorum, Patrologia Latina* 191. 1065–1235

Benedict, Saint, *RB 1980: The Rule of St Benedict in Latin and English with Notes*, ed. and trans., by Timothy Fry (Collegeville, MN: The Liturgical Press, 1981)

Bernard of Clairvaux, *Sermones de tempore, Patrologia Latina* 183. 35–360

Bernard of Cluny, *Ordo Cluniacensis per Bernardum Saeculi XI. Scriptorem*, in *Vetus Disciplina Monastica*, ed. by Marquard Herrgott (Paris: Caroli Osmont, 1726), pp. 134–364

Bibliorum Sacrorum cum Glossa Ordinaria, 6 vols (Venice: [n. pub.], 1603)

Bjarni Aðalbjarnarson, *Om de norske kongers sagaer* (Oslo: Dybwad, 1937)

Boccaccio, Giovanni, *Trattatello in laude di Dante*, ed. by Vittore Branca (Milan: Mondadori, 1974)

Bonaventure, *Bonaventurae opera omnia*, ed. by PP. Collegii S. Bonaventurae, 10 vols (Quaracchi: Collegium S. Bonaventurae, 1882–1902), v: *Quaestiones disputatae de perfectione euangelica* (1891)

—— *Commentary of the Gospel of Luke*, trans. by R. Karris, 3 vols (New York: Franciscan Institute Publications, 2001–04), i (2001)

—— *De assumptione B. Virginis Mariae*, in *Bonaventurae opera omnia*, ed. by PP. Collegii S. Bonaventurae, 10 vols (Quaracchi: Collegium S. Bonaventurae, 1882–1902), ix (1901)

Brennu-Njáls saga, ed. by Einar Ólafur Sveinsson, Íslenzk Fornrit, 12 (Reykjavik: Hið Íslenzka Fornritafélag, 1954)

Cassian, John, *De Coenobiorum Institutis Libri Duodecim, Patrologia Latina* 49. 53–476

Castiglione, Baldesar, *Il libro del cortegiano*, ed. by Vittorio Cian (Florence: Sansoni, 1947)

Cavalcanti, Guido, *Rime*, ed. by Roberto Rea and Giorgio Inglese (Rome: Carocci, 2011)

Caxton, William, *Gilte Legende*, ed. by Richard Hamer, EETS, old ser., 327–28, 339, 3 vols (Oxford: Oxford University Press, 2006–12)

Die Chronik des Klosters Lüne über die Jahre 1481–1530: Hs. Lüne 13, ed. by Philipp Stenzig (Tübingen: Mohr Siebeck, 2019)

Collectanea Anglo-Premonstratensia, ed. by Francis A. Gasquet, Camden Society, 3rd ser., 6, 10, 12, 3 vols (London: Camden Society, 1904–06)

Concilia Magnae Britanniae et Hiberniae, a Synodo Verolamiensi A.D. CCCC XLVI. ad Londinensem A.D. M DCCXVII, ed. by David Wilkins, 4 vols (London: R. Gosling, 1737)

Crispin, Gilbert, *Disputatio Iudei et Christiani*, in *The Works of Gilbert Crispin, Abbot of Westminster*, ed. by Anna Sapir Abulafia and Gillian R. Evans (London: Oxford University Press, 1986), pp. 1–53

Cursor Mundi: A Northumbrian Poem of the Fourteenth Century in 4 Versions, ed. by Richard Morris, EETS, orig. ser., 57, 59, 62, 66, 68, 99, 101, 7 vols (Oxford: Oxford University Press, 1961–66)

Danmarks middelalderlige annaler, ed. by Erik Kroman (Copenhagen: [n. pub.], 1980)

The Didascalicon of Hugh of St. Victor: A Medieval Guide to the Arts, trans. by Jerome Taylor (New York: Columbia University Press, 1961)

Documents Illustrating the Activities of the General and Provincial Chapters of the English Black Monks, 1215–1540, ed. by William A. Pantin, Camden Society, 3rd ser., 45, 47, 54, 3 vols (London: Camden Society, 1931–37)

Droplaugarsona saga, ed. by Jón Jóhannesson, Íslenzk Fornrit, 11 (Reykjavik: Hið Íslenzka Fornritafélag, 1950)

Du Bellay, Jean, *Correspondance du Cardinal Jean du Bellay,* ed. by Rémy Scheurer and others, 7 vols (Paris: Klincksieck; Société de l'histoire de France, 1969–2017)

Eckhart, Meister, *Werke,* ed. by Niklaus Largier, 2 vols (Frankfurt a.M.: Deutscher Klassiker Verlag, 2008), I, trans. by Josef Quint

Edmund of Abingdon, *Mirour de Seinte Egylse,* ed. by Alan D. Wilshere (London: Anglo-Norman Text Society, 1982)

—— *Speculum Religiosorum and Speculum Ecclesie,* ed. by Helen P. Forshaw (London: Oxford University Press for the British Academy, 1973)

Egils saga Skalla-Grímssonar, ed. by Sigurður Nordal, Íslenzk Fornrit, 2 (Reykjavik: Hið Íslenzka Fornritafélag, 1933)

Erasmus of Rotterdam, *Giulio,* ed. and trans. [into Italian] by Silvana Seidel Menchi (Turin: Einaudi, 2014)

—— *Opera omnia Desiderii Erasmi Roterodami* (Amsterdam: North-Holland Publishing; Leiden: Brill, 1969–)

—— *Opus epistolarum Des. Erasmi Roterodami,* ed. by Percy S. Allen and others, 12 vols (Oxford: Clarendon Press, 1906–58)

La Estorie del Evangelie: A Parallel Text Edition, ed. by Celia M. Millward (Heidelberg: Winter, 1998)

Eyrbyggja saga, ed. by Einar Ólafur Sveinsson and Matthías Þórðarson, Íslenzk Fornrit, 4 (Reykjavik: Hið Íslenzka Fornritafélag, 1935)

The First Grammatical Treatise: Introduction, Text, Notes, Translation, Vocabulary, Facsimiles, ed. by Hreinn Benediktsson (Reykjavik: Institute of Nordic Linguistics, 1972)

'La Folie Tristan (Oxford)', ed. and trans. by Samuel N. Rosenberg, in *Early French Tristan Poems,* ed. by Norris J. Lacy, 2 vols (Cambridge: Brewer, 1998), I, pp. 258–310

The Four Ancient Books of Wales, ed. and trans. by William F. Skene (Edinburgh: Edmonston and Douglas, 1868) <https://www.sacred-texts. com/neu/celt/fab/index.htm> [accessed 30 July 2020]

Geiler von Kaysersberg, Johannes, *Die aeltesten Schriften Geilers von Kaysersberg: XXI Artikel — Briefe — Todtenbüchlein — Beichtspiegel — Seelenheil — Sendtbrieff — Bilger,* ed. by Léon Dacheux (Freiburg i.Br.: Herder, 1882)

Geoffrey of Monmouth, *The History of the Kings of Britain,* ed. by Michael D. Reeve, trans. by Neil Wright (Woodbridge: Boydell, 2007)

——— *Life of Merlin/Vita Merlini*, ed. and trans. by Basil Clark (Cardiff: University of Wales Press, 1973)

Gottfried von Straßburg, *Tristan*, ed. and trans. [into modern German] by Rüdiger Krohn, 3rd edn, 3 vols (Stuttgart: Reclam, 1984)

——— *Tristan*, trans. by Arthur Hatto (London: Penguin, 1967)

——— *Tristan und Isold*, ed. and trans. by Walter Haug and Manfred Scholz, 2 vols (Frankfurt a.M.: Deutscher Klassiker Verlag, 2011)

Gregory the Great, *Moralia in Iob*, ed. Marc Adriaen, 3 vols (Turnhout: Brepols: 1979–85)

Grettis saga Ásmundarsonar, ed. by Guðni Jónsson, Íslenzk Fornrit, 7 (Reykjavik: Hið Íslenzka Fornritafélag, 1936)

Grosseteste, Robert, *Hexaëmeron*, ed. by Richard C. Dales and Servus Gieben (Oxford: Oxford University Press, 1982)

Gunnlaugs saga ormstungu, in *Borgfirðinga sögur: Hœnsa-Þóris saga, Gunnlaugs saga ormstungu, Bjarnar saga Hítdœlakappa, Heiðarvíga saga, Gísls þáttr Illugasonar*, ed. by Sigurður Nordal and Guðni Jónsson, Íslenzk Fornrit, 3 (Reykjavik: Hið Íslenzka Fornritafélag, 1938), pp. 40–108

Henry of Ghent, *Opera omnia*, 38 vols (Leuven: Leuven University Press, 1979–2018), VI: *Quodlibet II*, ed. by R. Wielockx (1983)

Hildebertus Cenomannensis Episcopus, *Carmina Minora*, ed. by A. B. Scott, 2nd edn (Munich: Sauer, 2001) <https://doi.org/10.1515/9783110963137>

Holsteinische Reimchronik, ed. by Ludwig Weiland, in MGH Deutsche Chroniken, 2 (Hanover: Hahnsche Buchhandlung, 1877), pp. 609–33

Honorius Augustodunensis, *Opera omnia*, *Patrologia Latina* 172

Hugh of St Victor, *De archa Noe, Libellus de formatione arche*, ed. by Patrice Sicard (Turnhout: Brepols, 2001)

——— *Didiscalicon*, ed. by Charles H. Buttimer (Washington, DC: Catholic University Press, 1939)

Iacopo da Varazze, *Legenda Aurea*, ed. by Giovanni P. Maggioni, 2nd edn, 2 vols (Florence: SISMEL, 1998)

Isidore of Seville, *Etymologies*, PL 82. 73–760

James of Viterbo, *De regimine christiano*, ed. and trans. by R. W. Dyson (Leiden: Brill, 2009)

Johannes de Caulibus, *Meditaciones Vite Christi*, ed. by C. Mary Stallings-Taney (Turnhout: Brepols, 1997)

Laxdœla saga, ed. by Einar Ólafur Sveinsson, Íslenzk Fornrit, 5 (Reykjavik: Hið Íslenzka Fornritafélag, 1934)

Lemmel, Katerina, *Pepper for Prayer: The Correspondence of the Birgittine Nun Katerina Lemmel (1516–1525); Edition and Translation*, ed. and trans. by Volker Schier, Corine Schleif, and Anne Simon (Stockholm: Runica & Mediaevalia, 2019)

Love, Nicholas, *The Mirror of the Blessed Life of Jesus Christ: A Reading Text*, ed. by Michael G. Sargent (Exeter: University of Exeter Press, 2004)

Ludolph of Saxony, *Vita Jesu Christi: Ex Evangelio et Approbatis ab Ecclesia Catholica Doctoribus Sedule Collecta*, ed. by Ludovic M. Rigollot, 4 vols (Paris: Palmé, 1878)

Machiavelli, Niccolò, *Edizione nazionale delle opere di Niccolò Machiavelli*, 6 parts (Rome: Salerno Editrice, 2001–)

Margery Kempe, *The Book of Margery Kempe*, ed. by Barry Windeatt (Cambridge: Brewer, 2000)

Marsilius of Padua, *Defensor pacis*, ed. by C. W. Previté-Orton (Cambridge: Cambridge University Press, 1928)

Mechthild von Magdeburg, *Das fließende Licht der Gottheit*, ed. by Gisela Vollmann-Profe (Frankfurt a.M.: Deutscher Klassiker Verlag, 2003

—— *Lux Divinitatis*, ed. by Ernst Hellgardt, Balázs Nemes, and Elke Senne (Berlin: De Gruyter, 2019)

Ménard, Philippe, *Le rire et le sourire dans le roman courtois en France au Moyen Âge (1150–1250)* (Geneva: Droz, 1969)

Miller, Max, *Die Söflinger Briefe und das Klarissenkloster Söflingen bei Ulm a.D. im Spätmittelalter* (Würzburg-Aumühle: Triltsch, 1940)

Mirk, John, *Festial*, ed. by Susan Powell, EETS, orig. ser., 334–35, 2 vols (Oxford: Oxford University Press, 2009–11)

Narrative and Legislative Texts from Early Cîteaux, ed. by Chrysogonus Waddell (Cîteaux: Commentarii cistercienses, 1999)

'Netzwerke der Nonnen: Edition und Erschließung der Briefsammlung aus Kloster Lüne (ca. 1460–1555)', ed. by Eva Schlotheuber and others, with Philipp Stenzig and others <http://diglib.hab.de/edoc/ed000248/start.htm> [accessed 26 October 2020]

Pascasius Radbertus, *Expositio in Matheo*, ed. by Beda Paulus, 3 vols (Turnhout: Brepols, 1984)

Patrologia Latina [PL], ed. by J.-P. Migne, 221 vols (Paris: Garnier, 1844–64)

Peter Comestor, *Historia Scholastica*, Patrologia Latina 198. 1045–1721

Peter of Poitiers, *Allegoriae super tabernaculum Moysi*, ed. by Philip S. Moore and James A. Corbett (Notre Dame: University of Notre Dame Press, 1938)

Peter the Chanter, *Verbum abbreviatum*, ed. by Monique Boutry (Turnhout: Brepols, 2004)

Peter the Venerable, *Adversus Iudeorum inveteratam duritiem*, ed. by Yvonne Friedman (Turnhout: Brepols, 1985)

Petrarca, Francesco, *Canzoniere*, ed. by Marco Santagata, rev. edn (Milan: Mondadori, 2010)

—— *Canzoniere, Trionfi: L'incunabolo veneziano di Vindelino da Spira del 1470 nell'esemplare della Biblioteca civica Queriniana di Brescia con figure dipinte da Antonio Grifo, INC. G V 15*, ed. by Giuseppe Frasso, Giordana Mariani, and Ennio Sandal (Rome: Salerno, 2016)

—— *Lettres familières*, 6 vols (Paris: Les Belles Lettres, 2002–15), VI, ed. by Vittorio Rossi (2015)

—— *Opere latine di Francesco Petrarca*, ed. by Antonietta Bufano, 2 vols (Turin: Unione tipografico-Editrice Torinese, 1975), ii, pp. 1255–83

—— 'Petrarch's Coronation Oration', trans. by Ernest Hatch Wilkins, *PMLA*, 68.5 (December 1953), pp. 1241–50 <https://doi.org/10.2307/460017>

—— *Petrarch's Lyric Poems: The 'Rime Sparse' and Other Lyrics*, ed. and trans. by Robert M. Durling (Cambridge, MA: Harvard University Press, 1976)

—— *Trionfi, Rime estravaganti, Codice degli abbozzi*, ed. by Vinicio Pacca and Laura Paolino (Milan: Mondadori, 1996)

Petrus Alfonsi, *Dialogue against the Jews*, trans. by. Irven M. Resnick (Washington, DC: Catholic University of America Press, 2006)

—— *Dialogus, Patrologia Latina* 157. 535–672

Pirckheimer, Caritas, *Quellensammlung*, ed. by Josef Pfanner, 4 vols (Landshut: Caritas Pirckheimer Forschung, 1966–67), ii: *Briefe von, an und über Caritas Pirckheimer (aus den Jahren 1498–1530)* (1966)

Pseudo-Jerome, *Commentarii in novum testamentum, Patrologia Latina* 30. 531–900

Pucelle, Jean, *The Hours of Jeanne d'Evreux, Queen of France* (c. 1324–28), Metropolitan Museum of Art, New York, The Cloisters Collection, Accession No 54.1.2, fols 15^v–16^r <https://www.metmuseum.org/art/collection/search/470309>

Saga Óláfs Tryggvasonar, ed. by Finnur Jónsson (Copenhagen: Gads Forlag, 1932)

The Saga of Olaf Tryggvason, trans. by Theodore M. Andersson (New York: De Gruyter, 2003)

The Saga of Tristram and Ísönd, trans. by Paul Schach (Lincoln: University of Nebraska Press, 1973)

Die Sangspruchdichtung Rumelants von Sachsen: Edition — Übersetzung — Kommentar, ed. and trans. by Peter Kern (Berlin: De Gruyter, 2014) <https://doi.org/10.1515/9783110343151>

Saxo Grammaticus, *Gesta Danorum*, ed. by Karsten Friis-Jensen, trans. by Peter Fisher, 2 vols (Oxford: Clarendon Press, 2015)

Sneglu-Halla þáttr, in *Eyfirðinga sǫgur*, ed. by Jónas Kristjánsson, Íslenzk Fornrit, 9 (Reykjavik: Hið Íslenzka Fornritafélag, 1956), pp. 261–95

A Stanzaic Life of Christ, ed. by Frances A. Foster, EETS, orig. ser., 166 (London: Oxford University Press, 1926)

A Talkyng of þe Loue of God, ed. by M. Salvina Westra (The Hague: Nijhoff, 1950)

P. *Terenti Afri Comoediae*, ed. by Robert Kauer and Wallace M. Lindsay (Oxford: Oxford University Press, 1963)

Þe Wohunge of Ure Lauerd, ed. by W. Meredith Thompson, EETS, orig. ser., 241 (London: Oxford University Press, 1958)

Thomas Aquinas, *Commentary on the Gospel of John: Chapters 1–5*, trans. by Fabian Larcher and James A. Weisheipl (Washington: Catholic University of America Press, 2010)

Thomas of Cantimpré, 'The Middle English Life of Christina Mirabilis by Thomas of Cantimpré', in *Three Women of Liège: A Critical Edition and Commentary on the Middle English Lives of Elizabeth of Spalbeek, Christina Mirabilis and Marie d'Oignies*, ed. by Jennifer N. Brown (Turnhout: Brepols, 2008), pp. 51–84 <https://doi.org/10.1484/M.MWTC-EB.4.00109>

Þórðar saga hreðu, in *Kjalnesinga saga: Jökuls þáttr Búasonar, Víglundar saga, Króka-refs saga, Þórðar saga hreðu, Finnboga saga, Gunnars saga keldugnúpsfífls*, ed. by Jóhannes Halldórsson, Íslenzk Fornrit, 14 (Reykjavik: Hið Íslenzka Fornritafélag, 1959), pp. 161–226

Þorleifs þáttr jarlsskálds, in *Eyfirðinga sǫgur*, ed. by Jónas Kristjánsson, Íslenzk Fornrit, 9 (Reykjavik: Hið Íslenzka Fornritafélag, 1956), pp. 213–29

Þorskfirðinga saga, in *Harðar saga: Bárðar saga, Þorskfirðinga saga, Flóamanna saga*, ed. by Þórhallur Vilmundarson and Bjarni Vilhjálmsson, Íslenzk Fornrit, 13 (Reykjavik: Hið Íslenzka Fornritafélag, 1991), pp. 173–227

Ulrich, *Antiquiores Consuetudines Cluniacensis Monasterii Collectore Udalrico Monacho Benedictino, Patrologia Latina* 149. 635–778

Visitations in the Diocese of Lincoln, 1517–1531, ed. by A. Hamilton Thompson, Lincoln Record Society, 33, 35, 37, 3 vols (Lincoln: Lincoln Record Society, 1940–47)

Visitations of Religious Houses in the Diocese of Lincoln, ed. by A. Hamilton Thompson, Canterbury and York Society, 7, 14, 21, 3 vols (London: Canterbury and York Society, 1915–27)

Visitations of the Diocese of Norwich, AD 1492–1532, ed. by Augustus Jessopp, Camden Society, new ser., 43 (London: Camden Society, 1888)

Vita Aedwardi Regis, ed. and trans. by Frank Barlow (Oxford: Oxford University Press, 1992)

Wackernagel, Philipp, *Das deutsche Kirchenlied von der ältesten Zeit bis zum Anfang des XVII. Jahrhunderts*, 5 vols (Leipzig: Teubner, 1864–77)

—— *Das deutsche Kirchenlied von M. Luther bis auf N. Herman und A. Blaurer* (Stuttgart: Liesching, 1841)

William of Ockham, *Dialogus*, ed. by John Kilcullen and others <https://www.thebritishacademy.ac.uk/pubs/dialogus/ockdial.html> [accessed 22 December 2019]

SECONDARY SOURCES

Abulafia, Anna Sapir, 'Jewish–Christian Disputations and the Twelfth-Century Renaissance', *Journal of Medieval History*, 15.2 (1989), pp. 105–25

Adams, Jonathan, 'Indledning: Østnordisk filologi — nu og i fremtiden', in
    Østnordisk filologi — nu og i fremtiden, ed. by Jonathan Adams (Copen-
    hagen: Universitets-Jubilæets danske Samfund, [n.d.]), pp. 11–13
Agamben, Giorgio, *The Highest Poverty: Monastic Rules and Form-of-Life*,
    trans. by Adam Kotsko (Stanford: Stanford University Press, 2013)
—— *The Open: Man and Animal*, trans. by Kevin Attell (Stanford: Stanford
    University Press, 2003)
—— *Opus Dei: An Archaeology of Duty*, trans. by Adam Kotsko (Stanford:
    Stanford University Press, 2013)
—— 'La parola e il sapere', *aut-aut*, September–December 1980, pp. 155–66
—— 'Postilla 2001', in *La comunità che viene* (Turin: Bollati Boringhieri,
    2001), pp. 89–93
—— *Potentialities*, trans. by Daniel Heller-Roazen (Stanford: Stanford Uni-
    versity Press, 1999)
—— *The Sacrament of Language: An Archaeology of the Oath*, trans. by Adam
    Kotsko (Stanford: Stanford University Press 2011)
—— *The Time That Remains: A Commentary on the Letter to the Romans*,
    trans. by Patricia Dailey (Stanford: Stanford University Press, 2005)
    <https://doi.org/10.1515/9781503619869>
Ahern, John, 'Binding the Book: Hermeneutics and Manuscript Production
    in *Paradiso* 33', *PMLA*, 97.5 (1982), pp. 800–09
—— 'Dante's Last Word: The *Comedy* as a *liber coelestis*', *Dante Studies*, 102
    (1984), pp. 1–14
Aichmayr, Michael, 'Taliesin: Literarische Überlieferung der Taliesin-Figur',
    in *Verführer, Schurken, Magier*, ed. by Ulrich Müller and Werner Wun-
    derlich (St Gall: UVK, 2001), pp. 903–14
Ainsworth, Maryan W., and Joshua P. Waterman, *German Paintings in the
    Metropolitan Museum of Art, 1350–1600* (New Haven, CT: Metropol-
    itan Museum of Art, distributed by Yale University Press, 2013)
Althoff, Gerd, *Spielregeln der Politik im Mittelalter: Kommunikation in Frieden
    und Fehde* (Darmstadt: Primus, 1997)
Altschul, Nadia R., *Geographies of Philological Knowledge: Postcoloniality
    and the Transatlantic National Epic* (Chicago: University of Chicago
    Press, 2012) <https://doi.org/10.7208/chicago/9780226016191.
    001.0001>
Amtower, Laurel, *Engaging Words: The Culture of Reading in the Later Mid-
    dle Ages* (New York: Palgrave, 2000) <https://doi.org/10.1007/978-1-
    349-62998-5>
Andersen, Elizabeth, 'Translation, Transposition, Transmission: Low Ger-
    man and Processes of Cultural Transformation', in *Transnational Ger-
    man Studies*, ed. by Rebecca Braun and Benedict Schofield (Liverpool:
    Liverpool University Press, 2020), pp. 17–41
Andersen, Per, 'Dating the Laws of Medieval Denmark: Studies of the Manu-
    scripts of the Danish Church Laws', in *Denmark and Europe in the Middle
    Ages, c. 1000–1525: Essays in Honour of Professor Michael H. Gelting*,

ed. by Kerstin Hundahl, Lars Kjær, and Niels Lund (Farnham: Ashgate, 2014), pp. 183–202

—— *Legal Procedure and Practice in Medieval Denmark* (Leiden: Brill, 2011) <https://doi.org/10.1163/ej.9789004204768.i-452>

Andersson, Theodore M., 'The First Icelandic King's Saga: Oddr Snorrason's "Óláfs saga Tryggvasonar" or "The Oldest Saga of Saint Olaf"?', *Journal of English and Germanic Philology*, 103.2 (2004), pp. 139–55

—— *The Growth of the Medieval Icelandic Sagas* (Ithaca: Cornell University Press, 2006)

Andersson-Schmitt, Margarete, '"Siælinna thrøst" und seine Varianten', in *Niederdeutsch in Skandinavien*, III, ed. by Lennart Elmevik and Kurt Erich Schöndorf, Beihefte zur Zeitschrift für deutsche Philologie, 6 (Berlin: Schmidt, 1992), pp. 70–76

Antonsson, Haki, 'Sanctus Kanutus rex', in *Medieval Nordic Literature in Latin: A Website of Authors and Anonymous Works c. 1100–1530*, ed. by Stephan Borgehammar and others <https://wikihost.uib.no/medieval/index.php/Sanctus_Kanutus_rex> [accessed 24 January 2020]

Appuhn, Horst, and Christian von Heusinger, 'Der Fund kleiner Andachtsbilder des 13. bis 17. Jahrhunderts im Kloster Wienhausen', *Niederdeutsche Beiträge zur Kunstgeschichte*, 4 (1965), pp. 157–238

Arnold, John, and Katherine J. Lewis, eds, *A Companion to the Book of Margery Kempe* (Woodbridge: Brewer, 2004)

Ascoli, Albert Russell, *Dante and the Making of a Modern Author* (Cambridge: Cambridge University Press, 2008) <https://doi.org/10.1017/CBO9780511485718>

Attridge, Derek, *The Singularity of Literature* (London: Routledge, 2004) <https://doi.org/10.4324/9780203420447>

—— *The Work of Literature* (Oxford: Oxford University Press, 2015) <https://doi.org/10.1093/acprof:oso/9780198733195.001.0001>

Austin, R. G., 'Ille Ego Qui Quondam', *Classical Quarterly*, n.s., 18 (1968), pp. 107–15 <https://doi.org/10.1017/S0009838800029153>

Baert, Barbara, 'The Pool of Bethsaïda: The Cultural History of a Holy Place in Jerusalem', *Viator*, 36 (2005), pp. 1–22

Bätschmann, Oskar, and Pascal Griener, *Hans Holbein* (Princeton: Princeton University Press, 1997)

Bale, Anthony, 'Richard Salthouse of Norwich and the Scribe of *The Book of Margery Kempe*', *Chaucer Review*, 52.2 (2017), pp. 173–87

Barański, Zygmunt G., 'Terza rima, "Canto", "Canzon", "Cantica"', in *Dante Now: Current Trends in Dante Studies*, ed. by Theodore J. Cachey, Jr (Notre Dame: University of Notre Dame Press, 1995

Barolini, Teodolinda, 'The Making of a Lyric Sequence: Time and Narrative in Petrarch's *Rerum vulgarium fragmenta*', *MLN*, 104.1 (January 1989), pp. 1–38 <https://doi.org/10.2307/2904989>

—— *The Undivine 'Comedy': Detheologizing Dante* (Princeton: Princeton University Press, 1992) <https://doi.org/10.1515/9781400820764>

Barthes, Roland, 'From Work to Text', in Barthes, *Image, Music, Text*, trans. by Stephen Heath (London: Fontana Press, 1977), pp. 155–64

—— *Image, Music, Text*, ed. and trans. by Stephen Heath (New York: Hill and Wang, 1977)

Baur, Kilian, *Freunde und Feinde: Niederdeutsche, Dänen und die Hanse im Spätmittelalter (1376–1513)* (Vienna: Böhlau, 2018) <https://doi.org/10.7788/9783412504380>

Beach, Alison I., and Isabelle Cochelin, eds, *The Cambridge History of Medieval Monasticism in the Latin West*, 2 vols (Cambridge: Cambridge University Press, 2020) <https://doi.org/10.1017/9781107323742>

Beadle, Richard, and Pamela King, eds, *York Mystery Plays: A Selection in Modern Spelling* (Oxford: Oxford University Press, 1984)

Beckwith, Sarah, 'A Very Material Mysticism: The Medieval Mysticism of Margery Kempe', in *Medieval Literature: Criticism, Ideology and History*, ed. by David Aers (Brighton: Harvester Press, 1986), pp. 34–57

Benjamin, Walter, 'On the Concept of History', trans. by Harry Zohn, in *Selected Writings*, 4 vols (Cambridge, MA: Harvard University Press, 2004–06), IV: *1938–1940*, ed. by Michael W. Jennings (2006), pp. 389–400

Bennington, Geoffrey, and Jacques Derrida, *Jacques Derrida* (Paris: Seuil, 1991)

—— *Jacques Derrida*, trans. by Geoffrey Bennington (Chicago: University of Chicago Press, 1993)

Benveniste, Émile, *Dictionary of Indo-European Concepts and Society*, trans. by Elizabeth Palmer (Chicago: Hau Books, 2016)

Berger, David, 'Gilbert Crispin, Alan of Lille, and Jacob ben Reuben: A Study in the Transmission of Medieval Polemic', *Speculum*, 49.1 (1974), pp. 34–47

Bersani, Leo, *The Freudian Body: Psychoanalysis and Art* (New York: Columbia University Press, 1986)

Bibire, Paul, 'On Reading the Icelandic Sagas: Approaches to Old Icelandic Texts', in *West over Sea: Studies in Scandinavian Sea-Borne Expansion and Settlement before 1300*, ed. by Beverley Ballin Smith, Simon Taylor, and Gareth Williams (Leiden: Brill, 2007), pp. 3–18

Bland, Mark, *A Guide to Early Printed Books and Manuscripts* (Chichester: Wiley-Blackwell, 2010) <https://doi.org/10.1002/9781444317855>

Blosen, Hans, 'Ein mittelniederdeutsches "Speculum humanae salvationis" in dänischem Gebrauch', in *Vulpis Adolatio: Festschrift für Hubertus Menke zum 60. Geburtstag*, ed. by Robert Peters, Horst P. Pütz, and Ulrich Weber (Heidelberg: Winter, 2001), pp. 71–88

Boccignone, Manuela, 'Un albero piantato nel cuore (Petrarca e Iacopone)', *Lettere italiane*, 52.2 (April–June 2000), pp. 225–64

Bolzoni, Lina, La rete delle immagini: Predicazione in volgare dalle origini a Bernardino da Siena (Turin: Einaudi, 2002)

Bomford, Kate, 'Friendship and Immortality: Holbein's *Ambassadors* Revisited', *Renaissance Studies*, 18 (2004), pp. 544–81

Borgolte, Michael, and others, eds, *Mittelalter im Labor: Die Mediävistik testet Wege zu einer transkulturellen Europawissenschaft* (Berlin: Akademie Verlag, 2008) <https://doi.org/10.1524/9783050047515>

Bowen, Barbara C., *The Age of Bluff: Paradox and Ambiguity in Rabelais and Montaigne* (Urbana: University of Illinois Press, 1972)

Braidotti, Rosi, 'Intensive Genre and the Demise of Gender', *Angelaki: Journal of the Theoretical Humanities*, 13.2 (2008), pp. 45–57

—— *The Posthuman* (Cambridge: Polity Press, 2013)

—— 'Writing as a Nomadic Subject', *Comparative Critical Studies*, 11.2–3 (2014), pp. 163–84

Brandenburg, Elena, *Karl der Große im Norden: Rezeption französischer Heldenepik in den altostnordischen Handschriften* (Tübingen: Narr Francke Attempto, 2019)

Brenkman, John, 'Writing, Desire, Dialectic in Petrarch's *Rime 23*', *Pacific Coast Philology*, 9 (April 1974), pp. 12–19 <https://doi.org/10.2307/1316564>

Brink, Stefan, '*Minnunga mæn*: The Usage of Old Knowledgeable Men in Legal Cases', in *Minni and Muninn: Memory in Medieval Nordic Culture*, ed. by Pernille Hermann, Stephen A. Mitchell, and Agnes S. Arnórsdóttir (Turnhout: Brepols, 2014), pp. 197–210 <https://doi.org/10.1484/M.AS-EB.1.101981>

Bruun, Henry, 'Rosenkrantz, Erik Ottesen', in *Dansk biografisk leksikon*, 3rd edn, ed. by Sv. Cedergreen Bech, 16 vols (Copenhagen: Gyldendal, 1979–84), xii (1982), pp. 332–33 <http://denstoredanske.dk/Dansk_Biografisk_Leksikon/Monarki_og_adel/Hofmester/Erik_Ottesen_Rosenkrantz> [accessed 13 March 2020]

Buck, Stephanie, and others, *Hans Holbein the Younger, 1497/98–1543: Portraitist of the Renaissance* (The Hague: Royal Cabinet of Paintings Mauritshuis, 2003)

Burckhardt-Biedermann, Theophil, 'Über Zeit und Anlaß des Flugblattes: Luther als Herkules Germanicus', *Basler Zeitschrift für Geschichte und Altertumskunde*, 4 (1905), pp. 38–44

Burrow, J. A., *Gestures and Looks in Medieval Narrative* (Cambridge: Cambridge University Press, 2002) <https://doi.org/10.1017/CBO9780511483240>

Burton, Janet, and Julie Kerr, *The Cistercians in the Middle Ages* (Woodbridge: Boydell, 2011)

Burton, Philip, *Language in the* Confessions *of Augustine* (Oxford: Oxford University Press, 2007) <https://doi.org/10.1093/acprof:oso/9780199266227.001.0001>

Bynum, Caroline Walker, *Dissimilar Similitudes: Devotional Objects in Late Medieval Europe* (New York: Zone Books, 2020) <https://doi.org/10.2307/j.ctv15r5dvj>

—— *The Resurrection of the Body in Western Christianity, 200–1336* (New York: Columbia University Press, 1995)

—— 'Violent Imagery in Late Medieval Piety: Fifteenth Annual Lecture of the GHI, November 8, 2001', *GHI Bulletin*, 30 (2002), pp. 3–36

—— *Wonderful Blood: Theology and Practice in Late Medieval Northern Germany and Beyond* (Philadelphia: University of Pennsylvania Press, 2007)

Byrne, Aisling, and Victoria Flood, eds, *Crossing Borders in the Insular Middle Ages* (Turnhout: Brepols, 2019) <https://doi.org/10.1484/M.TCNE-EB.5.109277>

Campbell, Lorne, and others, 'Quentin Matsys, Desiderius Erasmus, Pieter Gillis and Thomas More', *Burlington Magazine*, 120 (1978), pp. 716–25

Caputo, John D., 'Augustine and Postmodernism', in *A Companion to Augustine*, ed. by Mark Vessey with the assistance of Shelley Reid (Malden: Wiley-Blackwell, 2012), pp. 492–504 <https://doi.org/10.1002/9781118255483.ch37>

—— *The Weakness of God: A Theology of the Event* (Bloomington: Indiana University Press, 2006)

Caputo, John D., and Michael J. Scanlon, eds, *Augustine and Postmodernism: Confessions and Circumfession* (Bloomington: Indiana University Press, 2005)

Carey, Stephen Mark, 'Mittelniederdeutsche Weltchronik', in *The Encyclopedia of the Medieval Chronicle*, ed. by Graeme Dunphy, 2 vols (Leiden: Brill, 2010), ii, p. 1115

Carlquist, Jonas, *Handskriften som historiskt vittne: Fornsvenska samlingshandskrifter — miljö och funktion* (Stockholm: Sällskapet Runica et Mediævalia, 2002)

Carlson, Stephen C., 'The Accommodations of Joseph and Mary in Bethlehem: κατάλυμα in Luke 2.7', *New Testament Studies*, 56 (2010), pp. 326–42

Carruthers, Mary, *The Book of Memory: A Study of Memory in Medieval Culture*, 2nd edn (Cambridge: Cambridge University Press, 2008) <https://doi.org/10.1017/CBO9781107051126>

—— *The Craft of Thought: Meditation, Rhetoric, and the Making of Images, 400–1200* (Cambridge: Cambridge University Press, 2000)

—— *The Experience of Beauty in the Middle Ages* (Oxford: Oxford University Press, 2013) <https://doi.org/10.1093/acprof:osobl/9780199590322.001.0001>

Chappell, Julie A., *Perilous Passages: The Book of Margery Kempe, 1534–1934* (Basingstoke: Palgrave Macmillan, 2013) <https://doi.org/10.1057/9781137277688>

Cheney, Christopher R., *Episcopal Visitation of Monasteries in the Thirteenth Century*, 2nd edn (Manchester: Manchester University Press, 1983)

—— 'Norwich Cathedral Priory in the Fourteenth Century', *Bulletin of the John Rylands Library*, 20 (1936), pp. 3–30

Chinca, Mark, and Christopher Young, eds, *Orality and Literacy in the Middle Ages: Essays on a Conjunction and its Consequences in Honour of D. H. Green* (Turnhout: Brepols, 2005) <https://doi.org/10.1484/M.USML-EB.6.09070802050003050104050102>

Chism, Christine, '"Ain't gonna study war no more": Geoffrey of Monmouth's *Historia Regum Britannie* and *Vita Merlini*', *Chaucer Review*, 48 (2014), pp. 457–79 <https://doi.org/10.5325/chaucerrev.48.4.0458>

Ciaranfi, Anna Maria Francini, 'Iconografia', in *Enciclopedia Dantesca* (1970) <http://www.treccani.it/enciclopedia/iconografia_(Enciclopedia-Dantesca)/> [accessed 30 May 2020]

Cipollone, Annalisa, '"Né per nova figura il primo alloro ...": La chiusa di *Rvf* XXIII, Il *Canzoniere* e Dante', *Rassegna europea di letteratura italiana*, 11 (1998), pp. 29–46

Cixous, Hélène, *Illa* (Paris: Des Femmes, 1980)

—— *La* (Paris: Gallimard, 1976)

Clanchy, M. T., *From Memory to the Written Record*, 3rd edn (Chichester: Wiley-Blackwell, 2013)

Clover, Carol, *The Medieval Saga* (Ithaca: Cornell University Press, 1982) <https://doi.org/10.7591/9781501740510>

Clunies Ross, Margaret, *The Cambridge Introduction to the Old Norse-Icelandic Saga* (Cambridge: Cambridge University Press, 2010) <https://doi.org/10.1017/CBO9780511763274>

Coccia, Emanuele, *The Life of Plants: A Metaphysics of Mixture*, trans. by Dylan J. Montanari (Cambridge: Polity Press, 2019)

—— *La Vie des plantes: Une métaphysique du mélange* (Paris: Éditions Payot & Rivages, 2016)

Cohen, Jeffrey J., 'Inventing Animals in the Middle Ages', in *Engaging with Nature: Essays on the Natural World in Medieval and Early Modern Europe*, ed. by Barbara A. Hanawalt, Lisa. J. Kiser, and Julie Berger Hochstrasser (Notre Dame: University of Notre Dame Press, 2009), pp. 39–64

—— *Medieval Identity Machines* (London: University of Minnesota Press, 2003)

Collins, Raymond F., 'Inspiration', in *The New Jerome Biblical Commentary*, ed. by Raymond E. Brown, Joseph A. Fitzmyer, and Roland E. Murphy (London: Chapman, 1989), pp. 1023–33

Conklin Akbari, Suzanne, and Karla Mallette, eds, *A Sea of Languages: Rethinking the Arabic Role in Medieval Literary History* (Toronto: University of Toronto Press, 2013) <https://doi.org/10.3138/9781442663398>

Constable, Giles, *Letters and Letter-Collections* (Turnhout: Brepols, 1976)

Contini, Gianfranco, *Un'idea di Dante* (Turin: Einaudi, 1970)

Conybeare, Catherine, 'Reading the *Confessions*', in *A Companion to Augustine*, ed. by Mark Vessey with the assistance of Shelley Reid (Malden: Wiley-Blackwell, 2012), pp. 99–110 <https://doi.org/10.1002/9781118255483.ch8>

—— *The Routledge Guidebook to Augustine's* Confessions (New York: Routledge, 2016) <https://doi.org/10.4324/9781315726250>

Crevier Goulet, Sarah-Anaïs, 'Du jardin d'essai/*esse* à l'hortus conclusus: Figures de la naissance et du végétal dans l'oeuvre de Hélène Cixous', in *Des jardins autres*, ed. by Paolo Alexandre Néné and Sarah Carmo (Paris: Archives Karéline, 2015), pp. 257–80

Croce, Benedetto, *La poesia di Dante* (Bari: Laterza, 1921)

Dahlerup, Pil, *Dansk litteratur: Middelalder*, 2 vols (Copenhagen: Gyldendal, 1998)

—— *Sanselig senmiddelalder: Litterære perspektiver på danske tekster 1482–1523* (Aarhus: Aarhus Universitetsforlag, 2010). Saxo ebook

Danielsson, Tommy, *Sagorna om Norges kungar: Från Magnús góði till Magnús Erlingsson* (Hedemora: Gidlunds Förlag, 2002)

Davis, James, *Medieval Market Morality: Life, Law and Ethics in the English Marketplace, 1200–1500* (Cambridge: Cambridge University Press, 2012) <https://doi.org/10.1017/CBO9780511763366>

Deeming, Helen, and Elizabeth Eva Leach, eds, *Manuscripts and Medieval Song: Inscription, Performance, Context*, (Cambridge: Cambridge University Press, 2015) <https://doi.org/10.1017/CBO9781107477193>

Deleuze, Gilles, and Félix Guattari, *A Thousand Plateaus: Capitalism and Schizophrenia*, trans. by Brian Massumi (London: Bloomsbury Academic, 2012)

—— *A Thousand Plateaus: Capitalism and Schizophrenia*, trans. by Brian Massumi (Minneapolis: University of Minnesota Press, 1987)

Derendorf, Brigitte, 'Die mittelniederdeutsche "Historienbibel VIII"', *Niederdeutsches Wort*, 36 (1996), pp. 167–82

Derrida, Jacques, *Memoires for Paul de Man*, trans. by Cecile Lindsay and others (New York: Columbia University Press, 1989)

—— *Specters of Marx: The State of the Debt and the New International*, trans. by Peggy Kamuf (New York: Routledge, 1994)

Diem, Albrecht, and Philip Rousseau, 'Monastic Rules (Fourth to Ninth Century)', in *Cambridge History of Medieval Monasticism*, ed. by Beach and Cochelin, I, pp. 162–94 <https://doi.org/10.1017/9781107323742.009>

Dinshaw, Carolyn, *How Soon Is Now? Medieval Texts, Amateur Readers, and the Queerness of Time* (Durham: Duke University Press, 2012) <https://doi.org/10.1515/9780822395911>

Doob, Penelope, *Nebuchadnezzar's Children: Conventions of Madness in Medieval Literature* (New Haven, CT: Yale University Press 1974)

Echard, Siân, 'Palimpsests of Place and Time in Geoffrey of Monmouth's *Historia Regum Britanniae*', in *Teaching and Learning in Medieval Europe: Essays in Honour of Gernot R. Wieland*, ed. by Greti Dinkova-Bruun and Tristan Major (Turnhout: Brepols, 2017), pp. 43–59 <https://doi.org/10.1484/M.PJML-EB.5.113253>

Eco, Umberto, *The Open Work*, trans. by Anna Cancogni, intro. by David Robey (Cambridge, MA: Harvard University Press, 1989)

—— *Opera aperta: Forma e indeterminazione nelle poetiche contemporanee* (Milan: Bompiani, 1962)

—— 'The Poetics of the Open Work', in *The Role of the Reader: Explorations in the Semiotics of Texts* (London: Hutchinson, 1979), pp. 47–66

—— *The Role of the Reader: Explorations in the Semiotics of Texts* (Bloomington: Indiana University Press, 1979)

Eden, Kathy, '"Between Friends All Is Common": The Erasmian Adage and Tradition', *Journal of the History of Ideas*, 59 (1998), pp. 405–19

—— *Friends Hold All Things in Common: Tradition, Intellectual Property, and the Adages of Erasmus* (New Haven, CT: Yale University Press, 2001) <https://doi.org/10.12987/yale/9780300087574.001.0001>

Ekrem, Inger, 'Essay on Date and Purpose', in *Historia Norwegie*, ed. by Inger Ekrem and Lars Boje Mortensen, trans. by Peter Fisher (Copenhagen: Museum Tusculanum Press, 2006), pp. 155–225

Ellis, Roger, 'The *Northern Homily Cycle*: A Work in Progress', *Medium Aevum*, 88 (2019) <https://doi.org/10.2307/26889855>

Elmevik, Lennart, and Ernst Håkon Jahr, eds, *Contact between Low German and Scandinavian in the Late Middle Ages: 25 Years of Research* (Uppsala: Kungl. Gustav Adolfs Akademien för svensk folkkultur, 2012)

Enterline, Lynn, 'Embodied Voices: Petrarch Reading Himself Reading Ovid', in *Desire in the Renaissance: Psychoanalysis and Literature*, ed. by Valeria Finucci and Regina Schwartz (Princeton: Princeton University Press, 1994), pp. 120–45 <https://doi.org/10.1515/9781400821501.120>

'The *Eufemiaviser* and the Reception of Courtly Culture in Late Medieval Denmark', conference programme (Zurich, 2018) <https://www.ds.uzh.ch/_files/uploads/agenda/821.pdf> [accessed 4 March 2020]

Evangelisti, Silvia, *Nuns: A History of Convent Life, 1450–1700* (Oxford: Oxford University Press, 2007)

Evans, Gillian R., 'Alan of Lille's Distinctiones and the Problem of Theological Language', *Sacris erudiri*, 24 (1980), pp. 67–86

Expanding German Studies: An Interactive Bibliography for Teachers and Lecturers <https://germanstudiesbibliography.wordpress.com/> [accessed 18 September 2020]

Fabry-Tehranchy, Irène, 'Écrire l'histoire de Stonehenge: Narration historique et romanesque (XIIe–XVe siècles)', in *L'Écriture de l'histoire au Moyen Âge: Contraintes génériques, contraintes documentaires*, ed. by Etienne Anheim and others (Paris: Garnier, 2015), pp. 131–47

Faletra, Michael A. 'Narrating the Matter of Britain: Geoffrey of Monmouth and the Norman Colonization of Wales', *Chaucer Review*, 35 (2000), pp. 60–85 <https://doi.org/10.1353/cr.2000.0018>

Farrell, Jennifer, 'History, Prophecy, and the Arthur of the Normans: The Question of Audience and Motivation in Geoffrey of Monmouth's *Historia Regum Britanniae*', *Anglo-Norman Studies*, 37 (2014), pp. 99–114

Fauvelle, François-Xavier, *The Golden Rhinoceros: Histories of the African Middle Ages*, trans. by Troy Tice (Princeton: Princeton University Press, 2018) <https://doi.org/10.1515/9780691183947>

Febvre, Lucien, and Henri-Jean Martin, *The Coming of the Book: The Impact of Printing 1450–1800*, trans. by David Gerard (London: Verso, 1997)

Felski, Rita, *Hooked: Art and Attachment* (Chicago: University of Chicago Press, 2020) <https://doi.org/10.7208/chicago/9780226729770.001.0001>

Ferm, Olle, 'Lilla rimkrönikan', in *The Encyclopedia of the Medieval Chronicle*, ed. by Graeme Dunphy, 2 vols (Leiden: Brill, 2010), ii, p. 1032

Flint, V. I. J., 'The Career of Honorius Augustodunensis: Some Fresh Evidence', *Revue bénédictine*, 82.1–2 (1972), pp. 63–86

Foister, Susan, *Holbein and England* (New Haven, CT: Yale University Press, 2004)

—— *Holbein in England* (London: Abrams, 2007)

Frankopan, Peter, 'Why We Need to Think About the Global Middle Ages', *Journal of Medieval Worlds*, 1.1 (2019), pp. 5–10 <https://doi.org/10.1525/jmw.2019.100002>

Freccero, Carla, 'Ovidian Subjectivities in Early Modern Lyric: Identification and Desire in Petrarch and Louise Labé', in *Ovid and the Renaissance Body*, ed. by Goran Stanivukovic (Toronto: University of Toronto Press, 2001), pp. 21–37 <https://doi.org/10.3138/9781442678194-003>

Freccero, John, 'The Fig Tree and the Laurel: Petrarch's Poetics', *Diacritics*, 5.1 (spring 1975), pp. 34–40 <https://doi.org/10.2307/464720>

Frederiksen, Britta Olrik, '57. The Jutland Law', in *Living Words & Luminous Pictures: Medieval Book Culture in Denmark: Catalogue*, ed. by Erik Petersen ([n.p.]: Det Kongelige Bibliotek; Moesgård Museum, 1999), pp. 44–45

—— '61. Courtly Romances', in *Living Words & Luminous Pictures: Medieval Book Culture in Denmark: Catalogue*, ed. by Erik Petersen ([n.p.]: Det Kongelige Bibliotek; Moesgård Museum, 1999), pp. 48–49

—— 'Dyrerim, De gamle danske', in *Medieval Scandinavia: An Encyclopedia*, ed. by Phillip Pulsiano and Kirsten Wolf (New York: Garland, 1993), p. 145

—— 'The History of Old Nordic Manuscripts IV: Old Danish', in *The Nordic Languages: An International Handbook of the History of the North Germanic Languages*, ed. by Oskar Bandle and others, 2 vols (Berlin: De Gruyter, 2002–05), i (2002), pp. 816–24

Fredriksen, Paula, 'The Confessions as Autobiography', in *A Companion to Augustine*, ed. by Mark Vessey with the assistance of Shelley Reid (Malden: Wiley-Blackwell, 2012), pp. 87–98 <https://doi.org/10. 1002/9781118255483.ch7>

Freedman, Paul H., *Images of the Medieval Peasant* (Stanford: Stanford University Press, 1999) <https://doi.org/10.1515/9781503617537>

Fulton Brown, Rachel, *Mary and the Art of Prayer: The Hours of the Virgin in Medieval Christian Thought* (New York: Columbia University Press, 2017) <https://doi.org/10.7312/fult18168>

Gardini, Nicola, *Lacuna* (Turin: Einaudi, 2014)

Garipzanov, Ildar H., ed., *Historical Narratives and Christian Identity on a European Periphery: Early Historical Writing in Northern, East-Central, and Eastern Europe (c. 1070–1200)* (Turnhout: Brepols, 2011) <https://doi.org/10.1484/M.TCNE-EB.6. 09070802050003050303060704>

Gaunt, Simon, 'Discourse Desired: Desire, Subjectivity and *Mouvance* in *Can vei la lauzeta mover*', in *Desiring Discourse: The Literature of Love, Ovid through Chaucer*, ed. by James Paxson and Cynthia Gravlee (Selinsgrove, PA: Susquehanna University Press, 1998), pp. 89–110

'Gesta Danorum: Kulturhistorisk baggrund', in *Tekster fra Danmarks middelalder og renæssance 1100–1550 — på dansk og latin* <https://tekstnet.dk/gesta-danorum/about> [accessed 14 February 2021]

Gill, Katherine, 'Open Monasteries for Women in Late Medieval and Early Modern Italy: Two Roman Examples', in *The Crannied Wall: Women, Religion, and the Arts in Early Modern Europe*, ed. by Craig A. Monson (Ann Arbor: University of Michigan Press, 1992), pp. 15–47

Gillespie, Vincent, 'From the Twelfth Century to c.1450', in *The Cambridge History of Literary Criticism*, 9 vols (Cambridge: Cambridge University Press, 1990–2013), ii, ed. by Alastair Minnis and Ian Johnson (2005), pp. 145–235

—— 'Religious Writing', in *The Oxford History of Literary Translation in English: To 1550*, ed. by Roger Ellis (Oxford: Oxford University Press, 2008), pp. 234–83

Gillingham, John, 'The Context and Purposes of Geoffrey of Monmouth's *History of the Kings of Britain*', *Anglo-Norman Studies*, 13 (1990), pp. 99–118

Gísli Sigurðsson, 'Another Audience — Another Saga: How Can We Best Explain Different Accounts in *Vatnsdœla saga* and *Finnboga saga ramma* of the Same Events?', in *Text und Zeittiefe*, ed. by Hildegard L. C. Tristram (Tübingen: Narr, 1994), pp. 359–76

Giunta, Claudio, *Codici: Saggi sulla poesia del Medioevo* (Bologna: il Mulino, 2005)

Glauser, Jörg, 'Vorwort', in *Skandinavische Literaturgeschichte*, ed. by Jörg Glauser, 2nd edn (Stuttgart: Metzler, 2016), pp. viii–xviii <https://doi.org/10.1007/978-3-476-05257-5>

Gragnolati, Manuele, 'Authorship and Performance in Dante's *Vita nova*', in *Aspects of the Performative in Medieval Culture*, ed. by Gragnolati and Suerbaum, pp. 123–40

—— 'Insegnare un classico: La complessità di Dante e lo spirito critico', in *In cattedra: Il docente universitario in otto autoritratti*, ed. by Chiara Cappelletto (Milan: Raffaello Cortina, 2019)

—— 'The Lyric Poetry', in *Dante's 'Other' Works*, ed. by Zygmunt Baranski and Theodore J. Cachey, Jr (Notre Dame: Notre Dame University Press, 2022), pp. 1–34

Gragnolati, Manuele, and Francesca Southerden, *Possibilities of Lyric: Reading Petrarch in Dialogue; With an Epilogue by Antonella Anedda Angioy* (Berlin: ICI Berlin Press, 2020) <https://doi.org/10.37050/ci-18>

Gragnolati, Manuele, and Almut Suerbaum, eds, *Aspects of the Performative in Medieval Culture* (Berlin: De Gruyter, 2010) <https://doi.org/10.1515/9783110222470>

Green, D. H., *Medieval Listening and Reading* (Cambridge: Cambridge University Press, 1994) <https://doi.org/10.1017/CBO9780511518720>

—— 'Orality and Reading: The State of Research in Medieval Studies', *Speculum*, 65.2 (April 1990), pp. 267–80 <https://doi.org/10.2307/2864293>

Greene, Thomas M., *The Vulnerable Text: Essays on Renaissance Literature* (New York: Columbia University Press, 1986)

Gronert, Stefan, *Bild-Individualität: Die 'Erasmus'-Bildnisse von Hans Holbein dem Jüngeren* (Basel: Schwabe, 1996)

The Grove Encyclopedia of Medieval Art and Architecture, ed. by Colum P. Hourihane, 6 vols (Oxford: Oxford University Press, 2012)

Gumbrecht, Hans Ulrich, *Production of Presence: What Meaning Cannot Convey* (Stanford: Stanford University Press, 2004) <https://doi.org/10.1515/9780804767149>

Hallberg, Peter, 'The Syncretic Saga Mind: A Discussion of a New Approach to the Icelandic Sagas', *Mediaeval Scandinavia*, 7 (1974), pp. 102–17

Hamburger, Jeffrey F., *The Visual and the Visionary: Art and Female Spirituality in Late Medieval Germany* (New York: Zone Books, 1998)

—— ed., *Leaves from Paradise: The Cult of John the Evangelist at the Dominican Convent of Paradies bei Soest* (Cambridge, MA: Houghton Library of the Harvard College Library, 2008)

Hamburger, Jeffrey F., Eva Schlotheuber, and Susan Marti, *Liturgical Life and Latin Learning at Paradies bei Soest, 1300–1425: Inscription and Illumination in the Choir Books of a North German Dominican Convent*, 2 vols (Münster: Aschendorff, 2016)

Hamm, Berndt, 'Die "nahe Gnade" — innovative Züge der spätmittelalterlichen Theologie und Frömmigkeit', in *'Herbst des Mittelalters'? Fragen zur Bewertung des 14. und 15. Jahrhunderts*, ed. by Jan A. Aertsen and Martin Pickavé (Berlin: De Gruyter, 2004), pp. 541–57

Hansen, Niels Houlberg, 'The Transformation of the Danish Language in the Central Middle Ages: A Case of Europeanization?', in *Denmark and Europe in the Middle Ages, c. 1000–1525: Essays in Honour of Professor Michael H. Gelting*, ed. by Kerstin Hundahl, Lars Kjær, and Niels Lund (London: Routledge, 2014), pp. 111–38

Hansen, Reimer, 'Bruder Nigels dänische Reimchronik niederdeutsch', *Niederdeutsches Jahrbuch*, 25 (1899), pp. 132–51

Happé, Peter, ed., *English Mystery Plays: A Selection* (London: Penguin, 1975)

Hartmann, Sieglinde, and Stefanie Würth, eds, 'Deutsch-Skandinavische Literatur- und Kulturbeziehungen im Mittelalter', *Jahrbuch der Oswald von Wolkenstein Gesellschaft*, 16 (2006/07), pp. 1–346

Harvey, Barbara F., *Westminster Abbey and its Estates in the Middle Ages* (Oxford: Clarendon Press, 1977)

Hastrup, Kirsten, A Place Apart: An Anthropological Study of the Icelandic World (Oxford: Clarendon Press, 1998)

Haugen, Einar, '*First Grammatical Treatise*: The Earliest Germanic Phonology', *Language*, 26.4 (1950), pp. 4–64

Hawkins, Anne Hunsaker, 'Yvain's Madness', *Philological Quarterly*, 71 (1992), pp. 377–97

Heard, Kate, and others, *The Northern Renaissance: Dürer to Holbein* (London: Royal Collection Publications, 2011)

Heidegger, Martin, *The Fundamental Concepts of Metaphysics: World, Finitude, Solitude*, trans. by William McNeill and Nicholas Walker (Bloomington: Indiana University Press, 1995) <https://doi.org/10.2307/j.ctvswx8mg>

Heinzer, Felix, '*Claustrum non manufactum* — Innenräume normativer Schriftlichkeit', in *Schriftkultur und religiöse Zentren im norddeutschen Raum*, ed. by Patrizia Carmassi, Eva Schlotheuber, and Almut Breitenbach (Wiesbaden: Harrassowitz, 2014), pp. 141–65

Herman, Nicholas, *Le Livre enluminé, entre representation et illusion* (Paris: BnF Éditions, 2018)

Hermann, Pernille, 'Literacy', in *The Routledge Research Companion to the Medieval Icelandic Sagas*, ed. by Ármann Jakobsson and Sverrir Jakobsson (Abingdon: Routledge, 2017), pp. 34–47 <https://doi.org/10.4324/9781315613628-4>

—— 'Politiske og æstetiske aspekter i Rimkrøniken', *Historisk Tidsskrift* [Denmark], 107 (2007), pp. 389–411

Hervey, Mary F. S., *Holbein's 'Ambassadors': The Picture and the Men* (London: Bell and Sons, 1900)

Hill, Kat, 'Brotherhood, Sisterhood, and the Language of Gender in the German Reformation', *Reformation & Renaissance Review*, 17 (2015), pp. 181–95

Histories of Medieval European Literatures: New Patterns of Representation and Explanation (= *Interfaces: A Journal of Medieval European Literatures*, 1 (2015)) <https://doi.org/10.13130/interfaces-4960>

Hobson, Anthony, *Humanists and Bookbinders: The Origins and Diffusion of Humanistic Bookbinding 1459–1559* (Cambridge: Cambridge University Press, 1989)

Holck, Jakob Povl, 'Cultural Contacts and Genres of Runes — Danish Literacy around 1300', in *Literacy in Medieval and Early Modern Scandinavian Culture*, ed. by Pernille Hermann (Odense: University Press of Southern Denmark, 2005), pp. 151–63

Holman, Thomas S., 'Holbein's Portraits of the Steelyard Merchants: An Investigation', *Metropolitan Museum Journal*, 14 (1980), pp. 139–58

Holsinger, Bruce, 'Of Pigs and Parchment: Medieval Studies and the Coming of the Animal', *PMLA*, 124.2 (2009), pp. 616–23

Honess, Claire E., and Matthew Treherne, 'Introduction', in *Se mai continga … : Exile, Politics and Theology in Dante*, ed. by Claire E. Honess and Matthew Treherne (Ravenna: Longo, 2013), pp. 7–10

Howie, Cary, *Claustrophilia: The Erotics of Enclosure in Medieval Literature* (New York: Palgrave Macmillan, 2007) <https://doi.org/10.1057/9780230604148>

Hoyer, Jennifer M., and Jennifer Watson, eds, *Scandinavia and Germany: Cultural Crosscurrents* (= *Scandinavian Studies*, 91.4 (winter 2019)) <https://doi.org/10.5406/scanstud.91.4.0427>

Hudson, Benjamin, ed., *Studies in the Medieval Atlantic* (New York: Palgrave Macmillan, 2012) <https://doi.org/10.1057/9781137062390>

Hundahl, Kerstin, and Lars Kjær, 'Introduction', in *Denmark and Europe in the Middle Ages, c. 1000–1525: Essays in Honour of Professor Michael H. Gelting*, ed. by Kerstin Hundahl, Lars Kjær, and Niels Lund (London: Routledge, 2014), pp. 1–7

Hybel, Nils, *Danmark i Europa 750–1300* (Copenhagen: Museum Tusculanums Forlag, 2003)

Hybel, Nils, and Bjørn Poulsen, *The Danish Resources c. 1000–1550: Growth and Recession* (Leiden: Brill, 2007) <https://doi.org/10.1163/ej.9789004161924.i-448>

Imsen, Steinar, 'The Union of Calmar — Nordic Great Power or Northern German Outpost?', in *Politics and Reformations: Communities, Polities, Nations, and Empires: Essays in Honor of Thomas A. Brady, Jr.*, ed. by Christopher Ocker and others (Leiden: Brill, 2007), pp. 471–89 <https://doi.org/10.1163/ej.9789004161733.i-630.94>

Ingesman, Per, and Bjørn Poulsen, eds, *Danmark og Europa i senmiddelalderen* (Aarhus: Aarhus University Press, 2000)

Irigaray, Luce, and Michael Marder, *Through Vegetal Being: Two Philosophical Perspectives* (New York: Columbia University Press, 2016)

Jackson, Kenneth, 'The Motif of the Threefold Death in the Story of Suibhne Geilt', in *Féil-Sgríbhinn Eóin Mhic Néill/Essays and Studies Presented to Professor Eoin MacNeill*, ed. by John Ryan (1940; repr. Kill Lane: Four Courts Press, 1995), pp. 535–50

Jarman, A. O. H., 'Early Stages in the Development of the Myrddin Legend', in *Astudiathau ar yr hengerdd/Studies in Old Welsh Poetry*, ed. by Rachel Bromwich and R. B. Jones (Cardiff: University of Wales Press, 1978), pp. 326–49

—— 'The Merlin Legend and the Welsh Tradition of Prophecy', in *Merlin: A Casebook*, ed. by Peter H. Goodrich and Raymond H. Thompson (New York: Routledge, 2003), pp. 103–28

Jensen, Lars, and others, 'Denmark and its Colonies', in *A Historical Companion to Postcolonial Literatures — Continental Europe and its Empires*, ed. by Prem Poddar, Rajeev S. Patke, and Lars Jensen (Edinburgh: Edinburgh University Press, 2008), pp. 57–103

Jexlev, Thelma, 'Frille, Eggert', in *Dansk biografisk leksikon*, 3rd edn, ed. by Sv. Cedergreen Bech, 16 vols (Copenhagen: Gyldendal, 1979–84), v (1980), pp. 13–14 <http://denstoredanske.dk/Dansk_Biografisk_Leksikon/Samfund,_jura_og_politik/Myndigheder_og_politisk_styre/Rigsråd/Eggert_Frille> [accessed 13 March 2020]

Johnson, Ian, 'A Perspective from the Far (Medieval) West on Byzantine Theories of Authorship', in *The Author in Middle Byzantine Literature: Modes, Functions, and Identities*, ed. by Aglae Pizzone (Boston: De Gruyter, 2014), pp. 277–94 <https://doi.org/10.1515/9781614515197.277>

Jørgensen, Ellen, *Studier over danske middelalderlige Bogsamlinger* (Copenhagen: Bianco Lunos bogtrykkeri, 1912)

Jørgensen, Jens Anker, and Knud Wentzel, eds, *Hovedsporet: Dansk litteraturs historie* ([n.p.]: Gyldendal, 2005)

Jucknies, Regina, 'Through an Old Danish Lens? Precious Stones in the Late Medieval Danish Reception of Courtly Literature', in *The Eufemiavisor and Courtly Culture: Time, Texts and Cultural Transfer*, ed. by Olle Ferm and others (Stockholm: Kungl. Vitterhets Historie och Antikvitets Akademien, 2015), pp. 162–75

Justice, Stephen, 'Did the Middle Ages Believe in their Miracles?', *Representations*, 103 (2008), pp. 1–30

Kaczynski, Bernice M., ed., *The Oxford Handbook of Christian Monasticism* (Oxford: Oxford University Press, 2020) <https://doi.org/10.1093/oxfordhb/9780199689736.001.0001>

Kaufmann, Thomas, *Der Anfang der Reformation: Studien zur Kontextualität der Theologie, Publizistik und Inszenierung Luthers und der reformatorischen Bewegung* (Tübingen: Mohr Siebeck, 2018)

Kay, Sarah, 'Legible Skins: Animals and the Ethics of Medieval Reading', *postmedieval: a journal of medieval cultural studies*, 2.1 (2011), pp. 13–32

Keen, Catherine, 'Florence and Faction in Dante's Lyric Poetry: Framing the Experience of Exile', in *Se mai continga …*, ed. by Honess and Treherne, pp. 63–83

Keevak, Michael, 'Reading (and Conversion in) Augustine's *Confessions*', *Orbis litterarum*, 50 (1995), pp. 257–71

Kierkegaard, Søren, *The Sickness unto Death: A Christian Psychological Expos-ition for Upbuilding and Awakening*, ed. and trans. by Howard V. Hong and Edna H. Hong (Princeton: Princeton University Press, 1980)

Kirakosian, Racha, *From the Material to the Mystical in Late Medieval Piety: The Vernacular Transmission of Gertrude of Helfta's Visions* (Cambridge: Cambridge University Press, 2020) <https://doi.org/10.1017/9781108893657>

Kiser, Lisa J., 'Margery Kempe and the Animalisation of Christ: Animal Cruelty in Late Medieval England', *Studies in Philology*, 106.3 (2009), pp. 299–315

Kissinger, Norbert, and others, eds, *Anfangsgeschichten: Der Beginn volks-sprachiger Schriftlichkeit in komparatistischer Perspektive/Origin Stories: The Rise of Vernacular Literacy in a Comparative Perspective* (Paderborn: Fink, 2018)

Knowles, David, *The Monastic Order in England*, 2nd edn (Cambridge: Cambridge University Press, 1963)

—— *The Religious Orders in England*, 3 vols (Cambridge: Cambridge University Press, 1948–59)

—— ed. and trans., *The Monastic Constitutions of Lanfranc*, rev. by C. N. L. Brooke (Oxford: Clarendon Press, 2002)

'Knud den Helliges gavebrev, 1085', *danmarkshistorien.dk* <https://danmarkshistorien.dk/leksikon-og-kilder/vis/materiale/knud-den-helliges-gavebrev-1085/> [accessed 17 February 2020]

Knudsen, Anders Leegaard, 'Compendium Saxonis & Chronica Jutensis', in *Medieval Nordic Literature in Latin: A Website of Authors and Anonymous Works c. 1100–1530*, ed. by Stephan Borgehammar and others <https://wikihost.uib.no/medieval/index.php/Compendium_Saxonis_%26_Chronica_Jutensis> [accessed 20 February 2020]

—— 'Interessen for den danske fortid omkring 1300: En middelalderlig dansk nationalisme', *Historisk Tidsskrift* [Denmark], 100 (2000), pp. 1–32

—— 'Kongeriget Danmark i 1332 — et fallitbo', *Historisk Tidsskrift* [Denmark], 108 (2008), pp. 321–40

—— *Saxostudier og rigshistorie på Valdemar Atterdags tid* (Copenhagen: Museum Tusculanums Forlag, 1994)

—— 'The Use of Saxo Grammaticus in the Later Middle Ages', in *The Birth of Identities: Denmark and Europe in the Middle Ages*, ed. by Brian P. McGuire (Copenhagen: Reitzel, 1996), pp. 147–60

Kössinger, Norbert, and others, 'Introduction', in *Anfangsgeschichten: Der Beginn volkssprachiger Schriftlichkeit in komparatistischer Perspekti-ve/Origin Stories: The Rise of Vernacular Literacy in a Comparative Perspective*, ed. by Norbert Kössinger and others (Paderborn: Fink, 2018), pp. 7–8 <https://doi.org/10.30965/9783846763469_002>

Koster, Severin, *Ille Ego Qui: Dichter zwischen Wort und Macht* (Erlangen: Universitätsbibliothek Erlangen-Nürnberg, 1988)

Krummacher, Hildegard, 'Zu Holbeins Bildnissen rheinischer Stahlhofkau-fleute', *Wallraf-Richartz-Jahrbuch*, 25 (1963), pp. 181–92

Kundert, Ursula, 'Holsteinische Reimchronik', in *The Encyclopedia of the Medieval Chronicle*, ed. by Graeme Dunphy, 2 vols (Leiden: Brill, 2010), I, p. 812

Lähnemann, Henrike, 'Bilingual Devotion: The Relationship of Latin and Low German in Prayer Books from the Lüneburg Convents', in *Mysticism and Devotion in Northern Germany in the Late Middle Ages*, ed. by Elizabeth Andersen, Henrike Lähnemann, and Anne Simon (Leiden: Brill, 2013), pp. 317–41 <https://doi.org/10.1163/9789004258457_014>

—— '"An dessen bom wil ik stigen": Die Ikonographie des Wichmannsburger Antependiums im Kontext der Medinger Handschriften', *Oxford German Studies*, 34 (2005), pp. 19–46

—— 'Saluta apostolum tuum: Apostelvereherung im Kloster Medingen', in *Weltbild und Lebenswirklichkeit in den Lüneburger Klöstern: IX. Ebstorfer Kolloquium vom 23. bis 26. März 2011*, ed. by Wolfgang Brandis and Hans-Walter Stork (Berlin: Lukas Verlag, 2015), pp. 41–64

Laplanche, Jean, and Jean-Bertrand Pontalis, *The Language of Psycho-Analysis*, trans. by Donald Nicholson-Smith (London: Hogarth Press, 1973)

Lavinsky, David, '"Speke to me be thowt": Affectivity, *Incendium Amoris*, and the *Book of Margery Kempe*', *Journal of English and Germanic Philology*, 112.3 (2013), pp. 340–64

Lawrence, C. H., *Medieval Monasticism: Forms of Religious Life in Western Europe in the Middle Ages*, 2nd edn (London: Longman, 1989)

Lawton, Harold Walter, *Térence en France au XVIe siècle: Editions et traductions* (Paris: Jouve, 1926)

Lea, Anna, 'Lleu Wyllt: An Early British Prototype of the Legend of the Wild Man?', *Journal of Indo-European Studies*, 25 (1997), pp. 35–47

Leclercq, Jean, *The Love of Learning and the Desire for God: A Study of Monastic Culture*, trans. by Catherine Misrahi (New York: Fordham University Press, 1982)

Ledda, Giuseppe, 'L'esilio, la speranza, la poesia: Modelli biblici e strutture autobiografiche nel canto xxv del *Paradiso*', *Studi e Problemi di Critica Testuale*, 90.1 (2015), pp. 257–77

Ledo, Jorge, 'Erasmus' Translations of Plutarch's *Moralia* and the Ascensian *editio princeps* of ca. 1513', *Humanistica Lovaniensia*, 68 (2019), pp. 257–96

Leerssen, Joep, 'Literary Historicism: Romanticism, Philologists, and the Presence of the Past', *Modern Language Quarterly*, 65 (2004), pp. 221–43

Lewis, Robert E., and others, eds, *Middle English Dictionary*, online edition in *Middle English Compendium*, ed. by Frances McSparran and others (Ann Arbor: University of Michigan Library, 2000–18) <https://quod.

lib.umich.edu/m/middle-english-dictionary/dictionary> [accessed 21 March 2020]

Lochrie, Karma, *Margery Kempe and the Translations of the Flesh* (Philadelphia: University of Pennsylvania Press, 1991) <https://doi.org/10.9783/9780812207538>

Lönngren, Ann-Sofie, and others, eds, *Rethinking National Literatures and the Literary Canon in Scandinavia* (Cambridge: Cambridge Scholars Publishing, 2015)

Lombardi, Elena, *The Syntax of Desire: Language and Love in Augustine, the Modistae, Dante* (Toronto: University of Toronto Press, 2007)

—— *The Wings of the Doves: Love and Desire in Dante and Medieval Culture* (Montreal: McGill–Queen's University Press, 2012)

[Lund, Jørn] Professor Higgins, 'Tysk', *Folkeskolen*, 26 May 2006 <https://www.folkeskolen.dk/42837/tysk> [accessed 17 April 2019]

Lyotard, Jean-François, *La confession d'Augustin* (Paris: Galilée, 1998)

—— *The Confession of Augustine*, trans. by Richard Beardsworth (Stanford: Stanford University Press, 2000) <https://doi.org/10.1515/9781503618541>

Macola, Novella, 'I ritratti col Petrarca', in *Le lingue del Petrarca*, ed. by Antonio Daniele (Udine: Forum, 2005), pp. 135–57

—— *Sguardi e scritture: Figure con libro nella ritrattistica italiana della prima metà del Cinquecento* (Venice: Istituto Veneto di Scienze, Lettere ed Arti, 2007)

Mai, Anne-Marie, *Hvor litteraturen finder sted*, 3 vols ([n.p.]: Gyldendal, 2010–11), I: *Fra Guds tid til menneskets tid 1000–1800* (2010). Saxo ebook.

Mann, Nicholas, 'Petrarca giardiniere (a proposito del sonetto CCXXVIII)', *Letture Petrarce*, 12 (1992), pp. 235–56

[Manuscript Description of Stockholm, Royal Library, K 47], in *Tekster fra Danmarks middelalder og renæssance 1100–1550 — på dansk og latin* <https://tekstnet.dk/manuscript-descriptions/stockholm-k47-lang-beskrivelse> [accessed 28 January 2020]

Marder, Michael, *The Philosopher's Plant: An Intellectual Herbarium*, with illustrations by Mathilde Roussel (New York: Columbia University Press, 2014)

—— *Plant-Thinking: A Philosophy of Vegetal Life* (New York: Columbia University Press, 2013)

Margolis, Oren, 'Hercules in Venice: Aldus Manutius and the Making of Erasmian Humanism', *Journal of the Warburg and Courtauld Institutes*, 81 (2018), pp. 97–126

McDonald, Mark, ed., *Ceremonies, Costumes, Portraits and Genre*, The Paper Museum of Cassiano dal Pozzo: A Catalogue Raisonné: Series C, 1, 3 vols (London: Royal Collection Trust, in association with Harvey Miller, 2017)

McDonald, Peter, 'The Papacy and Monastic Observance in the Later Middle Ages: The *Benedictina* in England', *Journal of Religious History*, 14.2 (1986), pp. 117–32

McEntire, Sandra, ed., *Margery Kempe: A Book of Essays* (London: Garland, 1992)

McGinn, Bernard, *The Flowering of Mysticism: Men and Women in the New Mysticism* (1200–1350) (New York: Crossroad Herder, 1998)

McLaughlin, Martin, 'Biography and Autobiography in the Italian Renaissance', in *Mapping Lives: The Uses of Biography*, ed. by Peter France and William St Clair (Oxford: Oxford University Press, 2004), pp. 37–65 <https://doi.org/10.5871/bacad/9780197263181.003.0004>

McShane, Bronagh Ann, 'Visualising the Reception and Circulation of Early Modern Nuns' Letters', *Journal of Historical Network Research*, 2 (2018), pp. 1–25

Mecham, June L., *Sacred Communities, Sacred Devotions: Gender, Material Culture, and Monasticism in Late Medieval Germany* (Turnhout: Brepols, 2014) <https://doi.org/10.1484/M.MWTC-EB.5.106979>

Meeker, Natania, and Antónia Szabari, 'Libertine Botany: Vegetal Sexuality and Vegetal Forms', *postmedieval: a journal of medieval cultural studies*, 9.4 (2018), pp. 478–89

Meillassoux, Quentin, 'L'Inexistence Divine' (unpublished doctoral thesis, University of Paris, 1997)

—— 'Spectral Dilemma', *Collapse*, 4 (2008), pp. 261–76

Mertens, Volker, 'Bildersaal — Minnegrotte — Liebestrank: Zu Symbol, Allegorie und Mythos im Tristanroman', *Beiträge zur Geschichte der deutschen Sprache und Literatur*, 117 (1995), pp. 40–64 <https://doi.org/10.1515/bgsl.1995.1995.117.40>

Meyer, Johannes, 'Zur Reformationsgeschichte des Klosters Lüne', *Zeitschrift der Gesellschaft für niedersächsische Kirchengeschichte*, 14 (1909), pp. 162–221

Milis, Ludo J. R., *Angelic Monks and Earthly Men: Monasticism and its Meaning to Medieval Society* (Woodbridge: Boydell, 1992

Mitchell, Stephen A., 'Memory, Mediality, and the "Performative Turn": Recontextualizing Remembering in Medieval Scandinavia', *Scandinavian Studies*, 85.3 (2013), pp. 282–305

—— 'The Sagaman and Oral Literature: The Icelandic Traditions of Hjörleifr inn Kvensami and Geirmundr heljarskinn', in *Comparative Research on Oral Traditions: A Memorial for Milman Parry*, ed. by John Miles Foley (Columbus, OH: Slavica, 1987), pp. 395–423

Mize, Britt, 'The Representation of the Mind as an Enclosure in Old English Poetry', *Anglo-Saxon England*, 35 (2006), pp. 57–90 <https://doi.org/10.1017/S0263675106000044>

Mondin, Luca, 'Ipotesi sopra il falso proemio dell'Eneide', *CentoPagine*, 1 (2007), pp. 64–78

Morgan, Marjorie, *The English Lands of the Abbey of Bec* (Oxford: Clarendon Press, 1946)

Morris, Bridget, 'Christian Poetry: East Norse', in *Medieval Scandinavia: An Encyclopedia*, ed. by Phillip Pulsiano and Kirsten Wolf (New York: Garland, 1993), pp. 72–73

Mortensen, Klaus P., and May Schack, eds, *Dansk litteraturs historie*, 5 vols (Copenhagen: Gyldendal, 2006–09)

Mortensen, Lars Boje, 'Annales Ryenses', in *The Encyclopedia of the Medieval Chronicle*, ed. by Graeme Dunphy, 2 vols (Leiden: Brill, 2010), I, p. 85

—— 'Compendium Saxonis', in *The Encyclopedia of the Medieval Chronicle*, ed. by Graeme Dunphy, 2 vols (Leiden: Brill, 2010), I, p. 484

—— 'Latin as Vernacular: Critical Mass and the "Librarization" of Book Languages', in *Anfangsgeschichten: Der Beginn volkssprachiger Schriftlichkeit in komparatistischer Perspektive/Origin Stories: The Rise of Vernacular Literacy in a Comparative Perspective*, ed. by Norbert Kössinger and others (Paderborn: Fink, 2018), pp. 71–90 <https://doi.org/10. 30965/9783846763469_005>

—— 'Litteraturhistorisk tid — kan middelalderen afskaffes?', *temp — tidsskrift for historie* (forthcoming)

Mortensen, Lars Boje, and Tuomas M. S. Lehtonen, 'Introduction: What Is Nordic Medieval Literature?', in *The Performance of Christian and Pagan Storyworlds: Non-Canonical Chapters of the History of Nordic Medieval Literature*, ed. by Lars Boje Mortensen and Tuomas M. S. Lehtonen with Alexandra Bergholm (Turnhout: Brepols, 2013), pp. 1–41

Morton, Timothy, 'Guest Column: Queer Ecology', *PMLA*, 125.2 (2010), pp. 273–82

Mulder-Bakker, Anneke B., *Lives of the Anchoresses: The Rise of the Urban Recluse in Medieval Europe*, trans. by Myra Heerspink Scholz (Philadelphia: University of Pennsylvania Press, 2005) <https://doi.org/10. 9783/9780812202861>

Mundal, Else, 'How Did the Arrival of Writing Influence Old Norse Oral Culture?', in *Along the Oral–Written Continuum*, ed. by Slavica Ranković, Leidulf Melve, and Else Mundal (Turnhout: Brepols, 2010), pp. 163–81 <https://doi.org/10.1484/M.USML-EB.3.4282>

Muresan, Maria, 'Belated Strokes: Lyotard's Writing of *The Confession of Augustine*', *Romanic Review*, 95.1–2 (2004), pp. 151–69

Murray, Alan V., 'The Danish Monarchy and the Kingdom of Germany, 1179–1319: The Evidence of Middle High German Poetry', in *Scandinavia and Europe 800–1350: Contact, Conflict, and Coexistence*, ed. by Jonathan Adams and Katherine Holman (Turnhout: Brepols, 2004), pp. 289–307

Nash, Susie, 'Meditation and Imagination', in Nash, *Northern Renaissance Art* (Oxford: Oxford University Press, 2008), pp. 271–88

Nasti, Paola, 'Nozze e vedovanza: Dinamiche dell'appropriazione biblica in Cavalcanti e Dante', *Tenzone*, 7 (2006), pp. 71–110

Nedoma, Robert, 'Der Beginn volkssprachlicher Schriftlichkeit im alten Skandinavien: Eine Skizze', in *Anfangsgeschichten: Der Beginn volkssprachiger Schriftlichkeit in komparatistischer Perspektive/Origin Stories: The Rise of Vernacular Literacy in a Comparative Perspective*, ed. by Norbert Kössinger and others (Paderborn: Fink, 2018), pp. 275–301 <https://doi.org/10.30965/9783846763469_013>

Nelson, Jennifer, *Disharmony of the Spheres: The Europe of Holbein's Ambassadors* (University Park: Pennsylvania State University Press, 2019)

Newman, Barbara, review of Rachel Fulton Brown, *Mary and the Art of Prayer* (2018), *Speculum* 93.4 (2018), pp. 1169–71

Niederdeutsch in Skandinavien, vols 1–4, Beihefte zur Zeitschrift für deutsche Philologie, 4–7 (Berlin: Schmidt, 1987–1993), vols 5–6 [in one] (Frankfurt a.M.: Lang, 2005)

Nielsen, Marita Akhøj, 'Dværgekongen Laurin: Litteraturhistorisk baggrund', in *Tekster fra Danmarks middelalder og renæssance 1100–1550 — på dansk og latin* <https://tekstnet.dk/dvaergekongen-laurin/about> [accessed 12 February 2020]

Nordentoft, Mette, 'Zum (nord)europäischen Stemma des Passionstraktates Heinrichs von St. Gallen', in *Niederdeutsch in Skandinavien*, 6 vols (1987–2005), IV, ed. by Hubertus Menke and Kurt Erich Schöndorf, Beihefte zur Zeitschrift für deutsche Philologie, 7 (Berlin: Schmidt, 1993), pp. 168–95

Novikoff, Alex J., 'Anselm, Dialogue, and the Rise of Scholastic Disputation', *Speculum*, 86.2 (2011), pp. 387–418

Ó Béarra, Feargal, 'Buile Shuibhne: Vox Insaniae from Medieval Ireland', in *Mental Health, Spirituality, and Religion in the Middle Ages and Early Modern Age*, ed. by Albrecht Classen (Berlin: De Gruyter, 2014), pp. 242–89 <https://doi.org/10.1515/9783110361643.242>

O'Connor, Ralph, 'History or Fiction? Truth-Claims and Defensive Narrators in Icelandic Romance-Sagas', *Mediaeval Scandinavia*, 15 (2005), pp. 101–69

O'Donoghue, Heather, *Narrative in the Icelandic Family Saga: Meanings of Time in Old Norse Literature* (London: Bloomsbury Academic, 2021) <https://doi.org/10.5040/9781350167445>

Öberg, Jan, Erika Kihlman, and Pia Melin, eds, *Den mångsidige målaren: Vidgade perspektiv på Albertus Pictors bild- och textvärld* (Stockholm: Sällskapet Runica et Mediævalia, 2007)

Oksaar, Els, 'Eine neuentdeckte mittelniederdeutsche Weltchronik des 15. Jahrhunderts', *Niederdeutsches Jahrbuch*, 85 (1962), pp. 33–46

Olsson, Annika, 'Challenging the Bodies and Borders of Literature in Scandinavia: Methodological Nationalism, Intersectionality and Methodological Disciplinarity', in *Rethinking National Literatures and the Literary Canon in Scandinavia*, ed. by Ann-Sofie Lönngren and others (Cambridge: Cambridge Scholars Publishing, 2015), pp. 30–51

Orlemanski, Julie, 'Margery's "Noyse" and Distributed Expressivity', in *Voice and Voicelessness in Medieval Europe*, ed. by Irit Ruth Kleiman (Houndmills: Palgrave Macmillan, 2015), pp. 123–38 <https://doi.org/10.1007/978-1-137-39706-5_8>

—— *Symptomatic Subjects: Bodies, Medicine, and Causation in the Literature of Late Medieval England* (Philadelphia: University of Pennsylvania Press, 2019) <https://doi.org/10.9783/9780812296082>

Os, Henk van, 'The Monastery as a Centre of Devotion', in *The Art of Devotion in the Late Middle Ages in Europe 1300–1500*, ed. by Henk van Os, trans. by Michael Hoyle (London: Merrell Holberton, 1994), pp. 50–59

Ostrowitzki, Anja, 'Klösterliche Lebenswelt im Spiegel von Briefen des 16. Jahrhunderts aus dem Benediktinerinnenkloster Oberwerth bei Koblenz', *Studien und Mitteilungen zur Geschichte des Benediktinerordens und seiner Zweige*, 124 (2013), pp. 167–206

Otter, Monika, '1066: The Moment of Transition in Two Narratives of the Norman Conquest', *Speculum*, 74 (1999), pp. 565–86 <http://doi.org/10.2307/2886761>

—— *Inventiones: Fiction and Referentiality in Twelfth-Century Historical Writing* (Chapel Hill: University of North Carolina Press, 1996)

—— 'Neither/Neuter: Hildebert's Hermaphrodite and the Medieval Latin Epigram', *Studi medievali*, 3rd ser., 48 (2007), pp. 789–807

Panofsky, Erwin, *The Life and Art of Albrecht Dürer* (Princeton: Princeton University Press, 1943)

Paoli, Marco, '*Galeotto fu il libro e chi lo dipinse*: Ritratti di letterati e scienziati cinquecenteschi raffigurati con un libro. Primo censimento', *Rara volumina*, 22 (2015), pp. 5–28

Parks, Ward, 'The Textualisation of Orality in Literary Criticism', in *Vox Intexta: Orality and Textuality in the Middle Ages*, ed. by A. N. Doane and Carol Braun Pasternack (Madison: University of Wisconsin Press, 1991), pp. 46–61

Patota, Giuseppe, 'Petrarchino', *Bollettino di italianistica*, n.s., 13.1 (2016), pp. 53–69

Payen, Jean-Charles, 'The Glass Palace in the *Folie d'Oxford*: From Metaphorical to Literal Madness', trans. by Joan Tasker Grimbert, in *Tristan and Isolde: A Casebook*, ed. by Joan Tasker Grimbert (New York: Routledge, 2013), pp. 111–23

—— 'Le palais de verre dans la Folie d'Oxford', *Tristania*, 5 (1981), pp. 17–28

Peterson, Thomas E., '"Amor co la man dextra il lato manco" (*Rvf* 228) as Allegory of Religious Veneration', *MLN*, 135.1 (January 2020), pp. 17–33 <https://doi.org/10.1353/mln.2020.0013>

Petrucci, Armando, *Writers and Readers in Medieval Italy: Studies in the History of Written Culture*, ed. and trans. by Charles M. Radding (New Haven, CT: Yale University Press, 1995)

Petter-Wahnschaffe, Katrin, *Hans Holbein und der Stalhof in London* (Berlin: Deutscher Kunstverlag, 2010)

Picard, Jean-Michel, 'Merlin, Suibhne et Lailoken: A propos d'un livre récent', *Revue belge de philologie et histoire*, 80 (2002), pp. 1495–1503 <https://doi.org/10.3406/rbph.2002.4684>

Poulsen, Bjørn, 'Late Medieval Migration across the Baltic: The Movement of People between Northern Germany and Denmark', in *Guilds, Towns, and Cultural Transmission in the North, 1300–1500*, ed. by Lars Bisgaard, Lars Boje Mortensen, and Tom Pettitt (Odense: University Press of Southern Denmark, 2013), pp. 31–56

Price, David H., 'Hans Holbein the Younger and Reformation Bible Production', *Church History*, 86 (2017), pp. 998–1040

Przybilski, Martin, 'Denscke Kroneke', in *The Encyclopedia of the Medieval Chronicle*, ed. by Graeme Dunphy, 2 vols (Leiden: Brill, 2010), I, p. 516

Quinn, Judy, 'From Orality to Literacy in Medieval Iceland', in *Old Icelandic Literature and Society*, ed. by Margaret Clunies Ross (Cambridge: Cambridge University Press, 2000), pp. 30–60 <https://doi.org/10.1017/CBO9780511552922.003>

Rabitti, Giovanna, '*Nel dolce tempo*: Sintesi o nuovo cominciamento?', in *Petrarca volgare e la sua fortuna sino al Cinquecento*, ed. by Bruno Porcelli (= *Italianistica*, 33.2 (May/August 2004)), pp. 95–108

Rajendran, Shyama, 'Undoing "the Vernacular": Dismantling Structures of Raciolinguistic Supremacy', in *Critical Race and the Middle Ages* (= *Literature Compass*, 16.9–10 (September–October 2019)) <https://doi.org/10.1111/lic3.12544>

Ranković, Slavika, 'The Performative Non-Canonicity of the Canonical: *Íslendingasǫgur* and their Traditional Referentiality', in *The Performance of Christian and Pagan Storyworlds*, ed. by Lars Boje Mortensen, Tuomas M. S. Lehtonen, and Alexandre Bergholm (Turnhout: Brepols, 2013), pp. 247–72 <https://doi.org/10.1484/M.MISCS-EB.1.100758>

Rebecchini, Guido, 'Castiglione and Erasmus: Towards a Reconciliation?', *Journal of the Warburg and Courtauld Institutes*, 61 (1998), pp. 258–60

Rösli, Lukas, and Stefanie Gropper, 'In Search of the Culprit. Aspects of Medieval Authorship Introduction: Introduction', in *In Search of the Culprit: Aspects of Medieval Authorship*, ed. by Lukas Rösli and Stefanie Gropper (Berlin, De Gruyter, 2021), pp. 9–16 <https://doi.org/10.1515/9783110725339-001>

Rosand, David, and Michelangelo Muraro, *Titian and the Venetian Woodcut* (Washington, DC: International Exhibitions Foundation, 1976)

Roskill, Mark, and Craig Harbison, 'On the Nature of Holbein's Portraits', *Word & Image*, 3 (1987), pp. 1–26

Rouse, Richard H., and Mary A. Rouse, '"Statim invenire": Schools, Preachers, and New Attitudes to the Page', in *Renaissance and Renewal in the Twelfth Century*, ed. by Robert L. Benson and Giles Constable (Oxford: Oxford University Press, 1982), pp. 201–28

Rudolph, Conrad, 'First, I Find the Center Point': *Reading the Text of Hugh of Saint Victor's The Mystic Ark* (Philadelphia: American Philosophical Society, 2004) <https://doi.org/10.2307/20020367>

—— *The Mystic Ark: Hugh of Saint Victor, Art, and Thought in the Twelfth Century* (New York: Cambridge University Press, 2014) <https://doi. org/10.1017/CBO9781139583459>

Ruh, Kurt, 'Textkritk zum Mystikerlied *Granum sinapis*', in *Festschrift Josef Quint*, ed. by Hugo Moser and others (Bonn: Bouvier, 1964), pp. 169–84

Rushworth, Jennifer, *Discourses of Mourning in Dante, Petrarch, and Proust* (Oxford: Oxford University Press, 2016) <https://doi.org/10.1093/ acprof:oso/9780198790877.001.0001>

Rushworth, Jennifer, and Francesca Southerden, eds, *The Case for a Medieval Barthes* (= *Exemplaria*, 33.3 (2021)) <https://doi.org/10.1080/ 10412573.2021.1977514>

Saxl, Fritz, *Lectures*, 2 vols (London: Warburg Institute, 1957)

Schlotheuber, Eva, '*Gelehrte Bräute Christi*': *Geistliche Frauen in der mittelalterlichen Gesellschaft* (Tübingen: Mohr Siebeck, 2018) <https://doi. org/10.1628/978-3-16-156255-6>

—— 'Intellectual Horizons: Letters from a Northern German Convent', in *Mysticism and Devotion in Northern Germany in the Late Middle Ages*, ed. by Elizabeth Andersen, Henrike Lähnemann, and Anne Simon (Leiden: Brill, 2013), pp. 343–72 <https://doi.org/10.1163/9789004258457_ 015>

—— *Klostereintritt und Bildung: Die Lebenswelt der Nonnen im späten Mittelalter; Mit einer Edition des 'Konventstagebuchs' einer Zisterzienserin von Heilig-Kreuz bei Braunschweig (1484–1507)* (Tübingen: Mohr Siebeck, 2004)

—— 'Willibald und die Klosterfrauen von Sankt Klara — eine wechselhafte Beziehung', *Pirckheimer Jahrbuch für Renaissance und Humanismusforschung*, 28 (2014), pp. 57–75

Schmeidler, Bernhard, 'Einleitung', in Adam von Bremen, *Hamburgische Kirchengeschichte*, 3rd edn, ed. by Bernhard Schmeidler, MGH SS rer. Germ. (Hanover: Hahn, 1917), pp. vii–lxvii

Schmidt, Peter, 'Die Rolle der Bilder in der Kommunikation zwischen Frauen und Männern, Kloster und Welt: Schenken und Tauschen bei den Nürnberger Dominikanerinnen', in *Femmes, art et religion au Moyen Âge*, ed. by Jean-Claude Schmitt (Strasbourg: Presses Universitaires de Strasbourg, 2004), pp. 34–61

Schmitt, Carl, *Political Theology: Four Chapters on the Concept of Sovereignty*, trans. by George Schwab (Chicago: University of Chicago Press, 2005) <https://doi.org/10.7208/chicago/9780226738901.001.0001>

Schröder, Reinhold, 'Rumelant von Sachsen, ein Fahrender aus Deutschland in Dänemark', in *The Entertainer in Medieval and Traditional Culture: A*

Symposium, ed. by Flemming G. Andersen, Thomas Pettitt, and Reinhold Schröder (Odense: Odense University Press, 1997), pp. 15–44

Schumm, Johanna, 'Quoted Confessions: Augustine's *Confessiones* and Derrida's "Circonfession"', trans. by Jan Schönherr, *Comparative Literature Studies*, 52.4 (2015), pp. 729–56

Scribner, Robert W., *For the Sake of Simple Folk: Popular Propaganda for the German Reformation* (Oxford: Clarendon Press, 1994)

—— 'Why Was There No Reformation in Cologne?', *Historical Research*, 49 (1976), pp. 217–41

Shaw, Anthony N., 'The *Compendium Compertorum* and the Making of the Suppression Act of 1536' (unpublished doctoral thesis, University of Warwick, 2003)

Silver, Larry, *The Paintings of Quinten Massys, with Catalogue Raisonné* (Oxford: Phaidon, 1984)

Simpson, Otto G. von, '*Compassio* and *Co-redemptio* in Roger van der Weyden's *Descent from the Cross*', *Art Bulletin*, 25 (1953), pp. 9–16

Singleton, Charles S, *Dante's 'Commedia': Elements of Structure* (Baltimore: Johns Hopkins University Press, 1954)

Small, John, ed., *English Metrical Homilies from Manuscripts of the Fourteenth Century* (Edinburgh: Paterson, 1862)

Soifer, M., '"You say that the Messiah has come …": The Ceuta Disputation (1179) and its Place in the Christian Anti-Jewish Polemics of the High Middle Ages', *Journal of Medieval History*, 31.3 (2005), pp. 287–307

Somerset, Fiona, and Nicholas Watson, eds, *The Vulgar Tongue: Medieval and Postmedieval Vernacularity* (Princeton: Princeton University Press, 2003)

Southern, Richard W., *Western Society and the Church in the Middle Ages* (Harmondsworth: Penguin, 1970)

Spencer-Hall, Alicia, 'The Horror of Orthodoxy: Christina Mirabilis, Thirteenth-Century "Zombie" Saint', *postmedieval: a journal of medieval cultural studies*, 8.3 (2017), pp. 352–75

Spitzer, Leo, 'The Addresses to the Reader in the *Commedia*', *Italica*, 32.3 (1955), pp. 143–65

Staley, Lynn, *Margery Kempe's Dissenting Fictions* (Philadelphia: University of Pennsylvania Press, 1994)

Stark, Hannah, 'Deleuze and Critical Plant Studies', in *Deleuze and the Non/Human*, ed. by Jon Roffe and Hannah Stark (London: Palgrave Macmillan, 2015), pp. 180–96 <https://doi.org/10.1057/9781137453693_11>

Steel, Karl, 'Animals and Violence: Medieval Humanism, "Medieval Brutality", and the Carnivorous Vegetarianism of Margery Kempe', in *The Routledge Companion to Animal–Human History*, ed. by Hilda Kean (London: Routledge, 2018), pp. 1650–1716 <https://doi.org/10.4324/9780429468933-21>

—— *How to Make a Human: Animals & Violence in the Middle Ages* (Columbus: Ohio State University Press, 2011)

Steinberg, Justin, 'The Author', in *The Oxford Handbook of Dante*, ed. by Manuele Gragnolati, Elena Lombardi, and Francesca Southerden (Oxford: Oxford University Press, 2021), pp. 3–16 <https://doi.org/10.1093/oxfordhb/9780198820741.013.1>

—— *Dante and the Limits of the Law* (Chicago: University of Chicago Press, 2013 <https://doi.org/10.7208/chicago/9780226071121.001.0001>

Steinke, Barbara, *Paradiesgarten oder Gefängnis? Das Nürnberger Katharinenkloster zwischen Klosterreform und Reformation* (Tübingen: Mohr Siebeck, 2006)

Stock, Brian, *After Augustine: The Meditative Reader and the Text* (Philadelphia: University of Pennsylvania Press, 2001) <https://doi.org/10.9783/9780812203042>

—— *Augustine the Reader: Meditation, Self- Knowledge, and the Ethics of Interpretation* (Cambridge, MA: Belknap Press of Harvard University Press, 1996)

Stöllinger-Löser, Christine, '"Denscke Kroneke"', in *Die deutsche Literatur des Mittelalters: Verfasserlexikon*, 2nd edn, 14 vols (Berlin: De Gruyter, 1978–2008), xi (2004), cols 344–46

Strong, James, *The New Strong's Concise Dictionary of the Words in the Greek Testament and the Hebrew Bible* (Washington: Faithlife, 2009)

Sturm-Maddox, Sara, *Petrarch's Metamorphoses: Text and Subtext in the 'Rime Sparse'* (Columbia: University of Missouri Press, 1985)

Suárez, Francisco, 'De voto', in *Opera omnia*, 28 vols (Paris: Vives, 1856–78), xiv (1869), pp. 750–1179

Suerbaum, Almut, '*Es kommt ein schiff*, geladen: Mouvance in mystischen Liedern aus Straßburg', in *Schreiben und Lesen in der Stadt: Literaturbetrieb im spätmittelalterlichen Straßburg*, ed. by Stephen Mossman, Nigel F. Palmer, and Felix Heinzer (Berlin: De Gruyter, 2012), pp. 99–116 <https://doi.org/10.1515/9783110300581.99>

—— 'The Pseudo-Tauler *Cantilenae*', *Ons Geestelijk Eerf*, 84 (2013), pp. 41–54

Suerbaum, Almut, in collaboration with Manuele Gragnolati, 'Medieval Culture "betwixt and between": An Introduction', in *Aspects of the Performative in Medieval Culture*, ed. by Manuele Gragnolati and Almut Suerbaum (Berlin: De Gruyter, 2010), pp. 1–12

Suerbaum, Almut, and Annie Sutherland, eds, *Medieval Temporalities: The Experience of Time in Medieval Europe* (Woodbridge: Boydell & Brewer, 2021) <https://doi.org/10.1017/9781800101609>

Suerbaum, Almut, George Southcombe, and Benjamin Thompson, eds, *Polemic: Language as Violence in Medieval and Early Modern Discourse* (Farnham: Ashgate, 2015)

Sutherland, Annie, 'Þe Wohunge of Ure Lauerde and the House without Walls', in *Medieval and Early Modern Religious Cultures: Essays Honour-*

ing Vincent Gillespie on his Sixty-Fifth Birthday, ed. by Laura Ashe and Ralph Hanna (Cambridge: Brewer, 2019), pp. 3–19 <https://doi.org/10.1017/9781787445000.002>

—— 'Performing the Penitential Psalms: Maidstone and Bampton', in *Aspects of the Performative in Medieval Culture*, ed. by Manuele Gragnolati and Almut Suerbaum (Berlin: De Gruyter, 2014), pp. 15–38

Thaler, Peter, *Of Mind and Matter: The Duality of National Identity in the German–Danish Borderlands* (West Lafayette: Purdue University Press, 2009) <https://doi.org/10.2307/j.ctt6wq3c6>

Theben, Judith, *Die mystische Lyrik des 14. und 15. Jahrhunderts: Untersuchungen — Texte — Repertorium* (Berlin: De Gruyter, 2010) <https://doi.org/10.1515/9783484971097>

Thomas, Neil, 'The Celtic Wild Man Tradition and Geoffrey of Monmouth's *Vita Merlini*: Madness or Contemptus Mundi?', *Arthuriana*, 10 (2000), pp. 27–40 <https://doi.org/10.1353/art.2000.0017>

Thompson, Benjamin, 'Introduction: Monasteries and Medieval Society', in *Monasteries and Society in Medieval England: Proceedings of the 1994 Harlaxton Symposium*, ed. by Benjamin Thompson (Stamford: Watkins, 1999), pp. 1–33

—— 'Monasteries, Society and Reform in Late Medieval England', in *The Religious Orders in Pre-Reformation England*, ed. by James G. Clark (Woodbridge: Boydell, 2002), pp. 165–95

—— 'The Polemic of Reform in the Later Medieval English Church', in *Polemic: Language as Violence in Medieval and Early Modern Discourse*, ed. by Almut Suerbaum, George Southcombe, and Benjamin Thompson (Aldershot: Ashgate, 2015), pp. 183–222

Thorpe, Lewis, 'Merlin's Sardonic Laughter', in *Studies in Medieval Literature and Languages in Memory of Frederick Whitehead*, ed. by W. Rothwell and others (Manchester: Manchester University Press, 1973), pp. 323–39

Tomasek, Tomas, *Die Utopie im 'Tristan' Gotfrids von Straßburg* (Tübingen: Niemeyer, 1985) <https://doi.org/10.1515/9783111350103>

Tranter, Stephen M., 'Reoralization: Written Influence, Oral Formulation', in *Text und Zeittiefe*, ed. by Hildegard L. C. Tristram (Tübingen: Narr, 1994), pp. 45–54

Trillmich, Werner, 'Einleitung', in *Quellen des 9. und 11. Jahrhunderts zur Geschichte der hamburgischen Kirche und des Reiches*, ed. by Werner Trillmich and Rudolf Buchner, 7th edn, Freiherr vom Stein-Gedächtnisausgabe, 11 (Darmstadt: Wissenschaftliche Buchgesellschaft, 2000), pp. 137–58

Tronzo, William, *Petrarch's Two Gardens: Landscape and the Image of Movement* (New York: Italica Press, 2014) <https://doi.org/10.2307/j.ctt1t88w1b>

Turville-Petre, Gabriel, *Origins of Icelandic Literature* (Oxford: Clarendon Press, 1953)

Uexküll, Jakob von, *A Foray into the Worlds of Animals and Men: With a Theory of Meaning*, trans. by Joseph D. O'Neil (Minneapolis: University of Minnesota Press, 2010)

Uffmann, Heike, 'Inside and Outside the Convent Walls: The Norm and Practice of Enclosure in the Reformed Nunneries of Late Medieval Germany', *Medieval History Journal*, 4 (2001), pp. 83–108

—— *Wie in einem Rosengarten: Monastische Reformen des späten Mittelalters in den Vorstellungen von Klosterfrauen* (Bielefeld: Verlag für Regionalgeschichte, 2008)

Undorf, Wolfgang, 'Print and Book Culture in the Danish Town of Odense', in *Print Culture and Peripheries in Early Modern Europe: A Contribution to the History of Printing and the Book Trade in Small European and Spanish Cities*, ed. by Benito Rial Costas (Leiden: Brill, 2012), pp. 227–48 <https://doi.org/10.1163/9789004235755_010>

Urban, William L., *Dithmarschen: A Medieval Peasant Republic* (Lewiston: Mellen, 1991)

Varnam, Laura, and Laura Kalas Williams, eds, *Encountering the Book of Margery Kempe* (Manchester: Manchester University Press, 2022)

Voaden, Rosalynn, 'All Girls Together: Community, Gender and Vision at Helfta', in *Medieval Women in their Communities*, ed. by Diane Watt (Toronto: University of Toronto Press, 1997), pp. 72–91

Vollmann-Profe, Gisela, 'Mechthild von Magdeburg — deutsch und lateinisch', in *Deutsche Mystik im abendländischen Zusammenhang*, ed. by Walter Haug and Wolfram Schneider-Lastin (Tübingen: Niemeyer, 2000), pp. 144–58

Vosding, Lena, 'Gifts from the Convent: The Letters of the Benedictine Nuns at Lüne as the Material Manifestation of Spiritual Care', in *Was ist ein Brief? Aufsätze zu epistolarer Theorie und Kultur/What Is a Letter? Essays on Epistolary Theory and Culture*, ed. by Marie Isabel Matthews-Schlinzig and Caroline Socha (Würzburg: Königshausen & Neumann, 2018), pp. 211–33

—— 'Klösterliche Briefkunst: Die ars dictaminis im Kloster', in *Ars dictaminis: Handbuch der mittelalterlichen Briefstillehre*, ed. by Florian Hartmann and Benoît Grévin (Stuttgart: Hiersemann, 2019), pp. 493–517

—— 'Die Überwindung der Klausur: Briefkultur der Frauenklöster im Spätmittelalter', in *Zwischen Klausur und Welt: Autonomie und Interaktion spätmittelalterlicher Frauengemeinschaften*, ed. by Sigrid Hirbodian and Eva Schlotheuber (Ostfildern: Thorbecke, in press)

Vrieland, Seán, 'A Reunited Law: AM 6 8vo', *Manuscript of the Month*, 15 February 2020 <https://manuscript.ku.dk/motm/a-reunited-law-am-6-8vo/> [accessed 7 April 2020]

Waddington, Raymond B., *Aretino's Satyr: Sexuality, Satire, and Self-Projection in Sixteenth-Century Literature and Art* (Toronto: University of Toronto Press, 2004) <https://doi.org/10.3138/9781442670976>

Wakelin, Daniel, *Scribal Correction and Literary Craft: English Manuscripts 1375–1510* (Cambridge: Cambridge University Press, 2014) <https://doi.org/10.1017/CBO9781139923279>

Walker, Claire, '"Doe not supose ma well mortifyed Nun dead to the world": Letter-Writing in Early Modern English Convents', in *Early Modern Women's Letter Writing, 1450–1700*, ed. by James Daybell (Basingstoke: Palgrave, 2001), pp. 159–76 <https://doi.org/10.1057/9780230598669_11>

Wallace, David, 'Introduction', in *Europe: A Literary History*, ed. by David Wallace, 2 vols (Oxford: Oxford University Press, 2016), I, pp. xxvii–xlii

—— *Strong Women: Life, Text, and Territory, 1347–1645* (Oxford: Oxford University Press, 2011) <https://doi.org/10.1093/acprof:oso/9780199541713.001.0001>

—— ed., *Europe: A Literary History, 1348–1418*, 2 vols (Oxford: Oxford University Press, 2016)

Waller, Marguerite, *Petrarch's Poetics and Literary History* (Amherst: University of Massachusetts Press, 1980)

Ward, H. L. D., 'Lailoken (or Merlin Silvester)', *Romania*, 22 (1893), pp. 504–26 <https://doi.org/10.3406/roma.1893.5789>

Wetzel, James, *Augustine: A Guide for the Perplexed* (London: Continuum, 2010)

—— 'Augustine on the Will', in *A Companion to Augustine*, ed. by Mark Vessey with the assistance of Shelley Reid (Malden: Wiley-Blackwell, 2012), pp. 339–52 <https://doi.org/10.1002/9781118255483.ch26>

Whitehead, Christiania, 'Making a Cloister of the Soul in Medieval Religious Treatises', *Medium Aevum*, 67 (1998), pp. 1–29 <https://doi.org/10.2307/43629957>

Whittow, Mark, 'Sources of Knowledge; Cultures of Recording', *Past and Present*, 238, suppl. 13 (2018), pp. 45–87

Williamson, Beth, *Christian Art: A Very Short Introduction* (Oxford: Oxford University Press, 2004) <https://doi.org/10.1093/actrade/9780192803283.001.0001>

Wilson, Robert, *Prophecies and Prophecy in Dante's 'Commedia'* (Florence: Olschki, 2008)

Wind, Edgar, '"Hercules" and "Orpheus": Two Mock-Heroic Designs by Dürer', *Journal of the Warburg Institute*, 2 (1939), pp. 206–18

Winge, Vibeke, *Dänische Deutsche — deutsche Dänen: Geschichte der deutschen Sprache in Dänemark 1300–1800* (Heidelberg: Winter, 1992)

—— 'De denscke kroneke — der niederdeutsche Saxo', in *Vulpis Adolatio: Festschrift für Hubertus Menke zum 60. Geburtstag*, ed. by Robert Peters, Horst P. Pütz, and Ulrich Weber (Heidelberg: Winter, 2001), pp. 919–28

—— *Pebersvend og poltergejst: Tysk indflydelse på dansk* (Copenhagen: Gyldendal, 2000)

—— 'Zur Übersetzungstätigkeit Niederdeutsch-Dänisch und Dänisch-Niederdeutsch von 1300 bis Ende des 16. Jahrhunderts', in *Niederdeutsch in Skandinavien*, 6 vols (1987–2005), III, ed. by Lennart Elmevik and Kurt Erich Schöndorf, Beihefte zur Zeitschrift für deutsche Philologie, 6 (Berlin: Schmidt, 1992), pp. 30–36

Winston-Allen, Anne, *Convent Chronicles: Women Writing about Women and Reform in the Late Middle Ages* (University Park: Pennsylvania State University Press, 2004)

Wolf, Jürgen, *Die Sächsische Weltchronik im Spiegel ihrer Handschriften: Überlieferung, Textentwicklung, Rezeption* (Munich: Fink, 1997)

Woltmann, Alfred, *Holbein und seine Zeit*, 2 vols (Leipzig: Seemann, 1866–68)

Wormstall, Albert, 'Eine westfälische Briefsammlung des ausgehenden Mittelalters', *Zeitschrift für vaterländische Geschichte und Altertumskunde*, 53 (1895), pp. 149–81

Würth, Stefanie, 'Eufemia: Deutsche Auftraggeberin schwedischer Literatur am norwegischen Hof', in *Arbeiten zur Skandinavistik: 13. Arbeitstagung der deutschsprachigen Skandinavistik, 29.7.–3.8.1997 in Lysebu (Oslo)*, ed. by Fritz Paul (Frankfurt a.M.: Lang, 2000), pp. 269–81

Yates, Frances, *The Art of Memory* (Chicago: University of Chicago Press, 1966)

Zak, Gur, *Petrarch's Humanism and the Care of the Self* (Cambridge: Cambridge University Press, 2010) <https://doi.org/10.1017/CBO9780511730337>

Zumthor, Paul, *Essai de poétique médiévale* (Paris: Edition du Seuil, 2000)

—— *Merlin le prophète* (Lausanne: Payot, 1943)

—— 'Merlin: Prophet and Magician', trans. by Victoria Guerin, in *Merlin: A Casebook*, ed. by Peter H. Goodrich and Raymond H. Thompson (New York: Routledge, 2003), pp. 129–59

Notes on the Contributors

Philippa Byrne is Departmental Lecturer in Medieval History at Somerville College, Oxford. Her research focuses on scholastic thought in the twelfth and thirteenth centuries, the growth of schools and universities, and the translation of texts between Latin, Greek, and Arabic.

Nicolò Crisafi is Research and Teaching Fellow in Italian and Director of Studies in Modern Languages at Pembroke College, University of Cambridge. He researches medieval Italian literature, with a special focus on Dante. His interests lie in narrative theory, the role of the reader(s), the relation between language and affect, and the intersection between narrative forms and worldviews. He is the author of *Dante's Masterplot and Alternative Narratives in the 'Commedia'* (Oxford University Press, 2022).

Francesco Giusti is Career Development Fellow and Tutor in Italian at Christ Church, Oxford. He has published two books devoted respectively to the ethics and poetics of mourning and to creative and cognitive desire in lyric poetry: *Canzonieri in morte: Per un'etica poetica del lutto* (2015) and *Il desiderio della lirica: Poesia, creazione, conoscenza* (2016). He has co-edited, with Christine Ott and Damiano Frasca, the volume *Poesia e nuovi media* (2018); with Benjamin Lewis Robinson, *The Work of World Literature* (2021); and with Adele Bardazzi and Emanuela Tandello, the forthcoming *A Gaping Wound: Mourning in Italian Poetry* (2022).

Manuele Gragnolati is Professor of Medieval Italian Literature at Sorbonne Université, Associate Director of the ICI Berlin, and Senior Research Fellow at Somerville College, Oxford. His publications include the monographs *Experiencing the Afterlife: Soul and Body and Medieval Culture* (2005), *Amor che move: Linguaggio del corpo e forma del desiderio in Dante, Pasolini e Morante* (2013), and *Possibilities of Lyric: Reading Petrarch in Dialogue* (2020, with Francesca Southerden).

Oren Margolis is a scholar of the Renaissance. A historian of humanism, of history-writing and antiquarianism, and of the art and culture of the book, his interests range from epigraphy to Erasmus, and span Italy and the North, literary, intellectual, and art history. He is the author of *The Politics of Culture in Quattrocento Europe: René of Anjou in Italy* (Oxford University Press, 2016). Curator of the Bodleian Library exhibition 'Aldus Manutius: The Struggle and the Dream' (2015), he is now completing a book on the celebrated scholar-printer of Venice. Since 2019, he has been Lecturer in Renaissance Studies at the University of East Anglia.

Alastair Matthews is a translator and editor in Dunfermline, Scotland. Before leaving academia, he published monographs on the *Kaiserchronik* (Oxford University Press, 2012) and on the Middle High German *Lohengrin* (Camden House, 2016). He continues to pursue his scholarly interests, in particular the interface between German and Scandinavian literary history in the Middle Ages.

Brian McMahon is Associate Lecturer in English at Oxford Brookes University, co-convenor of the 'Old Norse Poetry in Performance' research project, and co-editor of *Old Norse Poetry in Performance* (forthcoming).

Monika Otter is an Associate Professor of English at Dartmouth College. Her research focuses on Latin, French, and English literature from England and northern France, 11th–13th centuries. She has worked on historiography, saints' lives, romance, and the complicated interfaces between these genres; the development of 'fiction' as an idea and as a category of literature; women's literature and gender issues; and translation theory. Her publications include *The Book of Encouragement and Comfort: Goscelin's Letter to the Recluse Eva* (Boydell and Brewer, 2004); *Inventiones: Fiction and Referentiality in Twelfth-Century English Historical Writing* (North Carolina University Press, 1996).

Damiano Sacco was a Fellow at the ICI Berlin from 2018 to 2020. His work focuses on continental and Italian philosophy, in particular on the works of Martin Heidegger, Giorgio Agamben, Jacques Derrida, and Emanuele Severino. He is currently translating some of Emanuele Severino's most important works into English. His articles have appeared in, among others, *Continental Philosophy Review*, *diacritics*, and *The European Legacy*.

Francesca Southerden is Associate Professor of Medieval Italian at the University of Oxford and Fellow of Somerville College. Her recent publications include *Possibilities of Lyric: Reading Petrarch in Dialogue* (2020, with Manuele Gragnolati) and *The Oxford Handbook of Dante* (2021, co-edited with Manuele Gragnolati and Elena Lombardi). She has a book forthcoming entitled *Dante and Petrarch in the Garden of Language*.

Almut Suerbaum is Fellow and Tutor in German at Somerville College, Oxford, and currently Chair of the Faculty Board of Medieval and Modern Languages. She has published extensively on the interrelationship between vernacular literature and Latin learned culture. As co-founder of the Somerville Medievalist Research Group, she has co-edited the volumes *Aspects of the Performative in Medieval Culture* (2010), *Polemic: Language as Violence in Medieval and Early Modern Discourse* (2015), and *Medieval Temporalities: The Experience of Time in Medieval Europe* (2020).

Annie Sutherland is Tutorial Fellow in Old and Middle English at Somerville College, Oxford, and Associate Professor in the English Faculty. She has published widely on medieval devotional literature and is currently working on thirteenth-century anchoritic culture.

Benjamin Thompson is Tutor in Medieval History at Somerville College and currently Associate Head (Education) of the Humanities Division in the University of Oxford. His work probes the interface between the medieval Church's core mission of prayer and ministry and its social and political presence. He has contributed to the previous Somerville medievalists' volumes and is currently writing a book about the nationalization and dissolution of the 'alien' (foreign) priories in late medieval England.

Edmund Wareham is a former Postdoctoral Research Associate on the 'Nuns' Network' project and a Fulford Non-Stipendiary Junior Research Fellow at Somerville College. He is now a Departmental Lecturer in Early Modern European Social and Cultural History at Oxford's History Faculty, and Director of Studies in History at St Benet's Hall.

Johannes Wolf is an independent researcher who has taught widely on Old and Middle English literature and specializes in Middle English religious writing. His Cambridge University PhD focused on the disciplinary techniques of pastoral and confessional material in Middle English. More recently, his research has turned to questions of experience, affect, and representations of the non-human in devotional medieval literature.

Index

Cultural Inquiry

EDITED BY CHRISTOPH F. E. HOLZHEY
AND MANUELE GRAGNOLATI

www.ingramcontent.com/pod-product-compliance
Lightning Source LLC
Chambersburg PA
CBHW030354130626
46549CB00004B/1488